The First Peacetime Draft

Modern War Studies

Raymond A. Callahan
Jacob W. Kipp
Jay Luvaas
Theodore A. Wilson
Series Editors

The First Peacetime Draft

J. Garry Clifford
and
Samuel R. Spencer, Jr.

University Press of Kansas

© 1986 by the University Press of Kansas

Published by the University Press of Kansas (Lawrence, Kansas 66045), which was organized by the Kansas Board of Regents and is operated and funded by Emporia State University, Fort Hays State University, Kansas State University, Pittsburg State University, the University of Kansas, and Wichita State University

Library of Congress Cataloging-in-Publication Data
Clifford, J. Garry (John Garry), 1942–
    The first peacetime draft.
    Bibliography: p.
    Includes index.
    1. Military service, Compulsory—United States—
History—20th century. 2. United States—Politics
and government—1933–1945. I. Spencer, Samuel R.
II. Title.
UB343.C564   1986   355.2'2363'0973   86-13328
ISBN 0-7006-0305-0

Printed in the United States of America
10 9 8 7 6 5 4 3 2 1

To
Carol K. Davidge
and
Ava C. Spencer

Contents

Illustrations

Preface

Like shadows on a parade ground, armies are usually a reflection of the larger sociopolitical forces and international conditions that shape military establishments. When the United States began conscripting citizens into the armed forces in the autumn of 1940, it marked the first time the nation had resorted to such procedures during peacetime. This revolutionary change in military format came about primarily because of the sudden changes in the international system occasioned by Nazi Germany's blitzkrieg victories in western Europe. Stunned by Hitler's conquests, Americans instinctively understood that a small army and good intentions counted for little in a world of totalitarian aggressors. Isolationist traditions soon crumbled. Whether they wanted to go to war with Hitler or not, a majority of Americans decided that a draft would be more efficient and equitable than volunteering if the country needed to raise armed forces large enough to defend interests at home and allies overseas. Passage of the Selective Service Act of 1940 took place after an intense three-month national debate in which nearly every segment of American society had an opportunity to influence the new defense system. This book examines in detail just how the first peacetime draft came to be.

This book has been nearly forty years in the making. The man most responsible for the draft law, Grenville Clark, began the project after World War II by asking Samuel R. Spencer, Jr., to help in writing his memoirs. The memoirs as such were never written, but the 1940 campaign for conscription, in which Clark was the central character, became the subject of Spencer's Ph.D. dissertation at Harvard, which was completed in 1951 and is based largely on Clark's private papers and interviews with key participants. For thirty-five years, Spencer's history has been available in manuscript form at Harvard's Widener Library and has frequently been used by scholars of United States policies prior to Pearl Harbor.

During the late 1970s, Spencer and J. Garry Clifford agreed that a collaborative work, updated and enlarged, would make a valuable contribution to the history of the period. Building on the basic structure and text of the original study, Clifford has therefore made extensive revisions and additions in the light of new scholarship and the many archival and manuscript collections that have become available in recent years. As part of a broader inquiry into the so-called Great Debate over United States intervention in the years 1939 to 1941, Clifford has enlarged the scope of the original study so as to give more attention to the opponents of conscription both inside and outside of Congress and to place the draft more clearly within the context of the Roosevelt administration's zigzag course toward war. Finally, the draft has also been evaluated in terms of the overall evolution of United States defense and foreign policies since 1940.

Acknowledgments

During the many years of research and writing, Spencer and I have incurred many obligations that we are happy to acknowledge. I wish to thank the late Mary Clark Dimond for first granting access to the Grenville Clark papers and for encouraging further research into her father's multiple activities as a "statesman incognito." Ruth Wight, formerly Clark's personal secretary and the cataloguer of the Clark papers at Dartmouth, has been a close friend and guide for nearly twenty years. Georgia Robison Beale, a fine historian in her own right, made available the correspondence files of Howard K. Beale that pertained to the 1940 draft opposition. Thomas V. Rankin provided hospitality and memories of his own nearly forgotten activities against the draft. John A. Danaher, Douglas Arant, Ruth Sarles Benedict, Kingman Brewster, Jr., James B. Conant, Lewis Hershey, Howard C. Petersen, and Walter Weible also granted personal interviews about their activities in 1940.

Many friends and colleagues helped at various stages. Walter LaFeber, Justus Doenecke, and James T. Patterson read and commented on one or more chapters. David Alvarez and Philip Ressler did preliminary research in distant repositories on our behalf. David Reynolds provided invaluable advice about manuscripts and archives in Great Britain. David Porter, a fellow scholar of the 1940 draft, generously shared notes from his research in numerous congressional manuscript collections. Larry Bland, editor of the *George C. Marshall Papers,* was very helpful in opening his "chronological file" of the general's papers at the Marshall Library. Thanks are also due to my department chairmen at the University of Connecticut—Louis Gerson, David Repass, and Larry Bowman—who arranged my teaching load so as to encourage research and writing. Michael Schwartz, Barbara Reno, Bill Anderson, Art Zilversmit, Vic Papacosma, Susan Riley, Lucien Vandenbroucke, Michael Ermarth, Jerry Handfield, Tony Hepburn, Jack Thompson, Ted Wilson, and Robert Ferrell gave food and lodging when it was most appreciated.

Librarians and archivists at numerous institutions were unfailingly efficient in meeting my requests for materials. The following deserve special commendation: Erika Chadbourne (Harvard Law School Library); Emmet D. Chisum (University of Wyoming Library); Judith Schiff and Patricia Stark (Sterling Library of Yale University); Connie Gallagher (University of Vermont Library); Robert Hessen (Hoover Institution on War, Peace, and Revolution); Nancy Bressler (Seeley Mudd Library at Princeton); Robert Wood (Herbert Hoover Presidential Library); Phil Cronenwett and Kenneth C. Cramer (Baker Library of Dartmouth College); and Vivian Shortreed (Quinebaug Valley Community College).

Five historians read the entire manuscript of this book and offered excellent criticism. Thomas Etzold and Gordon Warren were especially helpful in reiterating rules of grammar and style that we had learned in graduate school. Etzold also pointed out interpretive themes that were buried in detail. My UConn colleague Tom Paterson, a perceptive and diplomatic critic, wielded a sharp pen on all chapters and never once wrote "Ugh!" John Chambers, who knows the history of United States military formats better than anyone else, helped to place the developments of 1940 within a larger context. Ted Wilson, series editor at the University Press of Kansas, solicited the manuscript in the first place, helped to unsnarl tangled organization, and did what he could to clarify what was obscure.

My wife, Carol K. Davidge, enhanced this project in numerous ways. Together, we researched manuscript collections across the country and in the United Kingdom, stopping to see the Grand Canyon along the way. She also edited and typed the final manuscript on a word processor under emergency conditions. Without her love and support this book would still be unfinished.

A Young Humanist grant from the National Endowment for the Humanities provided support for a year of research in the Clark papers in 1973, and the University of Connecticut Research Foundation helped finance sabbatical research in 1980/81.

Any errors of fact or judgment are the authors' responsibility.

J. Garry Clifford

A note from Grenville Clark, whom I did not then know, asked me to meet him at the Hotel Vendome in Boston in the spring of 1947. Would I be interested in working with him on his memoirs? Having suffered a mild heart attack, he was under doctor's orders to slacken the intensive pace of his multifaceted activities.

So began the association and resulting five-hundred-page dissertation from which this book evolved. Within a matter of months after that first meeting, it was obvious that Grenville Clark would characteristically refuse to retire to the quiet pursuits of writing memoirs. Instead, he and the rows of file cases at his New Hampshire home (he saved everything) provided the lode of source material from which the dissertation was mined. His long-time secretary, Genevieve Maloney, helped immeasurably in the process. His wife, Fanny Dwight Clark, his daughters Louisa Clark Spencer (no relation to me) and the late Mary Clark Dimond—all contributed to a rounded view of the central figure in this story, a man guided by Lincoln's conviction—which Clark often quoted—that the people will save their government if the government does its job only indifferently well.

Further insights and information came from personal interviews with Julius O. Adler, Howard C. Petersen, Kenneth P. Budd, Lewis B. Hershey Mark Watson, J. McA. Palmer, Archibald G. Thacher, Felix Frankfurter, John D. Kenderdine, William Chadbourne, Philip A. Carroll, Edward R. Burke, Perley Boone, and McGeorge Bundy. Early access to both the Henry L. Stimson papers and the Franklin D. Roosevelt papers was both helpful and appreciated.

Arthur M. Schlesinger, Sr., of Harvard supervised and directed the writing of the dissertation. He and his wife, Elizabeth Bancroft Schlesinger, provided not only intellectual stimulation but also the warmth of hospitality and friendship to my wife and me during the long months leading up to the final product.

My wife, Ava Clark Spencer (no relation to Grenville Clark), deserves the accolade for which only the spouse of an aspiring writer can qualify. While pursuing her own career and caring for our first child, she not only served as a valuable critic but also preserved the household equilibrium which enabled my work to continue without interruption. In a very genuine way the dissertation—and therefore this book—belong partly to her.

Samuel R. Spencer, Jr.

1

The Lottery of War

Klieg lights blazed down on the huge ten-gallon fishbowl atop the stage of Washington's Departmental Auditorium. The glass container—the same one used in the draft lottery of 1917—contained 8,994 cobalt-blue capsules, each holding a different registration number. As newsmen and radio technicians buzzed among themselves, official cameras stood ready to photograph each number when it was drawn, along with a clock showing the exact time of each separate selection. Individual numbers would then be attached to a large gummed sheet of cardboard, which would become the master record, each sheet of which would also be photographed. Such elaborate procedures were meant to ensure that the first peacetime-draft lottery in American history would be fair and impartial.

The official ceremony began just before noon. Selective Service Director Clarence A. Dykstra and Brig. Gen. Lewis B. Hershey stepped onto the stage. Lagging behind came President Franklin D. Roosevelt, on the arm of his secretary, Edwin ("Pa") Watson. The blue-suited president looked tired and drawn, obviously exhausted by the 1940 presidential contest against Wendell L. Willkie, then in its final week. The famous "voice" still sounded strong and resonant, as FDR solemnly addressed a nationwide audience anxiously waiting for the fateful numbers to be drawn. He chose his words carefully. In describing the process about to begin under the Selective Training and Service Act, Roosevelt deliberately avoided the words *draft* or *conscription*, calling it instead a *muster*, thus evoking memories of Lexington and Concord and flintlock muskets. "Ever since that first muster," he emphasized, "our democratic army has existed for one purpose only: the defense of our freedom. It is for that one purpose and that one purpose only that you will be asked to answer the call to training." There was no mention, no hint, of another American Expeditionary Force to Europe. FDR also called upon religious support by reading letters from Catholic, Protestant, and Jewish leaders in "solemn recognition" of the occasion. The most eloquent came from Archbishop (later Cardinal) Francis J. Spellman, who wrote: "It is better to have protection and not need it than to need protection and not have it. . . .

1

Secretary of War Henry L. Stimson drawing the first capsule of the draft lottery on 30
October 1940. (Courtesy Franklin D. Roosevelt Library)

We really cannot longer afford to be moles who cannot see, or ostriches who
will not see.''[1]

Then the lottery commenced. The secretary of war, seventy-three-year-
old Henry L. Stimson, walked to the fishbowl. A nervous Lt. Col. (retired)
Charles B. Morris, who had blindfolded Secretary Newton D. Baker in 1917,
tried to perform the same function for Stimson. He fumbled with the
blindfold, which included a strip of yellow cloth cut from one of the chairs used
at the signing of the Declaration of Independence in 1776. Tense seconds
passed. Finally ready, Stimson reached his left hand into the jar, picked up the
first capsule he touched, and handed it to the president. Roosevelt opened the
capsule, paused for a signal from the newsreel men, then intoned: ''The first
number is one—five—eight.'' A woman in the auditorium screamed and
nearly fainted; her twenty-one-year-old-son Harry, along with some 6,175
registrants throughout the country, had the registration serial number 158. A
flurry of newsmen and radio announcers quickly appeared, bringing temporary fame to Mrs. Mildred Bell, her son Harry, and Harry's fianceé.

Roosevelt and Stimson exited after drawing the first number, and other
dignitaries, similarly blindfolded, selected the next eighteen capsules. Then,
as he would do for the next thirty years, General Hershey took over the draft
machinery. Assisted by a team of young women and volunteer Boy Scouts,
who had been practicing for days and could handle approximately fourteen

capsules and serial numbers per minute, Hershey supervised the rest of the drawings. It took seventeen hours—well into the morning of 30 October 1940—before the 16.4 million American males from the age of twenty-one to thirty-five, who had registered for the draft two weeks earlier, could learn the order in which they might be called for induction.[2] The lottery did not work perfectly. When General Hershey drew the last number shortly after 5 A.M., he discovered that six capsules had been inadvertently left out. A mini-lottery, conducted out of a felt hat, corrected this oversight. Another problem arose over the statistical fairness of the drawings. The plastic capsules had been dumped into the fishbowl in lots of one hundred, and officials periodically stirred the capsules with a large ladle carved from a rafter from Independence Hall. Pacifists in the Keep America out of War Congress, using mathematical tables, tried to prove that the numbers had bunched up and that the historic ladle was statistically dysfunctional. The protests came to naught, however.[3]

And so, for the first time when the United States was not officially at war, the drafting of American citizens into the armed forces had begun. It turned out that in New York City number 158 was held by registrants bearing such names as Faruggia, Chon, Cody, Weisblum, Stazzone, and Lichtenstein. Among those whose number came up 7,298th in the lottery was John Roosevelt, thus making it highly unlikely that the president's youngest son would be drafted during the next year. No draft protesters disrupted Lottery Day, and fears that hundreds, even thousands, would refuse to register proved unfounded; only thirty-six refused.[4] The press seemed more interested in the case of Reika Schwanke of Austin, Minnesota, who had mistakenly registered at her local draft board. "There ought to be some place for a woman in the army," she said on learning that women would not be drafted.[5] Most potential inductees took solace from the fact that if drafted, they would be required under the Selective Service Act to undergo only twelve months of military training, after which they would be subject to a ten-year obligation to serve in the reserves. Almost overnight the nation's number-one song became "Good-bye Dear, I'll Be Back in a Year."[6] Few Americans wanted or expected to fight in the European war that was raging across the Atlantic. The day after the lottery, President Roosevelt, speaking in Boston, gave his strongest assurance yet: "I have said this before, but I shall say it again and again: Your boys are not going to be sent into any foreign wars."[7]

Because the United States was catapulted into World War II by the Japanese attack on Pearl Harbor some thirteen months later, Franklin D. Roosevelt has been considered a poor prophet (or worse!) for the words he uttered in Boston on 30 October 1940. Although the president had assured parents that their sons were being drafted for defensive purposes only, these young men would soon be fighting—and dying—in such faraway places as Kasserine Pass, Guadalcanal, Anzio, and Iwo Jima. For the fifteen million men who constituted the armed forces of the United States during World War

II, the draft lottery of October 1940 became a lottery for war. For pacifist opponents of conscription it was also a lottery of death—not merely deaths suffered in battle but also the death of American ideals and institutions. By adopting peacetime conscription, the United States was allegedly imitating totalitarian governments abroad. "The beginning of the end will come with the passage of the Conscription Bill," lamented Oswald Garrison Villard, the grand old man of American pacifism. "After that, I think we might as well quit."[8] For the octogenarian senator from Nebraska, George W. Norris, this was "not a bill to prepare an army to fight tomorrow; it is a bill to prepare an army to fight men and peoples yet unborn. It is a step in the direction of fastening a dictatorship upon the American Government in time of peace."[9]

Nevertheless, given the reality of America's entry into World War II in December 1941, the passage of the Selective Training and Service Act in September 1940 proved to be one of the most decisive "steps" in the evolution of American policies prior to Pearl Harbor. Introduced into Congress two days before France's surrender and signed into law as Luftwaffe bombs were setting London afire, the conscription bill sparked an intense three-months' national debate that constituted America's first halting response to Hitler's domination of Europe. The conscription controversy coincided with the Roosevelt administration's policy of aiding Britain in steps short of war, most notably the destroyers-for-bases deal of 3 September 1940, and it affected the manner in which such assistance was carried out. Because the draft touched nearly every American family, no measure during the months before Pearl Harbor—not even the Lend-Lease Act of March 1941—generated as much public controversy. It was, as one Kansas congressman put it, "discussed very thoroughly in the press and over the radio and on the street corner as well as in the halls of Congress."[10] Described by its principal author as "a *sine qua non* to any real effort to stand up to Hitler et al.," the passage of the draft law helped to condition the country, both psychologically and militarily, for the war that lay ahead.[11] According to historian Forrest C. Pogue, "it was the Selective Service Act of 1940 . . . that made possible the huge United States Army and Air Force that fought World War II."[12] Without the trained manpower provided by the draft, American forces could not have taken the offensive in North Africa and the Pacific during 1942, and thus the entire outcome of the war might have been different.

Essential as it was for American participation in World War II, one might well assume that the Selective Training and Service Act was a product of White House planning. Nothing could have been more logical than for the president, directing the strategy of national preparation, to have urged the draft as the only effective means of obtaining the necessary manpower to run the defense machine. Nothing could have been more logical than for the General Staff, convinced of the inadequacy of the volunteer system as demonstrated in past wars, to have advocated compulsory training and service

with the White House. Curiously, however, the first peacetime draft originated neither with the army nor with the Roosevelt administration. Even
more curious is the fact that during the early stages, both the army and the
White House were at best apathetic to its passage.

Instead, the Selective Training and Service Act of 1940 was conceived,
written, and lobbied through Congress by a determined group of private
citizens who had no formal connection with the government. Failing to
persuade the leaders in the administration to support the measure, these men
had their bill introduced by a Republican congressman and by an anti–New
Deal lame-duck Democratic senator, neither of whom had seen it forty-eight
hours before their names were attached to it. Once the measure reached the
floor of Congress, this group of "amateurs" set about to educate the public
through a well-organized publicity campaign that was financed by private
contributions from all sections of the country. Eventually both the army and
the White House joined the fight—but not until they had been literally
prodded into the front lines.

The history of the Selective Training and Service Act of 1940 is therefore,
in one sense, the story of a pressure group; in an even narrower sense, it is the
story of one man—Grenville Clark—whose spirit and energy dominated that
group. As such, it is a vivid illustration of the power that a pressure group can
wield, for good or evil, in American political life. In its worst light, it might
suggest that a powerful minority interest can control the democratic processes
for its own ends, as proof of the political-science axiom "Who mobilizes the
elites, mobilizes the public."[13] Those who sponsored the bill, however, saw
the success of their four-months' campaign as vindicating their belief that a
peacetime draft was necessary, democratic, and in harmony with American
values. That it passed Congress without vigorous White House backing was,
in Grenville Clark's opinion, an expression of Abraham Lincoln's dictum that
"the people will save their government if the government itself will do its part
only indifferently well."[14]

In a larger perspective, the Selective Training and Service Act was
neither the product of an elitist conspiracy nor a clear pronouncement from
vox populi. Like most manifestations of public policy, the draft law evolved
through compromise, debate, bureaucratic tugging and hauling, differing
interpretations of public opinion, personality clashes, unforeseen contingencies, and partisan politics. Even though the original sponsors envisaged the
draft as being necessary for raising an army to participate in the European
war, Congress as a whole did not consciously enact the legislation for such a
bellicose purpose. Nor was President Roosevelt necessarily being insincere
when he pledged that American boys were not being drafted to fight in any
foreign wars. Although he welcomed selective service as the most desirable
and efficient method of obtaining manpower for the armed forces, FDR did
not in 1940 place conscription high on his list of priorities, not the least of

which was reelection to the White House for a third term. Likewise, the army, as it sought to mesh old mobilization plans with new strategic formulas for hemispheric defense, did not calculate that the draft would produce another generation of "doughboys" for a second American Expeditionary Force. The British ambassador later described the evolution of American policy as "rather like a disorderly line of beaters out shooting; they do put the rabbits out of the bracken, but they don't come out where you expect."[15] Opponents of the draft in 1940, in raising many legitimate questions about the consequences of peacetime conscription, were correct in predicting war but were wrong in perceiving the draft as part of some predetermined pattern.

The United States, as it were, went through a severe emotional trauma during the summer of 1940. British analysts of American politics noticed a phenomenon that was

> comparable only to the emotional experience which Britain went through at the time of "Munich," 1938. . . . The soaring temperature of a pathological crisis showed itself in the intensity of the feeling aroused; the quickening pulse, in the volume of comment elicited; and the lack of coordination, in a confusion of thought frequently commented upon at the time. Imminent in the crisis was the question of the existence of America either as a free and independent nation or as a prisoner fed through bars.[16]

Old notions of America's invulnerability gave way to nightmares of totalitarian menace from abroad. Military preparedness, which included conscription, was as much a reflex as it was a calculated response. This new quest for national security through military rearmament was, as the British observed, "a reaction to fear of aggression from Europe as fundamental as the fear of entanglement with Europe which had dominated the preceding months."[17] How the Roosevelt administration would integrate this new military power into its foreign policy in the months ahead remained an open question.

In a symbolic sense, however, whether it led inevitably to United States involvement in World War II or not, enactment of the Selective Training and Service Act in 1940 marked the effective end of the isolationist tradition in the United States. Hitler's blitzkrieg had jolted isolationists and internationalists alike into an instinctive realization that the broad Atlantic and Pacific no longer afforded sufficient protection in a world of totalitarian predators. John Quincy Adams had once pledged that the United States should not go "abroad in search of monsters to destroy," but air-age technology had so shrunk the globe that aggressors abroad might suddenly attack the hemisphere. The traditional distinctions between war and peace became inevitably blurred. While the nation remained officially at peace, it was deemed necessary to resort to a wartime measure—conscription—to raise military forces large enough to defend American interests at home and allies overseas. And like other weapons in the victorious war against the Axis, selective service remained a fixture in American defense policy long after the monsters of 1940 had been destroyed.

2

Plattsburg Revisited

The war in Europe still seemed far away to most Americans in early April 1940. A new baseball season was about to start; the sportswriters were marveling at Bob Feller's brilliant pitching, worrying about Joe DiMaggio's injury, speculating about a skinny young outfielder from Boston named Theodore Samuel Williams. New York sports fans were cheering their Rangers in the playoffs, not knowing that it would be forty years before another New York hockey team would capture the Stanley Cup. On Broadway, *Life with Father* was a fresh young play; and Monty Woolley was delighting theatergoers with the insufferable egotism of *The Man Who Came to Dinner*. In Washington that April, Norman Thomas accepted—for the fourth time—the Socialist party's nomination for president, while Republicans, most of whom had never heard the name Wendell Willkie, eagerly awaited the results of the first primaries. All over the country, people were making plans to see the World's Fair, scheduled to reopen for a second season at Flushing Meadow, New York, on 11 May.

The Second World War had begun with Hitler's lightning victory over Poland the previous September. Although Congress reacted by revising the Neutrality Act to permit the sale of arms and munitions to belligerents on a "cash-and-carry" basis, the average American remained determined to stay out of the Old World's troubles. The lack of fighting during the autumn and winter, which led pundits to speak of a "sitzkrieg" or "phony war," reinforced the general desire not to repeat the mistakes of 1917/18. A national poll in early March 1940 indicated that 96.4 percent of Americans opposed going to war against Germany.[1] As late as 3 April, the House Appropriations Committee cut back a modest armed-forces budget by 10 percent. The *Harvard Crimson* ran a series of editorials urging a negotiated peace between the Allies and Germany. As one of the student editors, a son of the American ambassador to England, informed his father: "Everyone is getting much more confident about our staying out of the war but that of course is probably because there is such a lull over there."[2] Young John F. Kennedy, like most members of his college generation, did not know how close the war actually was. Even before graduating cum laude from Harvard that June, the future commander of a PT-boat found himself taking an unpopular position on the most hotly debated American response to the war in Europe in 1940—that of military conscription. And by supporting a military draft in 1940, young Kennedy, like most Americans, did so in the hope that it would be the best insurance against attack, not as a step toward intervention.[3]

The lull ended with the rumble of Nazi armor across the border of Denmark on 9 April. Stunned Americans read about the desperate fighting in Norway. "I felt that familiar sick-at-the-pit-of-the-stomach shock," Anne Morrow Lindbergh wrote in her diary. "I keep forgetting—war is a thug's game. The thug strikes first and harder."[4] Though the British quickly intervened, within a month they were forced to abandon the Norwegians; the swastika soon flew over the Scandinavian coast from Narvik to Oslo.

On 10 May 1940, Hitler's legions invaded the Low Countries. Disaster. Duped into committing their reserves in Belgium, the French found themselves cut off as German armored divisions smashed through the Ardennes Forest, crossed the Meuse River between Sedan and Namur, and then began their wild dash across northern France, the first grey-green spearheads reaching the Channel port of Abbeville on 20 May. Americans, glued to their radios, could almost picture the scenes—refugees scrambling in panic as Stuka dive bombers, with sirens screaming, strafed crowded roads; the clatter of jackboots, as seemingly endless lines of blond Aryan youths marched through captured cities, their arms upraised in the "Heil Hitler" salute; the bitter, desperate struggle around the oil-blackened beaches of Dunkirk, as the trapped British Expeditionary Force miraculously fought its way to the hundreds of rescue ships just offshore.

The grim news continued. Holland surrendered after only four days of fighting; the Belgian Army capitulated on the eighteenth day. French armies tried to rally on the Somme, but again the Nazi armor broke through. The government of Premier Paul Reynaud evacuated Paris on 10 June, the same day that Italy ("the hand that held the dagger," in President Roosevelt's angry words) declared war on Britain and France. Three days later, German troops goosestepped past shocked, sobbing Parisian crowds. Americans heard what they thought was the defiant voice of Winston Churchill proclaiming England's determination to fight on:

> We shall not flag or fail. We shall go on to the end. We shall fight in France, we shall fight on the seas and oceans, we shall fight with growing strength and growing confidence in the air, we shall defend our island, whatever the cost may be, we shall fight on the beaches, we shall fight on the landing grounds, we shall fight in the fields and in the streets, we shall fight in the hills; we shall never surrender.

Neither Churchill's stirring oratory nor a British offer to merge the two empires could keep the French from capitulating. Reynaud's government fell, and a new regime under Marshal Henri Philippe Pétain negotiated an armistice. The formal terms were signed at 3:00 P.M. on 21 June, in General Foch's famous railroad car at Compiègne. Hitler allegedly danced his jig as the new master of Europe.

Most Americans reacted to the Nazi hurricane by sympathizing with the Allies and fearing for national safety. On 7 June the British ambassador reported:

> What hitherto had been at most a vague uneasiness that the Allies were not so sure after all of defeating Germany has turned almost overnight into a frightening persuasion that not only was Germany likely to defeat us, but it was quite in the cards that she would do so in short order. The feeling that . . . this hemisphere would no longer enjoy the time-honoured shelter of the British fleet and might find itself the last great citadel of Democracy in a world dominated by greedy and ruthless totalitarian Powers has shaken complacency and focused a sharp light upon the nation's own preparedness.[5]

A small minority actually called for a declaration of war against Germany by publishing a "Summons to Speak Out" in most of the country's major newspapers on Monday 10 June.[6] Few members of Congress, however, would agree with Senator Carter Glass's comment that "Germany should be wiped off the map and our disgraceful Neutrality Act . . . expunged from the federal statute books."[7] Senator Joseph C. O'Mahoney of Wyoming more accurately described Congress as "practically a unanimous unit in favor of complete national preparedness. The great majority want to extend every possible aid to the democracies . . . (but) feel it unnecessary and unwise to participate in the war by sending troops abroad."[8] Senator Theodore Bilbo of Mississippi summed it up best: "We are not going to send our boys to Europe to fight another European war, but we are going to get ready for the 'Big Boy' Hitler and 'Spaghetti Mussolini' if they undertake to invade our shores."[9]

Preparedness became a national obsession in those dark weeks of the Nazi conquest. When President Roosevelt asked a packed Congress on 16 May for fifty thousand airplanes a year, he received the loudest ovation he had heard in years. British analysts reported "near hysteria . . . in many sections of the [American] press and deep anxiety in practically all."[10] The National Legion of the Mothers of America organized a Molly Pitcher Rifle Brigade to shoot descending parachutists, and FDR was only half-facetious in telling his cabinet on 24 May that such tasks ought to be left to local volunteer fire departments.[11] The naval-minded Roosevelt was not alone in voicing genuine concern over the strategic threat that would be posed if Germany should gain control over the British and French fleets.[12] Americans were shocked to learn that when the Belgian Army surrendered on 28 May, the United States Army became the eighteenth-largest army in the world, just ahead of Bulgaria's. Republicans, looking for a campaign issue, wondered out loud what had become of the $7 billion appropriated for defense over the past seven years. By mid June, Congress had appropriated $5 billion more. Rumors of fifth-column activities in South America, as well as the possibility that Germany might demand Dutch and French colonies in a peace settlement, sent army planners scurrying to draw up new plans for hemispheric defense.[13]

While sometimes exaggerated, these fears did not lack substance. Treasury Secretary Henry Morgenthau confronted Army Chief of Staff George C. Marshall on 10 May, the day when the German blitzkrieg began. "I understand you could only put into the field today, fully equipped, 75,000 troops," charged Morgenthau. "That's absolutely wrong," Marshall retorted. "Well, how many could you put into the field today?" Morgenthau asked. "Eighty thousand" was Marshall's rueful reply.[14] Four days later, Morgenthau learned that "we haven't got one airplane today that has got the things we need if they went up against a German plane."[15]

Notwithstanding continued opposition from pacifist groups, several prominent isolationists joined with pro-Ally supporters in taking up the cry of preparedness. Henry Ford announced that his factories could turn out a thousand planes a day if given a free hand. Senator Arthur H. Vandenberg of Michigan repudiated the term *isolationist,* calling himself instead an *insulationist* who fervently supported hemispheric defense.[16] Gen. Robert E. Wood of Sears, Roebuck, Col. Charles A. Lindbergh, and publishers William Randolph Hearst, Robert R. McCormick, and J. M. Patterson all publicly endorsed compulsory military training before any such proposal was introduced into Congress.[17] "Everybody is for national defense," Senator Hiram W. Johnson of California admitted to his son, "and upon that point there is unanimity of sentiment." But Johnson, like many isolationists, believed that FDR, "with diabolical cleverness," was using the preparedness issue to "create terrible public clamor and hysteria" so as to "follow the line followed by us in 1917, which took us into the European conflict."[18] Heavy-jowled David I. Walsh of Massachusetts, chairman of the Senate Committee on Naval Affairs, exhibited a similar attitude as he supported increased expenditures for the navy but flew into "a towering rage about sale of navy stuff to Allies" and threatened to introduce legislation "prohibiting the sale of anything."[19] Although suddenly willing to vote vast sums for rearmament, most Republicans shared this distrust of FDR's motives, believing, as one congressman put it, that "the danger of our becoming involved in the European conflict really comes from the president more than any other source."[20] Congressman Karl Mundt of South Dakota reported to former President Herbert Hoover on 8 June: "Our minority group in Congress has gradually . . . gotten back its fighting spirit . . . to wage a head-on attack on FDR's steady usurpation of congressional powers and his sure march toward

LOUDER AND LOUDER THE WAR DRUM!

This critical cartoon from the Chicago *Tribune* illustrates the dilemma of isolationists like publisher Robert R. McCormick, who supported the idea of universal military training but feared that Commander in Chief Roosevelt would send draftees into the European war. (Reprinted with permission of the Chicago *Tribune*)

American involvement in the war.''[21] Deserved or not, such suspicion of the president's objectives meant that the consensus on preparedness could stretch only so far.

FDR held an equally jaundiced view of his opponents. To an old associate who had urged the shipment of modern arms to the Allies as quickly as possible, the president replied on 7 June: ''I am doing everything possible—although I am not talking very much about it because a certain element in the press . . . would undoubtedly pervert it, attack it, and confuse the public mind.''[22] Not until his commencement address at the University of Virginia, on 10 June 1940, did Roosevelt publicly pledge to ''extend to the opponents of force the material resources of this nation,'' while promising that ''we will . . . speed up the use of those resources so that we may have the equipment and training equal to any emergency.''[23] Acutely sensitive to isolationist obstruction, the president moved cautiously in those confused weeks before the fall of France. ''You will not be able to lead the American people unless you catch up with them,'' wired editor William Allen White on 5 June.[24] But FDR concentrated his appeals on less controversial issues of military rearmament, played down aid to England, and waited for public opinion to crystalize. When a group from New York sought a meeting to urge the president to support military conscription, FDR told his secretary on 14 June: ''The answer is No—the time is not ripe yet—put it off until a little later.''[25]

The fluidity of public opinion was further revealed in the Gallup polls of early June, according to which fully 65 percent of the American populace believed that if Britain and France were to surrender, Germany would eventually attack the United States. Five out of eight Americans expected the country to go to war eventually, and 75 percent believed that the United States should send more aid to the Allies. Nevertheless, only one citizen in fourteen advocated that war be declared against Hitler.[26] On the issue of military conscription, however, public opinion did seem to be moving. On 11 June, some 64 percent of Americans favored a year's compulsory service in the armed forces for all able-bodied males at age twenty; a month earlier only 50 percent had supported conscription.[27] White House mail on the subject rose in volume, but was still running two-to-one against a draft by late June.[28] Opinion seemed to be veering in two directions at once. A great gap existed between what Americans feared and expected to happen and what they thought should be done. Few Americans could plausibly deny the connection between the war in Europe and national safety, but how best to assure American defense without necessarily getting into the war remained the great issue.

Against the backdrop of blitzkrieg in Europe and concern for defense at home, it was probably inevitable that legislation for military conscription would be introduced into Congress in 1940. It was less predictable that such legislation would originate, not with the army, the White House, or Congress, but with a group of civilians whose own background and past services made them especially qualified to propose such a military solution.

On 8 May 1940, twenty-four hours before German panzers plunged into the Low Countries, some middle-aged men in their fifties and sixties gathered informally at the Harvard Club in New York City. These men, nine in all, constituted the Executive Committee of the Second Corps Area, Military Training Camps Association (MTCA)—an imposing title for an organization unknown to most Americans. Only slightly more familiar were the names of some of these gentlemen: Philip A. Carroll, a lawyer descended from the Carrolls of Carrollton; mustachioed Julius Ochs Adler, general manager and vice-president of the *New York Times;* Langdon P. Marvin, a former law partner of Franklin D. Roosevelt's; and Grenville Clark, founder of the great Wall Street law firm of Root, Clark, Buckner, and Ballantine.

The group had been called together by Dr. Adolph L. Boyce, chairman, and Alfred Roelker, secretary, of the New York MTCA headquarters, to discuss plans for the twenty-fifth anniversary of the Plattsburg training-camp movement, in which they had all actively participated. It was a boring meeting. Talk dragged on about a formal anniversary dinner or perhaps a parade at the World's Fair in Flushing. Then Grenville Clark interrupted. Had they all forgotten what the Plattsburg Movement stood for? Plattsburgers had always preferred action to talk. Prior to World War I they had demonstrated for military preparedness, initiating a program that trained nearly one hundred thousand officers for service on the Western Front. Now the world was even more menacing than in 1915. Why talk about reunions? Why not revive the Plattsburg Movement and do something practical? The army had expanded its officer reserves since the last war through the Reserve Officers' Training Corps (ROTC) and the Officers' Reserve Corps, but it was almost devoid of trained manpower to fill the ranks. Why not start a campaign for peacetime conscription? Clark reminded them that Plattsburgers had always supported the principle of universal military obligation.[29] In this informal way the idea of the first peacetime draft germinated.

That Grenville Clark should propose it at the Harvard Club in New York was no accident. The men who listened to him that evening might well have fancied the years turned back to 1915, when, nearly twenty-five years to the day, they had gathered angrily at the Harvard Club to talk over the sinking of the *Lusitania.* The parallels were striking. Americans in 1915, though shocked by the brutal consequences of German submarine warfare, had also resisted any counsels for war. In 1915, as in 1940, there had only been a slow awakening to the need for arming, a belated realization that the European war did have a distinct importance for the United States. In both cases, an interventionist minority tried vainly to persuade its fellow citizens of threats to

American interests and ideals, only to have the enemy accomplish, on his own initiative, what persuasion had largely failed to do.

The young men at the Harvard Club in 1915 had sent a telegram to the White House, pledging to "support the government in any measures, however serious, to secure reparations and guarantees" for the *Lusitania*.[30] Eager to do more and being of military age in their twenties and thirties, the young New Yorkers thought of training themselves for possible military service. Grenville Clark, Philip Carroll, and Theodore Roosevelt, Jr., took the ferry to Governors Island to see if the commanding general of the army's Eastern Department could give any assistance.

They had gone to the right man. A Harvard graduate, a *Mayflower* descendant, and a burly exemplar of the strenuous life, Maj. Gen. Leonard Wood was an outspoken advocate of military preparedness, the "patron saint, the guide and inspiration" of such organizations as the National Security League and the American Defense Society.[31] As army chief of staff in 1913, Wood had initiated special summer training camps for college students, a forerunner of the later ROTC program. To promote these camps, the "prodigiously busy" general worked eighteen-hour days, wrote articles and books, and spoke throughout the country, eventually urging a system of universal military training for the United States—that is, a small professional army on the Swiss model, backed by reserve troops who had undergone an obligatory six months of training at the age of eighteen or nineteen.[32] Wood's favorite quotation was from Demosthenes: "Go yourselves, every man of you, and stand in the ranks." Resented by many army people for his non–West Point origins and his civilian friendships, Wood aroused fears outside the service by his vigorous assertion of military views.[33] The delegation that visited him on Governors Island, however, were sons of men whom he had known for years. When Grenville Clark suggested a special training camp for older men at the Plattsburg Barracks in upstate New York, Wood became enthusiastic. If as many as a hundred professional and businessmen were to sign up for such a camp, he promised to provide the necessary officers and equipment.[34]

The Business Men's Camp at Plattsburg captured national attention that August. For four weeks some twelve hundred "tired businessmen" traded their plush offices and homes for sixteen rows of brown pyramid tents set on a sloping hill beside Lake Champlain. With the Adirondacks and the Green Mountains providing an attractive background, the trainees drilled, marched, fired rifles, and engaged in mock battles with regular troops. They took their training seriously and worked hard. In his official report, General Wood noted that the trainees "covered the ground ordinarily covered by our recruits in 4½ months and they received more hours of actual training than is received by the average militiaman in an enlistment of 3 years."[35] What attracted publicity to Plattsburg, however, was not the military results so much as the identities of the recruits. Among those carrying their 42-pound packs on maneuvers were such notables as war correspondent Richard Harding Davis, former Secretary of State Robert Bacon, Harvard football coach Percy D. Haughton, the mayor and the police commissioner of New York City, and three sons and a cousin of Theodore Roosevelt's.[36] The conspicuously aristocratic representation at Plattsburg came about deliberately. By recruiting primarily through university clubs and professional associations, the civilian organizers hoped to attract "the best and most desirable men . . . our kind of people."[37]

During their last week at Plattsburg, the civilian trainees formally organized themselves as the First Training Regiment and pledged to encourage "a system of military training camps throughout the nation" and to assist in providing "a reasonable amount of military training for the citizens of the United States."[38] In the autumn and winter of 1915/16 the First Training Regiment merged with a similar association, begun by General Wood's college trainees in 1913, to form the Military Training Camps Association; Grenville Clark was named secretary, and his close associates DeLancey Jay and J. Lloyd Derby became executive secretary and treasurer, respectively. Under Clark's prudent leadership, the MTCA avoided the shrill super-patriotism of some of the other preparedness organizations, kept from being too closely identified with General Wood, and worked closely with Congress and the War Department in shaping the National Defense Act of 1916. Under this legislation, during the summer of 1916, more than sixteen thousand volunteers took military training at twelve camps scattered around the country. In the remaining months prior to the United States' entry into war against Germany, the MTCA joined what historian John W. Chambers has called the "conscriptionist crusade."[39] The MTCA journal, *National Service,* began publication in February 1917 with the words "Devoted to the Cause of Universal Military Training" emblazoned on its masthead. The Platts-burgers' advocacy of this principle, reinforced by their own personal demonstrations for military training in the summer camps, undoubtedly made conscription more acceptable to Americans once war was declared in April.

On 5 April 1917, three days after Woodrow Wilson had delivered his war message, MTCA officials suggested that the Plattsburg camps scheduled for the next summer be converted to officer training camps. The army jumped at the idea and projected sixteen camps, which would train twenty-five hundred officers each in a three-months' course beginning in mid May. Since the army had neither the manpower nor the organization to handle the thousands of applications for the camps, Secretary of War Newton D. Baker gladly accepted the MTCA's offer to act as a recruiting agency.

Within three weeks the Plattsburg group set up volunteer-staffed offices throughout the country. The mailing lists that the MTCA had circularized for the 1916 camps were used again, as was the MTCA roster of more than twenty thousand persons who had attended federal training camps. The

MTCA hurriedly printed hundreds of thousands of application blanks, using its own funds for bulk mail, telephones, and telegraph. The total cost amounted to $350,000, none of which was paid back. In New York City, forty volunteer physicians examined applicants in groups of five in three-hour shifts from 8 A.M. to midnight. All told, the MTCA screened, examined, and certified to the army forty thousand out of more than one hundred and fifty thousand applicants; of these, some twenty-seven thousand completed the training and earned commissions.[40]

The army announced a second series of officer camps in early June. This time, War Department personnel supervised the recruiting, although the MTCA continued to distribute applications, serve as an information bureau, and provide clerical and medical help. Generally acting as "a liaison between the War Department on the one hand and the civilian population on the other," the MTCA, later in the war, helped to recruit for such specialized services as the American Ordnance Base Depot in France, the air force, the Army Corps of Engineers, the Quartermaster Corps, the Chemical Warfare Service, and the Tanks Corps. In some cities the MTCA provided preinduction training for men who wanted to learn the rudiments of military training before taking their oaths. The most notable example occurred in New York, where A. L. Boyce drilled thousands of prospective doughboys.

The total effect of the Plattsburg Movement went much farther than mere recruitment. The first twenty-seven thousand graduates of the first officer camps largely consisted of men who had attended the Plattsburg camps of 1915/16; these officers in turn trained and led the first increments of the National Army that the United States raised through the draft in the autumn of 1917. As believers in a citizen's obligation for military service, a large majority of the prewar Plattsburgers saw action in France, many winning medals at Belleau Wood and the Argonne Forest and some losing their lives. After the war a French officer observed that America's most remarkable achievement was, not in raising an army of two million men, but in finding and training in such a short time the officers to lead them. For this achievement the Plattsburg Movement can take much of the credit.

The Plattsburg method of officer procurement did not receive universal approval. When World War II came, the army studiously avoided a repetition of the officer-training system of 1917/18. The General Staff refused to accept potential officers directly from civilian life, insisting that the only avenue to Officer Candidate School should be through the ranks. This stand was prompted not only by the desire to condition future officers physically and psychologically by service on the enlisted level but also by a determination "to substitute a competitive and democratic system of procurement for the rather haphazard selection of young officers from a social and intellectual elite which had appeared necessary, for lack of a better means, in World War I."[41] The War Department defended its decision, and even Secretary of War Henry L.

Stimson, himself a graduate of the Plattsburg Camp of 1916, reluctantly concluded that the Officer Candidate Schools of World War II represented "the fair and democratic way."[42]

Charges that its members were seeking to create a military caste dogged the Plattsburg Movement in both World Wars. They find echoes in recent historical scholarship. John P. Finnegan has written that the Plattsburg camp of 1915 "was, in a way, a kind of secular retreat for a generation. There, amid simple martial surroundings, the upper-class elite underwent a conversion experience of patriotism, individual responsibility, and collective action. . . . The army camp had somehow become a paradigm for the good life in America."[43] John W. Chambers, the most careful student of the draft in World War I, has suggested that Plattsburgers thought "military training would help restore harmony, order, and vitality to a society that they believed was being fragmented and debilitated by individual selfishness, class and ethnic divisions, and local and regional parochialism."[44] Another scholar, focusing on General Wood's medical background, has even depicted the training-camp movement as "a public health program retaining the old tonic of regimen which medicine itself no longer emphasized."[45] Because so many Plattsburg veterans graduated to high positions in financial and government circles—most notably Henry L. Stimson, Robert P. Patterson, William J. Donovan, John J. McCloy, and Lewis Douglas—it has also been argued that the Plattsburg Movement constituted a nascent "power elite" that always advocated soldierly solutions and an imperialist foreign policy.[46]

Such criticisms of Plattsburg have some justification. Drawn to the bellicosity and swagger of men such as Leonard Wood and Theodore Roosevelt, some Plattsburgers were indeed susceptible to the peculiar attraction that the military seems to hold for a certain kind of authoritarian personality. During the First World War, such men roundly condemned first the "pacifism" and later the "internationalism" of Woodrow Wilson; still later they took pleasure in projecting military titles into civilian life and in promoting an extreme brand of "one hundred percent Americanism." Even his friends found it psychologically unsettling that future Secretary of War Robert P. Patterson always carried with him the belt of a German soldier whom he had killed in 1918.[47] Although the primary reason for advocating compulsory military training was to defend the United States against international dangers, some Plattsburgers also hoped that extramilitary benefits would be derived. "Heat up the Melting Pot," General Wood liked to say.[48] "Yank the Hyphen out of America," admonished another Plattsburger.[49] Even Grenville Clark, in his speech to the First Training Regiment at Plattsburg, had admitted that the camp "was not conceived merely as a means of obtaining security against external enemies, but of strengthening the nation internally against internal forces making for weakness and national disunity."[50] For subsequent generations, there is something both naïve and disturbing about Theodore Roosevelt's oft-quoted claim that "the military tent, where all sleep side-by-side, will rank next to the public school among the great agents of democratization."[51]

Several considerations help to place this critique of Plattsburg in perspective. First, by virtue of their own personal demonstration at Plattsburg and of their service abroad, the Plattsburgers occupied a philosophical position apart from the "more talkative" preparedness groups. Devoted as they were to the *compulsory* systems of selective service and universal military training, Plattsburgers emphasized this commitment by *voluntary* training and *voluntary* service. However romantic or naïve their beliefs, their sincerity could not be questioned. The dozen Plattsburg leaders who served as officers in New York City's Seventy-seventh Division, the so-called Melting Pot Division, thereafter believed that their shared military bond with immigrant Americans who served under them constituted "the national idea carried into practice."[52] Although Plattsburgers often behaved like aristocrats, they had no hesitancy in participating in the democratic process. They avoided partisanship. Whether it be recruiting for the camps, working with the War Department, or lobbying with Congress, the Plattsburgers went about their task with confidence. In an era when Harvard and Yale connections could automatically open doors, they knew the right people. If some of them put their faith in an unlikely hero—General Wood—the Plattsburgers did not follow their man on horseback to the Philippines when he failed to win the presidency in 1920. Conservative Republicans for the most part, they adapted easily to the era of Harding, Coolidge, and Hoover. Few of them joined the Roosevelt haters during the 1930s.[53] If the Plattsburg program of universal military training proved unacceptable to American institutions and values, they were willing to work within the system and abide by the results.

This ability to adapt to circumstances was particularly evident in the MTCA's reaction to the National Defense Act of 1920. The Plattsburgers originally had lobbied for a system based on universal military training, but Congress eliminated any such provision in the final bill. In its place the War Department was authorized to give *voluntary* training to any young civilians who desired it. Thus were born the Citizens' Military Training Camps (CMTC), an extension in principle of the Plattsburg idea. Grenville Clark argued that voluntary camps were "the only method whereby the public can be brought to consider the thing on its merits. . . . If it does not . . . produce a favorable sentiment, it is not adapted to the American people and we must revise our views."[54] Beginning in 1923, the army designated the MTCA as the official recruiting agency for the CMTC. During the ensuing two decades, more than half a million young men between the ages of eighteen and twenty-four emulated their Plattsburg predecessors in four-weeks' training courses.[55]

Despite the size and apparent success of the CMTC, universal military training seemed no closer to fulfillment in 1939 than it had been in 1920. The

CMTC was supposed to qualify graduates for reserve commissions through a three-years' ("Red-White-Blue") course, but only 4,630 such officers had earned commissions by 1934.[56] The camps, in President Calvin Coolidge's phrase, became "essentially schools in citizenship."[57] The MTCA continued to recruit for the CMTC during the interwar years, and Plattsburg officials in each of the army's nine corps areas were designated as civilian aides to the secretary of war. As part of the War Department establishment, the MTCA gradually evolved into a routine organization performing a limited, though valuable, function. This hardening of the arteries meant that members of the dynamic group that had organized the Plattsburg Movement lost much of their early interest. MTCA headquarters moved to Chicago in the early 1920s, and Charles B. Pike, a wealthy midwesterner who resembled the fictional George Babbitt, became chief civilian aide to the secretary of war. Chicago headquarters kept its enthusiasm for the CMTC, notwithstanding Gen. Douglas MacArthur's admission that "the camps do not directly serve to promote any military objective. The chief benefit to the army lies in the increased confidence in its personnel on the part of the civilian population."[58] A skeleton organization and memories of 1915 were all that remained in New York, as the "old Plattsburg crowd" returned to the law and other downtown professions during the 1920s and 1930s.

The Executive Committee of the Second Corps Area of the MTCA met at the Harvard Club on 8 May 1940. Most of these men had attended MTCA functions only infrequently in recent years, but the seriousness of the international crisis and their own involvement in the Plattsburg Camp of 1915 compelled their attendance this time. Grenny Clark's presence was another factor.

Clark has been described as a "statesman incognito"—known not at all to the millions but known very well to a few hundred persons of considerable influence in national affairs.[59] The historian Elting E. Morison has called Clark a man who "appeared, in critical or confusing times, as a lobby for particular impulses of the national conscience."[60] For someone who never held public office and who avoided the public gaze with a passion approaching obsession, Grenville Clark left an indelible imprint on important national decisions for more than half a century. The wellspring of his public service was an unshakable faith in American institutions that impelled him to act whenever those institutions were threatened—from without, as in the period 1915–17 and in 1940, and from within, because of attacks on civil liberties and on the Supreme Court. One of his last public efforts, providing money and legal services for jailed Freedom Riders in Alabama and Mississippi during the early 1960s, was done with his usual behind-the-scenes anonymity when Clark was in his eighties.[61] He wielded influence, in part, because of a social and economic heritage that placed him on terms of casual intimacy with the great and powerful; in part, because of a consistently held ideal of public service without thought of reward; and because of a fortuitous combination of personal qualities that matched vision with practicality and balanced courage and resolve with unselfish purpose.

The grandson of Le Grand Bouton Cannon, one of the founders of the Republican party, Clark was born a patrician. His New York home was an imposing mansion on Fifth Avenue; there were spacious summer homes in Vermont, a private railroad car, schooling at Pomfret and Harvard, where he graduated in the class of 1903 and belonged to the ultra-exclusive Porcellian Club. Later he became a member of the Somerset Club in Boston and the Knickerbocker Club in New York, bastions of tradition and ancient lineage.[62] In 1909 he married Fanny Dwight of Boston, whose family antedated the Revolution by several generations. Moving in such rarefied circles, Clark was called Grenny by presidents, cabinet members, ambassadors, military commanders, Supreme Court justices, university presidents—men who welcomed and sought his advice for more than sixty years.

After graduating from Harvard Law School in 1906, Clark spent two years as an apprentice law clerk in the New York office of Carter, Ledyard, and Milburn, where one of his fellow clerks was Franklin D. Roosevelt. In 1909 Clark and Elihu Root, Jr., opened their own one-room office at 31 Nassau Street, a partnership that grew over the decades into the prestigious firm Root, Clark, Buckner and Ballantine.[63] Although Clark excelled in the world of counsel, his legal practice often took second place to the ideals of public service that he had inherited from his Grandfather Cannon. This ideal had a unique twist in that public service for Clark never became equated with public office. Indeed, so finicky was he in avoiding the government payroll in any capacity that when Clark served a short term as a special adviser to Secretary of War Stimson during the autumn of 1941, he threw War Department lawyers into a dither by refusing to accept expenses or even the nominal "dollar-a-year" salary. Stimson had to make a special dispensation so that Clark could see classified material in his unofficial status.[64]

His passion for unofficial status stemmed from an ever-present fear that payment for services would compromise his independence, for Clark always conceived of himself in the role of independent critic, free to follow the evidence wherever it led. Clark thought it imperative that at least a few men who were interested in public affairs should remain amateurs, since the professionals, in their tendency toward "groovology" and bureaucratic routines, seldom had the creativity to produce new ideas in time of crisis.[65] This disdain for the "professionals" occasionally made Clark impatient with the fact that institutions and governments could not suddenly shift directions overnight. His urging of more dynamic policies sometimes ignored political realities. "Grenny Clark," an exasperated Franklin Roosevelt told an aide in

Grenville Clark in his best bulldog demeanor. (Courtesy of Dartmouth College Library)

1941, "could not get elected to Congress in any district—North, South, East or West."[66]

Fifty-seven years old in 1940, Clark was a sturdy six-footer, with a handsome, square-jaw New England face marred only by a slight birthmark above his left eye. His bushy eyebrows and general demeanor, not to mention his aggressive tenacity, reminded one of a bulldog. To his enemies, especially those who resented his strong hand in Harvard affairs, he seemed to hang on too hard. "The most powerful man in the United States" was one adversary's exaggerated description of Clark.[67] Though personally kind and gracious, the New York Brahmin could be relentless in overcoming obstacles to his purpose, sometimes enraging opponents by his self-confident indifference to dissenting opinions. He rather enjoyed the hostility that he aroused in behalf of a good cause.

And the causes mounted over the years. Even more than General Wood, it was Clark—"the man who thought of it all"—who achieved the success of the Plattsburg camps during World War I.[68] According to Ralph Barton Perry, the contemporary chronicler of the Plattsburg Movement, Clark's "initiative, persistence, public spirit and sagacity" made the camps what they were.[69] In 1931, together with Archibald Roosevelt, Clark founded the National Economy League to stop the raids on the Treasury which the voracious veterans' lobbyists were attempting. In the same year he became a member of the closely knit seven-man Corporation that governs Harvard University, a post he held until 1950. With Alphonse LaPorte, Clark wrote the brief on which the National Economy Act of 1933 was based, one of the key measures of President Roosevelt's First Hundred Days. Four years later, Clark turned against the president to lead, with Charles C. Burlingham and Douglas Arant, an independent committee of lawyers (all of whom had voted for FDR in 1936) which did much to block the plan to pack the Supreme Court.[70] As the head of the Bill of Rights Committee of the American Bar Association from 1938 to 1940, Clark challenged Jersey City Mayor Frank Hague's refusal to permit Norman Thomas to speak, and Clark defended the Jehovah's Witnesses in the widely publicized "flag salute" case. His successful campaign for conscription in 1940 and his unsuccessful effort in behalf of national service during World War II earned him the sobriquet "father of selective service."[71] After the war, however, Clark confounded some of his old military associates by taking up the cause of world federalism. His classic book *World Peace through World Law* (1958) and his backstage efforts for peace and disarmament almost won Clark the Nobel Peace Prize before his death at the age of eighty-five in 1967. "He is that rare thing in America," his friend Felix Frankfurter once remarked, "a man of independence, financially and politically, who devotes himself as hard to public affairs as a private citizen as he would were he in public office."[72]

Clark's proposal for compulsory training and service at the Harvard Club was not a spur-of-the-moment suggestion. He had been watching international affairs with growing concern ever since Japan had invaded Manchuria in 1931. In that year Henry L. Stimson, then secretary of state, had prophetically outlined to Clark the rise of Germany and Japan as dynamic powers and their parallel attempts to dominate Asia and Europe; he had warned that a coalition, including Russia and China as well as the Western democracies, would be necessary in order to stop the German and Japanese war machines. Urged by Stimson to become an assistant secretary of state and to help organize this coalition, Clark declined. His children were still young, and he had just joined the Harvard Corporation. But Clark did not forget

Stimson's prophecy as the war clouds loomed ominously during the late thirties.

In April 1940, after the invasion of Norway, Clark wrote an essay for the *Bill of Rights Review* that established his place in the interventionist minority who perceived Nazi conquests as a direct threat to the United States.[73] Later published in the *New York Times* and the *Boston Herald,* the essay contended that "the people of this country should have and do have a vital concern that Germany shall not decisively win this war." It thus followed logically that "we ought not to fool ourselves by pretending to be strictly neutral." What to do? Clark urged that the Johnson Act be repealed, so as to permit private loans to the Allies. American citizens should be permitted to enlist in the Allied armies, and the most modern arms and planes should be sent to Hitler's opponents. Clark also argued that the export of war materials to countries that might then sell them to the Axis should be banned. He advocated large increases in merchant shipbuilding, also suggesting that the United States make available government grants, not loans, to the Allied powers. Clark emphasized that simultaneously with this program of aid short of war, the country should greatly expand its own military facilities in order to meet the real geopolitical threat to the United States that a major Allied disaster would entail.

Shortly after writing this essay, Clark received notice of the Harvard Club meeting of 8 May. Thoughts of the MTCA automatically brought to mind the efforts of 1915–17. Then, as in 1940, Clark was convinced that the only equitable and efficient way to raise a large military force was through compulsory training and service. He therefore went to the Harvard Club prepared to urge that the Plattsburg Movement be revived. His old cohorts enthusiastically accepted his proposal for conscription, and they agreed to convene a much-larger gathering to determine how much support could be mustered, to define objectives, and to provide means for carrying out a concrete program. Clark chaired a planning committee for this next meeting, which was set for 22 May.[74]

On that same day, Neville Chamberlain was upheld by a shaky vote of confidence in the House of Commons. In the United States, people were talking about John Steinbeck's *Grapes of Wrath,* just awarded the Pulitzer Prize; Yankee baseball fans were moaning because their favorites, off to a dismal start, had dropped their fifth straight game and were languishing in the American League cellar. The ninety-five thousand racing fans who, the weekend before, had watched open-mouthed as a 36-to-1-shot named Gallahadion romped home first in the Kentucky Derby were wondering if he could do it again in the Preakness. But on 10 May the streamer headlines announced that the German armies were slashing into the Low Countries.[75]

The next two weeks, which saw German forces race across northern France to the Channel, were also taken up with intense planning for the meeting on 22 May. The Plattsburg sponsors deemed the support of the national MTCA imperative. As a functioning organization with branches throughout the United States, it would help in educating public opinion to the necessity for a draft bill. Washington officials in charge of military policy knew and respected the MTCA, not only because of its quasi-official status in the War Department but also because it was the legitimate embodiment of the old Plattsburg Movement; use of its name would eliminate the necessity of starting from scratch. Moreover, the fact that the MTCA had stood for universal military training since 1916 made it the logical vehicle through which to work. In 1940 Tom R. Wyles of Chicago was president of the MTCA and also the chief civilian aide to the secretary of war; and Robert H. Jamison of Cleveland was chairman of the Executive Committee. Clark invited both of these men to New York for the 22 May meeting, sending them a copy of three resolutions that the Planning Committee intended to offer. These resolutions would commit the MTCA to compulsory military training and service as "the only measure that will suffice to protect this country in the present world emergency"; "immediate and concrete measures, short of war, in aid to the Allies, including the sale of army planes"; and cooperation with a group (headed by Col. Frank Knox of the *Chicago Daily News*) that was proposing "Air Plattsburgs" to train selected civilians as army fliers.[76]

Notwithstanding these diplomatic overtures, it was difficult to avoid the appearance of trying to "use" the MTCA. Wyles and Jamison were taken somewhat aback by the sudden urgings from Clark; as it was, they balked at the second resolution, feeling that aid to the Allies lay completely outside the province of the MTCA. They did, however, submit the other two resolutions to the civilian aides in each of the nine corps areas, gaining their approval by a vote of nine to two. Backed by this favorable tally and by the approval of their National Executive Committee, Wyles and Jamison promised to attend the 22 May meeting and to bring the national MTCA behind the effort for conscription.[77]

Clark's Planning Committee also put careful thought into the list of those persons to be invited. The attendance of certain key individuals was considered indispensable: Henry L. Stimson, former secretary of both war and state and a consistent supporter of a firm military policy; Lewis Douglas, former congressman, director of the budget, and, later, ambassador to the Court of St. James; Gen. John F. ORyan, commander of the Twenty-seventh Division during World War I and a leading spokesman for the National Guard; William Allen White, the sagacious editor from Emporia, Kansas, who was then forming another "interventionist" organization, the Committee to Defend America by Aiding the Allies;[78] and Gen. John McAuley Palmer, a former adviser to the Senate Military Affairs Committee and the principal author of the National Defense Act of 1920.

The seventy-two-year-old Stimson, who had been embroiled for months in a wearisome lawsuit, at first tried to beg off. Clark, however, telephoned him persistently until the former secretary of state agreed to attend "for an hour or so."[79] Once there, Stimson wound up making a seconding speech in behalf of the resolution and, withal, became one of the meeting's most ardent participants. The seventy-year-old Palmer also hesitated because of his health. Having retired to his home in Hill, New Hampshire, to chronicle the military-policy decisions in which he had played a part, he at first declined the invitation sent to him by the Planning Committee. But Clark again got on the telephone, and Palmer agreed to come to New York.[80]

One more piece of preparatory diplomacy remained. It was obvious that a selective-service bill could not be considered in a vacuum. Having a direct and vital relation to the nation's military planning, any compulsory-training legislation would have to fit into the overall defense policies that the Roosevelt administration was busily reappraising.[81] Whether the president would commit himself on such a controversial subject as conscription during an election year was problematic. At this early stage, however, Clark and his friends considered White House support to be absolutely essential.

Clark accordingly sent a telegram to the president on 16 May 1940, the first of many attempts to elicit an endorsement. Since Clark was aware of Franklin Roosevelt's love of being personally "informed" about everything, this telegram recounted the plans that were taking shape in New York. Some of the old Plattsburg crowd, Clark explained, were considering "recommending and supporting compulsory military training," and "whether, as a matter of timing, it is opportune to put it forward publicly at this time."[82] This indirect attempt to sound out FDR's opinion brought back an oracular reply two days later. "I see no reason why the group you mention should not advocate military training," the president wrote, "but if it is to be called 'compulsory,' I am inclined to think there is a very strong public opinion for universal service of some kind so that every able-bodied man and woman would fit into his or her place." This statement seemed to indicate general, if cautious, approval of selective service, but it also foreshadowed Roosevelt's reluctance to abandon a plan that was very attractive to himself and to Mrs. Roosevelt, a program of vocational training designed to channel workers into defense industries. The sensitivity of the president's political antenna was reflected in his comment on the second MTCA resolution: "The difficulty of proposing a concrete set of measures 'short of war' is largely a political one—what one can get from Congress."[83]

What could be obtained from Congress was indeed a question mark. When Congressman Andrew J. May and Senator Claude D. Pepper proposed to relax the prohibition of the Johnson Act on loans to the Allies, they received heavy fire from isolationist batteries. Aviator hero Charles A. Lindbergh addressed the nation over CBS Radio on 19 May and urged Americans to concentrate on defending the hemisphere, rather than getting mixed up in European quarrels.[84] The lightning drive of the Nazi panzers jarred Americans into a realization that military and naval defenses needed immediate attention; and on 22 May, the day that the first German columns were reported at the Channel coast, a unified Senate passed the emergency appropriations for the War Department by a vote of seventy-four to zero.[85]

That evening, nearly a hundred prominent men met in the Biddle Room of the Harvard Club. Besides the original nine Plattsburgers and the MTCA officers from Chicago, the assemblage included Stimson; General Palmer; General ORyan; Lewis Douglas; DeLancey Jay, Kenneth P. Budd, and Archibald G. Thacher—all winners of the Distinguished Service Cross in World War I; Col. William J. Donovan; state supreme court Justice Philip J. McCook; George C. McMurtry, second in command of the "Lost Battalion" and a recipient of the Congressional Medal of Honor; Judge Robert P. Patterson; Archibald B. Roosevelt; Elihu Root, Jr.; and former Assistant Secretary of War Jonathan M. Wainwright.[86]

The homogeneity of the group is striking. Practically all belonged to the social elite and were graduates of Ivy League colleges. Thoroughly respected in business and the professions, these scions of WASP families were at home in such nonplebeian places as the Bankers' Club and the Downtown Association.[87] As a rule they possessed considerable means, and they were by nature and environment political conservatives. A few, such as Stimson, had participated in the international wing of the peace movement during the 1930s, as members of the League of Nations Association and the Council on Foreign Relations. All were Anglophiles. All were gentlemen to whom concepts of honor, dignity, and morality were as real as were those of politics and power. Having traveled widely and served abroad either in business or governmental capacities, such men had intense personal reactions to the gloomy news from Europe. One of them reported to the president's secretary, Marguerite ("Missy") LeHand:

> I am still feeling the thrill that I got last night at the dinner at the Harvard Club where the old Plattsburg group met once again in the same place that we met 25 years ago. . . .
>
> We met in the big paneled room that has a painting of Nick Biddle over the fireplace. There were about 100 men present. Every one of them is 100% behind the president in his Foreign policy and Defense plans. Many of them are his personal friends—Harry Stimson, Mayhew Wainwright, Lang Marvin, DeLancey Jay, Grenville Clark, Peter Bowditch, and a whole lot of others. I . . . regretted that the president could not have been there with us smoking his cigarette. He would have been very happy in that atmosphere. I felt proud of the breed that Plattsburg produced.[88]

The meeting began solemnly. With Clark presiding, A. G. Thacher moved the resolutions presented by the Planning Committee. Stimson, Wainwright, and McMurtry made seconding speeches. The resolutions dealing with compulsory training and "Air Plattsburgs" passed unanimously, but even in this like-minded gathering, opposition materialized to the proposal recommending immediate aid to the Allies. After Philip Roosevelt, Geoffrey Smith, Henry James, and A. Conger Goodyear objected, a large majority approved the resolution for "aid short of war," but only in the name of the Second Corps Area of the MTCA. An additional resolution called for the Regular Army and the National Guard to expand to full strength, pending the enactment of selective service.

New committees formed to carry out the three main resolutions. Archibald Thacher, an able lawyer who had long been interested in military affairs, headed a group to work on a selective-service bill; Philip Carroll, a veteran of both the French and United States air forces during the first war, was designated chairman of the "Air Plattsburg" committee; Cornelius Wickersham chaired the group dealing with aid to the Allies; and Julius Ochs Adler took charge of overall coordination. Though not formally organized as such until 3 June, the combined personnel of these committees constituted the National Emergency Committee (NEC) of the Military Training Camps Association, the title eventually given to the body that over the next four months organized and directed the campaign for the Selective Training and Service Act.

Thus, unknown to the General Staff, unknown to Congress, and unknown to the public at large, a movement began that would soon force a drastic reorientation of army plans, affect the political strategy of every elected official in Washington, and reach into every household in the United States. Not that the meeting was dark and secret, as subsequently charged! On the contrary, the Plattsburgers welcomed and even solicited wide publicity. Newsmen were summoned after the Harvard Club meeting, and readers of the *New York Times* found at the bottom of the front page on 23 May the story line: "Plattsburg Group Asks Conscription."[89] The article reported in detail the events of the night before, listed the leading persons involved, and gave a capsule history of the Plattsburg Movement.

This story in the *New York Times* foreshadowed the vital role that newspaper was to play in the coming drama. The connection came about naturally. The nation's most prestigious daily, which had endorsed the Plattsburg Movement of World War I, sympathized thoroughly with the efforts toward national defense in 1940.[90] Julius Ochs Adler, vice-president and general manager of the *Times,* formed an additional link as regimental commander of the Seventy-seventh Division and a prime mover in the 1940 campaign for conscription. In that era before television, whenever the *Times* gave favorable prominence to any particular group or cause, its lead was sure to be followed by hundreds of editors throughout the country. As two political scientists have put it, "The media may not tell us what to think, but they do tell us what to think about."[91] Even though the *Times* would push selective service for the next four months, it is nonetheless true that few who read of the Harvard Club meeting had any idea that something of national importance was afoot.

Even those who had been involved did not fully realize what lay ahead. The adopted resolutions revealed that the sponsors had not yet brought their ideas into sharp focus. As President Roosevelt implied in his letter to Clark, "aid short of war" was a nebulous term, and cooperation with a second group advocating "Air Plattsburgs" hardly constituted clear marching orders. The really tangible proposal, as Clark and his cohorts soon realized, was that of compulsory training and service. "It grows on me," Clark wrote to Adler, "that we have the constituency, the skeleton organization, the men and the brains to put over a big national movement."[92] But even this issue lacked sharp definition, for the Harvard Club meeting had spoken of compulsory training only in the most general terms; nor did those who were present know any details of the army's plans for manpower procurement. The next tasks were to determine just what they should advocate, to draft necessary legislation, and to present it to the people and to Congress.

On the same day as the Harvard Club meeting, President Roosevelt met with his secretary of agriculture, Henry A. Wallace. Usually calm about international affairs, Wallace excitedly told his chief that Germany "had definite designs on our [Western] Hemisphere." FDR replied: "Of course, what you say is true." Wallace insisted that it was " exceedingly important to arm for peace" and to create "an army with well-trained officers which could put large numbers of reserves into the field as soon as possible." The president thereupon described new military contingency plans to seize key British, French, Dutch, and Danish bases in the Caribbean.[93] The next evening, perhaps sensing the new mood in Washington, the British ambassador cabled London with the suggestion that England grant or lease whatever bases the United States might desire for hemispheric defense.[94] The next morning, 24 May, the first units of a ragtag armada began to move across the English Channel to pick up remnants of the British Expeditionary Force from the beaches of Dunkirk.[95]

Slowly, perceptibly, the connection between the war in Europe, England's survival, and national defense was taking form. As one isolationist told his constituents, "this country must modernize its armaments and prepare itself so well that the mailed fist of aggression cannot come to the Western Hemisphere."[96] Just how American forces would be raised was also becoming more apparent.

3

General Staff Planning:
The Background of Selective Service

The confidence of the New Yorkers on 22 May 1940 obscured an undeniable element of presumption, for it was presumptuous that a group of amateurs should consider itself better able than the War Department to determine military policy. Foreseeing possible friction between his civilian friends and the professional soldiers, General Palmer advised Archibald Thacher that before the latter's committee went ahead, its members should find out more about the army's mobilization plans. This advice was obviously sound, and the New York activists asked Palmer to visit Washington and to confer on their behalf with officers of the General Staff.

The army quite naturally had its own ideas about manpower procurement. By no means blind to the world crisis, the War Department had been laying plans since the early 1930s for a military and economic mobilization that every day was becoming increasingly probable. These plans reflected the experience of the army in meeting similar problems in the past, particularly the war of 1917/18; they also profited from observations of new techniques as practiced in the local wars of the 1930s. In short, army planning involved an analysis of the lessons that had been learned from various methods of recruitment in the past, plus an estimate of manpower required in the event of another war.

The history of the United States' military forces is in essence a history of two armies, a Regular Army, composed of professional soldiers, and a citizen army of draftees or volunteers committed to temporary service. "Selective service"—the term applied to the compulsory system used in the two world wars and from 1948 to 1972—is a specialized form of the more general term *conscription,* which has been a traditional method of raising military forces in America since the founding of the colonies. It should be emphasized, however, that the underlying basis of conscription—namely, the universal obligation of all able-bodied males to bear arms in defense of the community—was recognized and applied in colonial America primarily in terms of militia for home defense. Colonial volunteers marched with British regulars in storming Louisburg and Quebec, while local "minutemen," under a system of short-term compulsory service under local officers, defended scattered settlements from attack by French and Indians. This dual system of local conscription for home defense and of volunteer enlistment for foreign service accorded with an agrarian society's community structure of authority, its individualist values, and its distrust of centralized power.[1]

During the Revolution the Continental Congress extended this dual system by issuing calls upon the states for units of local militia and for voluntary enlistment in the Continental Army. Notwithstanding fluctuating and unpredictable manpower and glaring military inefficiency, there was no suggestion of conscription at the national level. Fears of standing armies were so ingrained in the republican ideology that all national forces disbanded after 1783, except for a single regiment. By 1787, however, the fifty-five notables who gathered at Philadelphia for the Constitutional Convention had grown more concerned about internal disorder and about border threats from England, Spain, and various Indian tribes. Accordingly, the new federal constitution granted Congress the unrestricted power to "raise and support armies." How these armies would be raised was deliberately left vague. Although a majority of the Founding Fathers probably favored some form of conscription, they declined to mention it because, in Edmund Randolph's words, "*draughts* stretch the strings of government too violently to be adopted."[2] During the 1790s the debates over military policy focused, not on conscription, but on the size, cost, and organization of the Regular Army and on the extent of federal control over the state militias.[3]

When the United States went to war in 1812, Congress repeated the Revolutionary experience by endorsing a policy of voluntary enlistments, coupled with requests to the states for militia units. The latter, which, on paper, consisted of some thousand regiments scattered around the country, had little more training than that obtained during the "grand spree" on the annual "muster day."[4] Moreover, state officials responded erratically to militia calls, and some federalized militia units refused to cross national boundaries, thereby preventing offensive operations in Canada. Meanwhile, despite a system of bounties to encourage enlistment, the Regular Army, authorized by Congress, was not able to recruit more than twenty thousand volunteers by the end of 1813. The resulting breakdown, combined with British military victories in 1814, spurred the first serious proposal to Congress for national conscription. Secretary of War James Monroe's plan of 14 October 1814 to raise forty thousand troops by means of a national draft embodied four principles later adopted in the twentieth century: universal obligation, individual selection, local administration, and national control.[5] A modified form of Monroe's plan passed Congress, but the war ended before the system could be instituted.[6]

Although the Mexican War did not put great strain on the nation's manpower, it did illustrate the inefficiency of volunteer methods. Two types of recruitment were employed: enlistments in the Regular Army for five years and enlistments in the wartime army for one year. At Puebla, midway on his march from Vera Cruz to Mexico City, Gen. Winfield Scott had to relinquish seven regiments of volunteers, nearly 40 percent of his army, because their terms of enlistment had run out.[7]

During the Civil War, both the North and the South eventually adopted conscription. The Confederacy, ostensibly formed because of states' rights and opposition to centralized power, ironically was the first to resort to conscription, in the spring of 1862. All told, approximately one-third of the nine hundred thousand Confederate soldiers who fought in the war were draftees.[8] The North, because of its larger population, did not feel the manpower pinch until 1863.[9] Even less so than in the South, however, did the draft become the principal means of raising troops for the Union armies. Voluntary enlistments continued, draftees could hire substitutes or purchase exemptions, and men were only drafted when districts failed to fill their quotas. Fewer than 8 percent of the 2.1 million men in blue were actually conscripted.

The Civil War drafts left a mixed legacy. Given the total nature of the sectional conflict, the adoption of conscription, however inefficient, permitted both Blue and Gray forces to reach a size and endurance unknown in previous wars. The costs were correspondingly high. As administered, the draft clashed with basic values of American political culture. Allowing rich men to buy substitutes underscored the inequity of both the Northern and the Southern systems. The fact that military—not civilian—authorities administered and enforced the draft offended democratic sensibilities on both sides. Also going against the grain was the way in which the draft operated under centralized control, ignoring local authorities and traditions. Widespread resistance occurred. In the South, every state except Florida reported that draft resisters were hiding in the mountains and swamps, and by the time of Lee's surrender at Appomattox, some 104,000 men had deserted from the Confederate Army. Opposition grew more violent in the North, especially in the cities. Beginning on 13 July 1863, when a mob from the Irish ghetto burned down draft headquarters, New York City suffered through the bloodiest riot in American history, upwards of twelve hundred deaths in four days.[10] Smaller riots erupted in Boston, Buffalo, and other cities. Some states did not even attempt conscription because of the extent of local hostility and the inability of federal troops to enforce the draft.[11]

Two posthumously published books testified to the ambiguous lessons of the Civil War. John A. Logan's *The Volunteer Soldier of America* (1887) celebrated the role that volunteers, commanded by local officers, played in the Northern victory. A congressman from Illinois when the war began, Logan had enlisted as a private, later had organized and commanded an infantry regiment, and eventually had won his general's stars at Vicksburg. Reflecting the powerful position of the Grand Army of the Republic in American politics after the Civil War, Logan's book eulogized citizen volunteers and criticized West Point professionals and conscript soldiers. Any system of compulsory service, he argued, was "too closely allied with the methods of monarchy to find any imitation in a republican government."[12] Although Logan's homilies probably represented the views of most Americans in the late nineteenth century, a more professional perspective could be found in the works of Gen. Emory Upton, the army's leading intellectual of the era.[13] More impressed by an inspection tour of European armies in the 1870s than by the volunteers who had served under him at Bull Run, Upton, in his writings, extolled West Point professionalism. Among his recommendations were a larger, expandable Regular Army, increased national control of state militias, a central General Staff, and universal military training. Upton's ideas, which he elaborated most extensively in *The Military Policy of the United States* (1904), became a veritable Bible for professional officers and military reformers before the First World War. Such professional views also engendered what historian Russell F. Weigley has called "Uptonian pessimism," for it was virtually impossible that nineteenth-century America would accept either large standing armies or compulsory training in peacetime.[14]

The "splendid little war" against Spain, fought with a tiny Regular Army, militia, and volunteers, did not last long enough to require large forces.[15] But the rather chaotic performance of the War Department helped to prompt a series of long-overdue reforms under Elihu Root, secretary of war from 1899 to 1904. Embodying the Progressive Era's concern for order, efficiency, and national control, Root's reforms sought to provide a military establishment befitting the United States' new role as a world power. The Dick Act of 1903 extended federal control over state militias by having the War Department provide arms and equipment without charge, in return for which militia units were required to hold drills, target practices, and summer encampments each year. The law further recognized the president's power to call militia troops into national service for nine months.[16] Root sponsored another bill that abolished the office of commanding general and made the secretary of war the supreme head of the army, under the president; the senior general at the War Department assumed the title of chief of staff as adviser and executive to the secretary. Further legislation in 1903 created the General Staff, which for the first time provided the United States with military specialists who were charged specifically with long-range strategic planning.[17]

Despite Root's reforms and subsequent efforts under Stimson and Wood from 1911 to 1913, the most important element in military planning, that of providing trained manpower in wartime, remained unsettled when World War I broke out in 1914. The choice lay, as it had throughout American history, between two approaches—an expandable professional army and a small professional force, supplemented by a wartime "citizen" army. Still influenced by Emory Upton's ideas, most professional soldiers favored an expandable standing army in which a relatively large professional force of skeletonized units could be filled to wartime strength by adding either Regular Army reserves or civilian volunteers and/or draftees. Under this system, Regular Army officers would command the same units before and after mobilization. Under the citizen-army theory, however, the principal mission of the Regular Army in peacetime would not be to command potential war units but to train citizen reserves that had already been organized into tactical forces. Once war began, citizen reservists would not merely fill Regular Army units, but reserve forces would also be activated as units, taking their assigned place in the field. The Regular Army would still compose the nucleus of any wartime army, but the activated reserve divisions, led by their own officers, would form the bulk of the fighting forces.

The National Defense Act of June 1916 represented a compromise between these two approaches. In 1912 the General Staff had published a report, "The Organization of the Land Forces of the United States," based squarely on the citizen-army approach. Its principal author was the youthful Capt. John McAuley Palmer.[18] When the Wilson administration espoused preparedness in the fall of 1915, however, Secretary of War Lindley M. Garrison put forward a more orthodox plan, the so-called Continental Army scheme. The proposal called for an enlarged Regular Army, plus a reserve force of four hundred thousand men (then considered a huge force), to be trained in three annual increments. The Continental Army, in theory, would flesh out Regular Army units in time of war. By constituting a national reserve under federal control, this new force would replace the state militias or the National Guard.

Despite agitation by the Plattsburgers and other preparedness organizations in behalf of universal military training, the legislative battle narrowed to a contest between advocates of Garrison's Continental Army and partisans of the National Guard, led by Congressman James Hay of Virginia, chairman of the House Committee on Military Affairs. Hay and other Southern progressives succeeded in blocking the Continental Army and in rescuing the National Guard from oblivion.[19] Secretary Garrison resigned, but the resulting Defense Act was a compromise in which the General Staff obtained its increase in the Regular Army, plus an Officers' Reserve Corps (ORC) and an Enlisted Reserve Corps (ERC), in harmony with the concept of an expandable army.[20]

Under the Defense Act of 1916 the United States seemed to have improved its military organization. To be sure, the new force could not match up to the German Imperial Army, but no one expected that it would.[21] The new reserves, moreover, existed almost entirely on paper. When the United

States entered the war in April 1917, the Regular Army Reserve numbered 4,767 and the ORC less than 2,000. Had the Plattsburg Movement not pushed through Section 54 of the Act, there would have been no legal mechanism for holding the Officer Training Camps in the spring of 1917. Even if the National Guard and various reserve components had provided a large-enough reservoir of manpower to raise Regular Army units to immediate war strength, the resulting army could not have fulfilled the demands of the American war effort. A citizen army had to be called in.

President Wilson wasted no time in deciding how to raise this new army. In his message of 2 April 1917 he stated categorically that the war would require "the immediate addition to the armed forces of the United States . . . [of] at least five hundred thousand men" and that these men should be chosen "upon the principle of universal liability to service."[22] Within a few days a draft bill, prepared at the War Department, was presented in Congress, and after a relatively short debate, it became law on 18 May, as the Selective Service Act of 1917.[23] The general plan was, first, to increase the Regular Army and the National Guard to war strength, as authorized under the National Defense Act, and, second, to draft additional forces of five hundred thousand as needed, the first increment to be raised at once. On 5 June more than nine and a half million men registered, and the building of the National Army began.[24]

The draft of 1917, based on service liability of all males between the ages of twenty-one and thirty-one (later widened to eighteen and forty-five), consciously profited from the Civil War experience.[25] The new law eliminated short-term enlistments by stipulating that military service should be for the duration of the war. The hiring of substitutes and the purchase of exemptions were forbidden. The bounty system was abolished. Most significantly, the draft of 1917 deftly blended local administration with federal control; more than five thousand local boards actually selected the draftees in each community according to federal guidelines and quotas. This last corrective had an enormous impact, for it helped to harmonize conscription with American tradition. A remote central government no longer seemed to be reaching into the local community to snatch away its citizens.[26] By designating precincts and counties as the bases for quotas, by utilizing local government machinery, and by having local civilian boards select their own neighbors for induction, the Selective Service System of World War I provided a successful model for the "new federalism" of the interwar years, in which national policies were carried out by state and local administrators.[27]

The draft seemed to enjoy wide public acceptance during the war. Except for a few shoot-outs in the mountains of North Carolina and Nevada, the closest approximation to violence Civil War–style came in the so-called Green Corn Rebellion in Oklahoma in August 1917, when some four hundred and fifty potential draft resisters were arrested without injury. The newly organized National Civil Liberties Bureau protested the harsh treatment accorded to conscientious objectors. Nevertheless, in a landmark case, *Arver* v. *United States,* the Supreme Court affirmed the constitutionality of national conscription. "As the mind cannot conceive an army without the men to compose it," Chief Justice Edward Douglass White wrote, "the objection that it [the Constitution] does not give power to provide for such men would seem to be too frivolous for further notice. . . . The very conception of a just government and its duty to the citizen includes the reciprocal obligation of the citizen to render military service in case of need and the right to compel it."[28] The *Arver* decision meant that when selective service was again proposed in 1940, little effective opposition to it could be organized on grounds of its unconstitutionality.

Despite the wartime success of selective service, the National Defense Act of 1920 contained no provision either for conscription or for compulsory training. That the new legislation contained the foundations of a citizen army owed much to John McAuley Palmer. Promoted to colonel in the American Expeditionary Force, Palmer had been sent back from France to represent Gen. John J. Pershing's views on postwar military policy, only to find that the General Staff had prepared a plan, based on the old principle of an expandable standing army, calling for 509,909 men in peacetime, to be increased to 1.25 million during an emergency.[29] The Senate Military Affairs Committee, headed by the young Senator James W. Wadsworth, Jr., of New York, instinctively shied away from the General Staff's bill. In the course of committee hearings the scholarly looking Palmer, carrying "a stack of papers a foot high," appeared in order to testify. Within minutes, everyone was alert. It was Palmer's assertion that the March bill was "not in harmony with the genius of American institutions," which startled the committee.[30] Asked to elaborate, Palmer spent nearly two days giving details of his own plan for a citizen army. "He was not domineering," Wadsworth remembered, "he wasn't offensive but he was philosophical."[31] "I think I have never seen a witness create as deep an impression."[32] Wadsworth thereupon asked the War Department to assign Palmer to the committee as a special adviser, and in this capacity he put his ideas into statutory form.

Palmer's blueprint for a citizen army had several essential features. He projected a small professional army, organized into three roles: garrisons for outposts and overseas bases; a few divisions at effective strength for strategic forces or for initial protection during emergency mobilization; and a force charged with the training of the civilian reserves. This citizen reserve would initially be composed of the National Guard and the National Army divisions of World War I; later a system of universal military training (UMT) would supply the necessary manpower. Finally, the United States would be divided into nine geographical areas, each serving as a framework for the administration, training, and mobilization of the citizen army.[33]

These principles were accepted wholeheartedly by the Senate Committee, but before the bill could be reported out, the Democratic party, in early February 1920, declared its opposition to any kind of compulsory military training. Other congressmen grumbled about the financial costs of universal training. Accordingly, the committee asked Palmer to rewrite the bill, discarding the UMT provision. In this abridged form it passed the Senate in April. Meanwhile, the House had passed a bill of its own in March, identical to the Senate version with respect to the Regular Army, but lacking any provision for a citizen reserve. For five weeks Senator Wadsworth worked at persuading the House conferees. Gradually he succeeded. Since the House bill, however, had been written in the form of amendments to the Defense Act of 1916, the House conferees insisted that the provisions for a citizen army be condensed into a few short sections. "It can't be done," Palmer complained. "It would be like asking Thomas Jefferson to write the Declaration of Independence in the form of amendments to the Book of Job."[34] Nevertheless, Col. Thomas M. Spaulding, an adviser to the House Committee, managed to "perform the miracle" by finding the necessary language.[35]

The resulting National Defense Act of 1920 bore little resemblance in form to Palmer's original plan. In the first place, the core of the citizen reserve—universal military training—had been excised before the bill left the committee. The remaining essentials, originally worked out in detail, had been crammed into a few clauses sketching the citizen army in broad outline. The product looked promising on paper. The principle of a national reserve, organized into tactical units, was recognized for the first time, and a skeleton provided as the basis for a fighting force in wartime. Nevertheless, despite initial optimism from Palmer, Wadsworth, and other reformers, the lack of compulsion meant that there would never be sufficient numbers to flesh out the skeletal divisions of the citizen army in the years between the two World Wars.[36] While it was a definite improvement over the 1916 Defense Act, the new system, undermanned as it was, could not easily adapt to large-scale mobilization in time of crisis. This fact had an obvious bearing on the 1940 campaign for selective service.

The army did not lack mobilization plans. Its blueprints for a possible war against any one of several potential enemies (designated as the Orange Plan, the Blue Plan, and other color plans) had given way under the impact of the 1939 crisis to five Rainbow plans, including possible full-scale war against the combined Axis powers.[37] Regarding manpower procurement, the General Staff's thinking reflected the lesson that a war army could not be raised by voluntary enlistments. But how did the General Staff resolve the inconsistency between this lesson and the fact that Congress had authorized no other machinery than the volunteer system? The answer involves a brief discussion of what happened to the idea of compulsory training and service between the wars, as well as what happened to the army itself.

A distinction must be made between universal military training (UMT) and "selective training and service," as employed during both World Wars. The key to the difference lies in the word *universal* as opposed to *selective*. UMT is universal in that it takes all able-bodied young men of a certain age, usually before they become established in their chosen vocations, and gives the entire age group the rudiments of a military education. Selective service, generally operating within wider age limits, *selects* from the eligible group those men who, because of occupation and dependency status, can best be spared from civilian life for military duty. Theoretically, selective service is better adapted to raising armies in an emergency, while UMT operates more efficiently as part of a permanent military system. By training *all* men at the lower age levels, UMT enables the army to depend upon a more youthful reserve for a much longer period, whereas under a selective-service system, many potential reservists soon pass beyond the military age. UMT is also eminently more equitable in that it does not take one man into the armed forces while leaving his neighbor in school or in some civilian job.[38] In theory at least, UMT requires a less complicated administrative process than does selective service, which must select recruits from millions of cases, each potentially different from the other. The larger numbers involved and the higher costs of a peacetime universal training program, however, helped to persuade Congress to reject UMT after World War II in favor of a modified Selective Service System.[39]

The only feasible time to introduce UMT is in peacetime, for such a system can build an effective reserve force only over a period of years. When faced with imminent wars that require large forces, as in 1917 and 1940, there was no time for gradual building. The armed forces needed all physically able men of all ages who could be spared from essentially productive tasks. Since the United States, at the beginning of both World Wars, had no large reserve as an established UMT system would have provided, it was forced to turn to selective training and service, which was looked upon in each case as an emergency measure only.

In the aftermath of World War I, in light of the general acceptance of the wartime draft, military reformers hoped that the American public would retain compulsory training in peacetime. This hope led the Senate committee to endorse Colonel Palmer's original plan. Nevertheless, as one Plattsburg veteran phrased it, the inevitable "widespread apathy, the reaction from the war" had set in, as Americans preferred jazz and automobiles over olive drab during the 1920s.[40] Once the Senate had rejected participation in the League of Nations, America's foreign-policy commitments did not seem to require large military forces. The antipathy to things military grew even deeper during the 1930s, as college students by the thousands took the Oxford pledge not to bear arms in any future war.[41] The abortive attempt of 1920 marked the only time prior to World War II that universal military training was seriously proposed to the American people or to Congress. The army itself meekly adapted. By 1934, even the chief of staff, Gen. Douglas MacArthur, observed that "the traditions of our people" would permit "no type of compulsory military service in time of peace."[42] As another officer put it: "To advocate the Swiss military system for America is just as absurd as to advocate the yodel as a substitute for the college yell, or goat's milk for coca-cola!"[43]

While UMT proved to be stillborn, there were periodic attempts between the wars to pass a form of selective-service legislation that would be directed, not toward making it part of the peacetime establishment, but merely toward expediting matters in the event of another war. The bills provided that upon a declaration of war by Congress, a Selective Service System like that of World War I would automatically begin to operate. These proposals added a new twist by urging *total* mobilization—that is, the conscription of the nation's entire resources, manpower and materiel, with each citizen assigned to his proper place in the war effort. Dating back to the French Revolutionary *levée* of 1793, such ideas also anticipated the national service policy adopted by Britain and considered by the United States during World War II.

The first bill of this type, the so-called Bok Plan, was introduced in the Senate by Republicans Arthur Capper of Kansas and R. C. Johnson of South Dakota in 1924. Two years later, Senator Capper offered a similar measure, written by the American Legion's Legislative Committee and endorsed by Bernard Baruch and such groups as the D.A.R. and the General Federation of Women's Clubs. A coalition of peace groups and the American Federation of Labor effectively opposed the measure. Another such effort came in 1928, when two bills providing for an automatic draft of manpower and industry in time of war, both supported by the legion, were introduced.[44] Again labor groups campaigned against it. The idea revived once more, still without success, in the late 1930s.[45]

It is problematical whether Congress would have passed any of these bills had they provided simply for the automatic reestablishment of the draft after a declaration of war. Even if it had, the practical value of such legislation would have been slight. Very few isolationists would have voted against a draft bill once war had been declared. The success of the World War I draft had settled the debate between conscription and volunteering as a *wartime* means of raising an army. The total effect of such legislation, therefore, would have been to save a week or two.

Such proposals do reveal the extent to which the thinking of both the people and their representatives rested on isolationist tenets. Americans assumed that in any future war, protected by the broad Atlantic and Pacific oceans, the country would have time for national deliberation and decision making in advance of formal hostilities. Few Americans then saw that even as a formality, the idea of a "declaration of war" belonged to the past. Painful memories of 1917/18 tugged hard at the American consciousness. Not wanting American boys to fight in European wars again, the average citizen would not urge war except in the case of a direct attack on the United States. Even Americans who were pro-Ally envisaged a scenario on the lines of 1914–17, in which the United States had ample time to prepare while England and France confronted Germany in the west. The blitzkrieg of May 1940 upset all calculations. "The USA had done exactly what we did," the British ambassador reported from Washington, "woken up about two years too late."[46] Not surprisingly, the General Staff had to wake up quickly as well.

Army thinking was conditioned to a large extent by the lean years of the 1920s and early 1930s, when military needs constituted unwelcome items in the federal budget. As early as 1922, niggardly appropriations from Congress forced the curtailment of many of the reserve programs set out in the National Defense Act. The 280,000-man Regular Army envisioned in 1920 was never realized during the interwar years, reaching a low of 120,000 in 1927. Historian Russell F. Weigley has written that the army during this period "may have been less ready to function as a fighting force than at any time in its history. . . . As anything more than a small school for soldiers the army scarcely existed."[47] Even when the Great Depression made recruitment an easier task, the army spent more time and money on relief programs such as the Civilian Conservation Corps than it did on training reserve components.[48] Not until the mid 1930s, when rumblings abroad raised the specter of mechanized war and aerial bombardment, did Congress begin to show concern over what the chief of staff called the "dangerous deterioration of the military establishment."[49]

The army suffered psychologically as well as materially during this period, so much so that by 1940 the so-called brass hats were nothing like the aggressive, demanding, bellicose stereotype often conjured up by pacifists.[50] General Staff officers made no concerted effort to push forward their own ideas on national defense, and instead of grasping for more money than Congress appropriated, the army for years had "engaged in continuing studies to determine the minimum strength at which the professional force could be expected to discharge with reasonable efficiency its vital missions in peace and emergency."[51] In short, the army had been so willing to take a back seat that its initiative and flexibility were somewhat impaired by the time an emergency arose demanding those qualities. In historian Robert Miller's words, the army had, by the late 1930s, developed a "built-in resistance to innovation."[52]

President Franklin D. Roosevelt did little to jar the military out of its peacetime lassitude. Always more interested in naval—not military—matters and more concerned with domestic needs than with international affairs during his first term, the mercurial president rarely consulted with his secretary of war, and he proclaimed fiscal orthodoxy in denying the army's modest requests for extra appropriations.[53] Even after the Munich crisis, when FDR began to move toward aiding the Allies with arms and equipment, he thought only reluctantly in terms of balanced increases for the army. Vast increases in air power became his "Aladdin's Lamp for instant and inexpensive national security."[54] When an open feud developed between Secretary of War Harry H. Woodring and Assistant Secretary Louis A. Johnson, Roosevelt declined to intervene. Even the president's famous confidence in Gen. George C. Marshall as army chief of staff came slowly: it took nearly two years after Marshall's appointment in September 1939 before the sternly professional general and the smiling squire of Hyde Park could work confidently together.[55] Given such circumstances, it is little wonder that the War Department suffered from bureaucratic inertia during the late 1930s.

The strategic thinking of the General Staff on the eve of World War II appeared most cogently in the Protective Mobilization Plans (PMP) of 1937-39. Developed under Secretary Woodring and Chief of Staff Malin Craig during these years, the war plans called for mobilization of the Regular Army and the National Guard into an Initial Protective Force (IPF) of four hundred thousand men, behind which would be "progressively mobilized, trained, and equipped much larger national armies as the defense of the United States demands."[56] This initial force aimed at reaching complete combat readiness within one month after M-Day. If this IPF proved insufficient, a PMF of more than seven hundred thousand would be mobilized within eight months of M-Day. Should still-larger armies be needed, the PMP provided for monthly increases of one hundred and fifty thousand until a four-million-man army had been attained. The bulk of such a force, curiously enough, would consist almost entirely of infantry, virtually ignoring air forces and armored forces. The PMP called for only one armored division in its ultimate projection of a four-million-man army.[57]

Since the National Guard numbered about two hundred thousand in 1939 and the Regular Army even less, how were the large forces envisaged in the PMP to be raised? This phase of mobilization bore the most direct relation to the 1940 campaign for conscription, and the army had been seriously working on it for nearly two decades. During the early 1920s the personnel section of the General Staff had prepared basic legislation and regulations for a Selective Service System to put before Congress after a declaration of war. A Joint Army and Navy Selective Service Committee was established in 1926; its task was to refine prospective legislation and to set up national and state headquarters for the system that would function in wartime. Keeping in touch with state officials and conducting correspondence courses and regional conferences for the civilian and reserve-officer personnel who would run the system, the Joint Committee formulated all plans "on the assumption that Congress, after considering past experience, will enact Selective Service very shortly after a National emergency arises. It is expected and hoped that any Selective Service thus instituted will resemble closely that of the World War.''[58] As the head of the Joint Committee later put it, ''everybody tried to take the last war as a basis for what you do in this war.''[59]

The Joint Committee's plan contained several essential features.[60] It authorized the president to order the registration and induction of ''such age groups between 18 and 45 as he prescribes.'' It also gave the president the authority to establish a Selective Service System, including local and appeal boards, and to use both state and local agencies in administering it. The proposed law stipulated that every registrant would become subject to military authority concurrent with the date on his induction notice. On the controversial subject of conscientious objectors, the Joint Committee's bill exempted, from combat service only, members of recognized religious bodies holding antiwar beliefs. Only members of the armed forces and foreign diplomatic personnel would be exempt from registration, with automatic deferment thereafter only for the highest federal and state authorities. The president would also have the authority to set rules for deferment due to dependency and occupational status. Like the 1917 draft law, the new proposal prohibited bounties, substitutes, and purchased exemptions. The Joint Committee's bill closely resembled the legislation later drawn up by the MTCA, except in one conspicuous respect: the army's bill would not be put before Congress until after a declaration of war; the Plattsburgers' bill would go into effect immediately.

No one knew better than the army that even if Congress were to pass a draft law without debate, it would take some time before a Selective Service System could actually process the first inductees at reception centers. The minimum estimate was sixty days. And yet, the PMP called for 750,000 men by M-Day plus sixty. The draft would not yet be functioning, and the first two months of World War I had produced only 290,000 volunteers.[61]

As to how these 750,000 men would be procured, the army had an answer in the form of an unprecedented recruiting campaign called the Civilian Volunteer Effort. This scheme projected that a nationwide drive for voluntary enlistments would be instituted by each governor as soon as an emergency should arise. The army, the navy, and the Marine Corps would allot quotas for each state; the governors, in turn, would make suballotments for each county or urban unit; a civilian committee in each community would then ''produce the results.'' Some states, the Joint Committee reported in 1939, had already made ''splendid progress'' in preparation for the Civilian Volunteer Effort, though others had done much less.[62]

Army experts knew that voluntary enlistments would probably fail to produce the necessary manpower during the first months of a war, but there seemed to be no alternative. In October 1939 an officer at the Army War College asked Gen. Hugh S. Johnson about possible peacetime conscription.

"If you are asking for my opinion as a mechanical question, I would say 'yes,'" answered the man who had helped to run selective service in World War I. "If you are asking my opinion as a political question as to whether you could get it through without being chewed up, I would say 'by all means, no.' Get it ready but keep it in the dark."[63] The Joint Committee was so dubious about the Civilian Volunteer Effort (CVE) that it tried to escape in advance from taking any responsibility for the likely failure of the plan. "The Army and Navy are not expected to produce money and supplies," the committee noted sententiously. "These things are furnished them, and their job is to use them in the war effort. The same principle applies to manpower." Recognizing that voluntary recruitment would vary greatly from state to state, the committee admitted that the CVE had been formulated "more in the hope than in the conviction that it will meet the situation for a couple of months until Selective Service can begin producing men at the training stations."[64] Nevertheless, it seemed to be the only way to solve the problem even partially, given the assumption that Congress would pass a draft law only after the country was at war.

Here, then, was the army's program for wartime mobilization as of early 1940: the Regular Army and the National Guard, numbering at best five hundred thousand effective troops, would go into action upon a declaration of war. This force would defend the country while an additional half-million raw recruits were being drafted and trained. To obtain these men, a selective-service bill, held in readiness, would be presented to Congress and passed quickly; the draft's administrative system, also in readiness, would operate as soon as Congress had acted. Meanwhile, during the first "couple of months" before the draft could begin producing men, the country would engage in a great campaign, full of brass bands and "Uncle Sam Wants You" posters, exhorting enough volunteers to bring the initial protective force to wartime strength.

There was nothing illogical about the army's mobilization plan. On the contrary, every piece of the jigsaw puzzle fit. But the fact that some pieces could not find their places until the country was already at war made the plan a dangerous gamble. The army was taking grave risks in depending on the initial protective force to hold off the enemy during the period of large-scale mobilization. "We place a tremendous responsibility on these first 400,000 defenders," Secretary Woodring had written candidly in 1938. "If they fail in their protective mission, the fate of the reinforcing citizens' armies is sealed."[65] Indeed, if the worst fears of army planners had been realized in the spring of 1940—namely, if a victorious Germany had acquired the French and British navies—the United States could have been "within a year . . . threatened by a vastly superior fleet in the Atlantic, strong in aircraft carriers, capable of protecting the transport of land troops to this hemisphere in appreciable numbers."[66] In the face of such a scenario, could a force of a few hundred thousand, or even a million, have defended the country adequately? And if so, for how long?

Even though the German blitzkrieg did not jolt the General Staff until May 1940, the vital importance of time was always recognized. Military experts usually argued that twelve to eighteen months would be necessary to train and equip large bodies of recruits.[67] General MacArthur had cited a basic lesson of World War I, that "hasty improvisation of an efficient fighting force is wholly impossible, even when the treasure of the Nation is spent without stint."[68] Similarly, General Craig had stressed, during the summer of 1939, "the time element in preparation for war. This is an immensely rich nation, but all of its wealth, all of its industry, all of its intelligent manpower, is helpless before the inexorable demands of *time* in manufacture and training. The period has long passed when ineffectively armed or insufficiently trained men can succeed in war."[69]

In view of this clear recognition of the time factor, especially as events abroad cast doubt upon the capacity of the Regular Army and the National Guard to protect the country while additional men were being mobilized and trained, why did the professional soldiers make no moves toward effective increases in manpower before 1940? One answer is that army officers were no more prescient than civilians. In the late 1930s the army of more than 2.5 million raised by the United States in World War I still seemed quite large. Not only was there no conception, even among the experts, of the vast mobilization that World War II would eventually require, but as the General Staff's plans indicated, many believed that even the "huge" masses of World War I were relics of the past. *Time* magazine, for example, explaining the army's defense plans to the public in 1938, praised the calculations that reduced mobilization figures to one million men: "This is taken to be all the men the U.S. could train and equip in time to be of use in a day when wars arise suddenly and are likeliest to be won by a country able to strike hardest and fastest."[70] In February 1940, General Marshall expressed satisfaction with an increase of seventeen thousand in the Regular Army and spoke against "plunging into a sudden expansion of personnel."[71] As the most recent historian of the Protective Mobilization Plan has shown, the General Staff gave priority to modernization and training over manpower expansion— at least until the spring of 1940.[72]

The defensive psychology that prevailed in both civilian and military circles also helps to explain the failure to focus on manpower. Americans fiercely proclaimed their purposes to be strictly nonaggressive; as Secretary Woodring wrote in 1939, "We visualize only the possible necessity of armed defense of our own domain."[73] Given the determination not to intervene in European affairs in the 1930s, there was no need for a large army. Carried to the extreme, this aversion to anything even suggesting attack produced the somewhat naïve though popular distinction between "defensive" and "offensive" weapons, together with the corresponding insistence that the United States should arm itself with nothing but defensive ships, guns, planes, and tanks. The outraged reaction, early in 1939, to FDR's remark that the Rhine might constitute America's first defensive frontier indicated the degree to which Americans abhorred the notion of another AEF. Until well into 1941, Roosevelt himself continued to believe that even if the United States should become a belligerent against Hitler, this would not necessarily mean sending a ground army to Europe. It was understandable, in such a context, that the War Department would put aside the old maxim "The best defense is a good offense" and continually emphasize, in General Craig's words, that the army was "purely defensive in character and nonprovocative in outlook."[74] Conversely, when the army did reverse itself in the summer of 1940 and supported the draft, isolationists thought that "the unseemly haste toward conscription [was] the best evidence that the president has an expeditionary force in mind."[75]

In retrospect, the lack of realism in this Maginot Line psychology seems obvious. Hindsight makes it clear that if the country should become involved in war, it would remain on the defensive only long enough to prepare a counteroffensive. American forces would have to carry the war to the enemy as soon as possible after an attack, or else the enemy might succeed in becoming virtually impregnable later. But the army, sharing the isolationist tenets held by most Americans until the fall of France, contemplated "a passive defense of the Continental United States and our overseas possessions."[76] Only in early 1939, with the formulation of Rainbow 1, did the General Staff widen its horizon to include the more dynamic strategy of "Hemisphere Defense."[77] Although this represented a distinct advance in contemplating action prior to a direct enemy attack, Hemisphere Defense nevertheless accorded with prevailing isolationist sentiment.[78] Even after the terrible events of May and June 1940 had caused President Roosevelt to consider such unneutral policies as sending fifty destroyers to England, the army did not suddenly become interventionist. When, in June 1940, FDR suggested contingency plans for possible naval and air action against German forces, the Joint Planning Board replied: "Our unreadiness to meet such aggression on its own scale is so great that, so long as the choice is left to us, we should avoid the contest until we can be adequately prepared."[79] During the ensuing months, General Marshall was constantly importuning the White House to consider rearmament needs at home before shipping vital equipment abroad.[80]

Other factors also accounted for the army's less-than-vigorous response. In 1940 the General Staff remained so small that "too much knowledge and too thorough appraisal" were expected of each officer. Few staff officers had been exposed to foreign military establishments, especially Germany's, where strategic thought had advanced far beyond 1918 concepts. Furthermore, the press of routine administration often diverted the staff from the more important task of planning.[81] A more important reason for the army's lethargy, however, was a thorough indoctrination in the principle of civilian leadership. Almost afraid of Congress and not at all intimate with the White House, the General Staff in 1940 still felt the effect of long years of bare subsistence.[82] Officers started from the assumption that it was absolutely impossible to persuade Congress to authorize, during peacetime, the compulsory system necessary for war mobilization.[83] Convinced that this was not mere opinion but unalterable fact, they made their plans accordingly. However laudable in constitutional terms, this hesitancy to "think big" might have had more military justification if the Initial Protective Force had actually been what it purported to be. But with half-strength units, inadequately trained reserves, shortages of guns, tanks, and war planes, the IPF existed mainly on paper. "As an army we were ineffective," General Marshall later admitted.[84]

The personal role of General Marshall dominated the War Department drama. Not yet the commanding personage of towering prestige, Marshall had moved cautiously during the months after his appointment as chief of staff in September 1939, feeling his way both with Congress and with President Roosevelt. Using Bernard Baruch as an intermediary, he began to cultivate senators on the Military Affairs Committee in the spring of 1940.[85] Marshall was slowly gaining the respect of White House intimates Harry Hopkins and Henry Morgenthau, Jr., but with the enigmatic Roosevelt his relations were still distant when the Nazi onslaught struck. In the emergency meetings at the White House prior to FDR's message to Congress on 16 May, the president seemed to be thinking only about factories and fifty thousand war planes per year, while the chief of staff was trying to give precise figures for manning and equipping the Initial Protective Force. "I know the navy gets to the president privately all the time. . . . Do you think I should?" Marshall asked Morgenthau.[86] Although Marshall followed the Treasury secretary's advice to "tell him [Roosevelt] what you think and stand right there," Marshall and Roosevelt were operating on different wavelengths.

During the dark weeks that followed, the president above all wanted to send planes and equipment to the embattled democracies without arousing isolationists in Congress; Marshall had to adapt to rapidly changing circumstances and to carry out mobilization plans as best he could. Mindful of the need for trained manpower, the chief of staff was still thinking primarily in terms of modernizing, expanding, and equipping the Regular Army.[87] He also wanted to "deal within the team of which the president was the head. . . . I had to be very careful," Marshall later recalled, "not to create the feeling that I, as the military leader . . . was trying to force the country into a lot of actions which it opposed."[88] Suspecting that the president regarded him as "the best of a bad bargain" during these months, the chief of staff did not want to offer unsolicited advice.[89]

The last days of May 1940 saw Washington engulfed in frantic activity, panicky rumors, and gloomy assessments. As reports pieced together the magnitude of the German breakthrough on the Meuse, experts soon predicted the total collapse of Allied opposition. Secretary of War Woodring observed, after one grim cabinet meeting, that "it would not be long until the British Navy would be sent to Canada convoying the King and Queen."[90] Despite pleas for assistance from Churchill and Reynaud, Assistant Secretary of State Adolf A. Berle summed up American reactions by noting "nothing we could do would get there in time."[91] The president told reporters off-the-record on 30 May: "It is extremely serious for England and France. . . . We are not saying so out loud because we do not want to intimate in this country that England and France have gone."[92] Compounding the dire news from Europe were growing fears of "fifth column" activities in Latin America ("the Trojan Horse," as FDR called it in his fireside chat on 26 May).[93] Apparently reliable reports reached Washington on 24 and 30 May of impending Nazi coups in Argentina and Uruguay, respectively.[94] Similar stories circulated about Chile and Brazil, where large German-speaking minorities were allegedly plotting to turn those countries into vassal states.[95] Reacting to these rumors and to the seemingly invincible panzers in Flanders, President Roosevelt, on 24 May, asked his naval and military advisers to draw up plans for landing an expeditionary force of at least one hundred thousand men on the northeast bulge of Brazil.[96] General Marshall was just starting to work on operation Pot of Gold, which later merged with the larger Rainbow 4 plans to occupy all European colonies in the Western Hemisphere in the event of an Allied defeat, when he received a telephone call from one of his oldest friends, asking for a conference to discuss immediate selective-service legislation.

4

Wooing the White House
and the War Department

As the movement for a peacetime draft took shape, Grenville Clark and his friends logically thought of enlisting support in the agencies most concerned with national defense—the War Department and the White House. Congress would hardly pass any legislation that the War Department disapproved; nor was it likely that vigorous action could be taken without the blessing of the president. Such considerations led to Clark's telegram of 16 May, informing FDR of "what was going on," and also to General Palmer's visit to the War Department as an emissary of the MTCA.

General Palmer left for Washington on 23 May, exactly a week after Roosevelt had asked billions for new weapons and equipment, including "at least 50,000 planes a year." But the president had failed to mention one significant fact—namely, that a vast force of trained men was needed to drive the tanks, pilot the planes, and shoulder the rifles. Taking into account the ground crews, intelligence and armament sections, administrative personnel, and other technicians, a 50,000-plane air force alone would number perhaps 750,000 men, more than twice the size of the existing Regular Army. Obvious or not, few at the time appeared to grasp the connection between materiel and manpower. The army itself, overwhelmed by "the rapidity of events" after 10 May, had not begun to think in such large terms.[1] New strategic plans by the General Staff for "hemispheric defense" did not envisage eventual intervention in the European war so much as they reflected widespread panic over possible "fifth column" uprisings in South America.[2]

Upon arriving in Washington, General Palmer was escorted directly from Union Station to General Marshall's home in Virginia. The two men were old friends, having served together on Pershing's staff during World War I, when Marshall, some ten years younger, had become a disciple of Palmer's in matters of military philosophy. Palmer was one of the few men who called the ramrod-stiff chief of staff by his first name. Marshall, though he received his friend cordially, was extremely busy. "I have no time whatever for anything more than business before Congressional Committees, the Budget

48

Bureau and the White House from daylight to dark,'' he noted at the time.[3] Instead of discussing the details of the MTCA proposals personally, Marshall told Palmer to consult with Maj. Lewis B. Hershey, executive officer of the Joint Army and Navy Selective Service Committee, as well as with other officers responsible for War Department planning. After two days of discussions, Palmer asked if Hershey could also confer with MTCA leaders in New York. Marshall assented, but issued these revealing instructions to Hershey: "Talk to these people. . . . Answer their questions. You may show them our manpower schedules and explain the draft system we would hope to operate if war should come. But do nothing that would constitute endorsement of their plans by the army. If any adverse publicity comes out of these meetings, I will disavow you. You are on your own.''[4]

Palmer returned to New York on 27 May, and the next day, Hershey and two other officers arrived at the Harvard Club for meetings with MTCA leaders. In explaining the army's plans, the professional soldiers emphasized that a compulsory draft would operate only after M-Day, with the Civilian Volunteer Effort to bridge the gap between the enactment and the effective operation of selective service. The New Yorkers, though they recognized the value of the Joint Committee's careful planning as to the mechanics of selective service, let it be known, with some finality, that they wanted compulsory-training legislation immediately and were not interested in any other plan.[5] The clash of perspectives in these initial encounters was obvious. Although they would later appreciate Hershey's affable humor and political acumen with Congress, the Plattsburg aristocrats found him dull and unimaginative on first impression. The seemingly rigid War Department blueprints recalled to Clark, in particular, the slow performance of the General Staff in 1917. Hershey, who had entered the service through the Indiana National Guard in 1913 and reputedly knew "as many men in the National Guard as [James A.] Farley knows in the Post Office," was simply not used to dealing with authoritative civilians of such elite standing.[6] Notwithstanding his later friendship with Clark, Hershey's first inclination was to view the New Yorkers as "usurpers" for having seized control of the MTCA from the national leadership in Chicago.[7]

These differences prompted Clark and Julius Adler to fly to Washington on 31 May to try to persuade General Marshall face to face. Newspapers were describing the retreat of Allied forces toward Dunkirk, as Clark and Adler were being ushered into the chief of staff's office in the old Munitions Building on Constitution Avenue. Marshall spoke as candidly as the circumstances would allow. War Department planning, he explained, was based on defending the Western Hemisphere. The Regular Army, still partly untrained and in the process of expansion, had to attain as rapidly as possible a degree of efficiency sufficient to meet any attack against the United States or South America. Twice he mentioned rumors of a pending German-backed coup in

Major Lewis B. Hershey, the chairman of the Joint Army-
Navy Committee on Selective Service, whose legislative blueprints formed the basis of the Plattsburgers' draft bill,' was
promoted to brigadier general in October of 1940. He later
served as the director of selective service for nearly thirty
years. (Courtesy of Franklin D. Roosevelt Library)

Uruguay. In such a context these plans for hemispheric defense took top
priority. Marshall even opposed mobilizing the National Guard at this point.[8]
Passage of a draft act would mean virtual abandonment of his program, for
the army would have to break up existing units to provide instructors for the
thousands of raw recruits. He was afraid, as he later put it, that the "small
nucleus of trained troops" would be "fatally diluted."[9]

Furthermore, it was not only doubtful that Congress would pass a
selective-service law in peacetime; the odds were decidedly against it.
Marshall had asked Congress for unprecedented sums during the past year,
and the past two weeks had been spent in interminable sessions at the White
House, drafting appropriations messages for Roosevelt. The president's

second emergency message went to Capitol Hill that very afternoon. Since Marshall was only beginning to gain the confidence of key members of Congress, he quite naturally did not wish to endanger these appropriations by stirring up controversy over a peacetime draft. Nor did Marshall want to disrupt his organizational planning by fighting for an apparent impossibility when the energies of the General Staff could be applied to a more realistic program.

In rebuttal, Clark and Adler claimed that the strategy of hemispheric defense was inadequate, that it was foolish to worry about coups in Uruguay when England and France were teetering on the verge of collapse, and that a German military victory would force a steep upward revision of all military estimates, the prerequisite of which was trained manpower. The current trickle of volunteers, they argued, would not fill the Regular Army quickly enough, not to mention the much greater forces that would be required. "No one had to tell me it [selective service] was necessary," Marshall later recalled. "I knew that full well, many times better than the man in the street."[10] But the chief of staff said it was not his place to advocate a legislative policy that the president had not authorized.

This was the cue for a gratuitous lecture from Clark about professional obligations. To his mind, he told the general, certain basic responsibilities rested upon every professional man, regardless of calling; his function was to give honest advice to the client who retained him. Since the president depended on the chief of staff for expert military counsel, it was Marshall's ethical duty, if he believed compulsory training necessary, to advocate it with the president, regardless of its chances in Congress. General Marshall reddened during these remarks but characteristically retained his self-control. He said shortly but courteously that he did not agree, that he did not consider it his obligation to volunteer unrequested advice, and that he did not intend to do so. The interview ended abruptly.[11]

While Clark had some justification for insisting that the army should move faster and think bigger, he made little effort to understand Marshall's position. The latter was no stranger to the Plattsburg Movement, having commanded civilian training camps in Utah and California in 1916. Nor was he indifferent to the need for trained manpower. As a scrupulous professional soldier with strong views about the army's subordination to civilian control, Marshall resented Clark's homilies about professional responsibilities. Clark, although he did not say so directly, was putting forward selective service on the tacit assumption that the United States would eventually intervene in the European War. Marshall's preoccupation with hemispheric defense and his reluctance, at least during May and June, to release vital war equipment to the British were based on the traditional United States policy of nonintervention in European affairs.[12] The general was not about to dictate what the geographic limits of national security should be. One of his aides explained

some weeks later: "We can't outline the plan of defense. That's the
government's job. We can outline the technical arrangements for anything
they decide on—whether it's intervention, hemisphere defense, Caribbean
defense. But we have to be told what they want done and what the foreign
policy is. And that we don't know. Do you wonder that what is being asked for
is enough to cover all possible contingencies?"[13] Even though Marshall saw
conscription as an eventual imperative, he did not wish to jeopardize his own
and the army's position prematurely. He would not emulate Leonard Wood.
"You might say the army played politics. . . . We had regard for politics," the
general explained in later years: "If I had led off . . . I would have defeated
myself before I started, and I was very conscious of that feeling. So if I could
get civilians of great prominence to take the lead in urging these things then I
could take up the cudgels and work it out."[14] Indeed, although Clark and
Adler thought differently at the time, the chief of staff's caution toward
conscription may have been a blessing in disguise. In light of Congress's
longstanding suspicion of army requests for expansion or innovation, the
Burke-Wadsworth bill may well have profited from the fact that it did not
originate with the "brass hats."[15]

Concurrent with their negotiations with the War Department, MTCA
leaders made a parallel assault on the White House. Clark's telegram of 16
May fired the opening gun; but it proved only the first of a long series of
unsuccessful attempts, throughout the spring and summer, to wrest from
Franklin Roosevelt an unqualified endorsement of selective service. Particularly during the early weeks the results were anything but fruitful.

The president's guarded statements on the draft were highly equivocal.
Because of his unwillingness to speak out, Democratic leaders in Congress
would have little or nothing to do with a conscription bill, and its sponsors had
to proceed on their own. FDR's equivocation raises the question as to his real
feelings. Did he sincerely want a draft bill, and if so, why did he not support it
vigorously from the first? Or was he really lukewarm, willing to back it only
after its adoption in some form had been virtually assured? Clark himself was
later to say, "Trying to guess the mental processes of the Great White Father
is a risky business."[16]

The evidence suggests that, in light of FDR's concern for building the
nation's defenses and of his awareness of their inadequacy, he came to regard
the enactment of a peacetime-draft law as desirable, but not necessarily urgent
or imperative.[17] During May and June, however, apparently more concerned
with material aid to the Allies and not at all sure about manpower needs, the
president was none too sympathetic to the idea. As late as 7 May he told
Henry Wallace that he saw no need for "an unusually large army. . . . No, all
we need is a sufficient force of men for a good expeditionary force to Brazil—
or some similar country—in case of invasion."[18] The German onslaught in

the West threw all military plans into disarray; but the incredible success of the panzers and Stukas seemed to illuminate, in one brilliant flash, the United States' paucity of the machines and weapons that could provide successful defense. Roosevelt, like most people, thought first in terms of material needs, with the result that his defense messages during these weeks, while urging speed in production with almost every sentence, said virtually nothing about manpower. When the president's thoughts did turn to manpower, moreover, he was first attracted by a broad program of vocational training for industrial workers rather than strict military training.

Ideologically, FDR had no objection to a draft law. Certainly a central tenet of the president's patrician philosophy was that every citizen had the responsibility to serve his or her country during wartime.[19] His subsequent protestations to the contrary notwithstanding, Roosevelt's earlier participation in the World War I campaign for preparedness had included several ringing endorsements of universal military training.[20] Only an emergency appendectomy had prevented the young assistant secretary of the navy from attending the first Plattsburg camp of 1915.[21] He could tell his wife Eleanor privately that it "is not a fact—that national defense can be manned by the volunteer system."[22] His reluctance to speak out publicly in the spring of 1940 seems to have stemmed primarily from considerations of political timing. When, in late May, the influential publisher of the *New York Herald Tribune* urged the president to endorse conscription, Roosevelt eloquently defended his noncommittalism, replying:

> You say you have been a pacifist all your life, but you are now for universal service. From what extremes do pendulums swing for us as individuals. Governments, such as ours, cannot swing so far or so quickly. They can only move in keeping with the thought and will of the great majority of our people. . . . Were it otherwise the very fabric of our democracy—which after all is government by public opinion—would be in danger of disintegration.[23]

The president would have been less than human if he had not had his eye on the November elections. Conscription during peacetime, necessary though it might become, was unprecedented. In an election year it was the proverbial hot potato. Some of FDR's strongest supporters warned that draft legislation was "fraught with political disaster," that it could not possibly be passed.[24] Eleanor Roosevelt thought that "the people themselves would never be willing to abide by it."[25] Although public-opinion polls indicated growing support for conscription during the spring and summer, they could not easily offset the flood of negative letters pouring into the White House.[26] "If you vote for conscription," one typical letter read, "my family will vote against you." Another opponent later scrawled: "I regret your insistence on the Draft. . . . My family and myself—hitherto Democratic voters—will not support you in the coming elections. We will urge our friends to do likewise."[27]

Personal ambition, it must be emphasized, was clearly a secondary motivation for FDR's political caution. Very likely, Roosevelt's concrete decision to seek a third term did not come until the fall of France some weeks later.[28] As commander in chief, FDR followed the battles in Flanders with intense concern. The fearful possibility that a victorious Hitler would gain control of the French and British fleets never left his thoughts. When Winston Churchill, now prime minister, urgently requested, on 15 May, that the United States proclaim nonbelligerency and make available as much war equipment as possible, including forty or fifty "older" destroyers, Roosevelt tried to respond positively. In his rearmament message the next day, he asked Congress "not to take any action which would in any way hamper or delay the delivery of American-made planes to foreign nations which have ordered them, or seek to purchase new planes. That, from the point of view of our own national defense, would be extremely short-sighted."[29] Roosevelt told the British, however, that he could not transfer destroyers without congressional authorization, and public opinion was not yet receptive. During the next two weeks, when it looked as though the entire British Expeditionary Force might be captured intact, the president sought—unsuccessfully—to obtain a British promise to send the fleet to Canada in the event of a German invasion.[30] Not until after the Dunkirk evacuation had been miraculously accomplished did FDR take a bold public lead in behalf of aid to England short of war.[31] If he moved too quickly, he rationalized to the British ambassador, "you will get another 'battalion of death' in the Senate like Wilson did over the League of Nations—a group which will exploit the natural human reluctance to war, excite the women . . . and get the Senate so balled up as to produce complete paralysis of action in any direction."[32]

This fear of an isolationist backlash may have been exaggerated, but it nonetheless inhibited Roosevelt's leadership during the ensuing weeks. Hardly an interventionist during this period, the president was trying to redefine United States policy in terms of hemispheric defense and to do what he could to keep the Allies fighting. FDR's eventual priority, once it became apparent that the Churchill government would continue the war alone, was to transfer defense equipment, including naval craft and war planes, to England as soon as it was politically feasible to do so. Isolationists in Congress, however, seemed to be willing to vote billions for defense but balked at giving aid that might lead to United States belligerency. When Senator Claude Pepper of Florida, with tacit White House approval, offered a resolution on 21 May that would have permitted the president to sell vital military supplies to the Allies, the Foreign Relations Committee tabled it.[33] Even army leaders dragged their feet when FDR, in early June, attempted to release bombers, rifles, and field equipment as surplus.[34]

The president chafed at the opposition. Just as some isolationists accused him of creating hysteria and secretly plotting to enter the war, Roosevelt tended to attribute diabolical motives to his opponents. "If I should die tomorrow," he told Morgenthau, "I want you to know this. I am absolutely convinced that Lindbergh is a Nazi."[35] However desirable in the long run, a peacetime draft was not an urgent priority in such a context. FDR later explained to his chief speech writer that "it would have been too encouraging to the Axis, too disheartening to Britain, and too harmful to his own prestige to make this [selective service] a matter of personal contest with Congress and be defeated."[36] Too controversial, it was one of those "irrevocable acts" that Roosevelt wanted to avoid until he was sure it could pass Congress.[37] Ironically, FDR might have rallied many isolationists and Republicans behind the draft at the time of France's surrender, when the national obsession for preparedness seemed to peak, especially if he had couched his support in terms of "fortress America" and hemispheric defense. But such a move might have alienated labor, peace liberals, and other elements of the New Deal coalition less than a month before the Democratic convention. The historian Robert A. Divine has compared the president's indecision during this period to a child's game of giant steps, in which he moved "two steps forward and one back before he took the giant step."[38] Wary of taking any irrevocable step until trends at home and abroad became more certain, FDR parried all initial attempts by the Plattsburgers to break through his indecision.

At this early stage they gave him every opportunity to declare himself. After their first exchange, Clark continued to bombard the president with telegrams. On 21 May, Clark sent to the White House the advance text of the resolutions for the Harvard Club meeting the next night. Three days later, he again wired that the MTCA had decided definitely to prepare and present a selective-service bill. On 26 May, with a fireside chat scheduled for that evening, Clark sent another telegram, exhorting the president to "clearly point out absolute necessity of compulsory military training now and of universal service on a broader basis if we are forced to war." A greatly enlarged arms program would have "no reality or substance whatever" without the manpower to back it up.[39]

This seed apparently fell on stony ground, for the fireside chat of 26 May stressed arms and equipment but virtually ignored personnel.[40] The president's press conference two days later was also discouraging. Disavowing any intention, as in 1917, of building an army of millions, FDR stated flatly: "We are not talking at the present time about a draft system, either to draft men or women or all three." (He also assured one female reporter that she would "not have to forego cosmetics, lipsticks, ice-cream sodas.")[41] When the president made his second emergency request for more than a billion dollars on 31 May 1940, he commented on manpower in exasperatingly general terms: "The expansion of our defense program makes it necessary that we undertake immediately the training and retraining of our people, and especially of our young people, for employment in industry and . . . in the army and navy."[42] This statement, though implying a slight shift toward selective service, was actually more reflective of plans for vocational training that were percolating within the administration.[43] Possibly, as Harry Hopkins hinted to Clark several weeks later, the president was thinking of a compromise between the two. Whatever the case, Roosevelt was proceeding intuitively, neither giving training plans careful scrutiny nor making his preferences clear to the bureaucracy.[44]

In view of FDR's hesitancy, the MTCA group had also sought a personal interview. After wiring FDR on 21 May that "request may be made to you for conference at early date," Clark had persuaded Felix Frankfurter to help obtain a hearing. On 28 May came a telegram from "Pa" Watson, the president's secretary, inviting Clark, Adler, and Patterson to the White House on 31 May. The next day, however, Watson wired to say that the president could not keep the appointment and had designated Harry Hopkins to receive them instead.[45] Clark, who did not think that an interview with Hopkins would accomplish their purpose, called Watson to say that it would be better for them to wait until the president himself could see them.

Instead, Clark turned to the War Department. The wire canceling the conference had reached him the day after the General Staff officers had visited New York to outline the War Department's plans on manpower. The seeming lack of vision in those views had strengthened a conviction that had been growing in Clark's mind for several days: before anything could be done about a draft bill or adequate national defense, something first had to be done about the weak and divided leadership in the War Department. Nothing would suffice, he concluded, but a vigorous new secretary of war. The unsuccessful interview with General Marshall clinched matters. Clark was thus in a disgruntled frame of mind on the morning of 31 May as he took a taxi from Marshall's office to the Supreme Court Building to see his old friend Justice Frankfurter.

The notion that all was not well at the War Department by no means originated with Clark, for the deplorable lack of harmony between the secretary of war and his assistant secretary had become a public scandal. For two years, Washington columnists had complained that the department lacked leadership, and the *Kiplinger Letter* had recently stated that Secretary Woodring was "plainly incompetent for the job."[46] The more hawkish members of Roosevelt's inner circle, most notably Interior Secretary Harold Ickes and Treasury Secretary Henry Morgenthau, constantly importuned their chief to clean up the War Department.[47] Even Republican presidential aspirant Thomas E. Dewey was publicly demanding Woodring's scalp.[48]

"Handsome Harry" Woodring, a former banker and "amiable, politically adroit" former governor of Kansas, had slipped into his cabinet post almost unnoticed.[49] In 1933 he had been made assistant secretary of war,

The cantankerous Harold Ickes, who as secretary of the Interior continuously prodded the president to move faster on preparedness and aid to Britain in 1940. (Courtesy of Franklin D. Roosevelt Library)

partly because he had supported Roosevelt "before Chicago," because he was particularly close to Postmaster General James A. Farley, and because the assistant secretaryship was by then considered virtually the property of the American Legion, in which Woodring had distinguished himself.[50] On the death of George H. Dern in August 1936, Woodring had automatically become acting secretary of war. FDR was preoccupied with the presidential campaign against Alfred M. Landon; so when he learned that the law required cabinet positions to be filled within thirty days of vacancy, he thereupon announced that Woodring would be his "temporary selection" as secretary, with a permanent appointment to be made after the November elections. Months passed, and Roosevelt made no new choice. Despite numerous candidates for the post, not to mention numerous assurances by Roosevelt to friends that he would replace Woodring, the president made the appointment "permanent" in April 1937. Woodring's familiarity with the

War Department, Roosevelt's own lack of urgency about military affairs at the time, and the overriding importance of the Supreme Court issue—all contributed to the president's lack of decision.[51]

From the first, Secretary Woodring had no peace in his job at the War Department. His assistant secretary, Louis A. Johnson, had coveted the secretaryship himself and had told the president so after Dern's death.[52] When Woodring won the top position, Johnson, who at first refused second place, accepted it only on the guarantee (allegedly from James Farley) that it would be a stepping stone to the secretaryship. Roosevelt, who knew about Johnson's ambitions and about Farley's alleged promise, made no effort to confront either man.[53] Blithely and deliberately, the president was following his usual pattern of putting "into the same office or job men who differed from each other in temperament and viewpoint."[54] Usually such administrative methods meant that the president would make all final decisions—except that in military matters during the late 1930s, Franklin Roosevelt was not inclined to act decisively. Chaos ruled the War Department. Adept at intrigue, Johnson cultivated congressmen and columnists, played favorites within the army, and openly aimed at displacing Woodring. "Louis is over-ambitious," Woodring later noted. "It is sort of like being oversexed."[55] Even General Marshall ran afoul of the feuding when Johnson, who had been instrumental in obtaining Marshall's appointment as chief of staff, became resentful of the general's impeccably correct relationship with Woodring.[56]

Woodring and Johnson differed on more than personal ambition. As the international picture darkened, Woodring veered increasingly toward an isolationist position; he was willing to build up American defenses, but he resisted any move that hinted at intervention. Johnson headed in the opposite direction, frankly preparing for the war that he believed would come. As the two men clashed over such issues as the sale of army planes to the Allies, Johnson thought he had Roosevelt's tacit support.[57] As the assistant secretary later remembered it, FDR told him: " 'Louis, you carry the flag and don't worry. I'll back you up. You go forward two feet and I'll not let you slide back more than one.' The way it worked out, I took all the hell, and Roosevelt approved of what I was doing."[58] Such rivalry may have suited the president's purpose, but it did little for efficiency in the War Department. In the frenzied meetings at the White House in mid May, according to Morgenthau's diary, "Woodring sat there in a corner and never opened his mouth. . . . Johnson and Woodring sat there and never talked to one another."[59] Another participant "came away with the feeling that General Marshall was the only one who knew what he was talking about."[60]

Roosevelt's responsibility for the confused administration of the War Department was obvious. Always reluctant to dismiss any subordinate outright, the president had let matters slide much too long.[61] For months he had been telling intimates that he intended to replace Woodring and Secretary of the Navy Charles Edison. In his maddening way, FDR would tease Ickes and Morgenthau by dangling names—appropriate and inappropriate—and gauging their reactions.[62] But as yet, FDR had made no changes, plainly enjoying the Byzantine atmosphere. Ickes wrote impatiently: "Those closest to him [Roosevelt], even including Missy [LeHand], do not know what is running in his mind as to important matters. Apparently he is taking absolutely nobody into his confidence. He promised a dozen people that he would get rid of Woodring, but he makes no move. . . . No one knows whom he has in mind for secretary of war or secretary of the navy."[63] Woodring himself knew of the rumors, but was determined to retain his position until the president formally requested his resignation.[64]

It was characteristic of a "dominating personality" such as Clark that, while he had no official voice whatsoever, he should have thought nothing of trying personally to force a replacement of Woodring.[65] The crisis plainly demanded a new secretary; the Roosevelt administration had apparently surrendered to inertia; therefore, someone had to act. The War Department's coolness toward selective service, confirmed by the unhappy interview with Marshall, strengthened Clark's resolve to take matters into his own hands.

Five years earlier, Clark might have gone directly to the White House, for he and Franklin Roosevelt had been casual friends since boyhood.[66] They had grown up during the same era and in the same New York circles; both had attended Harvard College, Roosevelt a year behind Clark. They became fellow clerks in the Carter, Ledyard, and Milburn firm in 1907, and historians still recount Clark's story of how FDR, in his disarming way, at that early date predicted his own subsequent rise through New York politics to Washington and ultimately to the White House.[67] The Plattsburg Movement brought them closer together during World War I, as FDR, then assistant secretary of the navy, instituted summer training cruises on board battleships as the navy's counterpart to military training camps. Roosevelt's election in 1932 saw Clark, as director of the National Economy League, providing needed assistance in outlining a program of reduced government expenditures. Clark's elaborate brief, modified by Roosevelt's budget director, Lewis Douglas, became the Economy Act of 1933, one of the first measures of the Hundred Days.[68] In 1935, Roosevelt asked Clark to become chairman of the National Labor Relations Board and later to head the Steel Board, but ever jealous of his amateur standing, Clark declined both requests. There exists a symbolic photograph of the Clark-Roosevelt relationship of these years—both men in formal attire, sitting apart from the rest of the crowd, in the rain, at the ceremonies commemorating Harvard's three-hundredth anniversary in 1936. His membership on the Harvard Corporation notwithstanding, Clark did not represent the majority of Harvard alumni when he voted for FDR for a second term.

A signed photograph of Franklin D. Roosevelt to "his old friend Grenny Clark." (Courtesy of Dartmouth College Library)

The friendship soured briefly in 1937, however, when Clark and Charles C. Burlingham organized a committee of lawyers to oppose Roosevelt's court-packing scheme. Clark also resented the president's public remarks criticizing elaborate family trusts, such as the one set up by Clark, as legal evasion of inheritance taxes. By 1939 the break began to heal, and as events abroad overshadowed domestic issues, Clark applauded the Roosevelt administration on foreign policy. Still, he was by no means a White House intimate; consequently, when it came to suggesting a new secretary of war, he quite naturally turned to Frankfurter.

Clark's connection with the Supreme Court justice formed one thread of the intertwined relationships that shaped the events to follow. There were others: Frankfurter's closeness to Roosevelt; the mutual regard of both Clark and Frankfurter for Stimson; the president's connection with Stimson. Each of these strands, winding back to the early years of the century, contributed to the final product. Had any one of them been absent, the pattern of history as woven in 1940 might well have unraveled. As Frankfurter later wrote, it was "another interesting illustration of Cleopatra's nose—the factor of contingency in history. If anyone were to tell me that it would have made no difference if FDR had appointed [New York Mayor Fiorello] LaGuardia as secretary of war, as he so strongly contemplated doing, he might equally well tell me that 2 and 2 makes 7."[69]

Clark had first known the bespectacled Jewish immigrant at Harvard Law School, where as members of the Class of 1906 they had been pleasant, though not close, friends.[70] Together they drank beer and ate cheese as young lawyers in New York, and their relationship grew stronger as the result of Frankfurter's close friendships with Elihu Root, Jr., and Emory Buckner, both of whom became Clark's law partners.[71] Frankfurter, a bachelor in those years, later confessed to Buckner that he had a "boulevard crush" on Fanny Dwight before she became Mrs. Clark.[72] Nevertheless, despite their old ties and wartime service together in Washington in 1917/18, Frankfurter developed a much more intimate friendship with the jovial Emory Buckner than with Clark. Not until the 1930s, when Clark joined the Harvard Corporation and defended Frankfurter against President A. Lawrence Lowell and others who were criticizing Frankfurter for his frequent trips to Washington, did the two men become closer.[73] Clark always tried to keep abreast of Cambridge affairs while on the corporation, and the lively, intellectual Professor Frankfurter proved to be the perfect academic gossip. Moreover, several of Frankfurter's prize students had joined the Root, Clark firm and then government service in Washington. And so the ties grew. When Frankfurter accepted the appointment to the Supreme Court in 1939, Clark made it a habit to visit him in Washington, as he had in Cambridge.

Frankfurter's connection with Roosevelt was bound up in the early years with his relationship to Stimson. Frankfurter had not known Roosevelt at Harvard but had been introduced to the young attorney by Clark in 1906. Thereafter, Frankfurter often lunched with FDR at the Harvard Club or met him at the Bar Association. At this time, Frankfurter first became associated with Stimson, then United States attorney for the Southern District of New York, who was recruiting able assistants to enhance the prestige of his office. On Harvard's recommendation, Stimson got in touch with Frankfurter, who soon became his right-hand man. Frankfurter thus began a lifelong friendship with the older man, who in turn treated the young lawyer like the son he had never had. When Stimson returned to private practice in 1909, his young protégé went with him, and together they worked on cases involving the sugar frauds and railroad rebates. As a one-man brain trust and speech writer, Frankfurter rode on Stimson's campaign train 1910, when the latter ran unsuccessfully for the New York governorship. Stimson's appointment the following year as secretary of war in the Taft administration found Frankfurter following his mentor to Washington. As law officer of the Bureau of

Insular Affairs, the twenty-nine-year-old Frankfurter argued his first case before the Supreme Court. Stimson, when he stepped down with the change of administrations in March 1913, urged his assistant to stay in Washington.[74]

Here the paths of Frankfurter and Roosevelt crossed again. The young state senator from New York joined the Wilson administration as assistant secretary of the navy, and because his office was in the same ornate State-War-Navy Building next to the White House, he saw Frankfurter frequently. Frankfurter went to Harvard Law School to teach in the autumn of 1914, but after two years he found himself back in Washington as a special assistant to Secretary of War Newton D. Baker. The increasing competition among the army, the navy, and other agencies in the field of industrial procurement brought about the formation in 1918 of the War Labor Policies Board (WLPB), of which Frankfurter became chairman. Franklin Roosevelt represented the navy on the WLPB, and the experience of working closely together in an important cause turned their earlier casual association into a closer relationship. The two men, one hastens to add, did not become intimate friends. Once when Roosevelt brought Frankfurter home for lunch, his wife wrote casually: "An interesting little man but very jew."[75] The gulf in backgrounds would always be present, and for Roosevelt, real intimacy with his fellow humans usually remained just beyond reach.

After Frankfurter's return to Harvard in 1919, he and FDR kept in touch occasionally, and the mutual affection and respect provided a basis for later renewal. When Roosevelt became governor of New York in 1929, Frankfurter paid court to his rising contemporary by sending FDR numerous flattering letters, to which he would usually receive one line of reply for every page sent. The Harvard professor worked enthusiastically for Roosevelt's election in 1932 and, after the victory in November, went several times to Albany as a confidential adviser. Although not a member of Roosevelt's inner "brains trust," Frankfurter rendered vital service in January 1933 when negotiations between Herbert Hoover and the president-elect had reached an impasse. By arranging a meeting between FDR and Stimson, then Hoover's secretary of state, Frankfurter helped to smooth the transition between administrations and to maintain continuity in foreign policy.[76] FDR's long talk with "Harry" Stimson on that occasion had considerable significance for the future.

Frankfurter's subsequent relations with the White House received much publicity. Opponents of the New Deal portrayed the Harvard professor as a sinister Svengali, giving advice and pulling strings from backstage. Although he held no official position until his appointment to the Court in 1939, Frankfurter did indeed exercise influence from afar—through letters, phone calls, flying visits, and especially the many bright young law graduates ("Frankfurter's Happy Hot Dogs") whom he recommended for New Deal posts. His own regard for Roosevelt grew enormously during these years, eventually bordering on hero worship. The president, in turn, increasingly valued Frankfurter's counsel and wit, but he never permitted Frankfurter the vast influence that critics imagined. When the Harvard jurist proved himself to be a good soldier by not criticizing the president's controversial court-packing plan, FDR repaid his loyalty by appointing Frankfurter to the Court when Benjamin Cardozo died in January 1939.[77]

The German victories in 1940 affected Frankfurter deeply. "Felix can't talk about the war without becoming highly emotional," noted his friend Ickes.[78] Concerned for the plight of Jews under Hitler and fearful that England might suffer the same fate as France, Frankfurter wanted desperately to do something. "There are no limits to . . . my willingness to be of help," he told the British ambassador, Lord Lothian. "You will know what are the limits of my capacity and the bounds of my restrictions."[79] To another English friend he complained about "the unwillingness of people to see the issues as I think they are in their stark clarity."[80] As a Supreme Court justice, Frankfurter could not take too public a role. But as a "kind of alderman-at-large for the better element," he could exhort and manipulate his many powerful friends from behind the scenes.[81] And he had access to the president. Like Morgenthau and Ickes, Frankfurter had already talked with Roosevelt several times about choosing a new secretary of war. Frankfurter had even suggested "the possibility of . . . setting up a bipartisan committee of two or three members of the cabinet with perhaps Senator [Warren F.] Austin and Congressman [James W.] Wadsworth, both of whom seem to appreciate the seriousness of the international situation."[82] FDR, as usual, had been noncommittal.

Clark found Frankfurter a willing fellow conspirator as they talked about the War Department over lunch at the Supreme Court Building. They agreed on the need for a new secretary, and quickly. Furthermore, he had to be committed to a positive policy of resistance to Hitler and to the immediate arming of the United States. Who would qualify?

Clark and Frankfurter bandied names about. Current rumors about a "coalition" cabinet eased any reluctance about discussing Republicans and conservatives. William J. Donovan, Lewis Douglas, Frank Knox—all of whom were associated with the Plattsburg revival—were tentatively considered. In a matter of minutes, however, Clark and Frankfurter seized on the perfect candidate: Henry L. Stimson. Like Frankfurter, Clark had known the elder statesman for years and often had visited Highhold, Stimson's estate near Huntington, Long Island. As a former secretary both of state and of war, Stimson would bring impeccable qualifications to the office. He commanded respect from Republicans and Democrats alike. His only drawback was age. Clark had thought the seventy-two-year-old Stimson "a very tired, decayed old man" at the Harvard Club dinner of 22 May.[83] Anticipating objections, Clark and Frankfurter hit on the idea of simultaneously suggesting a younger man to work with Stimson. This, they thought, might encourage Stimson to accept the office, for he would not have to trouble himself with finding a suitable assistant secretary. It would also appeal to Roosevelt, who would almost certainly raise the subject of Stimson's age.

The candidate for the second slot was not so obvious, but in listing possibilities, Frankfurter and Clark struck on the name of Robert P. Patterson, judge of the United States Circuit Court of Appeals in New York and formerly an associate in the Root, Clark firm. A tough, vigorous, capable man, Patterson fitted perfectly their conception of a strong assistant secretary. They were convinced of his "soundness" on the international situation. A winner of the Distinguished Service Cross in World War I, Patterson had attended the Harvard Club meeting of 22 May and, like Stimson, advocated aid to the Allies and immediate preparedness. Stimson-Patterson seemed to make a perfect team.

Before Frankfurter could place this dual ticket before the president, Clark attended to some last-minute details. Returning to New York over the Memorial Day weekend, the Plattsburg leader did what he afterward termed "an extraordinary thing."[84] He went to Stimson's family physician on Long Island (who also happened to be Clark's own physician) and requested a confidential report. The doctor demurred. He had never given out such information in the past, nor would he now if there were anything wrong with his patient. But Stimson's health was, in fact, sound; his haggard appearance stemmed from boredom and frustration, nothing else.[85]

Clark also called both candidates to learn whether they would accept if appointed. Patterson replied that he would look upon his appointment as a military order from the president. Stimson was less obliging. He did not like these goings on behind his back; the whole thing, he told Clark, was "a ridiculous idea." An hour later, after talking with his wife and his law partners, Stimson phoned back and said he would accept the office only under certain conditions. He would not, as a lifelong Republican, take any part in administration politics; he would use his position to push compulsory military training and service; he would pick his own subordinates; and he would be free to urge all necessary aid to the Allies to keep them from being defeated. Clark said they were being a bit high-handed in presenting Patterson's name in conjunction with his own. Although he did not know Patterson well, Stimson agreed to accept him on the unqualified recommendation of Clark and Frankfurter.

Frankfurter's task came next. The Supreme Court was scheduled to rise on Monday 3 June, and since the justice was leaving immediately thereafter to spend several weeks in Massachusetts, he arranged a farewell call on the president for Monday afternoon. FDR greeted Frankfurter and his wife, Marion, cordially. The president then made it easy by asking Felix if he had "any new ideas" about the War Department. Indeed he had, as the voluble jurist went on to present the case for Stimson and Patterson. Stimson, though well along in years, was vigorous and in good physical shape; he had already been sounded out and would accept the appointment under conditions that Frankfurter outlined. Patterson, too, would be willing to serve. The president said little, but from his benign expression when Stimson's name was mentioned, Frankfurter thought he had "struck fire."[86]

The two conspirators were still not satisfied. "We were trained to be careful lawyers, Grenny," Frankfurter said. One of the most accomplished and prolific letter writers of his generation, the justice took an elaborate brief, provided by "Sec" Root, Clark's law partner, and dictated two long letters to FDR, dated 4 and 5 June 1940. Folksy, eloquent, and subtle, the letters spelled out in attractive detail why Roosevelt should appoint the two men in question. Frankfurter even went so far as to stress the fact that Patterson had a farm on the Hudson, as did the president. "Some things click," he concluded, "they seem just right—and I cannot help but feel that the combination of Stimson and Patterson would take off your shoulders a very great burden. . . . Ideas are like men. One gets to know them after one lives with them for some time. The more I have lived with the idea of the Stimson-Patterson combination, the more right it seems."[87]

Frankfurter sensed correctly that he had "struck fire," for FDR was already well disposed toward Stimson. Roosevelt had seen little of the former secretary of state since 1933, but the conference between them that Frankfurter had arranged in January of that year had laid the foundation for mutual respect and cordiality. On that occasion, shortly before the new president's inauguration, Stimson had gone to Hyde Park in the morning and had talked with Roosevelt from 11 A.M., through lunch, until five o'clock that afternoon, as they drove together to New York. They had discussed a wide range of topics relating to foreign policy and had found themselves in substantial agreement on practically all basic issues. Twice before the inauguration they had met again.[88]

This friendly relationship continued throughout the 1930s, despite Stimson's public opposition to most of the New Deal, for Stimson's primary interest was in foreign policy, and in that realm he and Roosevelt thought much alike.[89] FDR appreciated Stimson's support on the issue of the World Court and on Cordell Hull's Reciprocal Trade Agreements.[90] Indeed, Stimson sometimes saw Hull when the latter and one or two aides fled the State Department early in the afternoon to play croquet on the broad green lawns of Woodley, Stimson's Victorian estate near Washington's Rock Creek. During the late 1930s Stimson frankly criticized the Neutrality Acts and what he considered to be inaction in the face of aggression in the Far East. Once FDR's diplomacy began to toughen, Stimson joined the president in publicly denouncing the Axis, and after hostilities had begun, he stood foursquare with the administration's attitude toward the war. On 3 May 1940, exactly one month before Frankfurter suggested Stimson's appointment to FDR, the justice had taken Stimson to the White House for an informal lunch with the president, who talked openly about a number of confidential developments in foreign policy.[91] Such a meeting of the minds was important, for in the delicate matter of taking a member of the opposition party into his cabinet, the president had to be absolutely sure of his man.

The widespread speculation about a "coalition cabinet" also worked in Stimson's favor. Frequently mentioned in this connection had been Alfred M. Landon of Kansas, the Republican candidate for president in 1936. Shortly after his defeat, Landon had stated that "politics should stop at the water's edge" and pledged to support Roosevelt's foreign policy. A year later he renewed that vow.[92] By no means an isolationist, Landon stayed on reasonably good terms with the administration as the international crisis deepened in 1939, and a visit to the White House that autumn started the rumor that he would become secretary of war.[93] Nothing came of this, but the rumors revived when he called at the White House again in May 1940. Such speculation proved idle, for the luncheon, which actually caused some embarrassment to both Landon and the president, resulted in little more than an exchange of frigid press releases.[94] Talk of a coalition cabinet continued, however, and at the time of the Landon incident, newsmen also reported that the president had offered the navy secretaryship to Frank Knox, Landon's running mate in 1936, who had called at the White House the week before.[95]

It was true that the president had already approached the sixty-six-year-old Knox. Indeed, FDR had a real fondness for this former Bull Moose progressive, whose pince-nez, piping voice, flashing teeth, and jerky movements reminded everyone of another Roosevelt whom Knox had followed up San Juan Hill in 1898. In 1937, when FDR had delivered his famous "quarantine" speech in Chicago, Col. Robert R. McCormick of the *Chicago Tribune* had erected a huge anti-Roosevelt sign facing the platform from which the president was to speak. Considering this an unpardonable discourtesy, Knox had written a special editorial in his own newspaper, the *Daily News,* condemning McCormick's action and praising the president's speech. FDR deeply appreciated the gesture and, only a short time later, phoned Knox and asked him to succeed Claude A. Swanson as secretary of the navy. Having run as Republican vice-presidential candidate only the year before, Knox considered such a move premature, so he declined.[96]

Knox remained in FDR's thoughts. Not only did the Chicago publisher continue to support Roosevelt's foreign policy, but Knox's old compatriot from Bull Moose days, Secretary Ickes, was constantly singing Knox's praises at the White House.[97] Late in 1939, during the period of the "phony war," the president again called Knox and offered him the navy position. Although the temptation was "almost irresistible," Knox again declined, saying that the "absence at the moment on the part of the public of any deep sense of crisis" would not justify his "completely forgetting and obliterating party lines." He delicately added that the appointment of only one Republican to the cabinet would not be considered as genuine a bid for nonpartisanship as would the addition of two or more. He had heard rumors that William J. Donovan, for whom he had the highest regard, was being considered as a possible secretary of war. If the crisis grew more serious in the future, a "team" appointment of two Republicans might make a decisive step toward national unity.[98]

Roosevelt reluctantly concurred with Knox's judgment. In the absence of "any deep sense of world crisis," the president admitted that "your coming into the Cabinet might be construed as a political move rather than as a patriotic move, which, as you know, was the only thing that actuated me." He added that "Bill Donovan is also an old friend of mine . . . and, frankly, I should like to have him in the cabinet," but he feared that "to put two Republicans in charge of the armed forces might be misunderstood in both parties!"[99] Such a move, when it came six months later, was indeed "misunderstood in both parties," but by then FDR was calculating the political repercussions differently. The president had ended his letter by saying that while he accepted Knox's decision for the present, he would not give up the idea as a future possibility. Knox replied: "Naturally, I am flattered to have you still feel you want me in your administration in the event that a new crisis comes."[100] They continued to correspond during the spring, and when the new crisis did come in May 1940, Knox was eager to serve. But when Knox visited the White House on 17 May to discuss "Air Plattsburgs," the president did not mention the cabinet position. By the end of the month, Knox was telling Republican friends that American, British, and French fleets should be consolidated so as to "starve Hitler into submission. . . . I don't know whether Roosevelt has the courage for that kind of leadership or not. If we do not act in this fashion then our only alternative is to arm to the teeth and get ready for the zero hour when Hitler will have brought the war to this world." Knox applauded the president's speech in Charlottesville on 10 June, wherein FDR promised to "extend to the opponents of force the material resources of this nation."[101] When Roosevelt did formally invite Knox into the cabinet a week later, he was adding probably the most aggressive interventionist of his administration.[102]

Curiously enough, despite persistent rumors and his own serious thoughts on the subject, the president continued to deny any intention of seeking a "coalition cabinet." "This coalition thing is made up of whole cloth," he snapped at a press conference. "It is not a case of barking up the wrong tree; it is a case of having gone out on a limb and then having sawed the limb off."[103] Whether the president or the press had crept out on a limb, the fact that Roosevelt announced the Stimson and Knox appointments within a

Secretary of the Navy Frank Knox. An original member
of the National Emergency Committee when it was
formed in June 1940, Knox's appointment to the cabinet
also gave impetus to the conscription campaign. (Courtesy of Franklin D. Roosevelt Library)

month made him seem, to say the least, inconsistent. FDR no doubt
rationalized the appointment of two Republicans as something other than a
true coalition cabinet. Stimson and Knox entered the government as individuals, not as representatives of the Republican party; indeed their appointments
caused a ''Roman holiday'' among Republican leaders, and the two men
were practically read out of the party for their apostasy.[104] In no sense did the
opposition as such gain a share in the government. Yet Roosevelt was
deceiving the press deliberately, for the phrase ''coalition cabinet'' was widely
thought to mean the addition of any Republicans. Many other Republicans,
several of whom were associated with the Plattsburg revival, later followed
Knox and Stimson into the administration.[105]

Although nothing happened immediately after Frankfurter's visit to the White House on 3 June 1940, undoubtedly the suggestion of Stimson made an indelible impression on Roosevelt's mind. Purely by coincidence, Stimson had written the president on 1 June, to send him an editorial by Knox supporting the administration's stand on European developments. "I think it is written in a fine courageous spirit," Stimson had said, "and I share his views."[106] On the day after Frankfurter's visit, the president acknowledged the former secretary's letter: "I wish to thank you very much indeed for your letter of June 1, with which you enclose the fine editorial Frank Knox published in the Chicago *Daily News*. I am very pleased to know that you are finding that public opinion is generally approving the attitude and policies which the administration has been following and will continue to follow. It is most encouraging to hear this from you."[107]

On the next day, 5 June, Stimson was still on the president's mind. Talking informally to representatives of the American Youth Congress, FDR delivered an impromptu lecture on the origins of current foreign policy, in which he gave particular attention to the achievements of "Harry" Stimson as secretary of state.[108] This did not necessarily mean that Roosevelt, that "most complicated human being," had irrevocably made up his mind on the appointment.[109] The idea that had originated with Clark and Frankfurter had to simmer for two more weeks before FDR took any action. Meanwhile the movement for selective service was gaining momentum without the support of either the president or the War Department.

5

New York:
The National Emergency Committee

It grew hot and sticky in midtown Manhattan on Monday 3 June 1940. As the temperature soared into the eighties on Times Square, perspiring journalists inside the Times Tower scurried about, preparing copy for the evening printers. The news looked better from the English Channel, where some nine hundred boats, large and small, were removing the last British troops from the Dunkirk area.[1] In Washington, President Roosevelt asked Congress for authority to call the National Guard into active federal service. The Senate that day passed the Pittman Resolution, reaffirming the Monroe Doctrine and refusing to recognize any transfer of territory in the Western Hemisphere that might result from Hitler's conquests. The Senate also shouted through, without dissent, a new appropriations bill that would increase the United States' naval tonnage by 11 percent. That day the navy announced that the cruiser *Quincy* was proceeding to Montevideo to monitor the volatile political situation in Uruguay, and final preparations were being made for the launching of the new 35,000-ton battleship *North Carolina* at the Brooklyn Navy Yard later within the week.[2] The event of greatest importance to national defense, however, took place at ten o'clock that morning in Julius Ochs Adler's spacious office on the top floor of the Times Annex. There, amid whirring fans and iced drinks, the leading proponents of conscription met to make concrete plans for "the big national movement" envisioned by Grenville Clark.[3]

Although the initial meeting at the Harvard Club two weeks earlier had set up several informal committees, it had provided no central directing force for an organized campaign. So far, the "movement" for selective service constituted little more than the expressed preferences of a few private citizens. Though earlier resolutions had passed in the name of the Military Training Camps Association, the MTCA seemed to be incapable of the kind of effort envisaged by the original sponsors. Hence the meeting in Adler's office, from which emerged a new organization known as the National Emergency Committee (NEC) of the MTCA. The amalgamation retained the advantage

70

of the MTCA's name while avoiding any veto or control from the parent organization. As chief organizer of the palace revolution, Grenville Clark became—almost automatically—chairman of the NEC, with four vice-chairmen: Adler; Tom Wyles and Robert Jamison, representing the national MTCA; and Frank Knox, who had come to New York to enlist support for the "Air Plattsburg" idea. A nine-member Administrative Committee, which possessed full power to act, was created to direct day-to-day activities. That afternoon at the Bar Association, a larger meeting of two hundred men approved the plan of organization, thus "officially" launching a second Plattsburg Movement for selective service.

At first the organizers intended that the NEC should have one hundred members, but the campaign gained momentum so rapidly that within four days the NEC expanded to one thousand. Although the generative power still flowed from New York City, this expansion took on national proportions; for the thousand members were allotted on a basis of one hundred for each of the nine corps areas, plus an additional one hundred from the nation at large. As in 1915, the Plattsburgers recruited mainly through alumni and professional associations. Twenty more vice-chairmen soon joined the four who had already been named. The list, when filled, boasted an impressive representation of influential men throughout the country.

The early June meetings also crystallized the focus of the NEC on the tangible goal of selective service. (Aid to the Allies and training camps for civilian pilots, two of the original objectives, passed to other groups, most notably William Allen White's Committee to Defend America by Aiding the Allies.)[4] In practical terms, the advocacy of conscription meant preparing a suitable bill, getting it introduced in Congress with the strongest possible backing, and building up public support to push the legislation through. One of the first requirements was to organize a publicity campaign to "educate" the public.

The new Plattsburg propaganda chief was a drawling, mischievous southerner named Perley Boone. Through Adler the NEC organizers had contacted Boone, a former *New York Times* newsman who had just resigned after four successful years as director of publicity for the New York World's Fair. Having planned, organized, and directed the media campaign that brought twenty-six million people to the fair, the Texas-born Boone had the reputation of being one of the ablest men in the public-relations field. The NEC could not offer him a lucrative salary, but Boone took the job because he shared the conviction that a draft bill was necessary for the safety of the country. By 7 June he had already recruited a staff of writers and cameramen. As he reported to the Administrative Committee, he was aiming not only at the metropolitan press but also at the small-town and rural papers in every corner of the United States.[5]

Naturally, such a publicity drive would take money, plenty of it. For this purpose, and to pay the overhead for an office at 28 West 44th Street, the NEC formed a Finance Committee, with subcommittees in each of the corps areas. The sponsors fixed a six-month budget at $285,000, of which the New Yorkers planned to raise $125,000 and the other corps areas $20,000 each. Of these $20,000 quotas, half would go to the NEC and half to promote the drive on the local level. Because the Selective Service Act was passed and signed by mid September, in three months rather than in six, the full $285,000 was never needed and thus was never raised. This high figure, however, stands in sharp contrast to the limited financial resources of the groups that opposed conscription in 1940. According to Frederick J. Libby, head of the National Council for the Prevention of War, the combined opposition did not expend more than $5,000 lobbying against the draft bill.[6]

The NEC's first fund raiser came at a luncheon held at the Bankers' Club in New York on Friday 7 June. Events moved so rapidly that the luncheon was almost on the spur of the moment; only two days earlier, Clark had sent out telegraphic invitations to business and professional men of substantial means. The strongly worded invitation asked the "personal financial support" of those attending and characterized the luncheon as important enough to attend "even at inconvenience or cancellation of other engagement."[7] More than a hundred men responded, and when it left the Bankers' Club, the NEC was richer by $30,000. Donations continued to come in from men who could not attend, and in three weeks the total had risen to $39,072.75.[8] Contributions ranged from $1 to $2,500, with larger offers declined on the assumption that it was preferable to spread the subscriptions among as many participants as possible.

To manage its finances the NEC called in Karl Behr, who had written to Clark after the first luncheon, offering to help in any further money-raising efforts. Assisted by William T. Stewart, an able young lawyer of the Root, Clark firm who had been "drafted" by the NEC, Behr went to work on plans for a second luncheon later in the month. This meeting also added substantially to the amount already collected. Meanwhile, with others attending to the details of administration, finance, and publicity, Grenville Clark turned to the task of writing an appropriate bill.

The bill that later was thrown into the Senate hopper as S-4164 took several weeks to gestate. Clark had sketched a preliminary draft as early as 24 May, and during the following month he prepared several more versions.[9] A number of persons assisted, among them Lewis Douglas, Joseph T. Ryerson of Chicago, Ralph Lowell of Boston, Douglas Arant of Birmingham, Presidents James Bryant Conant of Harvard and Harold W. Dodds of Princeton, General Palmer, "Sec" Root, William T. Stewart, and Howard Slade and Peter Jay, two junior officers of the Fiduciary Trust.[10] Even more direct contributions came from the NEC's subcommittee on legislation (A. G. Thacher, Philip A. Carroll, and Tompkins McIlvaine) and from Major Hershey's Joint Army and Navy Selective Service Committee. In the final analysis, however, the bill emerged primarily from the labors of two men: Grenville Clark and an assistant named Howard C. Petersen. The NEC had "drafted" this young lawyer from the firm of DeGersdorff, Swaine, Cravath, and Wood; five years later, Petersen was to become assistant secretary of war in the Truman administration.

In the initial stages of the draft movement, such terms as "universal training," "selective training and service," and "compulsory military training" had been used somewhat loosely. The MTCA, at least during its early years, had advocated a permanent system of universal military training (UMT) under which every able-bodied American male would undertake a year of military instruction. Tompkins McIlvaine, who had headed the MTCA lobby for UMT in 1919/20, remained the one NEC member who continued to insist, stubbornly and arrogantly, that such a system should be enacted even in 1940.[11] Clark, however, persuaded his colleagues that selective service was far more appropriate for the current emergency. "We did not sit down and draw a quiet peacetime training plan," he later explained to the Senate Committee on Military Affairs. "We approached it with the point of view that we were in a state of very great danger." UMT, which would build up a citizen reserve gradually through annual increments, could not produce the required number quickly enough. Nor was it fair to place the burden on only nineteen and twenty year olds. Clark told the senators that "it should be shared by a much wider age range and that this would also be more effective from a military point of view."[12]

Clark anticipated that the greatest hostility to selective service would come, not in opposition to the draft itself, but to its application in peacetime. He thus wrote a preamble to the bill, explaining its necessity. Although preambles were not at all common in United States legislation, Clark had been reading Froude and was struck by the military statutes of Henry VIII, in which preambles specifically set forth the reasons for the laws.[13] Accordingly, a three-part preamble to the NEC bill was aimed at meeting basic objections to the measure.

In a first premise the preamble argued that an endangered America could no longer stand idle and complacent behind the broad Atlantic:

> The Congress hereby declares that the integrity and institutions of the United States are gravely threatened and that to insure the independence and freedom of the people of the United States it is imperative that immediate measures be taken to mobilize the Nation's strength.

The second part stressed the inadequacy of the volunteer system:

> The Congress further declares that the Nation's strength depends not only
> upon the possession of modern arms but equally upon adequate forces of
> well-trained men and experience has shown that such forces cannot be
> obtained by voluntary enlistment.

The third argument tried to persuade those who saw conscription as a threat
to civil liberties, saying

> that in a free society it is just and right that the obligations and risks of
> military training and service be shared by all, so that every able-bodied man
> shall fit into his proper place under a fair system of compulsory military
> training and service.[14]

The New York sponsors, of course, had access to the legislative blueprints
of the Joint Selective Service Committee and benefited from the committee's
long study of the problem. Several well-defined differences emerged, however,
between the army's bill and the legislation presented by Clark's group. These
differences centered on age limits, the pay of inductees, the length of training,
and exemptions and deferments.

The issue of how large a proportion of the male citizenry should be liable
to registration and induction involved more than numbers. The army's bill
provided simply that the president might order the registration and induction
of such groups between the ages of eighteen and forty-five as he deemed
necessary; it would apply at the outset only to the twenty-one to thirty-one age
group.[15] The NEC's bill, however, mandated the registration of all male
citizens between eighteen and sixty-five. Those between the ages of twenty-
one and forty-five were liable for induction into the armed forces, while the
eighteen to twenty-one and the forty-five to sixty-five age groups could be
drafted for service in "home defense units of the land and naval forces of the
United States in or near the communities and areas in which they reside."[16]

Members of the NEC, mostly men of middle age, some of them
nostalgically yearning to fight again, were more optimistic than was the
General Staff about the potential military effectiveness of older men. Their
broader age range also resulted from a conviction, especially in Clark's mind,
that this range held psychological importance. In their optimistic view,
registration of all men between the ages of eighteen and sixty-five, virtually
the entire manpower of the country, would awaken the American people to the
need for preparation and at the same time would give every able-bodied man,
regardless of age, a sense of sharing in national defense. The NEC's bill also
included a detailed breakdown of the percentages of men to be called from
each age bracket (21–31, 31–38, and 38–45), with the youngest getting the
highest quota in order to maximize military effectiveness. The New Yorkers
did not realize, however, that the distinction between registration and actual
service did not always seem clear to the average American. Instead of

REVEILLE!

This cartoon from the Fort Wayne, Ind., *Gazette* suggests some of the larger ramifications of the draft bill as envisaged by its sponsors—the psychological preparation of the nation. (Reprinted with the permission of the Fort Wayne *Journal-Gazette*)

promoting national solidarity, the broad age ranges in the bill gave the misleading impression, in one pacifist's words, that "it would conscript for mil[itary] service all males 18–65—40,000,000 of us."[17] However laudable the purposes of wide registration, this part of the bill provided a rallying point for the opposition. President Roosevelt later told his cabinet that "95 per cent [of those] . . . [who] opposed . . . the draft bill" did so on the basis of false impressions that were "just plain nonsense."[18]

As to the period of training, Clark and his colleagues, perhaps influenced by the relatively short training they themselves had received in World War I, at first specified only six months. The Joint Army and Navy Committee urged an eighteen-month program that would allow for large-scale corps maneuvers as well as the training of individuals and small units. The NEC members budged only slightly, by lengthening the training period to eight months. Both bills contained a provision for extending the period of service in the event of a national emergency.[19] In the matter of pay, the NEC followed, without great enthusiasm, McIlvaine's suggestion that draftees should receive no more than a token $5 per month. McIlvaine argued that all men freely owed military service to their country and therefore should serve without pay, just as volunteers for the CMTC camps had done for the past twenty years. The Joint Committee's bill provided that draftees should receive the regular salary of their rank. The awkwardness of two different pay scales, not to mention aristocratic bias inherent in the $5 figure, should have been obvious to the New Yorkers. Nonetheless, the $5 provision remained in the bill as introduced in Congress, and it, too, aroused needless opposition.

The question of exemption from registration and deferment of service proved to be a knotty one. Clark's early drafts exempted from registration only foreign diplomatic personnel and certain high officials of the government; on the advice of Hershey's group, members of the armed forces were also exempted, thus having the two bills conform on this point.[20] The Joint Committee's bill also gave the president broad authority to defer service on the grounds of dependency or occupational status; administrative regulations would handle deferments of specific occupations. Clark realized the wisdom of such an approach, but the NEC received considerable pressure from President Conant and other educators, who feared that the sciences might be stripped of personnel unless the statutes were specifically to defer students and researchers.[21] The NEC's bill thus authorized the president to defer "those men whose employment in industry, agriculture, or other occupations or employment, or whose work in engineering, chemistry, physics, medicine, or dentistry, are found to be necessary to the maintenance of the national health, safety, or interest."[22]

The NEC followed the Joint Committee's bill in its handling of religion and conscience. The president might defer any ordained minister who was actively engaged in clerical duties.[23] In addition, members of recognized religious sects "whose creed or principles forbid its members to participate in war in any form" might be excused, not from registration or from all types of service, but from combat duty only.[24] Like the army's bill, the NEC's measure made all registrants subject to military law (and therefore to courts-martial) from the date they were ordered to report for induction.[25] Similarly, Clark's bill provided for a selection system based on local administration, as in the Selective Service Act of 1917.[26] Neither Clark's bill nor the Joint Committee's bill, however, gave any recognition to persons whose conscientious objection to military service derived from principles or beliefs that were not necessarily associated with religion in general or pacifist churches in particular. Nor would either bill protect "absolutist" objectors—namely, those who conscientiously refused to register or to perform noncombatant service. Since the British Conscription Act of 1939 contained much broader provisions for conscientious objectors, American pacifists concentrated on this issue during the following months.[27]

The NEC's bill underlined its peacetime application by authorizing the president to induct "such numbers of men as in his judgment, *whether a state of war exists or not,* are required in the national interest." This grant of power was hard for anti–New Deal members of Congress to swallow, for many of them already thought that the president was using the emergency to make himself a dictator.[28] To make selective service more palatable to FDR's opponents, Clark therefore added a clause prohibiting the induction of any men "until Congress shall appropriate the funds necessary for such a purpose."[29] Even though opponents later argued that the president would be able to circumvent such a provision, the bill clearly intended to hand Congress the reins. It also stipulated that "if and so long as the United States is not at war," men trained under the Selective Service Act should automatically become members of the army or navy reserve for ten years, or until they reached the age of forty-five. Reservists would be liable for further training of not more than one month in any one year and not oftener than three years in any five-year period. Finally, the entire act would expire on 15 May 1945, unless continued by Congress.[30]

Clark well understood the desirability of building up influential support for the measure before its introduction. While drafting the bill, therefore, he made a point of sending a copy of each version to Stimson, while inviting comments from other interested persons. On 11 June the first printed draft came off the press, and on the next day, Howard Petersen hand-carried copies to the White House, to General Marshall, and to Gen. John J. Pershing. While in the capital for these "courtesy" calls, Petersen also conferred with Major Hershey and Col. Victor O'Kelliher, each of whom made several further suggestions. Back in New York the next weekend, Petersen talked with Carroll, McIlvaine, and Thacher, and together they made such changes as the eight-months' training period and exemption of those already in the armed forces. On Monday 17 June the revised bill, substantially as it went to

Congress three days later, was printed. Across the Atlantic that day, Premier Reynaud gave way to the aged Marshal Pétain. The Germans had marched into Paris, and it looked as if France were finished.

Although a selective-service bill had become the primary goal of the National Emergency Committee, the enthusiasm generated by the 22 May meeting at the Harvard Club had sparked a parallel movement in early June—an effort, in Colonel Adler's words, to "raise the Plattsburg flag again." The veterans of 1915 proposed to establish the same type of training camps for business and professional men that had been the nucleus of the World War I officers' training program.

The army, however, opposed any renewal of Plattsburg-style officer training. The circumstances during the summer of 1940 were quite different from 1917, when a corps of officers had been needed in order to raise an army of any kind. (The first enlisted men who were inducted under the World War I draft were called in September 1917; the first "ninety-day wonders" had just graduated from the officer camps and were available to help train the new draftees.)[31] In contrast, the officer pool in 1940 seemed substantial. The Regular Army had more than thirteen thousand officers, and the National Guard could furnish twenty thousand more; in addition, college ROTC units were adding about eight thousand new second lieutenants each year to an Officers' Reserve Corps of more than one hundred thousand, on which the army could draw in an emergency.[32] While the General Staff could admit the need for vast increases in enlisted manpower, it could not justify "Plattsburg" camps to train more prospective officers.

General Staff opposition did not deter the enthusiastic laymen in New York, who were convinced that the coming emergency would require far more officers than the army had on the books, even if the entire hundred thousand in the ORC should prove to be individually fit and capable. Caught up in the anguish and emotion of 1940, the Plattsburg veterans believed that a revival of their old experiment would solidify the country and stimulate opposition to the Axis, thus performing a psychological function similar to that of the 1915/16 camps.[33] Leaders of the project, which the NEC undertook to sponsor along with the selective-service campaign, were two men who were themselves active reserve officers: Colonel Adler and Maj. John D. Kenderdine.

The initiative came from Kenderdine, whom the Plattsburgers had known before the first World War. MTCA leaders had asked Kenderdine, then a young staff writer on *McClure's,* to edit the association journal, *National Service,* which began publication in early 1917. Kenderdine did so for several months, then resigned to enter the army. After earning a commission at Plattsburg, he served as a regimental staff officer in the AEF. While not involved with the MTCA during the interwar years, he remained an active reservist and wrote several treatises on the officer problem.

In May 1940, as the selective-service campaign built up steam, Kenderdine approached Adler, whom he knew as a member of the same reserve brigade, with a plan for Plattsburg-type camps to train qualified civilians and to bring former servicemen up to date in tactics and techniques. Adler enthusiastically presented the idea to the inaugural meeting of the NEC on 3 June. Thinking that a revival of Plattsburg camps would not only contribute to national defense but also aid the conscription effort as a source of publicity, the NEC voted to ask the War Department to set up such a program. At the larger meeting that same afternoon at the Bar Association, more than two hundred New Yorkers formally resolved to seek training that would "perpetuate the spirit and success of the original Plattsburg Business Men's Training Camps of 1915" and "afford to business men at the present time opportunities to attend similar camps throughout the country."[34]

Especially among the younger men the idea caught fire, and during the next week, strong backing for the camps (despite the fact that they still had not been approved by official authority) developed in downtown New York under the leadership of Howard Slade and Peter Jay. It seemed like 1915 once again.[35] Spreading by word of mouth, news of the project reached the New York City alumni associations of several of the large eastern colleges, and on 13 June a group of young men, several of them sons of the original Plattsburg leaders, met in the auditorium of the Bar Association, with Slade as acting chairman.[36]

Slade said that he was completely ignorant of military matters except for the conviction that it was "a young man's job when the country is in danger." He then introduced Adler, who explained the plan and reported that negotiations with the War Department were in progress. (Kenderdine, by this time, was in Washington, trying to convert the General Staff.) Thacher and Clark spoke also, outlining the relationship of the Plattsburg idea to the conscription campaign and to an adequate defense program. Special impetus came from Lt. Gen. Hugh A. Drum, commander of the Second Corps Area and the senior officer in the army, who exuberantly avowed: "I believe that every man who wants this training should be given an opportunity to get it."[37] As a climax to the meeting, the participants sent telegrams to the president, the secretary of war, and the chief of staff, among others, urging that at least fifteen thousand volunteers be trained. Offering to help recruit for the camps, they declared that hundreds of young professional men would pay their own way if necessary.

This wave of enthusiasm broke against a rigid War Department. Army chiefs insisted that they did not need any more officers, that there were enough on the rolls for any foreseeable emergency.[38] It would be foolish, they argued, to waste energies on a civilian program when the thousands of officers in the ORC should be given first priority for training. They also claimed that Plattsburg camps would be too short to accomplish much. Moreover, so long as the army gave priority to building its regular units to full strength, it could not release enough officers to provide instruction for civilian trainees. Further opposition came from representatives of the Officers' Reserve Corps, who saw in the Plattsburg revival an attempt to by-pass their own organization.[39]

Thus, on 6 June the General Staff wired Adler, who was then handling the negotiations, that it considered the Plattsburg plan impractical and unacceptable. Adler thereupon appealed directly to General Marshall, wiring: "Military Training Camps Association is bitterly disappointed, and we appeal from it to you. . . . Those camps are auxiliary to our big movement for universal military training and . . . it is important to show . . . that older men . . . are prepared to give their service again to their country in an emergency. The example of even a few hundred of these older men before the youth of the country is vital in our judgment." Adler characterized complaints about "unfairness" to the ORC as coming from men with "a narrow viewpoint," saying that the "vast majority" of reservists would serve as corporals "if it were deemed by the War Department in the best interests of the country."[40]

To press this request for reconsideration, Kenderdine went to Washington on Monday 10 June. For four days he argued his case before officers of both the Personnel and the Plans and Training divisions, receiving cordial treatment from Maj. Walter Weible of G-3, who had been instructed to give Kenderdine every consideration. Other officers of the General Staff showed more resentment of "outside interference." If "that fellow Adler wants to run the army," they complained, "tell him to get himself appointed secretary of war." Kenderdine replied "with as much force as I could without being shot," shouting at one point that he believed 40 percent of reserve officers were inefficient. Gen. Frank M. Andrews, G-3, who had been listening to the skirmish from afar, came over and said to Kenderdine: "That's an incredible thing for you to say." The next day, meeting Kenderdine in the hall, he greeted him good-naturedly: "What, you still here? I thought my boys sent you back to New York last night."[41] Like his subordinates, Andrews opposed the camps but told Kenderdine that he would, of course, cooperate without reservation if the chief of staff were to approve them.

During his stay, Kenderdine had three interviews with Gen. William Bryden, deputy chief of staff, who brought up the practical problems of quotas, instructors, and finance. Would the camps, if authorized, be held in all nine corps areas or just at Plattsburg? Bryden did not want to single out one corps area, despite New York's obvious focal point. As to numbers, he set three thousand as the maximum figure the army could train in all camps. So that the machinery would be ready to go into operation if necessary, Bryden assigned a staff officer to work with Kenderdine in preparing such details as radiograms to commanders of corps areas, application blanks, and other forms.

The most difficult problem proved to be finance. Major Weible could not find any monies legitimately available to cover the estimated cost of $58.75 per trainee; thus, anyone who attended the camps for business and professional men would have to pay his own way. Keeping in daily touch with Adler by phone, Kenderdine succeeded in working out an agreement with the War Department and the NEC: each corps area's commander could exceed his regular CMTC allotment by $20 per man to provide for the special camps. Each trainee would furnish his own transportation and, upon arrival, would pay the extra cost of mess expenses and general overhead. The MTCA would underwrite the total amount by placing in the hands of the War Department nine checks, made out to the commanding generals of each corps area, totaling $76,500. If government funds were later provided for the camps (they were not), these checks would be returned, undeposited, to the MTCA.[42]

When Kenderdine attempted to persuade General Marshall on the morning of Thursday 13 June, he had five minutes, and five minutes only. When asked why Plattsburg camps were necessary and important, Kenderdine had three ready reasons: first, the world crisis made it imperative that the army build up an officer corps even larger than that carried on the rolls; second, to obtain officers, the army should go after men of proven leadership qualities rather than wait to get them through the ranks; and finally, from Kenderdine's own experience as a reserve officer, he was convinced that the pool of reservists on which the military counted had only 60 percent effectiveness. Marshall was digesting this reasoning when a phone call summoned him to Secretary Woodring's office. Sensing his chance, Kenderdine blurted out: "General, 800 young men are meeting in New York this afternoon on this very question; could I get a decision today so that I may transmit it to them by telephone?" The chief of staff hit the roof. "Major," he snapped, "you should know better than that. You know I can't give a snap decision without consulting my staff." Whereupon Marshall stomped out of the room.[43]

The next day, however, General Marshall approved the MTCA request unreservedly, a surprising move in view of his staff's outspoken opposition. In addition to bureaucratic reasons for opposing Plattsburg camps, the project would surely arouse public controversy as being playground soldiering on the part of Park Avenue elites. But Marshall, jolted by the collapse of France and "the lightning rapidity" of events abroad, had come a long way in the two weeks since his meeting with Clark and Adler.[44] On 4 June the chief of staff had asked that only four National Guard divisions be called to active duty, but by 22 June he was supporting selective service and urging the activation of all eighteen divisions of the Guard.[45] Although still thin-skinned about interference from "this important New York fellow and this other important New York fellow," Marshall was too politic to choke off well-intentioned support for building up preparedness.[46] Consequently, on 14 June he authorized all corps-area commanders to hold special four-weeks' businessmen's camps in conjunction with the regular CMTC camps beginning on 5 July.[47]

The army set the quota at three thousand trainees—three hundred for each corps area except the Second (New York) and the Seventh, which had five hundred and four hundred allotted respectively. The MTCA had the responsibility for selecting candidates on the basis of educational qualifications and demonstrated leadership in local communities. Applicants had to be between twenty-five and fifty years of age. The training course would consist of the basic CMTC program, modified for men of advanced age and experience. Marshall's directive only authorized businessmen's camps, leaving each corps-area commander to decide whether such a project was feasible.[48]

Having pushed their program through a reluctant War Department, the Plattsburgers found that they had nearly overreached themselves. Some MTCA officers, suddenly responsible for filling camps due to open in three weeks, doubted that they could meet their quotas. In Boston, Ralph Lowell, Mike Farley, and Benjamin Joy, all Plattsburg veterans of 1915, persuaded the local chapter of the Committee to Defend America to share office space and to help recruit for the camp at Fort Devens, Massachusetts. Officials of the First, Second, and Third corps areas accepted their tasks cheerfully, but open opposition developed in the Midwest, where Tom Wyles indignantly protested that the chief of staff must have "lost his mind." No sooner had Kenderdine returned from Washington than he boarded a plane for Chicago to mollify national officers in the Sixth and Seventh corps areas.[49] He received support from Joseph T. Ryerson, a Chicagoan on the Executive Committee. Against the objection that a hurried effort would be too feeble, Ryerson argued that success on a small scale would encourage later attempts of more consequence. When grumbling continued, Kenderdine forcefully pointed out that they had not met to discuss the merits of the plan but to implement the chief of staff's directive, at which point the assembled officials agreed, albeit in some cases with obvious reluctance, to begin recruiting for the camps.

Since applications for Plattsburg were already pouring in before approval from Washington, the task in New York involved selection rather than recruitment. To handle the three thousand aspirants for the five hundred allotted places, the NEC set up a special office on 44th Street, under Kenderdine's supervision, with Robert K. Haas and Robert Marks as volunteer assistants. Adler, as chairman of the NEC subcommittee on the camps, exercised general direction; and Col. Walter W. Metcalf headed the volunteer board that met every evening to evaluate the candidates. The success of the Second Corps Area's camp at Plattsburg was thus assured by the time when Clark and Petersen, having completed the final draft of their selective-service bill, were taking it to Washington for introduction in Congress.

6

Washington:
The Burke-Wadsworth Bill Debuts

The world is a stupendous machine, composed of innumerable parts, each of which in being a free agent, has a volition and action of its own; and on this ground arises the difficulty of assuring success in any enterprise depending on the volition of numerous agents. We may set the machine in motion, and dispose every wheel to one certain end; but when it depends on the volition of any one wheel, and the correspondent action of every wheel, the result is uncertain.

—Niccolo Machiavelli

The way in which the Selective Training and Service Act of 1940 first reached the floor of Congress illustrates how much important events may turn on trivialities. The day before its introduction in the Senate, the men who wrote it had no idea that within forty-eight hours their measure would be known throughout the country as the Burke-Wadsworth bill. That Congressman James W. Wadsworth of New York, in view of his long interest in military affairs, should introduce it in the House seemed logical, though by no means certain; that Senator Edward R. Burke of Nebraska, a bitter critic of the New Deal, should sponsor it in the upper chamber, came about largely as a matter of happenstance. Any one of a half dozen other senators might have had his name affixed to the bill. Because neither Burke nor Wadsworth had close ties with the White House, moreover, and because both men strongly supported Wendell L. Willkie in the presidential campaign that summer, the issue of peacetime conscription became more ensnarled in partisan politics than its sponsors wished.

NEC leaders met in New York on Monday 17 June to plan strategy for their draft legislation. Developments seemed to call for speed. The spectacle of German troops marching down the Champs Élysées three days before had made the war threat seem even more serious. Rumor also had it that Congress

83

might adjourn before the worst of the summer heat settled on Washington; some Republicans and isolationists feared that without Congress as a watchdog, President Roosevelt might somehow commit the country to war. FDR had said he would call Congress into special session if necessary, but his opponents thought otherwise.[1] With little time to lose, the NEC sponsors decided that their bill should be introduced, if possible, within the week. A telegram signed by Tom Wyles on behalf of the MTCA was sent to Congress, protesting early adjournment, while Howard Petersen flew to Washington that evening to confer with Major Hershey about the revisions made the preceding weekend. To help rally popular support, Elihu Root, Jr., agreed to prepare a pamphlet that contained, in addition to the text of the bill, arguments for compulsory training in general and the NEC's measure in particular. Seven or eight of the NEC sponsors arranged to rendezvous in Washington two days later to get the bill introduced into the Senate and the House.[2]

Several weeks earlier, Grenville Clark and his friends had hoped to have selective service adopted as part of the Roosevelt administration's expanding defense program; hence the efforts to woo President Roosevelt and the General Staff. This basic strategy had also led Clark, after his visit with Justice Frankfurter, to seek out Senator James F. Byrnes of South Carolina, reputedly one of the shrewdest political judges on Capitol Hill. Although Byrnes proved to be an effective floor leader in piloting the conscription bill through the Senate later that August, during the spring he had no inkling whatsoever that "His Excellency" (as he privately called FDR) would support such a measure.[3] To get a peacetime draft bill through Congress, he told Clark, would be difficult enough in an election year, but without the president's backing, it would not stand "a Chinaman's chance."[4]

This gloomy analysis presaged the negative attitude of many administration stalwarts throughout the conscription campaign. Coupled with White House caution and the War Department's apparent lack of interest during the first two weeks of June, it caused the sponsors to revise their strategy. By 17 June they had decided that, while still welcoming administration support, they would have their bill introduced, if possible, by a group of senators and representatives chosen from both sides of the political aisle.

This decision seemed wise in view of the political campaign then in the offing. Advance groups in Philadelphia were already preparing for the Republican Convention the next week; and while the various factions had a common bond in their opposition to the New Deal, they felt no unity on the international issues that were apt to dominate the convention. There seemed to be an excellent chance that the Republicans would officially go isolationist, nominating a candidate such as Senator Robert A. Taft of Ohio, who opposed Roosevelt's foreign policy.[5] If so, the GOP might condemn the draft as an interventionist measure; and with Republicans allied with Democratic isolationists, a conscription bill could scarcely pass.

In hasty preparation for Washington, Clark penned a memorandum that reveals the spur-of-the-moment flexibility of their plans.

> Complete and print today draft in form to present for consultation with leading members of Congress. Meanwhile, on Tuesday, June 18, make appointments with various leading legislators, including: in the House: Speaker [William B.] Bankhead, Representative [Sam] Rayburn (majority leader), Representative [Hatton] Sumners [sic] (Chairman Judiciary Committee) of Texas (Democrat) representing majority; Representative Joseph W. Martin, minority leader, and Representative James W. Wadsworth (former Senator and former Chairman of Senate Military Affairs Committee), representing the Republican minority. In the Senate: See Senator [Alben] Barkley, Majority Leader, Vice President [John Nance] Garner, Senator Byrnes, Senator [George] Norris (Nebraska), representing majority and Senator [Charles] McNary, Minority Leader, and Senator [Warren F.] Austin, of Vermont, representing the minority.
>
> Also in the House, see Representative Andrew May, Chairman of Military Affairs committee, and in the Senate, Senator Morris Sheppard, Chairman Senate Military Affairs Committee. Others to be considered are: Representatives [Bruce] Barton, [Clifton] Woodrum, and [M. J.] Merritt, in the House, and Senator [Carter] Glass, Senator [Warren] Barber [sic], Senator [Henry Cabot] Lodge, Senator [Edward R.] Burke, Senator [Tom] Connally and others.[6]

In addition to misspelling several names and thinking of Norris, who later opposed selective service, Clark interestingly listed Senator Burke simply as one of several "to be considered."

Clark, Adler, Petersen, Carroll, Lewis Douglas, and Douglas Arant, all of whom were in Washington by the evening of 18 June, established informal "headquarters" at the Hotel Carlton on 16th and K Streets. On Wednesday 19 June they set out to sell their bill. Since Wadsworth had emerged as the logical choice in the House, they got in touch with him first. General Palmer had worked closely with Wadsworth, then a forty-two-year-old senator, in formulating the Defense Act of 1920; and NEC member William Chadbourne, a close friend of Wadsworth's, had phoned the congressman two days earlier for an appointment.[7] Wadsworth said yes immediately. "Our trouble," he had written only a month earlier, "has always been that we have waited and waited and postponed and postponed and refused to believe what we saw, until all of a sudden we woke up and found ourselves unprepared."[8] Although not a member of the House Military Affairs Committee, Wadsworth suspected that members would be "glad to see an outsider stick his neck out," and he "didn't mind a bit."[9]

The bipartisan plan soon struck a snag, however, for most Democratic senators, mindful that no word had come down from the White House, refused to commit themselves. The attitude recalled Clark's interview with Senator Byrnes several weeks before. Senator Millard Tydings of Maryland told a familiar tale. Philip Carroll, a native Marylander, had talked to Tydings and had found him personally sympathetic. The senator complained, however, that the country was asleep; the moral fiber of the people had deteriorated; and no draft bill could pass under such circumstances. It simply could not be done.

Discouraged, the NEC members met again that evening at the Carlton. Speed still seemed important. With the Republican Wadsworth committed as a sponsor in the House, and with Senate Democrats lukewarm at best, they thought about a Republican senator. Henry Cabot Lodge, Jr., of Massachusetts seemed a possibility. When Clark talked with Lodge that day, the youthful senator had expressed a definite interest in introducing the bill, perhaps in conjunction with Tydings, a fellow member of the Military Affairs Committee. But Lodge would not commit himself absolutely, Tydings had pussyfooted, and results on the whole seemed meager.

At breakfast the next morning the NEC members vowed to get something done that day.[10] Clark and Adler took their list of senators and divided it between them, agreeing to see each senator until they found one who would introduce the bill. Clark had another appointment with Lodge at ten o'clock, after which Clark proposed to call on Senator Burke, with whom he had worked cordially during the court-packing fight of 1937. Because Burke's bitter feud with the White House had resulted in his losing the Democratic primary for the Senate that spring, the NEC had not considered the Nebraskan a likely candidate so long as they were seeking bipartisan sponsors. Adler, who had once been publisher of the *Chattanooga* (Tenn.) *Times,* decided to start with Senator Kenneth McKellar of Tennessee.

A simple misunderstanding eliminated Lodge. An avowed proponent of preparedness, the junior senator from Massachusetts might well have agreed to sponsor the bill, but when Clark called at his office that morning, Lodge had stepped out. Clark waited half an hour, then decided to see Burke and to return to Lodge later. After hearing Clark's explanation of the measure and its background, Senator Burke replied that he had been thinking along such lines for some time. A World War I veteran, Burke was willing, he said, to sponsor the bill in conjunction with Lodge, if the latter so desired, or with any other senator whose support might strengthen its chances for passage. Clark thereupon called Lodge's office and, when the secretary reported that the senator was still not available, left a message to the effect that Burke also wished to cosponsor the bill. Clark then phoned Adler in Senator McKellar's office. Adler was having a difficult time persuading McKellar, who was hard of hearing and well along in years. Burke, a vigorous personality who was well respected by his colleagues, seemed much preferable as a cosponsor. Hanging up the phone, Adler turned and said: "Senator, I'm sorry I pushed you so hard. I have this a little on my conscience." "On the contrary," said McKellar, "I'm just in the mood. I—." "Oh, no, Senator," Adler insisted to the gaping Senator. "We simply must not be precipitous." Adler then beat a retreat from McKellar's office.[11]

Meanwhile, hoping to build as broad a base as possible, Burke suggested that he and Clark go see Tydings, whose office was just across the hall, and sound him out once more. Tydings, however, repeated his conviction that peacetime conscription could not possibly pass. Furthermore, he had heard General Staff officers say that the army did not need a draft at this time. Clark tried to explain that in drawing up its bill, the NEC had worked with the army representatives, but Tydings refused to be persuaded.

Back in Burke's office, Clark called Lodge again, only to be told, with some emphasis, by his secretary that because of the "change in plans," Senator Lodge thought that perhaps Senator Burke should undertake the sponsorship alone. Apparently miffed, Lodge thought that Clark had intentionally by-passed him. Whatever the misunderstanding, Clark had no time to straighten things out. The Senate would convene at noon, in less than an hour, and was expected to recess after a very short session out of respect for Senator Ernest W. Gibson of Vermont, who had just died.[12] Burke then said that if introducing the bill had a higher priority than the identity of the sponsors, he would gladly go ahead on his own. Clark agreed that this would be best. In a matter of minutes, Clark called Wadsworth, who then discussed the matter with Burke by phone. On the spot they consented to present the measure to Congress as the Burke-Wadsworth bill.

The next half-hour was filled with frantic activity. To check the bill for proper form, Burke called in one of the Senate's drafting experts, who suggested that they revise the preamble and drop a nebulous section dealing with reemployment guarantees. Hastily they penciled in changes on the printed copy that Clark had with him. In the midst of this flurry, Petersen and Boone arrived, having been summoned by telephone. They quickly made corresponding notations and hurried off to be at the Capitol when the Senate convened. At a few minutes before twelve, the bill finally in order, Burke's secretary sprinted to the Senate chamber with the master copy, dropping it into the Senate hopper just at noon. Petersen and Boone were waiting in the press gallery with other copies of the bill to hand out to newsmen. It went into the record as S-4164; the next day, Wadsworth introduced the identical measure in the lower chamber as H.R. 10132.

Not content with handing copies to Washington correspondents, Boone determined also to have the text of the bill published in its entirety. This was no easy task. Few bills seemed important enough to warrant publication; most bills, even when they eventually became law, were amended beyond recognition. But Boone had laid his groundwork well. During the week he had sent advance texts to several influential editors whom he knew personally, together with notes explaining (with enthusiasm that stretched the truth) that the War Department had accepted it in principle and that the White House tacitly approved it. Boone clinched the matter by making personal visits to officials of the major wire services to emphasize the importance of the bill.

Consequently, just after the measure went to Congress, the entire text went out over Associated Press, United Press, and International News Service wires to almost two thousand newspapers from coast to coast. Persuaded by the wire-service coverage that this bill had unusual significance, many large metropolitan dailies printed the measure in full, and smaller papers printed excerpts. Editors who passed over the text were soon giving it editorial comment. Overnight, this successful publicity maneuver catapulted the Burke-Wadsworth bill into a major issue.[13]

The twentieth of June 1940 stood out as a significant date not only because of the introduction of the Burke bill in the Senate. Abroad, with the French army on its last legs, the Pétain government at Bordeaux was deciding whether to fight on in North Africa or to accept German armistice terms, while across the Channel the Luftwaffe was dumping bombs all along the south and east coast of England. "Wir fahren gegen England" ("We Are Sailing against England") was becoming a popular song among Nazi youths. In New York, pedestrians were looking curiously at a new tabloid on the newsstands: Marshall Field's altruistic venture in journalism, *PM*. That same day, Frederick Libby, the ebullient Quaker who headed the National Council for the Prevention of War, spent $17 on a long-distance phone call trying to persuade University of Chicago's President Robert M. Hutchins to head a new antiwar crusade uniting pacifists and isolationists.[14] Boxing fans were more interested in what round Joe Louis would knock out Arturo Godoy in their heavyweight fight that evening at Yankee Stadium.[15]

But the biggest story of the day broke just before noon. At that moment, just as Burke and Clark were scribbling last-minute changes on the Selective Service bill, someone burst into the senator's office with electrifying news from the other end of Pennsylvania Avenue—the president had just announced the nomination of two Republicans, Henry L. Stimson and Frank Knox, to head the War and Navy departments. Immediately grasping the implications for the conscription bill, Burke looked at Clark. "Any connection?" he asked with good-natured suspicion. Clark admitted that in the case of Stimson, there was.

For a time, notwithstanding Frankfurter's report that he had "struck fire" at the White House, the president appeared disinclined to do anything about the Stimson appointment. A week before, Clark had wired the justice: "Nothing whatever is happening to change the weak administration of the

War Department.''[16] Frankfurter tried to prod FDR from Massachusetts, but all they could do was wait.[17] Both Republicans and the Washington press were continuing to snipe at Woodring. Only a week before, Thomas E. Dewey had called loudly for the removal of the secretary of war "under whose guidance our military preparedness has been shockingly inadequate."[18] Columnist Drew Pearson observed, "If there is anything Roosevelt ought to know by now it is that only a blast of TNT will oust his Secretary of War."[19]

On 15 June, Stimson had phoned Clark to say he would deliver a radio address at the Yale commencement on 18 June. Did Clark have any suggestions? Indeed he had. With the NEC's bill to go to Congress within the week, Clark urged a particularly strong endorsement for compulsory military training and service, together with the advocacy of direct support to the Allies. How much Clark influenced the older man is a matter of conjecture, for Stimson had strong opinions of his own; but his speech three days later demanded the adoption of compulsory training "at once" and vigorously championed immediate aid to the Allied powers.[20] Though the address caused him some uncomfortable moments when suspicious senators cross-examined him during confirmation hearings several days later, it stood out not only for its influence on the public but also because it put Stimson unequivocally on record regarding these issues two days prior to his nomination as secretary of war.[21] Ever alert, Frankfurter wired the president, urging him to read Stimson's Yale speech.[22]

On 19 June, Stimson again phoned Clark, who was then in Washington. "Your ridiculous plot has succeeded," he announced. The elder statesman had been working at his law office when the president called that morning to ask him to become secretary of war. Stimson had demurred on account of his age, but FDR had insisted. Stimson also warned the president of his strong speech at New Haven the day before. FDR countered that he had already read the press accounts, and the Yale speech, far from being a deterrent, had clinched things. In addition, the president had repeated almost verbatim the conditions that Frankfurter had laid down as to his acceptance: Stimson would be free to express his own views on such issues as conscription and aid to the Allies; he would be excused from any partisan activities; and he would choose Patterson as his assistant secretary. With these stipulations understood and agreed to, Stimson accepted the job.[23]

Coy to the end, Roosevelt apparently made the final decision with his usual mix of shrewdness and superficiality. The navy post had become available late in May, when Secretary Charles Edison had agreed to run as the Democratic candidate for governor in New Jersey. Edison offered his resignation, effective 15 June. When Roosevelt called Knox early on the morning of 19 June, he casually asked if Knox preferred navy or war. Fortunately, Knox professed to know little about army matters and chose the navy.[24] Knox then asked the president to delay announcing his nomination

until after the Republican Convention, where Knox intended to press hard for
an interventionist plank on foreign policy. Roosevelt wisely decided otherwise,
arguing that an announcement before the convention would emphasize
patriotism over partisanship and that any belated appointments would be
interpreted as "an act of disgruntlement and bad sportsmanship."[25] FDR still
had not dismissed Woodring or approached Stimson. Nor was he telling
White House intimates what was afoot. (He did hint to Morgenthau on 17
June that an important change would be announced in two days. When
Morgenthau, early on the nineteenth, reminded Roosevelt that the "two days
are up," the president replied: "That's right, and I am going to do something
today." The "very self-possessed" Roosevelt would say nothing more.)[26] The
perfect excuse to dismiss Woodring presented itself on 17/18 June, when the
secretary of war refused to approve the sale of twelve B-17 bombers to
England.[27] Alluding vaguely "to a succession of events both here and
abroad," the president thereupon asked for Woodring's resignation on 19
June, suggesting that it would be "of the utmost importance to this country"
if Woodring were to become governor of Puerto Rico.[28] He formally
announced the appointments of Stimson and Knox the next day.

Despite earlier rumors of a coalition cabinet, the dual nomination hit
Washington like a "bombshell."[29] In Philadelphia, Republican leaders, who
were preparing for the convention, were dumbfounded. The president had
said that the appointments reflected the "overwhelming sentiment of the
nation for a national solidarity in a time of world crisis and in behalf of
national defense and nothing else," but the outraged opposition denounced
the move as being nothing but "petty politics." Dewey called it an act of
"weakness and desperation," a "political raid" on the Republican party. On
Capitol Hill there was shocked disbelief. "Is this true?" shouted Missouri
Democrat Bennett Champ Clark on the floor of the Senate.[30]

Many Republicans raged as furiously at Stimson and Knox as they did at
the president. John D. M. Hamilton, chairman of the GOP National
Committee, reportedly read the two nominees out of the party, saying they
were "no longer qualified to speak as Republicans or for the Republican
organization."[31] On the Senate floor, denunciations of Knox and Stimson
became so vitriolic that Senator Alben W. Barkley had to remind his
colleagues that the power to declare war did not lie with members of the
cabinet. A fellow Chicagoan fumed about "Benito Knox."[32] "I would back
Judas Iscariot against our peerless leader in the White House," wrote one
Republican.[33] One of the few temperate voices belonged to William Allen
White, who argued that Stimson and Knox had "done the patriotic thing."
"If the Republican party . . . bleats like a sheep for peace at any price,"
White warned, "my beloved party will not even carry Maine and Ver-
mont."[34] White later used the machinery of the Committee to Defend
America to send fifteen thousand telegrams in support of Stimson and Knox.

Secretary of War Harry H. Woodring. His dismissal from the cabinet and replacement by Henry L. Stimson was a turning point in the campaign for selective service in 1940. (Courtesy of Franklin D. Roosevelt Library)

"I feel like Father Coughlin or Frankenstein," he confided to Alf Landon, "and I am duly and properly scared, humble, and a bit ashamed."[35] Senator Warren F. Austin of Vermont, the ranking Republican on the Senate Military Affairs Committee, called a hasty conference of fellow GOP colleagues and told them to stop acting like fools and to give Stimson a fair hearing after the Republican Convention. The senators sheepishly agreed.[36]

Isolationists of both parties suspected that Woodring had been forced out because he had opposed secret steps toward war. The departing secretary reportedly had told friends that a "small clique of international financiers" were trying to oust him because he opposed "stripping our own defenses for the sake of trying to stop Hitler, 3,000 miles away."[37] A Washington editor informed former President Hoover that Woodring, on resigning, had written a "hot letter" to FDR, defending his conduct and claiming that Roosevelt had consistently cut military estimates while granting "all kinds of money for the raking of leaves and like worthless projects."[38] Suspicions increased when the White House refused to release Woodring's letter of resignation on the grounds that it was "too personal."[39]

What Woodring actually wrote in his letter to FDR was a plea to "maintain your pronounced non-intervention policy. I trust you will advise those who would provoke belligerency—a state of war for our nation—that they do so with the knowledge that we are not prepared for a major conflict. Billions appropriated today cannot be converted into preparedness tomorrow."[40] A soothing reply came back from the White House. "Don't worry about maintaining the non-intervention policy," Roosevelt promised. "We are certainly going to do just that—barring, of course, an attack on the validity of the Monroe Doctrine."[41] The president continued to smooth Woodring's ruffled feathers over the next few days, obtaining Woodring's pledge not to make the resignation a political issue. When Woodring and his family paid a farewell call at the White House on 26 June, the façade of friendship remained intact.[42] Roosevelt, of course, did not dismiss Woodring simply because FDR was plotting intervention and the departing secretary opposed such a course. But the two men did differ on priorities. Woodring sincerely believed that the transfer of modern arms to Britain constituted an unwarranted "stripping" of America's defenses, and he was therefore dragging his feet on policies that Roosevelt considered vital. If not exactly disloyal to FDR, Woodring saw himself as a watchdog against intervention. Even Woodring's sympathetic biographer has concluded that the President "had no alternative to dismissing him . . . and had sufficient reason to act as he did."[43]

If FDR found it difficult to replace Woodring, even though he had contemplated the move for several years, ousting Louis Johnson as assistant secretary became almost impossible for the president. Despite FDR's commitment to Stimson to appoint Robert Patterson, Roosevelt said nothing publicly at the time of Stimson's nomination. Johnson, who had done a good job of planning for industrial mobilization, thought the top slot should have been his. "But, Mr. President, you promised me not once but many times," the former National Commander of the American Legion pleaded.[44] FDR admitted his obligation to Johnson but said that "the political situation had not worked out that way." When Johnson offered his resignation, Roosevelt refused to accept it, saying that "they could not educate a new assistant and Louis had to go on and do the work, and all would be well."[45] Johnson later told friends that FDR would choose him as his vice-presidential mate if he ran for a third term.[46] The president was borrowing trouble by not facing the issue at the time. In addition to his usual distaste at firing subordinates, Roosevelt did not want to alienate the West Virginia Democrat's many powerful friends (among them James A. Farley, Bernard Baruch, and several conservative Democrats on Capitol Hill).[47] Retaining Johnson would also enable the president to continue his "divide-and-rule" methods of administration. Whatever the primary reason, FDR did nothing, and Johnson still held his post when the Senate confirmed Stimson as secretary of war almost three weeks later.[48]

These complications notwithstanding, the appointments of Knox and Stimson marked a vital turning point in the country's burgeoning defense effort. Whether or not they amounted to a "War Cabinet," as isolationists charged, they added to the government two men who were eager to pursue policies that might lead the United States into war. As the British ambassador reported to London, "the president has now strengthened his national position . . . by securing two outstanding Republican personalities to fill two key defence positions . . . [that] notoriously needed strengthening."[49] Appointed as a sort of team to administer the two service departments during one of the most dangerous periods in United States history, the two men fortunately brought to their tasks a warm and cordial appreciation for one another. As early as 20 May, before any hint of his own appointment, Stimson had written to Knox of his "deep gratification" that the publisher was reportedly being considered for the navy post. "I cannot conceive," the older man added significantly, "of any more effective step which he [Roosevelt] could take towards the creation of such real national solidarity than to place in the hands of responsible leaders of the opposition party the two departments which have direct supervision of the navy and army."[50]

The revitalized leadership of the War Department had, in addition, a decisive impact on the selective-service campaign. Until that time, the army had been lukewarm, if not hostile, to immediate conscription. Although its representatives had passively cooperated with the New Yorkers in drafting the bill, they had shown no faith in the possibility of its passage. Harry Woodring, in fact, strongly opposed a peacetime draft. The General Staff, with its fixation on hemispheric defense, remained committed to a policy that entailed smaller estimates as to the requirements for future military action. In contrast, the newly appointed secretary of war and his assistant-secretary-to-be had both actively participated, as had the new navy secretary, in the initial stages of the conscription campaign in New York. Indeed, Stimson had specifically made the advocacy of selective service a condition of his acceptance. Through Stimson's influence, especially his relationship with General Marshall, the army soon formed ranks behind the Burke-Wadsworth bill.[51]

On Friday 21 June, morning headlines announced the appointments of Stimson and Knox and the introduction of the Burke bill in the Senate. That same day, Hitler dictated armistice terms to France in the famous railroad car at Compiègne. At the end of its afternoon session, Congress recessed for a week to permit Republicans to attend the GOP Convention in Philadelphia. Back in New York, the members of the National Emergency Committee took advantage of the temporary lull to raise more money and to prepare for hearings before the Military Affairs Committee when the Senate reconvened.

On Tuesday the twenty-fifth the Steering Committee and the Administrative Committee of the NEC met jointly to hear a report from Clark on the happenings in Washington. In a minor revolt, Tompkins McIlvaine insisted on advocating a universal, rather than a selective, training program. But his colleagues voted down a proposal to substitute a three-year training period for youths eighteen to twenty-one. The NEC also agreed to double its membership, to two thousand.[52]

The sponsors of the Burke-Wadsworth bill glumly followed the progress of the Republican Convention. To their disappointment, Governor Harold Stassen of Minnesota had seemed to condemn conscription in his keynote address of the night before. Stassen's shafts, however, were aimed not so much at military conscription as at the president's recently announced proposal for compulsory vocational training.[53] On Wednesday the isolationists seemed to be gaining, as they converted the platform plank on foreign policy into a stronger declaration against any kind of intervention. Former President Hoover declared that "the spirits of American boys buried in Flanders twenty years ago rise before us today to warn us that we can make war but we cannot assure liberty in the Old World."[54] The NEC leaders had only a slight inkling that behind the scenes a coalition of Republican leaders, mostly easterners, was preparing to stampede the convention for Wendell L. Willkie of Indiana.[55] Despite columnist Arthur Krock's opinion that Willkie was the "only spot of color" at the convention thus far, Willkie had said nothing positive about the draft and was still considered a dark horse.[56] Some of the Plattsburgers' New York friends, including "Sec" Root's nephew Oren, the chief organizer of the national Willkie Clubs, had joined the Willkie campaign because of his espousal of aid to the Allies short of war.[57] But none of the NEC leaders knew the Indiana candidate well enough to guess that he privately supported more interventionist measures than did FDR and that he would give vital backing to their selective-service bill later that summer.[58]

On Thursday 27 June, with tension building toward the first ballot scheduled for that evening, the NEC held a second fund-raising luncheon at the Broad Street Club in Manhattan. During this luncheon, at which Governor Herbert H. Lehman, Lewis Douglas, and General Drum spoke, an incident occurred that was packed with ruinous possibilities for the Burke-Wadsworth bill. As master of ceremonies, Clark was introducing the speakers when a waiter brought an urgent message that Stimson was calling. Clark excused himself and hurried to the telephone.[59] Stimson said: "I've just received a letter from the President. He encloses a letter sent to him by the War Department, signed by Louis Johnson as Acting Secretary, requesting him to put into effect a full scale volunteer recruiting drive planned by the army. In an attached note the president says he supposes it should be approved, but he asks my opinion. What do you think I should do about it?"[60]

Johnson was requesting presidential authority to start the machinery of the Civilian Volunteer Effort. This proposal by the General Staff exemplified its cautious attitude toward conscription. A month earlier, General Marshall and his staff had not even intended to call the National Guard to active duty; instead, they planned to expand and train the Regular Army as the first step in an orderly, gradual mobilization.[61] When Marshall, on 4 June, at the time of Dunkirk, had urged that four divisions of the Guard be activated, he had also recommended the immediate use of the CVE to procure the additional one hundred and twenty thousand men then authorized. Officers of the Personnel, Plans and Training, and Supply divisions of the General Staff had worked out the details of the recruitment program during the next three weeks. On 22 June, two days after the introduction of the Burke bill in the Senate, confidential radiograms alerted the commanding generals of all corps areas that the president might authorize the CVE as soon as Congress had passed the most recent appropriation bill. The commanders should stand by to initiate the program in their areas at any time after 1 July.[62]

Yet, in response to the fall of France as well as to prodding from the NEC, the General Staff was slowly coming around to the idea of peacetime conscription. For one thing, expansion of the army through the draft would make it easier for General Marshall to justify the retention of planes and other equipment that the president seemed so eager to give to the British.[63] Beginning early in June, Major Hershey's committee had modified the Joint Army-Navy Selective Service bill for peacetime enactment, and Marshall and Adm. Harold R. Stark had included such a recommendation in the Army-Navy "Joint Estimate" of 22 June 1940. But when the chief of staff and the chief of naval operations had brought their revised plans to the White House two days later, President Roosevelt had breezily dismissed a strictly military bill and had "outlined at considerable length the character of the Selective Service Act he was proposing: to wit—one that would require a year of service to the government out of each young man between the completion of high school (18 years) and the completion of a professional course in college . . . ; that all should be entirely away from home (. . . 'in camp') for such a period; that it was important that it should be optional as to time on account of family obligations or responsibilities."[64] Thus, in lieu of the president's support for a draft at this juncture and in recognition of the need to recruit manpower quickly, the General Staff was recommending, over Johnson's signature, the next best solution—namely, the Civilian Volunteer Effort. Fortunately, FDR had asked Stimson's advice before setting the machinery in motion.[65]

Clark grew alarmed as he listened to Stimson over the phone. "I hope you will disapprove, and strongly," he urged. "If that plan goes into effect, our opponents will have a ready-made case. They'll insist that the volunteer program, since it's already under way, be given a trial, and a selective service bill then couldn't possibly go through until the next Congress."

Secretary of the Treasury Henry Morgenthau, Jr., who
thought that President Roosevelt's ideas about voluntary
national service ''sounded awfully good.'' (Courtesy of
Franklin D. Roosevelt Library)

Stimson had doubts about the propriety of his turning thumbs down.
''I'm in a difficult position,'' he pointed out. ''I haven't even been confirmed
yet, and the president undoubtedly sent it to me just as a matter of courtesy. I
don't know but that I'd better just let it go through.''

''I've got to get back to the speakers at this luncheon,'' Clark replied
hurriedly. ''But believe me, that plan would be fatal to any chance for a draft
bill. I want to urge you just as strongly as I can to disapprove it.''[66]

This analysis was probably accurate. The passage of draft legislation in
the ensuing weeks turned on the question of whether or not volunteering
would work. If the country had been in the midst of a great patriotic
campaign, with brass bands, exhortations of ''Uncle Sam Wants You,'' and
the like, there is little doubt that the advocates of ''giving the volunteer system
a try'' would have won, postponing a compulsory system for perhaps a year.
The effects of such a delay would have been far-reaching and possibly
disastrous if the United States had found itself at war in 1941.

The telephone conversation proved decisive. Later that day, Stimson called again. "You were right," he told Clark. "The thing had to be stopped, in spite of the fact that it put me in a rather awkward situation." He had sent the letter back to the White House with an adverse recommendation, and the CVE proposal had "died forthwith."[67]

Stimson's intervention also helped to bridge the gap between the NEC and the professional soldiers at the War Department. Without any publicity, General Marshall flew to Mitchel Field on Long Island to spend the night of 27 June with the secretary-designate at Highhold. Never one of Stimson's intimates during the latter's first stint at the War Department from 1911 to 1913, the chief of staff phoned their mutual friend, Gen. Frank R. McCoy, and asked for "a tip" about Stimson's "special ideas and what advice you would give me in my approach to him."[68] The meeting went off splendidly, and the two men "talked until almost midnight,"[69] with selective service undoubtedly part of the conversation. A week later, on 2 July, testifying at his confirmation hearings, Stimson officially let it be known that he officially favored the draft. He urged "the arousal of a national spirit which will grasp the emergency and be willing to make the effort and sacrifice involved in carrying out the program in the shortest possible time." As the first and most effective step, he advocated "the prompt enactment of a statute establishing a system of selective compulsory training and service. Such a statute is imperatively needed at this moment to secure the men necessary to meet the strength of our present peacetime military establishment. It is also imperatively needed to raise the men necessary for the larger program of emergency defense . . . which the president has recommended and the Congress authorized."[70] Meanwhile, the army chiefs of staff were busily revising their plans.[71]

The reversal of War Department attitudes toward selective service that came with Stimson had no parallel at the White House. The president, as the British ambassador reported, was still "frightened of a die-hard bloc in Congress, has permitted no real trial of strength, and continues to encourage a seeping process in favour of the Allies by letting facts, the Press, his friends, and his opponents speak so."[72] Roosevelt refused to commit himself on conscription and actually showed more interest in a compulsory vocational training program that would feed young men into defense industries.[73]

At his 7 June press conference he made an apparent slip. The *New York Times* that morning had endorsed conscription in a vigorous editorial, and a reporter asked what the president thought of it.[74] "I only read the first paragraph," FDR answered, "and I liked it."[75] He said nothing more, but it seemed to be an endorsement of sorts, and some newspapers snatched up the remark as proof of presidential blessing. Some of the peace groups at this point began to organize against conscription.[76] But Roosevelt had not meant to show his hand. When Clark wired, urging the president to make an "unequivocal declaration" in his Charlottesville speech on 10 June, FDR's words dealt with manpower only in general terms: "The program unfolds swiftly and into that program will fit the responsibility and the opportunity of every man and woman in the land to preserve his or her heritage in the days of peril."[77] Four days later, when Clark and other NEC leaders asked to see him about their bill, FDR told his secretary: "The answer is No—the time is not ripe yet—put it off until a little later."[78]

On 18 June, pushed into a corner at another press conference, the president reneged on even the mild support he had intimated on 7 June. "Perhaps I should not have spoken so fast," he said. "I did not, frankly, intend to imply that there should be compulsory military training for every boy in this country." He had been using *military* in a very broad sense to connote all phases of defense preparation. He did think that youth needed discipline, however, and that the country was coming "to some form of universal government service."[79]

FDR then sketched the broad objectives: trained men for actual service with the army and the navy; a behind-the-lines, uniformed reservoir of communications and aviation technicians; nonuniformed technicians in production of essential items; and a training program for agricultural workers. All the nation's young people, male and female, would take their proper places within this framework.[80] While the idea seemed fuzzy in the president's mind when he presented it to reporters, his statement did reflect proposals for "coordination of all government activities now dealing with various types and phases of civilian training," worked out by Secretary of Labor Frances Perkins and Sidney Hillman, who had recently taken charge of employment for the defense program.

On the next day, 19 June, Stephen T. Early, FDR's press secretary, called attention to the president's remarks the day before and announced that Sidney Hillman, assisted by Harry Hopkins, had been appointed to draft a plan for training two million young people through such existing agencies as the National Youth Administration (NYA), the Works Progress Administration (WPA), the Civilian Conservation Corps (CCC), and the Office of Education. Curiously enough, considering FDR's listing of "service in the army and navy" in his statement, Early emphasized that "the program intended by the president was one of peacetime training in which military preparedness would have no part."[81]

If FDR hoped to deflect criticism by playing up nonmilitary purposes, he had miscalculated. A comprehensive national service plan seemed to be a more drastic departure from traditional American practice than did a peacetime military draft. Congressman James Oliver of Maine observed that "compulsory military service in and of itself is not so bad, but . . . I cannot conceive of American youth being regimented under the leadership of those individuals.''[82] Congressman Wadsworth thought the president had taken leave of his senses. ''Frankly,'' he confided to a constituent, ''I have never known of such a system being put into effect in any country . . . not even in Germany.''[83] Protests also poured in against the appointment of a ''foreign-born'' ''avowed Communist'' such as Hillman.[84] At the Republican Convention, Governor Stassen blasted the president's scheme in his keynote address, while John L. Lewis called it ''a fantastic suggestion from a mind in full intellectual retreat.''[85] From Democratic Congressman Eugene Cox of Georgia came the anguished cry: ''God alone can save this Republic if our youth are put under a man like Sidney Hillman.''[86]

Although some support for the idea materialized, most notably among youth organizations, the furor of opposition apparently had its effect.[87] Only four days after his appointment, Hillman outlined to the press a program that seemed mild compared with the specter of national service that the president had conjured up. A million and a half workers would undergo training in special courses, Hillman explained, but the source of most of the trainees would be the NYA, the CCC, and the WPA. Most significantly, he said nothing about compulson of any kind; the program would be voluntary, worked out in cooperation with private industry.[88] At this time, too, the White House asked Clarence Pickett, a prominent Quaker and a friend of Mrs. Roosevelt's, to take part in the manpower planning. Pickett's participation, which was quickly communicated to other leaders in the peace movement, permitted many liberal opponents of the draft to think that the president actually did not want military conscription.[89] Roosevelt's more apparent motives were not surmised for several weeks.

FDR's vision of ''some form of universal government service'' never did fully develop. On 9 July the president denied to the press that he had abandoned plans for vocational training, and as late as mid August, after he had quietly told administration floor leaders to line up support for the Burke-Wadsworth measure, FDR still insisted privately that he preferred some kind of vocational training to military conscription.[90] Whether he intended it as a fall-back alternative in case selective service failed or whether he genuinely favored vocational training, the poker-faced president let the pot fill up before he played his cards. Even after the United States had entered the war, when a much more determined movement for a National Service Act was launched, the president, while supporting the bill in principle, never exercised the leadership necessary to ensure its passage.[91] Until FDR's sensitive antennae had picked up favorable public opinion, the impetus for selective service would have to come from outside the administration.[92]

In fact, the president's concern for political repercussions may have caused him to miss a glittering opportunity at this juncture in late June 1940. During the Republican Convention in Philadelphia, Wendell Willkie's chief foreign-policy advisers were proposing that their candidate, if nominated, should approach FDR with a grand scheme for bipartisan agreement on issues of foreign policy and defense. Seen and approved by such officials as Gen. George V. Strong, chief of the War Plans Division of the General Staff, and Assistant Secretary of State Stanley K. Hornbeck, the GOP proposals included: the promise of fifty flying fortresses, one thousand army planes, and one hundred destroyers to the British; the repeal of the Neutrality Act and the Johnson Act; the use of United States shipyards to repair British navy vessels; the diplomatic recognition of Gen. Charles de Gaulle's Free French Committee; the "support of conscription and speeding up of our own rearmament program, including the lengthening of the work week to 50–60 hours"; the renunciation of a third term by President Roosevelt; and the creation of a special post of minister of munitions, to be filled by Willkie.[93] Although the evidence is fragmentary, it appears that FDR never knew of these possible overtures from Willkie. Very likely because the isolationist wing of the Republican party would have repudiated him, Willkie chose not to approach the White House. Nevertheless, a meeting nearly took place. Roosevelt himself asked Edwin Watson to schedule an appointment with Willkie two days before the latter's nomination, and on the following weekend, New Dealers Benjamin V. Cohen and Harold Ickes talked with columnist Joseph Alsop about arranging a secret rendezvous or finding a trusted intermediary so that FDR could communicate safely with his opponent.[94] Whatever the reason, however, no face-to-face meeting occurred until after Roosevelt's reelection in November. Partisan perceptions prevailed, for on the day of Willkie's nomination, the president told Henry Wallace that Willkie was a "totalitarian at heart" and went on to comment sarcastically about the Wall Street crowd that had bought him the nomination.[95]

Instead of dealing with Willkie, the ever-cautious Roosevelt had Harry Hopkins meet with Grenville Clark on 28 June. NEC leaders had thought it best to wait until they had introduced their bill before renewing their courtship of the White House. Again, FDR avoided direct contact, having Clark see Hopkins instead. In biographer Robert Sherwood's words, it marked "one of Hopkins' first appearances in a role that was to become of major importance—the confidential contact man between Roosevelt and private citizens who were advocating some policy of which the president approved but which he did not want to advocate publicly for political reasons at the time."[96] Hopkins and Clark agreed that the world crisis was worsening, and that a German victory might pose even greater perils within a few months. Hopkins then asked Clark what "recipe" the president should offer to Congress. Clark suggested a flat presidential declaration that the institutions, economic life, and even the physical integrity of the country were seriously endangered. FDR should urge the immediate passage of selective-service legislation, as well as an eventual National Service Act to back up the strictly military part of national defense. Hopkins showed special interest in the last suggestion, indicating that the president still hoped to dovetail the provisions for military and for vocational training. They discussed the possibility of introducing a vocational-training bill along with the Burke-Wadsworth measure, but Clark demurred. In view of the recent outbursts against Hillman's plan, Clark contended that opposition to universal service would certainly delay and possibly kill any bill for conscription that summer. A military draft had to come first.[97]

The conference, though cordial, left Clark with mixed feelings, for Hopkins refused to commit his chief to any endorsement of selective service. Yet the presidential aide did give his personal encouragement, and he did hint that support might be forthcoming from the Oval Office later.[98] Thus, at the end of June, with Senate committee hearings scheduled for the following week, the New Yorkers still were operating on their own, and FDR, like Mr. Micawber, was still waiting for something to happen.

7

Washington:
Hearings and Harmony

General of the Army John J. Pershing remained much in the public eye during the spring and summer of 1940. For a time it looked as though the seventy-nine-year-old war hero, then quite ill and occupying a fourth-floor suite at Walter Reed Hospital, would die and be accorded an extravagant state funeral. But Pershing, who had helped to plan his own funeral, refused to die. The former commander of the AEF rose from his sick bed and paid a well-publicized visit to the White House in late May, as if to remind Americans that they had fought alongside the French in 1918 to repel German armies. He maintained regular contact with his one-time protégé General Marshall, and in early August, Pershing delivered a nationwide radio address in which he advocated the transfer of destroyers, bombers, and other vital war equipment to England. He also gave the conscription campaign a much-needed boost.[1]

The Plattsburgers had kept in touch with Pershing from the beginning of their activities. General Palmer, Pershing's chief of operations during World War I and a lifelong friend, had visited the old general at Walter Reed on his first trip to Washington in late May. Grenville Clark had also known Pershing for years, most recently from summer visits by the retired general to Dublin, New Hampshire, where Clark lived.[2] When Howard Petersen had taken the first printed drafts of the NEC's bill to Washington during the week of 10 June, Clark had sent a covering letter, requesting Pershing's "comments and criticisms."[3] The general replied favorably, saying that "without a plan for universal service before war comes we will be caught again as we were in the last war and as we have been, in fact, in all our wars. . . . This should never happen again."[4]

Clark and Palmer visited Walter Reed Hospital again in late June, hoping to persuade Pershing to testify at the Senate hearings. The general said he would testify gladly, but his doctors advised against another personal appearance at that time. He would, however, certainly write a favorable letter, provided the Senate committee first officially requested his opinion. At this point, General Palmer, who had drafted many documents for Pershing in the past, offered to compose a statement for his former chief. The old gentleman's grey eyes turned cold and he snapped, "Palmer, I compose my own statements."[5] Clark quickly assured Pershing that the Senate committee would formally request his views.

The NEC leader then took a taxi to the Senate Office Building, where he called on Morris Sheppard, the Texan who headed the Committee on Military Affairs. Sheppard, as he did throughout the campaign for conscription, told Clark that he would do whatever he could to help. His colleagues most assuredly wanted to know what General Pershing thought about military conscription. Since Clark knew what the general expected, would Clark mind, Sheppard drawled, "drafting a letter to the general from the committee?" Clark returned to the Hotel Carlton, where he and Palmer composed the letter and then sent it over to Sheppard that afternoon. The senator, after having it typed on his Senate stationery, dispatched it by messenger to General Pershing. The general, satisfied that the proprieties had been observed, set about preparing his statement.[6]

Formal hearings began on Wednesday 3 July 1940, the same day that the British Navy attacked the French Mediterranean Fleet at Mers el Kebir, Algeria, near Oran, to prevent it from falling into German hands. Burke and Wadsworth both attended the opening session in the Senate committee room, along with Clark, Adler, William J. Donovan, President Conant of Harvard, and General Palmer. A small army of reporters and photographers also jammed inside, having been summoned by Perley Boone, who personally handed out printed copies of General Pershing's letter to the committee members. Senator Sheppard's dramatic reading of Pershing's letter produced the desired effect. "If we had adopted compulsory military training in 1914," the general wrote, "it would not have been necessary for us to send partly trained boys into battle against the veteran troops of our adversary. . . . Certainly we could have ended the conflict much sooner, with the saving of many thousands of lives and billions of treasure."[7] Although the general seemed to be advocating universal military training, rather than selective service, he endorsed "the principles embodied in Senator Burke's bill" without equivocation. Chairman Sheppard then called on Wadsworth, whose informal remarks drew a round of applause. The congressman from Geneseo, New York, recalled that both he and Sheppard had sat on the Senate Military Committee nearly twenty years before when they dropped compulsory training from the National Defense Act of 1920. "We . . . could not get anywhere with it," Wadsworth remembered, "and I may remind you, Senator Sheppard, you and I supported that bill at that time, and the answer that was given to us was, 'Oh, well, there will not be any more wars.' "[8]

Clark then took the stand. In his usual slow, deliberate manner, he explained how the "old Plattsburg crowd" (among them two recipients of the Congressional Medal of Honor and five of the Distinguished Service Cross) had come to prepare the bill. The group, he explained, had become convinced that Hitler's victories posed a direct threat to the United States, and only through a system of compulsory military training and service could the country, in their estimation, adequately prepare to meet the threat. In a veiled allusion to President Roosevelt's talk about vocational training, Clark emphasized that theirs was a "simon-pure, 100 per cent military training and service bill. It contemplates no . . . training for any but military purposes: nothing whatever."[9]. They did not claim perfection for their bill by any means, but they argued that it represented considerable thought on the part of mature and experienced men.

The case for the bill, as Clark and the other witnesses elaborated it, turned on the basic premises of the preamble, now designated as section 2. They stressed above all "that the integrity and institutions of the United States [were] gravely threatened." This was difficult to prove, and opponents maintained time and again that the nation faced no immediate danger. Sponsors retorted that the lightning events in Europe demanded a new orientation in American thinking. Clark warned: "We have got to wake up to the fact that . . . if the British fleet is either destroyed or taken over, instantly the whole situation changes, and, instead of our having the balance of naval power, the weight of naval power is or shortly would be against us. If you include Japan, which is very possible, it might be heavily against us."[10] The sponsors cited the real possibility that European colonies in Latin America could fall into German hands, and air-age geography made bombing attacks something other than hysterical fantasy.[11] Clark frankly admitted that if the United States were not "subject to a major threat," there was "no point to this bill at all."[12]

This led to the second premise: that "to insure the independence and freedom of the people of the United States," mobilization of the nation's strength became imperative, that such strength depended "not only upon the possession of modern arms but equally upon adequate forces of enlisted men," and that "such forces cannot be obtained by voluntary enlistment."[13] The emphasis on manpower was aimed at counteracting the current tendency to think mainly of materiel requirements. The dramatic victories by mechanized forces in Europe had stimulated, among Americans, a demand for modern weapons, especially tanks and planes, a demand that was reflected in the president's arms program. But as to obtaining the thousands of trained men who would use the products of a great armament program, the country seemed to have developed a blind spot.

NEC witnesses judged that volunteering would be inadequate for two reasons—it could not obtain the required numbers, and even to the extent that it did produce recruits, it would remain uneven and wasteful. The sponsors argued that history had demonstrated the failure of voluntary enlistments; so, too, did the armed forces' current difficulties in increasing their strength.

During the five months from January to June, the army had succeeded in enlisting some forty-seven thousand men, but because most were reenlistments and because of losses due to deaths, the expiration of old enlistments, and other reasons, the total personnel had increased by at most fifteen thousand.[14] Maj. Gen. William N. Haskell of the New York National Guard testified: "We have been struggling in New York to increase from 21,000 to approximately 27,000 since last October. There was quite a hullabaloo about getting all of those men in one month, but we have not gotten them yet, and we have put on every kind of pressure we can to get them."[15]

Supporters of the Burke-Wadsworth bill also criticized the volunteer system because of its alleged inequities. "Under our system of government," they contended, "the right and fair way is not to throw the burden on the few who will come forward as volunteers, perhaps disturbing industry, but to have a carefully planned system under which you get the right men."[16] General Palmer pointed out that conscription would enable the War Department to make its plans with "scientific precision," an impossibility when the results of volunteering were "always uncertain." He likened the government to "an engineer called upon to plan a great bridge without knowing whether he will be able to procure a third or even a tenth of the steel required to complete the structure. To plan an effective national defense under the volunteer system is literally absurd."[17]

Palmer also defended the sponsors' third premise, namely, that selective service represented the most equitable and democratic method. Nearly all proponents touched on this point, but here Palmer was in his element. As in his published works, he traced compulsory military training back to the beginnings of the nation, emphasizing particularly that George Washington had urged such a system as the cornerstone of national defense.[18] Far from being an instrument of foreign militarism, compulsory training was, Palmer insisted, with some exaggeration, "really an American invention," for the Father of His Country had proposed it "long before the modern Nation in arms was thought of in France and Germany."[19]

The NEC also arranged for other influential and articulate witnesses. William J. Donovan, commander of the "Fighting Sixty-ninth" in World War I, described how doughboys had come to him in France without knowing how to put on gas masks, some of them having never opened the bolts of their rifles.[20] Lewis Sanders, a consulting engineer and colonel of artillery in the Army Reserve, discussed at length the problems connected with training men to operate the machines of modern warfare. He expressed confidence that civilians who would be inducted under selective service could be molded relatively quickly into effective fighting forces of the new type.[21] From Frederick Palmer, the noted war correspondent, came a reminder that infantry was not obsolete, that the Germans had by no means relied exclusively on armor, and that the United States Army, if called upon to fight again, would also need large numbers of foot soldiers.[22] A most eloquent voice belonged to President Conant of Harvard, who, at Clark's urging, had abandoned the political neutrality usually expected of university presidents.[23] "First things come first," said Conant. "Today I believe mobilization of the Nation's forces for defense takes precedence over all other considerations." Since the Burke-Wadsworth bill contained adequate safeguards necessary for educational interests, Harvard's president supported it as the most "efficient" and "just" method of "building an army in a free democracy."[24]

The question inevitably arose as to the number of men the army would require. To dampen the inevitable charges of "militarism," Clark denied at the outset that the bill meant to create a "giant army." "It has no purpose of that sort at all," he explained. Selective service would simply provide "a flexible instrument by which small numbers or moderate numbers, or big numbers, can be drafted."[25] Admittedly, the New Yorkers were envisaging a larger army than the present institution; Adler and Sanders spoke of bringing two million men into training as soon as possible. They did not advocate, however, an expanded Regular Army. Senator Edwin C. Johnson of Colorado had asked General Palmer: "General, there has been some talk in the Senate of increasing the Regular Army to 700,000 men. If you had your choice to accept the pending bill or increasing the Regular Army to 700,000 men, which in your judgment would be preferable?" "This present bill," replied Palmer, because "a Regular Army of 700,000 men would be too small, entirely, to meet our needs in this crisis and . . . much too large a force to serve as a nucleus for a peacetime establishment."[26]

This exchange emphasized anew the commitment of the "old Plattsburg crowd" to the idea of a "citizen army," as opposed to an "expansible standing army." Some senators understood, at least partly, that a basic conflict existed here. Senator Sheridan Downey of California, an advocate of a small mechanized army, protested that Regular officers were saying confidentially that they did not want a draft—that a small, hard-hitting professional force would be more effective.[27]

This claim had the ring of truth. The General Staff, under the impact of events abroad and the change in administration at the War Department, was gradually revising its thinking. As yet it had not abandoned the expandable standing army as the basis of its mobilization planning, but it was going higher and higher in its estimate of the force that would be necessary for hemispheric defense. As these estimates ballooned upward, they would eventually pass the point that would be compatible with a regular force, skeletonized though it might be. At a meeting on 1 July, Acting Secretary Johnson indicated that President Roosevelt wanted an army of "4 million men," whereupon General Marshall threw up his hands and said "he had no notion as to what they would do" with such an outlandish figure.[28] Budget Director Harold Smith quickly intervened, and Johnson admitted that he had given his own personal estimate. Nevertheless, strategic requirements remained so fluid that the laymen sponsors of the Burke-Wadsworth bill had at the time a more accurate conception of the size of a war army than did the professionals.

Before the NEC spokesmen could complete their case, they had to smooth out a minor conflict with the National Guard. Gen. Milton Reckord of the Maryland National Guard had testified that the "Guard was being relegated to the status of a home guard."[29] Officials of the Guard obviously feared that the Burke-Wadsworth bill, by building up a trained reserve on a national basis, might prejudice the National Guard's traditional status as the "second line" of defense behind the Regular Army.[30] Clark, Palmer, and Petersen thereupon agreed to amend the bill to allow trainees, after serving four months, to "commute" the other four months by joining the active National Guard.[31]

Clark returned to New York after a second day of hearings ended the sponsors' presentation. Thus far the senators had no official inkling of what the army thought about the proposed legislation. Clark had taken pains to stress that while his group had conferred with and received valuable advice from such officers as Hershey, Weible, and O'Kelliher, they did not pretend to anticipate the views of the General Staff.[32] Therefore the committee adjourned on Friday 5 July with the understanding that representatives of the War Department, in response to Senator Sheppard's routine request, would testify on the following Tuesday, 9 July. With Stimson not yet approved as secretary of war, the army's reaction could not be certain. As Wadsworth later remembered: "Their mouths were closed and in turn the mouths of the chief of staff, of the chief of naval operations, and of all the subordinates down the military line were closed. The two committees sat waiting."[33]

Meanwhile the thinking of the General Staff was undergoing considerable change. The series of revised manpower estimates had crystallized by mid June into a projected PMP force of 1,166,715 men, with a Regular Army nucleus of 400,000 to be raised and trained first. In contrast with earlier plans, M-Day now loomed as an imminent possibility, and General Marshall proclaimed it of "imperative importance" that materiel and equipment for a million men be on hand before 1 October 1941.[34] The chief of staff was moving toward this goal when he recommended the Civilian Volunteer Effort to fill the Regular Army.

Even this program, bold and sweeping though it seemed, proved to be short-lived.[35] Hardly had Marshall approved it when it was overtaken and supplanted by a new blueprint drawn, not by the General Staff, but by Lt. Col. James H. Burns, executive officer for the assistant secretary of war, and William Knudsen, production authority on the recently formed National Defense Advisory Commission.[36] Though this plan also ran into snags, most notably President Roosevelt's reluctance to ask for huge appropriations in one lump sum, the groundwork was being laid in late June and early July for an army of at least two million men.

Such changed thinking accorded perfectly with the shifting attitudes of the civilian population. The war news was making Americans increasingly jittery. After France's surrender the British ambassador to the United States, Lord Lothian, reported "a wave of pessimism passing over this country to the effect that Great Britain must inevitably be defeated"; two weeks later, after the naval action at Mers el Kebir, he described "nothing but approval and admiration for the way the cabinet and Royal Navy have dealt with the problem of the French fleet."[37] Congress and the country, though by no means eager to intervene, were suddenly insisting that the armed forces be vastly increased. "I am heartily in favor of making this country strong," wrote Senator Burton K. Wheeler of Montana, "as strong as our military and naval experts believe is necessary."[38] According to Senator Lodge, it was "the general feeling of Congress, and . . . among public opinion throughout the country, to provide all the money for the National Defense, and so all you have to do is ask for it."[39] "An appropriation a day keeps the dictator away," quipped the *New Yorker*.[40] Like quotations on a bull market, estimates of men and money were rising daily. Almost overnight, reversing everything the professional soldiers had experienced for two decades, the nation wanted to give the army more men and money than it had ever dreamed of requesting in peacetime.

General Marshall, who was struggling hard "to keep our heads above the flood of these critical weeks," expressed pleasant surprise at the national publicity for the Burke-Wadsworth bill.[41] When President Roosevelt, on Stimson's recommendation, killed the army's proposal for a Civilian Volunteer Effort, there seemed no other way to raise the necessary manpower except through conscription. Marshall's flying visit to Highhold on 27 June produced a meeting of minds on the general desirability of army support for selective service, but not necessarily on the timing or details.[42] Even though the White House had still not endorsed conscription officially, Marshall instructed his staff officers to prepare favorable testimony for the Senate hearings.

On Sunday 7 July 1940, two days prior to the expected testimony, the *New York Times* "authoritatively reported" that the General Staff would support the Burke-Wadsworth bill "in principle."[43] That same weekend in Washington, Howard Petersen met a friend of his at dinner, Col. William Draper, a reserve officer who had been called to temporary duty from his civilian position at Dillon-Read in New York.[44] Draper, then working in the Personnel Division of the General Staff, told Petersen that the army's report on the bill was ready to go to the Senate committee. "Could I see it?" asked Petersen. "Certainly," Draper said. "Come over to the office tomorrow."

The army report, when Petersen read it, thoroughly alarmed him. Despite an opening statement that the War Department was "in full agreement with the broad purposes" of the Burke-Wadsworth bill, it offered as "available for comparison" a far-better measure prepared by the Joint Army and Navy Selective Service Committee. Although identical in many provisions, the Burke-Wadsworth bill contained alleged defects which the Joint Committee's bill avoided. S-4164 (the Burke bill) seemed unclear as to whether it was to be permanent or temporary legislation. Moreover, its provisions for registration and selection, based on wide age limits and a complicated percentage system, would prove "unworkable." S-4164 took an unrealistic view on length of training, which would last eighteen months, rather than eight. Nor did the provision for home defense units seem desirable. Such units did not need to be conscripted, and their inclusion, in a measure designed to raise troops for the armed forces, would create confusion. The registration of all men eighteen to sixty-four would double the cost of the first year's program. Finally, while praising "the high patriotic motives of the authors and sponsors" of the NEC bill, the report concluded "that the purpose will be best achieved by substituting the complete text of the Selective Service Committee's bill for the text of S-4164."[45]

Petersen quickly phoned Clark in New York to tell him that the army was about to give the NEC bill the "kiss of death." The General Staff, heretofore uninterested in their campaign, was now patting them on the back and planning to "take over" by substituting their own legislation. Actually, despite the immediate alarm of Petersen and the NEC, the army's proposal would not have caused any catastrophe. Their main concern, after all, was to pass a workable selective-service law to build up the nation's defenses, and either of the two bills would have achieved this purpose. The NEC had already scored in getting the movement successfully started; furthermore, as time went on, their bill was amended to conform in most respects to the Joint Committee's ideas. At the time, however, the Plattsburgers considered certain provisions of their bill to be vital, and having carried the matter thus far without any official support, they did not relish having the Burke bill completely struck out.

Clark at once got in touch with Stimson, who was then preparing to move to Washington. An old Plattsburger himself and a participant in the selective-service campaign from the outset, the secretary-designate naturally wanted to prevent friction between the NEC and the General Staff. He told Clark he would try to iron things out. Stimson arrived in Washington on 8 July; that evening he asked General Marshall to Woodley, Stimson's Washington home. They decided to call a conference of all concerned parties the next day. As a result, General Marshall telephoned Senator Sheppard and canceled the appearance of the representatives of the General Staff that had been scheduled for the next morning.

Clark flew to Washington on Tuesday morning 9 July and went with Petersen to Woodley about noon. General Marshall, General ˘Andrews, General William E. Shedd, Colonel O'Kelliher, and Major Hershey represented the army. The professional soldiers found themselves somewhat overwhelmed by the no-nonsense civilians, not to mention the spacious splendor of Stimson's eighteenth-century mansion, which looked out over the natural beauty of Rock Creek Park.[46] Stimson did most of the talking, emphasizing his previous endorsement of selective service and stating that strong and unequivocal support would henceforth be the policy of the War Department. He then asked each side to give its views. Marshall, realizing "they were in Dutch with the Secretary of War right from the start," tried to stress the army's balanced needs.[47] Hershey voiced particular concern with the wide age range in the NEC bill.[48] Stimson thereupon stated that he could see no insuperable difficulties. The army would withdraw its report, and compromises between the NEC and the General Staff bills would be worked out in further conference. They would then give united backing to the Burke-Wadsworth bill as modified.[49] "We were given our marching orders," Hershey later remembered.[50]

The testimony before the Senate committee on Friday 12 July reaffirmed the Woodley agreement. General Marshall explained: "The War Department is strongly of the opinion that some such bill is necessary, and particularly at the present time; that the bill . . . put forward by the Training Camps Association is in general accord with the War Department's ideas as to selective service and training; that it can be accommodated to the several more or less minor points that we think should be adjusted by the process of amendment."[51]

The chief of staff discussed his earlier efforts to build up the Regular Army as a prerequisite to further expansion. This first phase of the Protective Mobilization Plan (PMP) had by no means been completed by 12 July. Marshall proposed to move directly to the second phase, the "balanced force" of a million men, by training such a force at one time, instead of in two installments. The first increment of draftees, instead of forming homogeneous groups, could funnel directly into the under-strength units of the Regular Army and the National Guard, thus obviating the need to strip regular units to provide training cadres. Such a plan would entail calling the National Guard into active federal service, for the Regular Army had neither the equipment nor the personnel to begin the job alone. Therefore, on 12 July, the day of Marshall's Senate testimony, President Roosevelt announced that he would activate the Guard as soon as Congress gave him the authority to do so.[52]

Marshall and his staff elaborated on the new plan to the Senate committee.[53] The Regular Army then comprised approximately 255,000 men and was trying to recruit to its authorized strength of 375,000. The National Guard numbered about 230,000. If the draft law were passed, they would induct about 400,000 selectees during the autumn, enough to increase the Regular Army to 500,000 and the Guard to 400,000. This would fill all existing units. To provide for the second increment of 400,000 the following spring, the army would institute the Replacement Training System envisaged by the PMP, to which trainees would go rather than to permanent organizations. By the autumn of 1941, when the National Guard would have completed its year of training, the Regular Army would be proficient enough to furnish cadres for the organization of new units; to these new units the second increment of draftees would report after basic training in the replacement centers. By April 1942 the initial objective—the balanced force of two million men—would have been trained and equipped. Thereafter the army could apply the Selective Service System to building up a reserve.

Had the war not intervened, this plan might have produced a trained reserve such as that desired by General Palmer and the Senate committee in 1920. The army, however, believed that selective service was not well adapted for permanent use. As a vehicle for creating a large army quickly, it was urgently needed; but if the United States remained at peace, staff officers planned to change the entire basis of selection by the autumn of 1942 so as to call out men by age groups, thus transforming the system into one of universal military training.[54] As General Marshall summed it up, for the immediate future the draft would procure men "for actual service in the ranks," but in the long run the army hoped to use it for reserve purposes.[55]

"In other words," Senator Lister Hill of Alabama asked, "what you really contemplate at the present time, General, is to bring these men into the Regular Army or into the National Guard . . . you would build your basic army out of your Regular Army and out of your National Guard. Is that not true?" "Exactly that," General Marshall replied. Senator Hill commented: "Then after you build up your basic army, then you take that basic army, if need be, and break it down and build this larger army." "That is the idea," agreed the general.[56]

The chief of staff also tried to discourage Senator Lodge's proposal to increase the Regular Army to 750,000. "We would have either to organize units from the ground up without any trained personnel to leaven the mass, which would require about a year," Marshall declared, "or we would have to emasculate existing units in the Regular Army . . . to provide nuclei for new units." He did not "think we should take such a hazard."[57] Lodge's proposal would also entail stripping the National Guard, which, in Marshall's estimate, would subvert the entire system of national defense established in 1920.[58]

Marshall and his staff added the weight of their expertise against voluntary enlistment. When critics pointed out that recruiting was running at an unprecedented pace, the chief of staff readily admitted that the quota for

June had been reached ten days before the end of the month.[59] Nonetheless, as Marshall pointed out, they had set quotas in accordance, not with the army's needs, but with its expectations, which they had determined on the basis of far-smaller manpower requirements than they now were contemplating.[60] Even assuming a continued enlistment of 18,000 per month (the current figure), the army could not hope to reach the authorized 375,000—much less the new projection of 500,000—fast enough to meet a threat that required immediate readiness. Finally, even if higher pay and shorter enlistments could obtain the necessary numbers, a selective-service system would "insure procurement of the required number of men at the proper time in an orderly and efficient manner" so that the results would be "predictable and determinable."[61]

As to specific provisions of the bill, representatives of the General Staff hoped for modifications on such questions as age limits, length of training, and pay for trainees. They planned to work out the necessary compromises in compliance with Stimson's directive at Woodley. The War Department, unlike the White House, now unequivocally and vigorously favored an immediate draft. General Marshall had finally "taken up the cudgels."[62]

Confirmed by the Senate on 9 July, Stimson took his oath of office at an unpretentious White House ceremony the next day. On Thursday 11 July, the day before Marshall's Senate testimony, Clark sent the new secretary specific recommendations for carrying out the mandate of the Woodley conference. It was a matter of "harmonizing views," Clark wrote, "getting them in definite written shape, producing an amended bill as soon as possible, getting it reported out of both Committees on the floor and getting it voted on." With Congress due to recess the following week for the Democratic Convention, Clark proposed that representatives of the War Department, the Navy Department, the National Guard Association, and the MTCA work out, in precise language, the necessary amendments.[63] Stimson accepted the suggestion. Daily meetings at the Army War College ensued, with Howard Petersen, General Palmer, and Malcolm Langford sitting in for the MTCA. The conferees thrashed out their differences while the Democratic Convention was running its course in Chicago. Line by line they went over the Burke-Wadsworth bill. With Major Hershey acting as chief draftsman and conciliator, the group produced for the Senate committee a document that had enough amendments to necessitate an entirely new printing of the bill.

The major compromises centered around the alleged deficiencies cited in the War Department's report. The army's objection to Home Defense units prevailed, albeit with only grudging acceptance by the MTCA. The revised language stated that men eighteen to twenty-one and forty-five to sixty-four should be liable for duty in "such home defense units of the land and naval forces of the United States as may hereafter be authorized by Congress."[64]

Both sides compromised on the length of training, settling on twelve months. The revised bill also allowed trainees to discharge their reserve obligations by enlisting in the Regular Army or in the active National Guard for two years.[65] In the matter of pay the MTCA deferred to the War Department. Never enthusiastic about the $5-per-month token stipend, the NEC accepted language whereby selectees would receive "the same pay, allowances, and other benefits as are provided by law for enlisted men of like grades and length of service." A section guaranteeing draftees the opportunity "to qualify for officer rank" was weakened, under pressure from the General Staff, to read that such inductees should have "an opportunity for promotion."[66]

The MTCA did manage to keep its cherished registration of all men from the ages of eighteen to sixty-five.[67] Similarly, Plattsburgers retained the liability for service to the age of forty-five, while conceding to the army that the twenty-one to thirty-one age group should be called first. At the army's suggestion, administrative regulations would govern the method of selection, but the MTCA's stipulation for drafting certain percentages of each age group, so as to secure a representative cross section, remained in the bill.[68]

The Plattsburgers still balked at eliminating certain specific groups in the provision for deferments. Army representatives argued that all deferments should be left to the regulations, which could be drawn to cover all cases and could be easily changed if necessary. This judgment prevailed. But the MTCA, persuaded by President Conant that technicians and scientists had to receive deferments, reserved the right to disagree.

The conferees also added two new sections. The first, taken from the 1917 act, prohibited the payment of bounties for enlistment and the hiring of substitutes. The second called for certificates for satisfactory fulfillment of duty, stating further that it was the "purpose and intent" of Congress that employers should rehire, without loss of seniority, any former employee holding such a certificate.[69] This declaration in regard to reemployment became even more explicit before the bill was finally passed.

The draftsmen tried specifically to conciliate the National Guard. To assuage General Reckord's fear that under the new policy the members of the Guard might be sent home after a year's service, the conferees drafted an entirely new section stating that "whenever the Congress shall determine that troops are needed for the national security in excess of those of the Regular Army and of men in training and service under this Act, the National Guard of the United States, or such part thereof as may be necessary, shall be ordered to active Federal Service and continued therein so long as such necessity exists."[70] The Senate committee wrangled over this point in executive session, but it remained in the bill that reached the Senate floor.[71]

The National Guard still fretted. Perceiving a loophole in the phrase "whenever the Congress shall determine that troops are needed . . . in excess of those of the Regular Army *and of men in training and service under this Act,*" the

Guard still thought it might have to take a back seat. General Reckord made a determined effort to amend this passage, sending strong pleas to Wadsworth and to Chairman May of the House committee, but the bill eventually became law with the declaration unchanged.[72] Palmer and Wadsworth both believed that their old friend Reckord was being unduly alarmed.[73] For Palmer, the proposed year's training for the Guard was the real crux of the matter. If they stood up well in this test, there was little danger that the old "minute-men" would be sidetracked once war came.[74] Events proved this judgment to be accurate.

The "harmonizing of views" at the War College ended the conflict between the sponsors of the bill and the army.[75] The General Staff continued to press its ideas with respect to age limits, but the Burke-Wadsworth bill itself remained intact when Congress reconvened during the final week of an oppressively hot July.

Although the Plattsburg laymen had won over the army on the draft, they ran into a stone wall on the matter of the procurement and training of officers. The vast enlargement in manpower plans had not changed the General Staff's thinking on officers; the 120,000 in the Officers' Reserve Corps were still deemed sufficient for any wartime expansion.[76] While admitting the lack of materiel and enlisted manpower, an army spokesman testified that 90,000 Reservists were "eligible for service and physically qualified to perform field duties."[77] For General Marshall, reserve officers represented a great source of pride. "The products of the ROTC are in great contrast to 1917," he later told the House committee. "We have young graduates from the ROTC in an artillery unit, for example. . . . They have an artillery preparation that we did not dream of when we rushed through the three months camp at the time of the World War."[78] Such fixed views did not bode well for the Plattsburg camps that opened on 5 July.

Pressure to enlarge the camps mounted nonetheless. The camp at Plattsburg, publicized almost daily by the *New York Times,* was attracting much media attention, for the trainees included such prominent citizens as Judges William F. Clark of Philadelphia and Robert P. Patterson; Newbold Morris, president of the New York City Council; DSC winner Robert K. Haas, vice-president of Random House; socialite Jock Whitney; Winthrop Rockefeller (whose immediate relegation to K.P. duty made good news copy); William McChesney Martin, later to become head of the New York Stock Exchange; and various others.[79] Again, as these men field-stripped machine guns, sprawled on the ground for range firing, and hiked the dusty roads around Plattsburg, it seemed that the years had rolled back to 1915. Mayor Fiorello H. La Guardia visited the camp to speak.[80] And President Roosevelt sent a message of encouragement, expressing "the whole-hearted appreciation of the American people for those patriotic impulses which prompted the

Julius Ochs Adler "raising the Plattsburg flag" again at the Businessmen's Training Camp, Plattsburg Barracks, N.Y., in July 1940. (Courtesy of John D. Kenderdine and Dartmouth College Library)

voluntary services of the Plattsburgers of 1915, and which now prompt the Plattsburgers of 1940."[81]

The camp at Plattsburg, however, proved to be the shining exception to an otherwise lackluster performance. The apathy of the army, the lack of enthusiasm among MTCA personnel outside of eastern cities, and the short three-week's recruiting period—all combined to dampen interest in the camps elsewhere. Plattsburger Ralph Lowell had a disconcerting talk with the commander at Fort Devens. Lowell noted: "He was very polite, but he doesn't believe in these camps . . . he thinks the army has all the officers it can possibly need. . . . It is inconceivable that an officer of his standing can be so shortsighted. He cannot visualize an army of over 300,000 men, while I feel that the very minimum is one million." The camps at Fort Devens, Fort Sam Houston, and Fort Leavenworth were approximately filled; but of the original quotas of 300 each, only 142 men attended Fort McPherson; 144, Fort Benjamin Harrison; 225, Fort Sheridan; 233, Fort Meade; and a low of 112, Camp Ord in California.[82] General Staff officers considered the experiment a "flop."[83] One of General Marshall's friends inspected Company A at Fort Sheridan and reported that "none of them know exactly why they are there or what the purpose may be of their training."[84]

The New York activists, however, intoxicated by their own exuberance and all too ready to blame the army for any shortcomings, set about to expand the program even before the July camps opened. The NEC appointed a subcommittee, consisting of Adler, Kenderdine, and Wickersham. Urged on by a meeting of eight hundred applicants for Plattsburg on 1 July, this committee proposed a second series of officer-training camps, which would attract some three to four thousand candidates per corps area, to begin in September.[85] They forwarded the proposal to Acting Secretary of War Louis Johnson. The covering letter stated that a few weeks of basic training obviously could not produce fully trained officer personnel, but the camps could provide "an essential nucleus" from which capable officer material could be developed. Such camps would also "demonstrate to the people of our country, especially to our youth, the need for national unity and morale of the citizens of the United States in the crisis confronting us." The plan called for a four-weeks' course in September for men twenty-one to fifty years of age, with the government to pay all expenses and with reserve officers, under Regular Army supervision, to provide the instruction.[86]

This proposal reached the War Department before Stimson was confirmed. On 10 July, the day after the conference at Woodley, Clark, Adler, Sanders, Thacher, Wickersham, and Kenderdine discussed the matter in New York. On the next day, Clark sent a long memorandum to Stimson, now secretary of war, calling his attention to the formal request to Johnson, which was still pending. "The thing can be done with great success," Clark emphasized, "if an early decision is reached. If the announcement is delayed, however, there will be a scramble and rush which would seriously handicap the effort."[87]

On 16 July, Stimson talked with General Shedd of the Personnel Division and General Andrews of Plans and Training, both of whom flatly opposed the camps because the army could not spare enough officers. They stated further that since the MTCA had not filled quotas for the camps then in progress, they could not logically meet the expanded authorizations for September.[88] At a meeting with the civilian aides on the next day, Stimson and General Marshall both strongly urged that the Burke-Wadsworth bill be passed but did not comment on the proposed September camps. The General Staff's view was presented instead by Major Weible, who reiterated that there were not enough officers, either regular or reserve, to make it practicable to have camps in the fall. The civilian aides, apparently dominated by the New Yorkers, overwhelmingly passed a resolution reaffirming their support for the September camps.[89]

NEC leaders were in no mood to compromise. "I am convinced," Lewis Sanders wrote to Clark, "that we have in our Regular Officers the finest body of military leaders in the world, but at present they work in mental straight jackets."[90] Another Plattsburger fumed: "What matter if the War Department says men of 40 or 50 are too old? Poppycock!"[91] Clark, then in Plattsburg, walked over to the Western Union Office and wrote out an indignant telegram to Stimson:

> Training Camps Association has given its assurance that tens of thousands of picked men throughout the country will volunteer for these camps. . . . I understand argument was made that two or three corps areas failed to fill quotas. . . . If this statement was made as . . . alibi for not proceeding with September camps it is no less than outrageous. Every conceivable obstacle was interposed. . . . To cite inability to meet impossible conditions everywhere as reason for not proceeding now . . . is utterly without justification to put it mildly.[92]

The secretary was caught between two fires. He obviously did not want to throw cold water on his Plattsburg comrades, but at the same time it was difficult, even presumptuous, for a newly appointed cabinet officer to override the expert advice of his department. On 18 July, Stimson had a visit from Tom Wyles, who reported confidentially that although the Western Corps Areas could probably fill the quotas in time, they did not have nearly so much enthusiasm for September camps as did the New York group.[93] This seemed to settle the matter, as Stimson on 24 July announced that the War Department did not contemplate further training camps in the fall.[94]

The project flickered to life again two weeks later, just as debate on the Burke-Wadsworth bill began in the Senate. William J. Donovan had returned from a special White House mission to England, and he was asked by Stimson if he might be interested in heading up a series of officer camps in September. Donovan said he would.[95] Stimson then phoned NEC representative Malcolm Langford with a message for Clark. "Tell him I want 25 Bill Donovans to run the businessmen's camps in September," he said, "not just men who know the drill book, but fellows like Donovan with real leadership ability and enthusiasm." If he could find enough qualified commanders, the secretary thought the camps might be feasible after all.[96]

Two days later, however, after a long talk with General Marshall (who "gave me all the contrary reasons"), Stimson phoned Clark in New Hampshire. Since he had given them the "go" signal, Stimson would hold the camps if the New Yorkers insisted, but in view of Marshall's objections, he "hardly thought it wise to do so."[97] Clark, too, was doubtful, for time was running short. After canvassing the matter with NEC members, General Drum, and veterans of the July Plattsburg camp, Clark agreed to scrap the September camps but suggested that one single camp be held at Plattsburg. General Drum assured them that he could handle such a camp "quite nicely."[98] Stimson, though he would dearly have loved to relive his earlier experiences at Plattsburg, bowed to Marshall's wishes. "Not inclined to consider the proposition of a single camp at Plattsburg," he wired on 14 August: "It involves sectional differences which in my opinion render it inadvisable."[99]

This ended the matter. But the earlier camps, despite opposition from the General Staff, the apathy of midwestern officials of the MTCA, and the hypercritical attitude of the New York sponsors, had served their purpose. As an adjunct to the selective-service campaign, they provided an excellent source of publicity for Perley Boone and his staff. They also demonstrated to the country that there were men past college age who were ready to contribute their time and energy to the nation's defense when such a spirit was badly needed.

As later events revealed, the abortive campaign for a large-scale revival of the Plattsburg Movement presaged a much better organized effort in 1941. When he made the final decision against the September camp, Stimson told Clark that "if an opportunity comes up in future when it may seem that the general cause of national defense will be furthered by a renewal of this project, I shall be glad to take it up again."[100] Once the Burke-Wadsworth bill had safely passed, Clark and his cohorts, still convinced that the army would need officers in ever-increasing numbers and that such officers should come from civilian life as well as from Officer Candidate Schools, pressed the subject anew. For Stimson, it became "one of the hottest spots I am sitting on" in 1941.[101] Sympathetic to a renewal of Plattsburg camps, Stimson and Assistant Secretaries Robert P. Patterson and John J. McCloy (both Plattsburg veterans) tried to persuade General Marshall and his staff. Finally, in August 1941, Marshall did what he later called a "very reprehensible thing." "Very well, Mr. Stimson," he said. "I have done my best and I have my entire staff with me. They all see this thing alike. . . . I tell you now that I resign the day you do it."[102] Marshall thus had his way, and the army never instituted Plattsburg camps for officer training in World War II.[103]

General Palmer, who regarded both Clark and Marshall as "younger brothers of whom I am very proud," found the dissension distressing. If "I were in his [Marshall's] position," Palmer wrote to Clark in July 1940,

> and the secretary should take his advice from some outside source to the extent of deranging a carefully digested program that I had prepared for him, after prolonged study by my subordinates, I would tender my resignation— not from personal pique but because it would be contrary to the spirit of the General Staff law for me to bear the burden of responsibility in such circumstances. Nor would I retain the respect and confidence of my subordinates. . . . I am sure that you too would resign in such a situation. . . . When you were in the Adjutant General's Office in 1917, you ruptured the inhibitions of the hide-bound War Department of that day and through your defiance of fuddy-duddy superiors you accomplished a great

reform and performed a great public service. This naturally made you impatient of red-tape and narrow routine. But, in spite of my repeated assurances, you refuse to believe that the War Department of 1940 is entirely different from the War Department of 1917.[104]

"Don't take my criticisms . . . too seriously," Clark replied. "I think the C. of S. is a grand character, but I have to hold to my view that it really was a mistake not to find some way to hold some more camps for older men. . . . Anyhow, our bill is now well known to the public. . . . A big struggle impends, but I have faith that we will come out all right on it."[105]

Much of the wrangling over the businessmen's camps took place during the week in which NEC and army representatives were hammering out an amended selective-service bill at the War College. The public eye, however, was focused, not on Washington, but on Chicago, where a listless and resentful Democratic Convention was going through the motions of nominating a presidential candidate. Until the last minute, Franklin Roosevelt had left the matter of the third term in doubt, and as late as 12 July, three days before the convention opened, the press still carried such conjectural headlines as "Roosevelt Willing, Democrats Hear."[106] Not until the seventeenth, with the convention in session, did Alben Barkley give an "official" explanation of the president's position; only then did it become public that Jimmy Byrnes was engineering the third-term "draft."[107] Roosevelt's headquarters were firmly established in the Blackstone Hotel, presided over by Harry Hopkins, with a direct telephone hookup from the lavatory to the White House. Although not at all happy about it, the delegates followed the only course open to them and nominated Franklin Roosevelt on the first ballot.[108]

The selection of a vice-presidential candidate caused near rebellion. Also at the last moment, FDR made known his choice: Henry A. Wallace. Since the secretary of agriculture was by no means a popular figure to all factions of the Democratic party, it seemed at first that the delegates would throw over the traces. But the president insisted: "Well, damn it to hell, they will go for Wallace or I won't run and you can jolly well tell them so."[109] Again, having no real alternative, the delegates sullenly acquiesced. But the convention left a bitter taste in the mouths of several party stalwarts who had gone to Chicago with their eyes on the vice-presidency. Among the disenchanted were some Democrats who later battled hard against selective service, most notably Senator Wheeler of Montana.[110]

Logically, one might expect that the two major political parties would give some guidance to public opinion on such a crucial question as peacetime conscription. Unhappily, little logic was involved. A month before, the Republicans at Philadelphia had said in their plank on national defense:

> The Republican party is firmly opposed to involving this nation in a
> foreign war. . . .
>
> We declare for the prompt orderly and realistic building of our national
> defense to the point at which we shall be able not only to defend the United
> States, its possessions, and essential outposts from foreign attack, but also
> efficiently to uphold in war the Monroe Doctrine.[111]

Now, at Chicago, the Democrats uttered only a cautious paraphrase of their
rivals' banalities:

> The direction and aim of our foreign policy has been, and will continue
> to be, the security and defense of our own land and the maintenance of its
> peace. . . .
>
> Weakness and unpreparedness invite aggression. We must be so strong
> that no possible combination of powers would dare to attack us. We proposed
> to provide America with an invincible air force, a navy strong enough to
> protect all our seacoasts and our national interests, and a fully equipped and
> mechanized army.[112]

In the one apparent difference, the Republicans blamed the president for not
preparing the country more adequately, while the Democrats praised him for
doing so much in the face of constant obstructionism.

The single mention of the draft came from the president himself, who
found good use for the word in accepting the nomination. Speaking into
network microphones from the White House after much of the nation had
fallen asleep, he pointed out that "during the past few months, with due
Congressional approval, we have been taking steps to implement the total
defense of America." Millions of Americans were contributing to the defense
effort, some of them "drafted" from their homes and jobs into government
service. "Most right-thinking persons," FDR continued, "are agreed that
some form of selection by draft is necessary and fair today as it was in 1917
and 1918." Applying the principle to himself, he could not decline to serve in
his own "personal capacity" if "called upon to do so by the people of my
country."[113]

With the convention over, Congress straggled back to work on Tuesday,
23 July. With the temperature soaring into the nineties, progress on defense
measures slowed. The Burke-Wadsworth bill remained tied up in committees.
The senators deliberated on the amended bill that was presented to them when
they returned, while the House committee settled back for a long siege by
opposition witnesses. The Detroit Tigers and Cincinnati Reds were battling
for first place in their respective leagues, and announcements by such
prominent Democrats as Al Smith, John W. Davis, and Senator Burke that
they were supporting Willkie filled the papers.[114]

On Thursday 25 July came news that made Washington forget the heat
for a moment. A week before, ostensibly in the president's good graces,

Assistant Secretary of War Louis Johnson had gone to Chicago, hopeful of gaining the vice-presidential nomination. He had been denied that honor, just as he had been denied the post of secretary of war. Now the White House announced that he would no longer be assistant secretary—Judge Robert P. Patterson would take his place.

Johnson made no secret of his bitterness. In his public letter of resignation he explained how he had offered to resign when Stimson was appointed but that the president had urged him to stay. "I am now informed that Mr. Stimson had already made different plans. For three long years," Johnson complained, "I have given my energy . . . to . . . adequate national preparedness. Today I presented our program to Congress and . . . that for which we have striven seems on the way. It is with keen regret, therefore, that I tender my resignation again."[115] With obvious discomfort, President Roosevelt replied: "You have severed the formal ties that make you a member of my official family, [but] there are closer bonds of friendship and affection which will grow stronger as time passes."[116]

FDR took the final step with great reluctance and only after considerable prodding. Stimson had "chafed a good deal" during the preceding weeks, for Johnson's continued presence "kept a much disorganized Department in a continual state of disorganization."[117] Stimson went to the White House several times to remind the president about his commitment. FDR kept asking for time, evidently hoping that Stimson would weaken, that Johnson would retire voluntarily, or that somehow things would work out. Stimson poured out his troubles to Henry Morgenthau on 17 July, saying that Johnson seemed to have the idea that he would stay on as assistant secretary and that Patterson would become a special assistant. Morgenthau, who had seen the president vacillate before, suggested that Stimson himself send Patterson's name to the Senate.[118] Instead, Stimson wrote a strong letter to the president, stating that in the interests of the War Department, the appointment of a new assistant secretary should be made promptly.[119] At the same time, Clark and Adler tried to help matters along by leaking to the press a report that Patterson, then a "buck private" at the Plattsburg businessmen's camp, was being considered for assistant secretary.[120] Finally, almost in desperation, Stimson turned again to Morgenthau, who agreed to phone Roosevelt at Hyde Park on 23 July.[121] Roosevelt promised to ask for Johnson's resignation, but cowardly to the end, he had "Pa" Watson break the bad news. Watson later told Morgenthau that "Louie broke down and cried like a baby."[122] The public announcements came two days later.

At first glance it seems mildly surprising that the Plattsburg crowd objected so strongly to Louis Johnson. In contrast to Harry Woodring, Johnson was a decided interventionist; his hundreds of speeches in behalf of preparedness hardly suggested any lack of sympathy with their efforts to build a larger army. By coincidence, he had even served at one time as MTCA

Undersecretary of War Robert P. Patterson inspecting a machine gun in 1942. Patterson's promotion from Plattsburg private to assistant secretary of war in July 1940 made headlines. (Courtesy of Franklin D. Roosevelt Library)

civilian aide for West Virginia. But the New Yorkers were a homogeneous, upper-class, somewhat snobbish group who had been educated at the best eastern colleges, and Louis Johnson, considered "loud" and indiscreet, a professional veteran, professional joiner, and professional politician, was simply not of their ilk.[123] In addition, Stimson could scarcely relish an ambitious assistant secretary who was embittered because he had not received the top post himself.

The president tried to soften the blow by offering Johnson a position as one of his six "administrative assistants," with the specific duty of acting as his chief's "eyes and ears" on "the entire question of national defense."[124] Johnson declined this offer, much to Stimson's relief.[125] During the next month, especially after a conference with the president on 15 August, rumor had it that Johnson was about to become assistant secretary of commerce.[126] This, too, Johnson declined, remaining out of government service until he became the president's personal representative to India in 1942.[127]

The public, of course, knew little about what had transpired behind the scenes relative to Johnson's replacement by Patterson, whose acquaintance most Americans first made through a news photograph of the judge in his Plattsburg dungarees. Perley Boone saw to it that Patterson was on K.P. when the official announcement of his appointment was made, and naturally, photographers recorded "trainee" Patterson's discharge to become assistant secretary of war.[128] The press reported that "the manner in which Judge Patterson was selected was not clear," and Steve Early tersely commented that Stimson had requested his appointment "in line with the traditional right of cabinet members to name their assistants."[129] One of Johnson's Democratic friends commented: "I don't like it a damn bit the way he [FDR] keeps dragging in Republicans who . . . like the camel that gets his nose into the tent, moves all the way in, and then they start kicking the Democrats out."[130] Once in Washington, however, the energetic Patterson won acceptance quickly. Within a month, Harold Ickes told the president that "I would have asked for Patterson myself if I had been made secretary of war."[131] Morgenthau told Stimson that the new assistant secretary "has made a tremendous hit with me."[132] Roosevelt exulted: "Bob Patterson is a grand fellow and I think the War Department has become a happy shop again."[133]

Patterson showed his mettle over the next seven years, first as assistant secretary, then as undersecretary, and finally as secretary of war. For the selective-service campaign, his appointment added to the president's official family another uncompromising proponent who at once made known his full support. On 4 August 1940, during his first week in office, Patterson delivered a strong address over CBS Radio, endorsing the Burke-Wadsworth bill.[134] The Plattsburg team, now intact, girded itself for a determined attack from the opposition.

8

The Organized Opposition: "A Good Ship with Not Enough Crew to Make It Sail"

Howard K. Beale, a forty-year-old historian at the University of North Carolina, had planned to spend the summer of 1940 at the Library of Congress, researching a biography of Theodore Roosevelt. The selective-service controversy soon diverted him from scholarly pursuits. A liberal activist and philosophical pacifist, Beale had joined the American Civil Liberties Union (ACLU) in the early 1930s, had written several pamphlets and articles about academic freedom, and had become good friends with Roger Baldwin, the national director of the ACLU. When Baldwin asked Beale to represent the ACLU at the Senate hearings on the Burke-Wadsworth bill, Beale threw himself into the fray. From early June until mid September, taking time off only to read graduate dissertations and to take his mother to Vermont for a short vacation, Beale devoted his considerable energies to the anticonscription campaign. Testifying personally before committees in both houses, buttonholing senators and congressmen, lobbying with Major Hershey and other army representatives, and ghostwriting speeches for opposition senators, Beale, "more than any other single person," shaped the liberal provision for conscientious objectors (COs) in the final Selective Training and Service Act.[1] "I shudder to think," Beale wrote facetiously at one point, "what Theodore would think of me if he knew what had taken his biographer's attention from TR himself. How he would denounce me!"[2]

Beale faced a dilemma that in many ways symbolized the awkward choices that were confronting most pacifist opponents of conscription in the summer of 1940. Although personally opposed to conscription, Beale was representing the ACLU, itself a broad coalition of groups and interests that were united by a commitment to constitutional rights. Roger Baldwin, a conscientious objector himself in World War I, also considered that conscription in any form was reprehensible, but he did not think that the ACLU could

124

take such an uncompromising stand without disintegrating.[3] Because he also feared that broad opposition was "licked" from the start, Baldwin would commit the ACLU only to protecting the rights of conscientious objectors.[4] With Baldwin's tacit approval, Beale therefore assumed a double identity. As the official ACLU spokesman, Beale testified specifically about protecting conscientious objectors. When he briefed opposition witnesses or talked to sympathetic senators, however, he encouraged broader opposition to the draft itself. His interview with Senator Burton K. Wheeler of Montana on 23 July provides a case in point. Wheeler, having gone to the Democratic Convention with hopes of attaining either the nomination or the vice-presidential slot, had returned in a sour mood. "How can you expect me to vote for a man," he asked Beale, "who pretends to be a liberal and yet stirs up hysteria to put over a fascist measure of this sort?" Wheeler then phoned Senator Sheppard, who said that his committee would soon report out the Burke bill favorably. Wheeler shouted that "there would be a terrific fight on the floor" and slammed down the receiver. In reporting this conversation to Roger Baldwin, however, Beale predicted that there would be "not more than 5 or 6 votes" against the bill.[5] Although he later prepared speeches for Wheeler and other opposition senators, Beale never thought that they could actually defeat selective service.[6]

Beale's pessimism stemmed in part from an unsentimental assessment of congressional and public opinion. He also found discouraging the inevitable differences of opinion among leaders of the various peace factions which were lobbying in Washington. Whether emphasizing the protection of conscientious objectors instead of all-out opposition or supporting amendments that would give voluntary enlistments a further trial or proposing substitute legislation for voluntary national service, the opponents of conscription sometimes resembled the eighteenth century Polish Parliament in their inability to agree on a common strategy.[7] Beale became especially irritated with the antics of some student witnesses. "Smart alecs" like the "president of the senior class at George Washington," he informed Baldwin, had "convinced the senators that youth has no sense of obligation to the country, but merely demands license and support for its own irresponsible ways." If such witnesses could be "tied up" and kept away from Capitol Hill, "it would do more good than all the witnesses all the rest of us can send."[8] Beale found himself similarly frustrated when self-appointed spokesmen for religious groups and influential laymen testified about conscientious objectors without having any real understanding of the subject.[9] Mayor La Guardia's testimony on 26 July "nearly jammed the works for us" by suggesting that all objectors could be dealt with after four months of basic training.[10] Fortunately, as a close friend of La Guardia's, Baldwin persuaded the mayor to write to the House committee to the effect that most "CO's" object to training as well as

President Roosevelt and the man he nearly appointed secretary of war in 1940—Mayor Fiorello La Guardia. The mayor thought that the Burke-Wadsworth bill was "not so hot." (Courtesy of Franklin D. Roosevelt Library)

fighting, and that appropriate status should be determined by a civilian authority before they were inducted.[11]

Beale, as the summer wore on, joined with other pacifists in concentrating on the issue of conscientious objectors. Seeing conscription as inevitable and American intervention in the war as probable, these pacifists were seeking, in historian Charles Chatfield's phrase, "to prepare in pacifism a refuge from the floodtide of violence."[12] Paul Comly French and Raymond Wilson, of the American Friends War Problems Committee, became Beale's most indomitable allies. Along with representatives of the historic peace churches, the Friends had met with President Roosevelt in January 1940 and had urged broad protection for conscientious objectors in wartime, including nonreligious objectors and "absolutists" whose beliefs forbade noncombatant or alternative service.[13] French and Wilson testified before the House and the Senate committees, and together with Beale, they attempted to use quiet Quaker persuasion behind the scenes. Colonel O'Kelliher and Major Hershey were startled to learn that not all Quakers sought conscientious-objector status, that military service would be a matter of individual conscience.[14] Although unwilling to protect "absolutists" lest Communists and "fifth columnists" gain exemption, the army representatives did seem willing to recommend language that would recognize conscientious objectors on the basis of "religious training and belief."[15] Through further conversations with members of the Senate committee, most notably Edwin Johnson of Colorado, John Thomas of Idaho, Elbert Thomas of Utah, and—much to their surprise—Sherman Minton of Indiana, they succeeded in amending the bill to protect all religious objectors. The Senate bill, reported favorably on 5 August, also provided for a national register for conscientious objectors, with each individual claimant to be investigated and heard by the Department of Justice. It called either for noncombatant military service or for "work of national importance under civilian direction" for those objectors judged to be sincere.[16]

The House committee was not so easily swayed. With Chairman Andrew May apparently trying to rush the bill through with only perfunctory hearings and with Congressman Charles Faddis of Pennsylvania hectoring all opposition witnesses, the prospects for a broad CO amendment seemed poor.[17] Gradually, however, working through Congressman W. D. Byron of Maryland and "a friendly fine young Congressman [John J.] Sparkman of Alabama," Beale and the Quakers made headway.[18] Beale even tried to convert Faddis when they bumped into one another in the Capitol washroom. "Oh, you're just a lot of people who want all the advantages and protection America can give you without doing anything for her. . . . You don't know the danger we are in and what's more you don't any of you give a damn," the congressman snorted. Paul French visited Faddis's office the next day. After much shouting from the congressman and persistent persuasion from French, the former blurted out: "I think you fellows are crazy, just plain crazy . . . but I'll have to hand it to you, you are persistent cusses and I at least admire your sincerity, and I think, damn you, I'll probably vote for your CO clause and even for your absolutist objector."[19] Chairman May also assured French that he was "a CO and a good Baptist and we could rest assured that neither he nor any other member of the committee wanted to shoot COs or put them in jail."[20] The House bill, when it was reported out favorably at the end of August, contained a CO clause identical to the Senate version.

The preoccupation of some pacifists with conscientious objectors reflected the despair and disarray that had overtaken the American peace movement during the past two years. It seemed that only a short time before, a grand coalition of pacifists, peace advocates, isolationists, and internationalists had backed the Senate Munitions Inquiry, lobbied for "permanent" neutrality laws, and supported a national referendum (the so-called Ludlow Amendment) in the event of war.[21] College students by the thousands had taken the "Oxford Pledge" not to participate in any future war, and revisionist historians had been arguing that the United States had entered the Great War in 1917 for false and insufficient reasons.[22] The outbreak of fighting in Asia and Europe soon brought defections. By 1939, internationalist groups such as the League of Nations Association and the Foreign Policy Association were supporting collective security and the revision of the neutrality laws.[23] Most liberal internationalists followed Clark Eichelberger and William Allen White as they formed, first, the Non-Partisan Committee for Peace through Revision of the Neutrality Act and, then, in May 1940, the Committee to Defend America by Aiding the Allies.[24] The list of those who recanted their earlier antiwar stands included columnist Dorothy Thompson, journalist-historian Walter Millis, and prominent Protestant theologian Reinhold Niebuhr.[25] Most pacifists, moreover, were isolationists only in the narrow sense of wanting to avoid war, and their proposals in 1939/40 for neutral mediation and efforts to rescue and feed the victims of Nazi conquest pleased neither isolationists, "with their fear of foreign involvement," nor "advocates of collective security, with their support of an Allied coalition against the fascists."[26] Pacifist doctrine certainly opposed conscription, but most strict pacifists accepted the inevitability of conscription, along with war, and thus redoubled their efforts to protect their own constituency through conscientious objection. "If only the Peace Movement were not so weak and so poor," one peace worker wrote despairingly in July 1940. "It is like a good ship, with not enough crew to make it sail."[27]

Two pacifist organizations, the War Resisters League and the Fellowship of Reconciliation (FOR), cooperated with Beale and the Friends in pressing the conscientious-objector issue. Each group numbered approximately ten thousand members. Founded in 1914, the FOR constituted the main body of Christian pacifism in the United States, outside the historic peace churches (Friends, Mennonites, and Church of the Brethren). The War Resisters League, founded in 1924 as an offshoot of the FOR, aimed at enlisting political, philosophical, and humanitarian pacifists who were dedicated to opposing war and to eradicating its causes. Both groups had been looking inward since the mid 1930s, strengthening their organizations at the local level, building up "pacifist teams," and preparing literature and advisory boards to counsel COs in the event of war.[28] Representatives of the Fellowship and of the War Resisters League testified eloquently against the draft before both committees, although the thrust was primarily in behalf of the conscientious objectors.[29] One especially impressive set of witnesses responded to an eleventh-hour appeal from Howard Beale and spent the week of 25 July to 2 August testifying before committees and canvassing individual congressmen. Headed by the War Resisters' secretary, Abraham Kaufman of New York City, these pacifists persuaded Congressman Wadsworth to support a provision for nonreligious objectors and to keep his mind open on protection for absolutists.[30] Even though Secretary Stimson mistakenly called them "mushroom peace societies," the efforts of dedicated pacifists to expand CO protection made for a more equitable bill and may actually have facilitated the enactment of selective service in the end.[31]

The most effective opposition came from groups that were not so strictly pacifist in orientation. Formed in 1938, the Keep America out of War Congress (KAOWC), led by Norman Thomas, served as an umbrella organization that linked the financial resources and legislative contacts of the peace societies with the national political appeal of the Socialist party.[32] Until the formation of the America First Committee in September 1940, the KAOWC was the only broad antiwar coalition in existence. Although declining in membership and money, the KAOWC still provided a convenient vehicle for coordinating the activities of a hundred or so liberal peace advocates, many of whom had worked in tandem for various causes since the 1920s and were skilled in the techniques of mobilizing public opinion through local affiliates around the country. With such prominent and persuasive spokesmen as Norman Thomas, journalists Oswald Garrison Villard and John T. Flynn, and lobbyists Frederick Libby and Dorothy Detzer, the KAOWC network hoped to "terrorize" the Roosevelt administration on the draft, just as it had on neutrality legislation three years earlier.[33]

The antiwar network responded belatedly but vigorously to the threat of conscription. Beguiled at first by President Roosevelt's vague talk about voluntary national service, peace advocates initially underestimated the appeal of the Burke-Wadsworth bill. "Lame-duck, lame argument," sniffed one opponent, in an apparent reference to Senator Burke's defeat in the primary.[34] Beginning in mid June, however, the KAOWC's Governing Committee in New York sought to organize a broadly based Committee against Conscription. Several prominent individuals, including historian Charles A. Beard and Boston University's President Daniel Marsh, were asked to head the committee, but they declined.[35] Edwin C. Johnson, secretary of the Committee on Militarism in Education, eventually assumed the duties. As a long-time activist against compulsory ROTC in the nation's schools and colleges, Johnson used his educational contacts to get some three hundred signatures from university presidents and professors to a "Declaration against Conscription," which Johnson read before the Senate Military Affairs Committee on 11 July.[36] The declaration, which condemned selective service as the opening wedge of totalitarianism, a negation of democracy, and a departure from American tradition, was also dramatically endorsed by Oswald Garrison Villard, who, despite a painful attack of kidney stones, testified as treasurer of the Committee on Militarism in Education.[37] Johnson also published the declaration in selected newspapers and magazines, exhorting readers to oppose conscription by writing to the president, senators, and congressmen.[38] Throughout the summer, Johnson kept up a steady correspondence with key members of Congress, helped to coordinate opposition witnesses, served on a joint strategy committee with Howard Beale, Frederick Libby, and Dorothy Detzer, and did what he could from his New York office at 2929 Broadway.[39] One of Johnson's more stimulating contributions was his discovery and reprinting of Daniel Webster's 1814 speech against conscription, a copy of which went to every member of Congress and to assorted editors across the country.[40]

An even more important figure in the anticonscription campaign was the executive secretary of the National Council for the Prevention of War (NCPW), Frederick J. Libby.[41] "A round-faced, scrubbed little man, full of vigor and zeal, shining with sureness, compact, tidy," the 65-year-old Libby had been running the National Council's Washington headquarters since the inception of the organization in 1922.[42] Formerly a Congregationalist minister and currently a practicing Quaker, Libby was the only strict pacifist on the National Council, an organization that actively supported disarmament and neutrality during the twenties and thirties but had lost membership in recent years and, after falling some $70,000 in debt in 1939, had cut its staff to a skeleton force on reduced salaries.[43] Gregarious and energetic, Libby had no qualms about dealing with conservatives and isolationists, and on the day that the Burke-Wadsworth bill was introduced, he was trying to organize a broad "Anti-War Crusade" that included such Republicans as John Foster Dulles and Theodore Roosevelt, Jr.[44] Libby and his equally dedicated wife, Faith, worked at a furious pace that summer. The last week in June saw him testifying at the Philadelphia Convention in behalf of a strong peace plank in the Republican platform. Libby and Oswald Villard, also at Philadelphia, found Wendell Willkie attractive and impressive, and for the next three months they urged the candidate—through telegrams, letters, and Republican intermediaries—to speak out against the Burke-Wadsworth bill.[45] Returning to his office in Washington, Libby "geared into" the conscription campaign by telephoning Senator Sheppard and demanding time to "organize the opposition." Between 3 July and his own Senate testimony a week later, the pacifist warhorse mimeographed anticonscription letters to seventeen hundred local branches of the National Council; sent separate letters, urging protest, to one hundred and fifty editors of religious journals; lobbied with several antiwar senators; and attended a KAOWC committee meeting in New York on 9 July.[46]

Libby's hastily prepared statement before the Senate committee the following afternoon gave rise to one of the hearings' more curious moments.

> " 'In time of peace prepare for war.' Did you ever hear that saying?"
> interjected Senator Minton.
> "I have heard it many times," Libby replied.
> "Do you believe it?"
> "No."
> "No?"
> "I do not. I would prefer to say—"
> "In summertime, do not get ready for winter?"

"In time of peace, prepare for peace," Libby shot back. "Why should we not do that?"[47]

The fast-moving Libby journeyed to Chicago the following week, accompanied by a contingent from the Youth Committee against War (YCAW, the youth affiliate of the KAOWC). They sought a strong peace plank in the Democratic platform. While Libby found a friendly audience in Senators Wheeler, Walsh, and Pat McCarran on the Platform Committee, the young people picketed local headquarters of the Committee to Defend America by Aiding the Allies. The demonstration took on an anticonscription coloring as the male students wore prison stripes with nooses around their necks and the women dressed in deep mourning. One placard read: "I am 20; William Allen White is 72."[48] After obtaining a satisfactory antiwar plank ("weakened w. clause . . . 'except in case of attack' "), Libby returned to the conscription battle in Washington.[49] Suddenly another crisis! Roosevelt's remark about being "drafted" for a third term persuaded Libby that the White House secretly supported the Burke-Wadsworth bill.[50] Chairman May was telling peace workers that the House committee would close without hearing testimony from the opposition. Newspapers were predicting swift passage, and a reporter for the *Kiplinger Letter* boasted to Libby that fewer than ten senators would vote against the draft.[51] Urgent appeals for money went out to local affiliates of the National Council as well as to other past contributors.[52] Working closely with Howard Beale and the Friends, Libby pressed May to keep the hearings open, while he alerted Norman Thomas, Mayor La Guardia, and several prominent religious leaders to apply to present testimony in person.[53] Thomas, in turn, wrote to President Roosevelt, charging that "you are willing to put it through without adequate discussion or explanation."[54] Stung, the president replied: "I have taken no part in the details of any proposed legislation. . . . There is no unfair rushing of this legislation. You for one are having an excellent chance to have your say just like a lot of other people."[55] The hearings thus continued into early August. Meanwhile, Libby, Detzer, and other peace workers in Washington notified local chapters of the KAOWC network to bombard senators and congressmen with letters, telegrams, and postcards against the draft.[56] Slowly the momentum seemed to turn.

Libby's charismatic colleague in peace lobbying, Dorothy Detzer of the Women's International League for Peace and Freedom (WILPF), did not immerse herself in the anticonscription campaign until the last week of July. Like Libby, she had not anticipated the strength of the Burke-Wadsworth bill and had concentrated on lobbying for strong peace planks at the Democratic and Republican conventions. As a good friend and supporter of Senator Wheeler's, Detzer also diverted her energies to his quixotic quest for the Democratic nomination at Chicago.[57] Upon returning to the Jackson Place headquarters of the WILPF, however, she jumped wholeheartedly into the battle. In her testimony before the House committee on 30 July, Detzer spoke extemporaneously in favor of a six-months' trial for voluntary enlistment, arguing that the rush toward conscription merely masked the administration's desire for intervention in the European war.[58] Especially close to members of the Senate peace bloc because of her lobbying for the Nye Committee in the mid 1930s, the WILPF's representative remained flexible and optimistic throughout the draft fight, eventually prodding her legislative allies to push voluntary enlistments rather than all-out opposition to the draft principle. "We still have time," Detzer wrote to local branches on 31 July. "There seems to be a real chance to win if the pressure from the country continues and increases—it is this pressure which at present is turning the tide."[59]

The high point of the counterattack came on 1 August, with the anticonscription rally at the Hotel Raleigh in Washington, sponsored by the Youth Committee against War. Despite sweltering temperatures of close to 100 degrees, more than a thousand persons jammed inside the Raleigh's auditorium to hear speeches by Norman Thomas and Senators Wheeler, Nye, and Holt.[60] Nearly three hundred members of the Youth Committee from twenty-three states attended the rally, including executive secretary Fay Bennett and national officers John Swomley and James L. Farmer.[61] Although hampered by financial difficulties, the youth affiliates of the KAOWC proved to be the most imaginative of the antidraft activists. At various times during the summer, the Youth Committee's leadership considered such ideas as hiring a gigantic "peace train" to crisscross the country, forming an "Army of Peace," with officers and enlisted ranks as a parody of military organization, and a continuous three-man picket of the White House, employing Gandhian nonviolent discipline. Each proposal had to be abandoned for lack of money.[62] As it was, the YCAW concentrated on local activities, in terms both of generating letters and telegrams against the draft and of counseling potential conscientious objectors.[63] Among Fay Bennett's contributions was a six-page pamphlet, *Democracy Betrayed,* which analyzed the Burke-Wadsworth bill and was sent to some ten thousand youths during August.[64] To help polish her prose, Bennett called upon her then-unemployed Brooklyn friend, journalist Richard Rovere, for which task Rovere received the princely sum of five dollars.[65]

Rovere also worked briefly that summer for the antiwar newsletter *Uncensored,* which similarly fought the good fight against conscription.[66] Launched the previous autumn with a donation of $300 from Libby's National Council, *Uncensored* served as a mouthpiece for the liberal Writers Anti-War Bureau, with the young Socialists Sidney Hertzberg and Cushman Reynolds as editor and associate editor respectively.[67] Frank C. Hanighen, the rumpled, chain-smoking coauthor of the 1934 best seller *Merchants of Death,* acted as a one-man Washington bureau. As a veteran on Capitol Hill,

Hanighen knew everyone in the Washington press corps, had contacts in the Congress and the executive branch, and was close to Detzer, Libby, and other peace advocates. Several times a week, Hanighen would type out the latest rumors and inside information and send the copy to New York, where Hertzberg would shape it into the most authoritative antiwar statements then being published.[68] Although *Uncensored* never achieved a circulation of much more than two thousand, many on Capitol Hill read it, and opponents constantly cribbed from it during the debates over the draft in August and early September. Helping Hanighen after mid July as an unofficial liaison with Congress was Thomas V. Rankin, a twenty-four-year-old Harvard law student who was working that summer in the Library of Congress Reference Service. A founder of the Veterans of Future Wars as a Princeton undergraduate, Rankin strongly opposed conscription.[69] In his job as a researcher he quickly made contacts with most congressional opponents and became especially friendly with young Ed Wheeler, who was serving as an aide to his father the senator. Scrupulous about not showing favoritism during regular hours, Rankin worked overtime and evenings researching historical arguments against conscription, and it was he who hit on the idea in early August of taking extra copies of *Uncensored* to key Senate offices to circulate as debate material.[70] Rankin later played a vital role in helping Republican Congressman Hamilton Fish to coordinate his opposition to the draft with liberal Democrats whom he scarcely knew.[71]

Because Norman Thomas feared "Hitlerism more than Hitler," he also did yeoman's work against conscription in 1940.[72] Although he spent much of his time speaking around the country as the Socialist party's candidate for president, he always reminded audiences of his pacifist principles, and as chairman of the KAOWC, he made two important forays to Washington to testify against the draft.[73] In his appearance before the Senate committee on 11 July, he excoriated Senator Burke for once having said that "Hitler was greater than Bismarck," thus implying that support for the draft was support for fascism.[74] His second visit to the Capitol came at the end of the month, when it looked as if the draft bill might be rushed through without full debate. "The emergency warrants a virtual filibuster," Thomas told Senator Wheeler, and the Socialist leader did what he could to arouse opposition from labor unions and farm organizations outside the eastern states.[75] Thomas also worried that schisms within his own party over the European war were causing many older Socialists to defect. "Our Socialist Party today is so much a young man's party," he admitted, "that we could be pretty well broken up by the draft."[76] In his campaign speeches in August and September he continually emphasized his opposition to the draft, while heckling Willkie and Roosevelt for their failure to do likewise.

Other prominent members of the KAOWC network included Benjamin C. Marsh, executive secretary of the People's Lobby, who "fulminated"

Thomas V. Rankin, Princeton University, 1938, was a founder of
the antiwar organization Veterans of Future Wars. Although he
worked against the draft in 1940 as an employee of the Library of
Congress Reference Service, he became a close associate of Grenville Clark in the 1950s and 1960s. (Courtesy of Thomas V.
Rankin)

before both committees against the draft.[77] The doughty New Englander
Oswald Garrison Villard resigned from the *Nation* in June, after forty-six years
with the magazine, when its editors endorsed compulsory military training.
Drawing upon his journalistic reputation as a military analyst, Villard told the
Senate committee that the threat posed by Nazi Germany to the United States
was long range at worst and certainly did not justify conscription. He pointed
out: "I have written three books on Germany alone. If I felt that there was the
slightest danger, immediate danger, I should, of course, not be here today.
There is no immediate danger. There cannot be."[78] The liberal journalist
John T. Flynn emulated Villard by later quitting the *New Republic,* when it
supported the draft and other interventionist measures. In his column in the
New York World Telegram, Flynn warned about a war plot that was being
hatched in the White House, built on the hysterical premise that Hitler was
about to attack the United States. "That scare is a fraud—pure and simple,"
he wrote. "But conservatives have fallen for it, hook, line and sinker."[79]

Beyond the individuals and groups associated with the Keep America out
of War Congress, the remnants of the so-called peace movement had mixed

attitudes toward the draft. As noted, most internationalists joined William Allen White's Committee to Defend America by Aiding the Allies, and while that organization took no official position on conscription, local chapters in New England supported it strongly.[80] The older, more conservative peace organizations, such as the Carnegie Endowment for International Peace and the American Peace Society, avoided taking a stand either out of principle or because its officers were "not wholly in agreement among themselves."[81] The National Peace Conference similarly found that its member organizations were too divided to take an official position on selective service.[82] Of all the organizations sometimes categorized as part of the "peace" movement, the only ones that supported conscription unequivocally were the veterans—the American Legion, the Veterans of Foreign Wars, the Reserve Officers Association, and the like.[83] The hard core of the antiwar forces, however, the hundred or so professional peace workers who directed their organizations in New York and Washington and knew one another by name, almost unanimously "lined themselves up against the whole business."[84]

An important and usually impassioned adjunct of the peace forces was the loosely organized but articulate youth movement. While college presidents such as Conant of Harvard, Charles Seymour of Yale, and Dodds of Princeton made forceful appeals for preparedness, many of their students were demonstrating loudly for peace. The Williams College *Record* denounced Professor Frederick L. Schuman for his outspoken pro-Ally position; at Harvard, tin soldiers arrived in the mail boxes of five interventionist professors; and the *Daily Kansan* at Lawrence caustically reminded faculty that more students than professors died in wartime.[85] Much to the embarrassment of President Ernest M. Hopkins, a delegation of Dartmouth students took a peace petition to Washington and presented it to Congressman Foster Stearns.[86] At Yale, nearly fifteen hundred students sent a petition to the White House opposing any kind of aid to England and France.[87] For his part, FDR wrote a letter to his old Harvard teacher Roger Merriman, praising him for calling student pacifists "shrimps." "I think the best thing for the moment is to call them shrimps publicly and privately," he noted. "Most of them will eventually get in line, if things should become worse."[88]

The nation at large took notice of the youth movement during the week of 4 July, when the American Youth Congress (AYC) held its sixth national gathering at College Camp, Wisconsin.[89] This amorphous body attracted more than five hundred delegates, who represented, according to its own report, some five million young people, to say nothing of ninety-five "observers," representing two million more. The American Youth Congress had gained notoriety the previous February when some of its members had hissed the president during a Washington meeting, notwithstanding the fact that Mrs. Roosevelt had done her best to give the organization guidance and respectability.[90] During the July convention the Youth Congress made the front pages again because of a bitter fight between right-wing and left-wing factions. The leftists, having finally ousted their opponents, sent their executive secretary to Washington to testify before the House committee. Secretary Joseph Cadden avowed: "We declare our readiness to contribute our energies, our services, and if need be our lives, to . . . defending our country . . . against any attack of enemies from without our country and against any betrayal from within." But the Burke-Wadsworth bill evidently posed such a "betrayal." Since the only effective "first line of defense" consisted of a "free, unregimented and happy youth," the AYC condemned "all proposals which have been made for compulsory military training or conscription."[91]

Such opposition typified most of the other organized youth groups that sent witnesses to Washington. The National Intercollegiate Christian Council warned against the "so-called mobilization bills" that tended to "destroy the labor movement, abrogate civil liberties, and move this country away from democracy toward fascism."[92] The American Student Union, boasting members from two hundred and fifty colleges, told the Senate committee that more than one million students had attended its annual peace demonstrations in the past six years.[93] On its board the Youth Committee against War, which was so effective in organizing the anticonscription rally in Washington on 1 August, included representatives of the National Council of Methodist Youth, the Farm YMCA, the Student Peace Service, the Youth Section of the Fellowship of Reconciliation, and several others.[94] A minister who represented one million young Methodists informed senators that "in conference after conference . . . from southern California to New England, our young people have stated in straightforward resolutions their opposition to conscription."[95] A nineteen-year-old witness for the Geneva Peace Fellowship of the International Council of Religious Education pleaded with the House committee on behalf of voluntary service: "American youth is ready to make a sacrifice. They are ready to give their time, energy, and even money to build a greater America. . . . American youth awaits and hopes for an American answer."[96]

Kingman Brewster, Jr., and R. Douglas Stuart led a group of students opposed to war who chose deliberately not to take a position on conscription.[97] During the spring these two Yale students had begun to explore the idea of a national antiwar organization that would link pacifists, youth, conservatives, isolationists, and noninterventionists of all political shadings. Finding initial interest, Stuart continued throughout the summer to sound out potential patrons such as Henry Ford, Gen. Robert Wood of Sears-Roebuck, Governor Philip F. La Follette of Wisconsin, and Charles Lindbergh.[98] It soon became apparent, however, that many of those who were willing to join, especially in the Midwest, favored a strong national defense and either supported conscription or hesitated because they feared that Roosevelt would use a conscript army for intervention. Under such circumstances, the committee organizers (which included a young Yale law student and assistant football coach named Gerald R. Ford) avoided any stand on the draft and at first gave the name Defend America First to their proposed organization.[99] When Frederick Libby balked at joining an antiwar organization that preached strong defense until after the conscription fight had ended, Stuart said he understood and "only hope your efforts will be successful in this direction."[100] Even though it later worked closely with Wheeler, Taft, Vandenberg, and other senators who fought hard against the draft, the America First Committee did not formally establish itself until after the Burke-Wadsworth bill had been passed. Thomas Rankin, an undergraduate classmate of Stuart's at Princeton, gave Stuart periodic reports from Capitol Hill and assured him that "the same people who favor full aid, even war, were the proponents of conscription."[101]

What lay behind this deep-seated set of attitudes that identified the upper stratum of American youth with the isolationists and the pacifists? Justice Frankfurter thought he knew the answers. College students, he informed the British political scientist Harold J. Laski, had been corrupted by the "sloppy, sleazy stuff that has been handed out by most historians and most political scientists in most American colleges and universities since Versailles." He added: "Of course, the scape-goat theory of history, all this debunking negativism without any guiding criteria and indeed the denial that there are any moral validities give a sense of sophistication extremely flattering to the naïve and intellectually immature."[102] Frankfurter's interventionist friend the poet Archibald MacLeish strongly agreed. If Americans considered all words and moral judgments "phony," MacLeish wrote to the *New York Times* in May, "then there is nothing real and permanent for which men are willing to fight." He confessed that writers of his own generation, himself included, had created the distrust of "the tags, the slogans, and even the words." They had "immunized the young generation against any attempt in its own country by its own leaders to foment a war by waving moral flags and rhetorical phrases. But," he concluded in his indictment, "the irresponsibles . . . have left it defenseless against an aggressor whose cynicism, brutality and whose stated intention to enslave presents the issue of the future in moral terms."[103]

Later developments proved that the jeremiads of Frankfurter and MacLeish were exaggerated. Eleanor Roosevelt, for example, even while she supported conscription and severed ties with the American Youth Congress in 1940, maintained her friendship with the youths whom she knew best and did not lose faith in student idealism.[104] Indeed, the commencement orators who proclaimed in June 1940 that the "Yanks Are Not Coming," would be winning Silver Stars and Navy Crosses two years later.[105] When the crisis arrived, American youth overcame the handicap of disillusion and cynicism. Straws in the wind were already evident in 1940. The activism of men in their

Neal Anderson Scott, Davidson College, 1940, was one of many commencement orators in 1940 who proclaimed that the "Yanks Are Not Coming." Nearly two years later, as an ensign in the navy, he was killed in the Battle of Santa Cruz Island. (Courtesy of Scott's family)

twenties and thirties at the Plattsburg camps served partly to balance the larger numbers at anticonscription rallies. With the pledge that American youth stood "ready to assume whatever defensive burdens an unkind fate has compelled," the Junior Chamber of Commerce threw its weight behind the Burke-Wadsworth bill.[106] A Youth Division of the Committee to Defend America by Aiding the Allies had already begun to function by early June, and in the autumn the interventionist Student Defenders of America, headed by Adam Yarmolinsky, soon made inroads on campuses across the country.[107] The National Committee of Young Democratic Clubs, meeting in Chicago in July, recorded its sympathies for the democracies of Europe and endorsed FDR's policy of "translating these sympathies into an active program of giving all aid to those countries."[108]

In sum, one may fairly conclude that the pacifistic attitudes that MacLeish and Frankfurter deplored were neither permanently fixed nor typical of American youth in general. To be sure, dedicated pacifist witnesses such as David Dellinger and seven other students at the Union Theological Seminary refused even to register for the draft in the autumn of 1940 and spent a year in jail.[109] (Dellinger was to figure in an even-more-famous antiwar trial nearly thirty years later.) Nevertheless, the total number of conscientious objectors during World War II seemed quite small compared to the many thousands who had taken the Oxford Pledge during the 1930s. The fact that the "youth movement" came largely from the upper stratum in education did not necessarily reflect the sentiments of the less articulate majority who had never read a college textbook. In a poll prompted by the anticonscription resolution of the American Youth Congress, the Gallup Institute asked a sampling of the twenty-one to twenty-five age group early in July, "Do you think every able-bodied young man twenty years old should be made to serve in the army or navy for one year?" Fifty-two percent answered yes; 48 percent answered no. In a second poll a month later, 62 percent of Americans between the ages of twenty-one and thirty favored conscription. Late in August, Gallup conducted a third poll that asked directly: "If the draft law is passed, will you, personally, have any objection to spending a year in some branch of the military service?" Of the young men aged twenty-one to twenty-four, some 68 percent replied that they would have no objection; in the younger group, from sixteen to twenty-one years old, 81 percent were willing to serve.[110]

Of course, when the United States finally did enter the war, young Americans did not assume military duties with the same idealistic patriotism as in 1917. Just as the war novels of Irwin Shaw and Norman Mailer differed from those of Ernest Hemingway and John Dos Passos, journalist William L. White caught the mood of a young Kansas farm boy, who told him: "I suppose if we've got to go, we ought to have training. . . . The best thing you can say about this new war is that if we win it, things will stay the same. . . . But you can't expect Irving Berlin to write a very stirring marching song about how swell it is to go out and die for the status quo."[111] Years later the literary critic Alfred Kazin recalled how smugly he had spent the summer of 1940 living with a group of political radicals on Cape Cod: "We were all Socialists still, and Socialists stayed out of capitalist wars." The next and last scene of Kazin's memoir shifts to a movie theater in Piccadilly in 1945, where an older and apparently wiser Kazin is viewing the first newsreels of the newly liberated concentration camp at Belsen. As the "sticks in black-and-white prison garb" shuffled across the screen, Kazin remembered, "it was unbearable. People coughed in embarrassment, and in embarrassment many laughed."[112] A respectable Boston lawyer, who later opposed the Vietnam War, also reminisced about 1940: "It was as though a curtain came down after Pearl Harbor. If I hadn't seen copies of my correspondence, I would not have believed I worked so hard against the draft back then."[113]

As it was with American youth, religious opinion in the United States remained divided, with perhaps a slight majority of Catholic and Protestant spokesmen being opposed to the Burke-Wadsworth bill. Although ecclesiastical leaders showed primary concern for conscientious objectors, in most cases a strong religious feeling against war produced an active hostility to the bill itself.

The editors of the most widely circulated Catholic periodical, *Commonweal,* disagreed about the European war. In June 1940, associate editor C. G. Spalding proclaimed that "the hour has come to announce irrevocably our determination to oppose the extension of fascism throughout the world; by war if necessary."[114] The general tone of the magazine, however, remained much less bellicose, and on the specific issue of the draft, another editor wrote in August that such legislation was "obviously a long leap toward entry into the war. . . . Periodicals such as this one, that do not want to get the United States into the war, ought to oppose the draft."[115] The *Catholic Worker* took a more resolute stand. Editor Dorothy Day, a member of the KAOWC governing committee, proclaimed that war was "again the Folly of the Cross."[116] Both Day and business manager Joseph Zarella warned the Senate committee that Pope Pius XI had described conscription as "scarcely better than war itself, a condition which tends to exhaust national finances, to waste the flower of youth and poison the very fountain heads of life, physical, intellectual, and moral."[117]

Because the Burke-Wadsworth bill, unlike the 1917 act, did not automatically exempt all clergy, including seminarians and teaching brothers, much of the Catholic hierarchy rallied in opposition. Historian George Q. Flynn has written: "From the *Boston Pilot* to the *Inland Catholic* of Spokane and from *True Voice* of Omaha to the *Sign* of Union City, New Jersey, editorials rang with the same tone of denunciation."[118] The Reverend Barry O'Toole of Catholic University testified that conscription violated a "Christian principle that vocations should be optional."[119] Monsignor Michael J. Ready of the National Catholic Welfare Conference wrote to President Roosevelt, Postmaster General Farley, and other prominent Catholics, urging an amendment to exempt all clergy.[120] Although Catholics usually disclaimed any intention of resisting the draft, the ensuing deluge of letters and petitions served to prod Congressman John W. McCormack and such senators as Walsh of Massachusetts, Joseph Guffey of Pennsylvania, Francis T. Maloney of Connecticut, and others to sponsor amendments requiring all clergy (including students and brothers) to register, but effectively exempting them from subsequent military service.[121] At one point in mid August, some three hundred and fifty priests, nuns, and brothers appeared on Capitol Hill.

Dividing into groups of five, they saw all ninety-six senators in one day. "The next morning," an astonished Howard Beale recorded, "as soon as the Senate sat 11 senators rushed forward trying to be the first in presenting a bill exempting all theological students. The House was handled in the same way. It made our hard work seem inexperienced and ineffective."[122] Once the clerical amendment passed, Catholic opposition tended to dissipate.

Among Protestants, the most authoritative voice belonged to the Federal Council of Churches of Christ in America, which represented more than twenty-five denominations and twenty-two million church members. Working through its Department of International Justice and Goodwill, the Federal Council had drunk deeply at the well of Christian pacifism during the 1920s and 1930s. Hitler's blitzkrieg, however, jolted the council into putting aside its longstanding goal of international disarmament. Without immediately turning interventionist, it tried to remain impartial on the draft. The Federal Council did create a special committee for conscientious objectors, and it testified strongly for protection of nonreligious as well as religious scruples.[123]

Many leaders of American Protestantism, however, expressed vehement opposition. From the pulpit of Riverside Church in New York, Dr. Halford E. Luccock of Yale preached that the passage of a draft in peacetime would mark "the end of the United States as it has been known since the birth of the Constitution."[124] John Haynes Holmes, the long-time head of the Community Church in New York, wrote despairingly: "We are witnessing the break-up of everything that we have known as our world; and the members of our generation . . . witness only dishonor, disaster, and death."[125] Bishop G. Bromley Oxnam served on the Methodist Commission on World Peace, which voted unanimously for "unalterable opposition" to the Burke-Wadsworth bill.[126] After finishing an essay about conscientious objectors, Oxnam noted in his diary: "How strange to be writing about conscience with the American Legion parading in the streets from early morning until late at night. I would feel a little bit better if the Legion were as much interested in driving out fascism as it is in driving communism out."[127]

Highly respected clergymen stood just as resolutely on the other side of the question. Episcopal Bishop William T. Manning of New York publicly urged that Congress immediately pass "the bill for compulsory military training and service. . . . The call is imperative."[128] Dr. Daniel A. Poling, a leading Baptist minister, asserted in August that "the only efficient, adequate, democratic program is universal service with each citizen related to the defense at the point of maximum effort."[129] A strong supporter of aid to the Allies, President Henry Sloane Coffin of the Union Theological Seminary intervened with Secretary Stimson to give pacifist clergy an opportunity to testify before the House committee. "I am all for giving conscientious objectors a fair deal," Coffin assured Norman Thomas, "but if some of you . . . would as fairly . . . say that the selective draft is a just way of defending the country, that the crisis is serious, that Britain should be given every help we can, I would feel very differently towards working with you. The trouble with the pacifists is that they want favors but are not willing to see and assist the other point of view."[130] Coffin's colleague Henry Van Dusen bitterly assailed the "irresponsible idealism" of the influential *Christian Century*, whose editors in June 1940 had naïvely proposed a world conference to end the war on the basis of local self-government, global federation, and immediate and complete disarmament.[131] "Would Hitler consider such a proposal?" they asked. "Many will shout 'No!' But does anyone know until it is put up to him? And to the German people?"[132]

The *Christian Century*, as expected, opposed the Burke-Wadsworth bill from the outset, calling the MTCA "one of those mysterious and well-financed letterhead organizations which springs to the aid of official agencies when there is a propaganda job to be done."[133] At the height of the opposition's assault later in the summer, the journal warned that conscription would "Prussianize" America. "Fashion, music, our magazines, our movies, the Sunday sermon, the plays of our children, Christmas gifts for youngsters, art and literature," lamented assistant editor William Hubben, "the very dreams of our boys, once colorful with wild west schemes, will assume the terrifying aspect of modern mechanized warfare."[134] When the Selective Training and Service Act was finally passed in mid September, the *Christian Century* attributed its margin to machinations by "the president, the army, and most of the metropolitan press, [and] by skillful manipulation of the psychology of emergency."[135] Its editor, Charles Clayton Morrison, blamed the defeat on the suddenness of the issue and the difficulty of organizing effectively during the vacation season. He took some solace in that the clergy and church press had "shown a unanimity of opposition seldom achieved on any issue," a unanimity that "included the Roman Catholic Church."[136] Although this judgment was a little exaggerated, it was true that Protestant and Catholic leaders formed a strong bulwark in the anticonscription army.

The educational world was divided on the draft as well, although the balance on American campuses tended to tip in favor. The considered judgment of Guy E. Snavely, executive director of the Association of American Colleges, was that university administrators seemed "friendly" to the Burke-Wadsworth bill.[137]

Similar to the churchmen's concern for conscientious objectors, most educators showed less interest in the draft per se than they expressed anxiety about the relationship of colleges and universities to national defense, especially in the event of a large-scale mobilization. George P. Zook, president of the American Council on Education, promised the Senate committee full cooperation and hoped that the federal government would reciprocate: "Adequate consideration must be given to the conservation of educational values, resources, and personnel, [and] all agencies of education must be utilized for the most effective meeting of any national emergency. These are not in opposition. . . . They are equally vital and correlative."[138] As for conscription itself, the American Council left the issue to Congress.

President Walter Hulihan of the University of Delaware ridiculed the isolationist contention that no immediate danger to the United States existed and declared that "those of us . . . endorsing this bill are more impressed with the threat . . . unless such a measure as this is adopted and preparation is made."[139] Snavely read to the Senate committee the results of a poll of 555 of the nation's 600 accredited four-year liberal-arts institutions. To the question "Do you favor selective compulsory military training in peacetime for those 21 years of age and above?" 141 college presidents answered no; 43 others said they were undecided, but were leaning toward endorsement; and 331 answered yes. With this poll expressing the unofficial feeling of his constituency, Snavely put his organization on record "in favor of a certain amount of conscription in peacetime."[140] This stand accorded with the defense pronouncements of the Educational Policies Commission and the American Youth Commission, both of which openly supported selective service later in the summer.[141]

The interventionist/isolationist controversy had, of course, been raging in different forms in academic circles long before the summer of 1940. The usual pattern on college campuses saw a line-up of students against professors, with a sprinkling of faculty ready to give advice and encouragement to the younger generation. The opposition received valuable aid from historian Charles Beard, who in May published a small volume proclaiming that the United States should avoid "world adventures" and concentrate on solving "the grave social and economic crises at home."[142] (President Roosevelt jotted in his copy of Beard's book: "40 years hard and continuous study has brought forth an inbred mouse.")[143] Other revisionist historians, such as Harry Elmer Barnes, C. Hartley Grattan, and Charles C. Tansill, wrote impassioned warnings against repeating "the deadly parallel" of 1917.[144] Former revisionist Walter Millis argued just as earnestly that "1939 is not 1914," while such historians as Henry Steele Commager, Marquis James, Carl L. Becker, Charles M. Andrews, Allan Nevins, and Dumas Malone organized a subsidiary division of the Committee to Defend America by Aiding the Allies.[145]

At commencements in June a flurry of interventionist and proconscription rallies occurred on eastern campuses, chiefly among alumni groups. On 8 June, General Adler addressed a gathering of about two hundred and fifty Princetonians, who proceeded to vote unanimously in support of compulsory military training. Stimson delivered his important speech of 18 June to a similar alumni group at Yale, while Lewis Douglas spoke in behalf of the draft at Harvard's commencement.[146] Amherst and Williams also had rallies of this type, each endorsing the conscription bill. At Harvard, more than a hundred faculty members banded together to form the American Defense Group under the leadership of Professors James Landis and Ralph Barton Perry, who corresponded with like-minded academics across the country that summer, making a particular effort to obtain petitions and statements in favor of the draft.[147] The establishment of a similar faculty group at Northwestern University, almost in the shadow of the *Chicago Tribune*'s tower, showed that preparedness sentiment did not confine itself to the East.

That a large minority of educators still opposed the draft seemed evident by the many distinguished signatures on the "Declaration against Conscription," presented to the Senate Committee on 11 July. Within a week, Perley Boone, with help from the Harvard Defense Group, issued a statement, signed by 189 educators, refuting the "notion that a system of universal training and service enforced by the State is in itself inconsistent with the principles of freedom."[148] In addition, on the same day the "Declaration against Conscription" was published, the presidents of twenty-three colleges voted unanimous support for the Burke-Wadsworth bill at a meeting in New York.[149] A similar unanimous vote came out of another conference of twenty-two college representatives, convoked by President William M. Lewis of Lafayette.[150] Just how much college presidents could speak for their faculties and students, of course, remained a matter of opinion. Later in the summer, Howard K. Beale protested furiously when a press release from the Harvard Defense Group claimed that there was "practically unanimous support" for the draft at the University of North Carolina. Beale wondered about the scholarly standards of distinguished Harvard professors who could make such a claim on the basis of scanty evidence; he doubted that the Chapel Hill faculty could reach unanimous agreement on anything, although he admitted that members of the History Department were split, with his own antidraft views being held by a minority.[151] The Harvard dons, their faces probably crimson, apologized.

While the world of academe seesawed from approval to opposition, organized labor leaders, with few exceptions, were arrayed against selective service. As James Wechsler wrote in *PM*, "the organized labor movement finds itself more solidly aligned against conscription than against—or for— anything else." Such a stance did not come as a surprise. Having won the right to organize during the New Deal, labor leaders quite naturally feared for their unions once the "nation puts on uniforms and manpower is registered." They feared that military priorities might result in no-strike edicts and "work-or-fight" orders, and even more subtle, according to Wechsler, was "the fear that large-scale military psychology will evoke anti-union vigilantism."[152] Sponsors of the Burke-Wadsworth bill tried, early in their campaign, to forestall opposition from labor. On 14 June, Archibald Thacher met with

David Dubinsky, the powerful head of the International Ladies Garment Workers' Union. Not at all unfriendly, Dubinsky gently reminded Thacher that labor had always opposed conscription as a matter of principle. Thacher assured him that they did not intend the bill to be a strike-breaking measure. "What we're trying to do," he said, "is to defend this country, and in that defense organized labor has just as vital an interest as any other group." Dubinsky, who had been born in Poland, replied: "I realize what it means to be an American citizen. I came here myself as an immigrant, and I often tell my younger friends, when they're inclined to be overcritical, that they ought to get down on their knees and thank God they're living in this country. But you and your organization should be satisfied if labor doesn't come out actively against your bill; that's the most you can hope for."[153]

Even this hope proved futile, as the president of the United Mine Workers' Union (UMW), John L. Lewis, became the first of many labor leaders to damn conscription. Engaged in a bitter feud with President Roosevelt in 1940, Lewis told the House committee that a peacetime draft "involves a very definite departure from the basic principles of the Constitution . . . and the Declaration of Independence." Not only would conscription cause dislocations "among the lives of millions of individuals," but also "freedom of speech and freedom of the press and freedom of individual initiative and enterprise would be seriously threatened."[154] William Green, president of the American Federation of Labor (AFL), came out against the bill on 5 August because he believed that it was premature. His unions would support a draft "when such action becomes necessary to defend, protect, and preserve America," but Green had seen no proof that the volunteer system had failed. Two weeks later he told a meeting of the AFL that the Burke-Wadsworth bill was "not well-planned." He promised support for national defense, so long as troops did not go abroad, workers' jobs remained protected, maintenance to families was extended, and conscription was instituted only after the volunteer system had failed to produce sufficient manpower.[155] Throughout August and early September, AFL affiliates supported compromise proposals to postpone the operation of the draft.[156]

The railway workers did not budge an inch in their opposition. Presidents of the Switchmen's Union and the so-called four brotherhoods sent a strong letter to Chairmen Sheppard and May, blasting peacetime conscription as "the very antithesis of democracy."[157] Similar support came from Julius Luhrsen, executive secretary of the Railway Labor Executives Association, who wrote letters to Senators Johnson of Colorado and La Follette of Wisconsin and actually lobbied on Capitol Hill in mid August.[158] In the same camp stood the Brotherhood of Sleeping Car Porters, which censured conscription in its Fifteenth Annual Convention in September.[159]

Although the Congress of Industrial Organizations (CIO) did not act with complete unanimity, its affiliates generally closed ranks with other labor groups. The national convention of the United Auto Workers (UAW), the first major union to meet after the Burke-Wadsworth bill had been introduced, was in session in St. Louis on 2 August when news flashed that FDR had endorsed the draft at his morning press conference. Delegates almost immediately shouted through, without dissent, a resolution damning conscription as being "foreign to our mode of life and existence." They urged union members to send "an avalanche of telegrams and letters" to Congress.[160]

The National Maritime Union publicly avowed that conscription could "only be construed as an attack on labor under the cover of the defense program."[161] Its president, Joseph M. Curran, helped to organize the Emergency Peace Mobilization in Chicago over the Labor Day weekend.[162] Locals of the Steel Workers, the United Auto Workers, and other CIO unions joined him in the rally, but Sidney Hillman's Amalgamated Clothing Workers and the Textile Workers' Union, two of the largest CIO affiliates, refused to participate.[163] As labor's representative on the new National Defense Advisory Commission (and privy to President Roosevelt's ideas about voluntary national service), Hillman stood virtually alone in endorsing selective service. "No man," he told the UAW on 31 July, "can say he is for labor, if he is not ready to defend democracy to the utmost."[164]

The National Farmers' Union, which claimed to represent more than one hundred thousand farm families, also dug in against the Burke-Wadsworth bill. The union's spokesman, Robert Handschin, testified before both committees, arguing that the draft would hit "the class of young men and young women whom we represent—the lower income farmers and their boys of military age." Meeting in August, the executive board of the union sent to every member of Congress letters of protest, signed by farm officials of seven of the Great Plains states.[165]

Although they were never in the vanguard of opposition, the farm organizations and the labor unions gave valuable political support to the antidraft activists in Washington.

Vociferous women's groups, some of them representing obscure constituencies, also swelled the opposition's ranks. Ida B. Wise Smith, president of the Woman's Christian Temperance Union, recited the charge that the draft constituted "the first step toward a totalitarian state."[166] The national chairperson of the Ladies of the Grand Army of the Republic feared that men would be drafted before cantonments could be completed, testifying that in 1917 "thousands of the flower of this nation were drafted and placed in camps with no uniforms, arms or blankets . . . where they suffered and died like flies."[167] Countless "mothers' " organizations—the National Legion of American Mothers, the Silver Star Mothers, the American Mothers' Neutrality League, and so on—joined in the chorus.[168] The most conspicuous called themselves the Mothers of the United States of America, a group of black-veiled matrons from Detroit who began a "death watch" against conscription in late August. In terms of media attention, such women's organizations tended to overshadow the more professional efforts of such peace workers as Dorothy Detzer, Jeannette Rankin, Fay Bennett, Alice Dodge, and others affiliated with the KAOWC.[169]

In some cases the opposition received support from nondescript letterhead organizations such as the Islands for War Debts Committee, which free-lance writers Prescott Dennis and J. Frank Webber ran from a two-room downtown office in Washington. Denouncing the draft bill, they mailed out reprints of Senate speeches and explained that Prussia had assisted Lincoln's administration during the Civil War and that today's enemies could become tomorrow's friends.[170] The Islands for War Debts Committee, it later turned out, was secretly financed by agents of Hitler's Germany.[171] Another obscure group, the New York Committee to Keep America out of War, sent mimeographed letters to Congress, warning that conscription was part of a Rooseveltian plot to intervene in the war on the side of atheistic Russia.[172] The Lawyers' Committee to Keep the United States out of the War submitted an elaborate brief, questioning the bill's constitutionality; the committee's chairman, Louis McCabe of Philadelphia, led a delegation of one hundred lawyers to Capitol Hill, where Senator Wheeler received them cordially.[173] And there was also the clever (but anonymous) Hoosier, who sent to his congressman a handsomely bound sixty-page booklet entitled, "Arguments in Favor of the United States Entering the European War," in which all the pages were blank![174]

Several groups that were concerned primarily with civil rights also lined up with the anticonscriptionists. In addition to Howard Beale's yeoman efforts for the ACLU, a representative for the National Federation of Constitutional Liberty denounced the peacetime draft as "abhorrent to free men."[175] Josephine Truslow Adams of the Philadelphia Committee for People's Rights testified against the draft and especially the principle of alien registration contained in the Burke-Wadsworth bill.[176] Ironically, this part of the bill received fulsome praise from President Royal C. Stephens of the National Club of America for Americans, a nativist group reminiscent of the Know-Nothing era. Not only did Stephens testify in favor of the draft, but he also urged further amendments denying immigration to everyone "seeking to enter the United States in competition with American citizens." Stephens bellowed: "We are going down the line for America."[177]

The mails also brought sinister letters from men and women whom the historian Arthur M. Schlesinger, Jr., has described as "pathetic people in back parlors who hated themselves or their lives."[178] Quite a few letters resembled the one from Sam Porter, who scrawled to Grenville Clark on a sheet of notebook filler: "Why not go to England your kind are not wanted or

needed here. Have not the guts—you want other to do your fighting for you—
is that it?''[179] From Illinois came a mock certificate:

Know All Men by These Presents—

> This Coupon entitles *Grenville Clark* to one honorary graveyard plot in
> Dreamland Cemetery [*sic*], Boody, Illinois.

> This great national cemetary is designed as a final rotting place for those
> who made the supreme sacrifice of their ideas and sympathies so that
> civilization might live.[180]

Even less amusing was a one-page letter in longhand on the stationery of a
hotel in La Crosse, Wisconsin: ''The time has passed . . . when War Mongers
. . . can stay at home with their over-sexed sons and daughters (like your over-
sexed Chief in the White House & his family of Degenerate Sons and
Daughters . . . financed by the Revenge Crazed Jews of England. . . . The
Oriental Vermin the Jews . . . will be exterminated with you—their Gentile
Stooges.''[181] President Roosevelt received his share as well, including one
from ''A Mother'' who warned: ''The day will come when you will be on *your
death bed* and you will have to answer for all these boys. *I* would hate to be in
your place.''[182]

Besides letters from individuals, anti-Semitic organizations were busy
mailing out cheap mimeographs, such as one flier that purported to expose a
secret meeting at the Harvard Club. ''Twenty years ago the late Adolph Ochs
. . . became imbued with the idea [conscription]; and last May Julius Ochs
Adler carried out the wishes of his late uncle. To please this Jew you are being
forced to leave your job . . . and alter the whole course of your life.''[183]
Material of this type might have slipped off a press in the headquarters of any
number of native fascist organizations then in existence. It might have come
from St. Albans, West Virginia, the point of origin for the Knights of the
White Camellia; from Father Charles E. Coughlin's Christian Front offices in
Michigan; from the hundreds of squalid shacks that passed for Ku Klux Klan
offices; from the Washington office of James True, the ''dean'' of American
Jew baiters; or from Asheville, North Carolina, the headquarters of William
Dudley Pelley, the goateed astrologer who headed the Silver Shirts.[184]

Father Coughlin, the ''Radio Priest'' whose sermons from the Shrine of
the Little Flower in Royal Oak, Michigan, had stirred millions during the
1930s, probably remained the most influential of the native fascists. Although
he was no longer master of the airwaves, Coughlin still preached against
Communists and Jews in his weekly newspaper, *Social Justice.*[185] He labeled
the draft bill a ''communist plot to place every adult between the ages of 18
and 64 in the military . . . at the mere nod of a Hitlerized president and his
American Gestapo.''[186] Once the Burke-Wadsworth bill had become law,
Coughlin urged retaliation against those congressmen who had sacrificed

American sons "to an international clique which, in his hatred, is prepared to sacrifice the Gentile world for retention of its control."[187]

This kind of diatribe raises the question as to how much the opposition to the Burke-Wadsworth bill benefited from subversive support. Congressional investigations, sedition trials, and forty years of historical research in both American and foreign sources have shown that the connection between totalitarian governments abroad and American extremist groups was not nearly as extensive and as sinister as most people believed at the time.[188] That Americans should have manifested a sudden great fear of subversive activity seemed understandable. After the conquest of Norway and France, the term *fifth column* became a household phrase in the United States—for government officials and ordinary citizens alike.[189] When Ambassador William C. Bullitt spoke over nationwide radio on 18 August and pointedly described the chaos that he had seen in France, which had been caused by fifth-column subversives, many isolationists who had no affection for Nazi Germany believed that Bullitt was also labeling them subversives and traitors by implication.[190] In the heated atmosphere of 1940/41, it sometimes became difficult to distinguish between responsible and irresponsible opposition, between debate and diatribe, between anti-Semitism and anti-interventionism. Perhaps the greatest irony that was perpetrated by extremists on both the Right and the Left was that by pledging to save America by mimicking the rhetoric and methods of totalitarian masters abroad, they actually speeded up American intervention by discrediting noninterventionism at home. In historian Geoffrey Smith's phrase, the subversives became "Roosevelt's unwitting allies."[191]

The German-American Bund provided a case in point—this most notorious organization of native Fascists, whose membership Congressman Martin Dies estimated at more than one hundred thousand.[192] In fact, only two thousand Bundists remained by August 1940.[193] Bundesführer Fritz Kuhn had gone to jail for grand larceny the previous December, and his self-appointed successor, G. Wilhelm Kunze, had to cope with mounting debts, surveillance from the FBI, feuding and factionalism within the Bund, and laws barring Bundists from federal employment. At the Bund's annual convention in Chicago in late August, only thirty-eight delegates attended for fear of "insane persecutions."[194] Notwithstanding this feebleness, Bund publications scored the Burke-Wadsworth bill, saying that Roosevelt meant to solve unemployment by sending young Americans to Europe to die for England. When a provision in the final law prohibited Bund members from holding jobs in defense industries, an indignant Kunze ordered all Bundists to refuse induction into military service.[195] These antics, plus scores of swastika-adorned telegrams to Congress, gave the sponsors of conscription an opportunity to make more of the Nazi-Fascist opposition than was actually warranted.[196]

Although it was surprising to find them both in the same bed, Fascist extremists in 1940 could claim American Communists as strong allies. This incongruity did not come to pass without considerable pain for party members in the United States. V. I. Lenin had once said that the locomotive of history might make hairpin turns, but after the Nazi-Soviet Pact of August 1939, many loyal comrades had trouble hanging onto the caboose. Most fellow travelers, attracted to Moscow's espousal of collective security after 1935, left the ranks in disillusion. But after recovering from the first shock, the remaining faithful readjusted obediently, and by 1940 they were doing battle alongside their new Fascist allies against the Washington preparedness effort. Calling on the radical antiwar tradition of an earlier generation, Elizabeth Gurley Flynn contributed the pamphlet *I Didn't Raise My Boy to Be a Soldier— for Wall Street,* and the *Daily Worker* began to serialize Dalton Trumbo's *Johnny Got His Gun,* a bitter novel about an American amputee veteran of 1918.[197]

At the national convention of the Communist Party in early June, delegates supported United States neutrality and denounced the "militarization and armaments program of the administration and Congress."[198] The Burke-Wadsworth bill, almost by definition, became a milestone on the road to "imperialist war." In New York, party officials claimed to raise more than $113,000, much of which went into their anticonscription drive.[199] "Since the main campaign of the Communist Party at this time is to block all efforts to conscript labor's blood and toil," the chief fund raiser stated, "a considerable part of these funds will be used to fight the . . . conscription bill now pending in Congress."[200] From the *New Masses,* party loyalists could learn the true story about the origins of the draft. The editors reported that on 19 June "the Roosevelt-Hillman Plan as ready to be sent to Congress," whereupon "Senator Burke rushed the army's conscription bill into the congressional hopper." The War Department and labor-hating congressmen had allegedly been "thrown into a frenzy by the thought of a labor union official having a hand in the training program." The draft thus became "war, Wall Street's war on freedom in America."[201]

Joining in the attack, the *Daily Worker* excoriated the Senate Military Affairs Committee for passing "this storm trooper measure without a whimper."[202] The Young Communist League ground out "Stop Conscription" handbills that warned: "You are about to be regimented to die for Wall Street."[203] The Communist unit in Red Hook, Brooklyn, hoped to catch the eye of Italian workers with a broadside, written half in Italian and half in English, claiming that 95 percent of the American people were opposed to the Burke-Wadsworth bill.[204] The Emergency Peace Mobilization Committee in Rochester, New York, tried to picket in Congressman Wadsworth's hometown of Geneseo, New York. "The villagers were genuinely angry," Wadsworth's son Jerry reported. "As it was, some of these Communist kids got pushed around a little and Sheriff Bean heaved a sigh of relief when the last car disappeared down the Avon road."[205]

Ironically, the Communists' most bitter enemies in 1940, those dwindling numbers of Marxist intellectuals who called themselves Trotskyists, also opposed the Burke-Wadsworth bill. Writing from Mexico City before a Stalinist pickax ended his life, Leon Trotsky himself told his American comrades: "Conscription? Yes. By the Bourgeois state? No. We cannot trust this work . . . to the state of exploiters."[206] The slogans that were adopted at the party's plenary session on 10/11 August included: "Down with the war and the warmongers! Down with conscription! For a people's army and a workers' government!! Record your vote against the war, against conscription!"[207] The young Trotskyist intellectual Dwight Macdonald, writing on the "Willkievelt Campaign," later charged that "on the crucial issues of war and conscription our 'democratic' political system provides no channel for the expression of opposition to the Roosevelt policies."[208]

The efforts of extremists—Communists, nativists, Fascists, Trotskyists, or anti-Semites—undoubtedly made slight impact on the vast majority of the American people. Unfortunately, some of the Plattsburgers who sponsored the draft bill overreacted to the subversives and tried to link the latter's activities to the more mainstream opposition to the draft. Although this search for subversives never went very far, it became part of a pattern that many interventionists followed in the months before Pearl Harbor so as to attribute the worst-possible motives to their noninterventionist adversaries. To be sure, pacifists and isolationists, Nazis and Communists (at least before 22 June 1941)—all wanted the United States to stay out of the European war. But this correlation of goals obscured the fact that the large majority of Americans who opposed conscription and intervention did so out of motives as patriotic and principled as those of their interventionist opponents.[209]

In the final estimate, the success or failure of the organized opposition depended on whether its arguments could persuade Congress and the country to reject the Burke-Wadsworth bill. In hearings, broadsides, radio speeches, newspaper columns, demonstrations, petitions, and Congressional debate, the outcome of the opposition's counterattack rested on the persuasiveness of its argument. And while the message varied in emphasis and eloquence, most opponents subscribed to a threefold set of contentions, namely, that conscription was not necessary, that it was un-American, and that the volunteer system could provide adequate defense.

Opponents hit repeatedly at the central premise of the Burke-Wadsworth bill—namely, that the country was facing a grave threat. Despite Hitler's sudden success and their own loathing of Nazism, most opponents played down the danger to the United States. "The protecting oceans remain unchanged," Oswald Garrison Villard assured Norman Thomas. To such pacifists, the interventionists were jumping at phantoms, "convinced that Hitler was going to land four or five divisions of death in New England by way of Iceland and Greenland under cover of fog."[210] Fred Burdick, of the Voice of the People Committee, testified that no "nation or a combination of nations can successfully invade and supply an invading army across 3,000 miles of water" and claimed that "we would have plenty of time to train a strictly defensive army" before enemy troops could be massed against "our well fortified posts and adequately mined harbors."[211] Witness after witness, with only minor variations in theme, reiterated this faith in "the doctrine of American invulnerability."[212]

A corollary to the emphasis on invulnerability was a more sophisticated argument reflecting on the recent blitzkrieg in Europe. Until Hitler overran Poland and, indeed, until the incredible campaign against the Low Countries and France, most Americans still thought of war in terms of endless trenches, with a stark no man's land of barbed wire and shell craters beyond. Remembering the war movies of the 1920s and 1930s, they pictured military action in the form of sudden "over the top" charges, a breakthrough if successful, and a realignment after each engagement. Tanks still seemed awkward, lumbering "land battleships," moving with tortoiselike speed. Pilots were medieval knights of the air, flying rickety biplanes, dueling opponents, and shouting "tally-ho."

The newsreels of swift panzers, backed by screaming Stukas, brought a revolution in American thinking. Germany's sudden technological prowess both impressed and frightened a nation of tinkerers and automobile fanciers. "We have gone into an entirely new era of warfare," Senator Sheridan Downey proclaimed, and first priority should be cadres of "young and vigorous men to handle these machines we are going to provide for them."[213] Armchair analysts began to proclaim, with more assurance than knowledge, that "masses of infantry" had become obsolete in modern warfare. Opponents eagerly seized upon this logical and apparently unanswerable talking point. They applauded Downey's advocacy of a "hard-hitting, professional, well-trained army of four to five hundred thousand men, mechanized troops . . . who know how to take care of their cars or equipment, tear it down and put it together again."[214]

The argument gained currency because several leading authorities, including some professionals, seemed to endorse it. Frank Knox had made an early statement supporting the "small army" idea, and one witness quoted Senator Tydings as having favored "the strongest navy in the world, the strongest air force in the world, and a relatively small but highly trained and well-equipped army."[215] In addition, the influential military columnist George Fielding Eliot had given the opposition ammunition by saying that the Burke-Wadsworth bill would not provide much security. "There would be only masses of partially trained men whom we could not arm, equip, or provide leaders for in any reasonable time," he testified.[216] John McAuley Palmer tried to answer with an open letter to the *New York Herald Tribune,* and Eliot later testified that he did not oppose conscription in principle but that he wanted a defined and limited objective.[217] By that time, however, the damage had been done.

The most authoritative advocate of the "small mechanized army" turned out to be Hanson W. Baldwin, the young military analyst of the *New York Times.*[218] Witnesses quoted Baldwin so often that Congressman Faddis peevishly inserted in the *Congressional Record* some biographical data that was intended to show that the *Times*'s journalist had no special qualifications as a professional military expert.[219] Numerous opponents cited Baldwin's article in the August issue of *Harper's,* especially the paragraph that read:

> Conscription in time of war can be justified. But at a time like the present it cannot be justified on the basis of hemispheric defense, for no such mass of men as conscription would provide can be effectively used in this hemisphere—with one possible exception: If we were preparing for a death struggle with a Japanized Asia and with a completely Germanized Europe in which all the navies and merchant marines and ship-building facilities on the continent were in German hands—a possibility which we have . . . considered to be most unlikely.[220]

Opponents of conscription, like Baldwin himself, dismissed his one exception, but by 1942 that exception proved to be the most accurate part of his analysis.

Time and again, opponents belabored the point before the committees. "Unless we are to go in for foreign military adventures," declared Norman Thomas, "we are concerned for a relatively easy defense primarily to be entrusted to the Navy, the air force, and the highly trained operators of mechanized warfare."[221] "Would not this country be better defended by a smaller army trained to use these new weapons," another witness asked, "than by millions whose unfamiliarity and experience with these new tools were limited by books and blueprints?"[222] Convinced that the conscriptionists were seeking to create a second AEF, Villard even argued that large numbers of draftees would "swamp" the army and actually detract from national defense.[223]

It also followed logically, opponents argued, that with only a small, highly trained force needed, the ranks could easily be filled by volunteers if the government would offer such inducements as higher pay, short terms of service, and rapid advancement. Quoting former Secretary Woodring's assertion that a large army "was not an essential part of our defense against any possible invasion," a witness for Labor's Non-Partisan League asserted that until the army offered pay equal to that of an enrollee in the Civilian Conservation Corps, "it cannot be said that . . . voluntary enlistment has failed."[224] One student witness vowed that American youth stood ready to "make a sacrifice." He pleaded: "Before scrapping the American inclination for sacrifice . . . you try it out."[225]

This appeal to give the volunteer system a fair trial dogged the Burke-Wadsworth bill in its entire journey through Congress. Much of its allure derived from the fact that many senators and congressmen saw in the proposal an opportunity to dodge the touchy issue of conscription until after the ballots had been counted in November. Proponents made numerous attempts to argue against postponement, most notably Walter Lippmann, in his sharp column in mid August, where he pointed out that volunteers would come in sufficient numbers only when the "threat of conscription" lurked in the background. He predicted "an ingratiating campaign to pin white feathers on young men who did not volunteer, and the young ladies would . . . call them slackers. . . . In practice it is a moral horror."[226] Even President Roosevelt quietly warned nervous Democrats to "think this through in terms of national safety and not just in terms of votes."[227]

Finally, of all the arguments advanced against the Burke-Wadsworth bill, nearly every witness proclaimed one with special fervor. Nearly every magazine or newspaper article, every letter to the editor, and every telegram to Congress or the White House at least touched on the keystone of the anticonscription case—that selective service would become a totalitarian device to destroy civil liberties and take America down the road to dictatorship. The revulsion was genuine. The journalist William Henry Chamberlin, returning home after covering the fall of France for the *Christian Science Monitor,* noted in his diary that he had a "feeling of almost physical sickness when I see prospect of conscription in America. . . . America's great and complicated dilemma: to resist attack . . . without any such totalitarian measure as complete military individual conscription."[228] Villard, whose family had escaped military conscription by emigrating from Germany in 1849, told William Allen White that "universal service is but the entering wedge, for that is the cornerstone of all dictatorial structures. . . . [If] a state can exercise a peacetime right to levy on the bodies of its young men and put them to work or in military camps . . . it can take other steps . . . as have Hitler and Mussolini."[229]

Witnesses before the committee spoke with equal earnestness. "Compulsory military service is against the principles of the citizens of the United States," one woman told the House committee.[230] It is "a thoroughly European device," asserted another.[231] Arguing that the bill itself posed "more of an emergency than a threat from Hitler," Frederick Libby claimed that its real purpose aimed at creating "discipline throughout the Nation; disciplined men; but disciplined men means regimented men; obedient men; and Germany has been much criticized in our country . . . justly and rightly so, because of its regimentation."[232] Norman Thomas contended that the greatest danger to America came, not from "conquest by Hitler, but the adoption of Hitlerism in the name of democracy." No proposal "could be more in line with Fascist regimentation and less in accord with American tradition."[233] As if to fulfill their worst nightmares, Senator Minton interjected at one point: "We can beat Hitlerism. I think that Hitlerism is the greatest threat to civilization we know today, and the way to meet Hitlerism is with Hitlerism."[234] Although Minton may have intended his remarks to be humorous, the anticonscriptionists thought he was deadly serious.[235]

Some peace advocates tried to spell out in detail how the subversion of civil liberties would proceed. John Nevin Sayre, of the Fellowship of Reconciliation, predicted that the draft would "set in motion forces certain to infringe 'the liberty to know, to utter, and to argue freely according to conscience.'" Even religious liberty would be "drastically curtailed."[236] A representative of the Friends' General Council testified that Quakers also considered conscription to be the "negation of the right of conscience and a denial of religious freedom."[237] Dorothy Day pointed out that "a cardinal Catholic principle is the right of a man to choose his vocation. . . . And to take the young men . . . from the opportunity to do constructive work . . . we consider a cruel wrong and a violation of natural rights."[238] Perhaps the most impassioned plea came from Eugene M. Lerner of George Washington University, who begged the senators to vote nay on a bill that would "turn this country into a horrifying holocaust" and "destroy American democracy." "Only in the hearts of young people," he declaimed, "remains the American dream . . . and when those hearts are hardened by the hammer blows of the force psychology on which this bill is based and when those hearts are blasted to bits by the cannon of war, the American dream is gone forever; and with that disappearance, America, the true America, will have vanished. . . . We must not let that happen."[239]

Because they represented such a wide diversity of opinions, the arguments against the Burke-Wadsworth bill did not always come across so concisely or convincingly as the neat and skillful case of its advocates. But the very intensity and sincerity of the opposition, coupled with the wishful desire of many Americans to believe that such a measure was indeed unnecessary, gave weight to their contentions and rallied thousands of converts. As this momentum peaked in late July and early August, opponents began to hope that they might, after all, prevent the bill from being passed.

9

Prelude
to the Congressional Debates

Impatiently, James V. Forrestal was chafing in his job as a White House administrative assistant. Forrestal had left his lucrative position as president of the Wall Street firm of Dillon, Read for governmental service just after the fall of France, but he was bored by his initial duties dealing with Latin American economic coordination. On a hot afternoon in late July, he dashed off a note to financier Bernard Baruch: "What are your views on the chances of the conscription measure going through? That seems to me now to be one of the most important things to get done."[1] Baruch, who had directed the War Industries Board in World War I, gave an experienced answer: "You will find, the longer you are there, that many people talk about a thing, but they do nothing about it. But I bet you the conscription bill can be put over. Wanna bet?"[2]

A week later, on the same day that the Senate Military Affairs Committee reported favorably on the Burke bill, President Roosevelt appointed Forrestal to the newly created post of undersecretary of the navy. The wager with Baruch about conscription was quickly forgotten as Forrestal immersed himself in his new naval responsibilities, not the least of which were the pending negotiations for the transfer of fifty destroyers to England. Nevertheless, the fate of the selective-service bill still remained "one of the most important things" in Washington, and its supporters, both in and out of Congress, were mobilizing to "put it over." Its opponents were also organizing.

Despite mounting signs of opposition, the events of July had been encouraging to advocates of the draft. At the War Department, "a happy shop again," both the new secretary and his assistant were vigorously pushing selective service.[3] The General Staff had reversed its previous stand. Public-opinion polls continued to show growing majorities. When the Senate Military Affairs Committee adjourned for the weekend on Friday 26 July, prospects for early enactment seemed bright. Having added the final touches,

156

the committee planned to give the Burke bill its official endorsement on Tuesday, then to take it to the Senate floor. Debate was tentatively scheduled for Wednesday 31 July, and optimists were predicting passage by a substantial majority within ten days. The army, according to a front-page article in the Sunday *Times*, was "poised" to conduct the "giant lottery" that a draft law would activate.[4]

As it stood, the bill remained faithful to the original in essentials. Home-defense units had been left to future legislation, but all American males from the age of eighteen to sixty-four were required to register, and those aged twenty-one to forty-five were liable for a year's training. The Senate committee had voted only minor variations thus far, strengthening the penalties against draft dodgers, making the exemption of ministers mandatory, and revising the section on reemployment.[5] The committee had postponed a vote only because several members were out of Washington until Tuesday.[6]

Grenville Clark was already preparing for the floor debate. Confident that both committees would report favorably, Clark regarded the Senate contest as crucial. As early as 23 July he had urged Lewis Sanders, who was then organizing local committees in the Midwest, to "bring pressure from home states of the various senators to encourage their support of the bill where they are already favorable, and to remove or minimize their opposition where they are unfavorable." He planned to "canvass with Burke and Wadsworth" as to which senators needed to be "worked on, whether they are favorable but want support, or unfavorable and need to have their hostility diminished."[7] If the Senate were to vote favorably, Clark reasoned, the House would follow easily because of the commanding influence that Wadsworth exercised in the lower chamber.[8]

By this time, Howard C. Petersen and William T. Stewart had returned to their law offices. To take their places, Clark managed to obtain two more young men from New York law firms on a similar "loan" basis. Malcolm Langford of Cadwalder, Wickersham, and Taft joined the NEC from mid July to late August, running the headquarters at the Hotel Carlton after Clark left on 1 August. Franklin Canfield came from the firm of Sullivan and Cromwell, which he had been a Paris representative for until the Nazi invasion had forced him to return to the United States. Canfield thereupon offered his services to Clark and stayed with the NEC through the next winter. Able, articulate, and energetic, these young NEC volunteers, as Lewis Hershey later put it, "practically wore out shoe leather" in the next several weeks as they buttonholed senators and congressmen.[9]

The first step came on the afternoon of 24 July, when Clark, Senator Burke, and Langford together went over the entire roster of ninety-six senators, trying to predict each vote. After careful appraisals, they set up five classifications: (1) definitely favorable; (2) probably favorable, but "worth checking up on''; (3) probably unfavorable, but worth some effort; (4) attitude unknown; and (5) definitely unfavorable. The three men hoped that ''personal interviews by just the right men with certain senators and careful reasoned letters in other cases'' would be the most effective method of persuasion.[10]

A twelve-page mimeographed document recorded the results of this first canvass. A table divided the senators into six regional groupings: New England, Middle Atlantic, South, Middle West, Northwest and Mountain, and Southwest and Coast states. A duplicate estimate on the twenty-two southern senators was also sent to Douglas Arant, a native of Birmingham, who agreed to assume responsibility for the southerners. Clark, Langford, and Burke produced the tally shown in Table 1.[11] This analysis shows that the sponsors felt reasonably certain about only thirty-two senators—those in the ''definitely favorable'' and ''definitely unfavorable'' categories. They planned to focus most intensely on the sixty-four men in the three middle groups.

TABLE 1

Class	South	New England	Middle Atlantic	Midwest	Northwest/ Mountain	Southwest/ Coast	Totals
Definitely favorable	7	5	1	7	2	2	24
Probably favorable	10	3	6	3	5	4	31
Probably unfavorable	0	1	0	5	2	2	10
Unknown	5	3	5	3	4	3	23
Definitely unfavorable	0	0	0	4	3	1	8
Totals	22	12	12	22	16	12	96

Their estimates, it turned out, erred badly in some instances. For example, the entry for Johnson of Colorado read: ''Senator Edwin C. Johnson—Dem. Class 2—probably favorable. *Remarks:* Important man as member of Military Affairs Committee. G. C. and M. S. L. to see him.'' This optimistic appraisal seemed to be confirmed by Lewis Sanders, who wrote that a Colorado friend of the senator's had said that Johnson was ''originally opposed to the Burke-Wadsworth bill but . . . his objections have now been taken care of.''[12] Johnson, ''a great bull moose of a man'' who certainly looked militant, in actuality became the one member of the Senate committee who worked closely with Howard Beale and other pacifist opponents.[13] His hostility to conscription, while not as loud as that of Burton Wheeler or Rush

Holt, proved just as consistent. Other similar errors occurred: both Prentiss Brown of Michigan and Frederick Van Nuys of Indiana were labeled "definitely favorable," whereas both eventually voted nay. In contrast, Matthew M. Neely of West Virginia, listed as "unfavorable" because he would allegedly fall under the influence of John L. Lewis, wound up voting for the bill.

In general, however, Clark and his cohorts determined fairly accurately where support and opposition lay. In New England they expected strong backing from such men as Wallace White of Maine, Styles Bridges of New Hampshire, Warren F. Austin of Vermont, and Henry Cabot Lodge of Massachusetts. The Middle Atlantic region looked doubtful, although such senators as Warren Barbour of New Jersey, Robert F. Wagner of New York, and Joseph Guffey of Pennsylvania eventually voted aye. Tydings of Maryland, who had thrown cold water on the project originally, gave the bill a timely boost by coming out for it in the midst of floor debate. The South stood almost as solidly for conscription as it was Democratic: even such reputed isolationists as Robert Reynolds and Josiah Bailey, both of North Carolina, supported the bill. Although administration stalwarts like Byrnes and Barkley showed only mild enthusiasm, the NEC could count on Sheppard of Texas, Lister Hill of Alabama, and Pepper of Florida to be wholehearted proponents.

They anticipated that the strongest opposition would be from the West. In the central states, proponents had to reckon with Bennett Champ Clark of Missouri, Taft of Ohio, and Vandenberg of Michigan. The conscriptionist cause also suffered when the Senate's most respected member, octogenarian George W. Norris of Nebraska, refused to support the draft, despite his much-publicized break with the isolationists the preceding year. Norris told his constituents that he believed in the sincerity of President Roosevelt's pledges against war, but peacetime conscription smacked of the totalitarian systems he opposed abroad; he would not vote for it.[14] Gerald P. Nye of North Dakota, Wheeler of Montana, and Johnson of Colorado loomed as formidable opponents in the mountain states. West Coast opposition included Lewis B. Schwellenbach of Washington, Pat McCarran of Nevada, and Sheridan Downey and Hiram Johnson of California. Partly offsetting this phalanx, however, were such friendly senators as Burke of Nebraska, Minton of Indiana,[15] Scott Lucas of Illinois, Josh Lee of Oklahoma, and Joseph C. O'Mahoney of Wyoming. Republican Chan Gurney of South Dakota neutralized Nye's opposition by coming out strongly for the bill. Gurney later told Stimson that he had received only one negative letter from his constituents and that all eight South Dakota dailies applauded his stand.[16]

With this roster as a starting point, Clark and his colleagues set to work on individual senators. They "farmed out" some of the personal contact. Ralph Lowell was asked to get in touch with Walsh of Massachusetts, a doubtful supporter; Cornelius Wickersham agreed to write to James M. Mead of New York; Pattsburger Duncan Harris assumed the task of following up earlier efforts with James J. Davis of Pennsylvania; Kenneth Budd promised to prod Warren Barbour of New Jersey; and Adler and James Thomson tried to soften Bennett Clark's opposition. An unexpected bonus materialized when former New Hampshire Governor Robert Bass came to Washington on other business, spent four hours with Senator Charles Tobey, and finally persuaded the crusty isolationist to support selective service. Grenville Clark suggested that someone in St. Louis be asked to write to junior Senator Harry S. Truman.[17] For the most part, however, Clark and two or three assistants in Washington carried the burden; as each senator was interviewed, they summarized his position just as Langford recorded a visit with Chavez of New Mexico: "Senator Dennis Chavez—Dem. Class 2. Interviewed Wednesday, July 31, a.m. Noncommittal as to position. Will read bill and hearings carefully. Very much bothered by heavy mail in opposition to the bill. Says representative cross-section of all his people are writing him urging him to oppose. Conclusion: Essential that as many good letters as possible be written from New Mexico."[18]

The flood of oppositionist mail that worried Senator Chavez had begun to pour in during the last week of July, and by 1 August it was reaching overflow proportions. Senator Wheeler said he had received two thousand letters over the weekend; Vandenberg reported ten thousand.[19] Chairman Sheppard later counted more than forty thousand letters, most of them expressing opposition.[20] That this deluge was washing away any chance for early passage of the Burke bill became evident from conversations with several opposition senators.

Vandenberg, for example, seemed to be friendly enough, willing to listen to their arguments. "But look at this mail," he protested, pointing to a stack of letters on his desk. "I couldn't possibly support a bill when ninety percent of my constituents are against it."[21] From Senator Taft came much the same reception. The controlling factor in the Ohioan's position was the belief that the United States had little to fear from the Axis. He was no pacifist; rather, he simply contended that the absence of a real threat made large-scale preparation unnecessary.[22] Taft later commented to Clark: "I don't know that I have ever voted on a measure with as much confidence that my view is the correct one."[23] Clark and Arant also interviewed Wheeler, with whom they had worked during their common fight against FDR's court plan in 1937. This time they found no basis for cooperation. The "emergency," Wheeler insisted, was completely artificial, a war hysteria whipped up by the interventionists. Volunteering had not been given an adequate trial. Once men were drafted, no one could tell where Roosevelt would send them. Wheeler boasted that he had received thousands of encouraging letters that supported his stand.

The torrent of opposition mail, of course, did not have entirely spontaneous origins. Liberal peace workers, especially Frederick Libby and Dorothy Detzer, had stepped up their efforts since the Democratic Convention in Chicago. Norman Thomas's challenge to President Roosevelt to allow the opposition further hearings resulted in the appearance of such prominent clergymen as Bishop W. Appleton Lawrence, Monsignor Michael Ready, and Dr. Harry Emerson Fosdick before the House committee on 30 July.[24] Over the weekend of 27/28 July, thousands of letters were mailed from the National Council for the Prevention of War (NCPW) and from WILPF headquarters in Washington to branch members around the country, urging them to send wires and letters to senators and congressmen.[25] Howard Beale dispatched mimeographed letters, requesting similar responses, to more than three hundred of his friends.[26] Local protests were already occurring: in Hartford, Connecticut, before an audience of five hundred, Oswald Garrison Villard debated conscription with Republican Congressman William J. Miller; Villard won the debate, notwithstanding the crowd's initial sympathy for his opponent, a double-amputee veteran of World War I.[27] In Akron, scores of women from the Ohio Peace Council besieged the district office of Congressman Dow Harter, despite 100-degree temperatures, to urge him to vote against the draft.[28] In Montana, veteran peace worker Jeannette Rankin, renowned for her vote against war as a congresswoman in 1917, won the Republican nomination for that state's second congressional seat by a thousand-vote margin; the victorious Rankin arrived in Washington on 29 July to participate in the anticonscription rally sponsored by the Keep America Out of War Congress.[29]

The climax of this initial onslaught against the draft came on Thursday 1 August 1940. Frederick Libby's diary tells the story:

All a.m. delegates pour in. They pass through my office in droves of 20–25. Warren [Mullen, NCPW secretary] tells them about their senators, what he knows. I tell them what questions they must be able to answer—'Isn't this Democratic?' etc. They ask questions too. Then they go to the Hill, and another group comes in. 260 delegates from 23 states register at our office. . . . P.M. Delegates come and go and leave reports. Confer w. some. Cars bearing signs ad[vertising] the m[eeting] go to big govt. b[uildings] and parade back & forth. 8:15 Mass rally at the Raleigh [Hotel]. 1100. Some turned away. Charles Boss [Methodist minister] chairman. Does well. . . . Rt. Rev. M[onsignor] Barry O'Toole. Fay Bennett [official of Youth Committee against War]. Sen. Rush Holt. Norman Thomas. . . . Sen. [Gerald P.] Nye. Sen. [Burton] Wheeler. While Rush Holt is speaking, an ex-marine who in elevator said he had 'come to throw tomatoes at Wheeler' makes a disturbance, comes to front & threatens Holt & is taken out. No harm done except reports in press. A good m[eeting], enthusiasm genuine. Not on radio. Too long.[30]

The upsurge of opposition clearly worried the NEC leaders. Grenville Clark at first thought the opponents were obtaining "canned" telegrams, "largely based on misstatements and misunderstanding." Congress needed to be "made aware of the real and solid opinion," he wired to New York headquarters. "Important. . . . Get everyone possible to wire or write their Senators today." From Gen. Sherman Miles, chief of intelligence, Clark also received permission to publicize a letter that Miles had written emphasizing that, despite the success of mechanized forces in the German blitzkrieg, "infantry was still the basic arm" and that sufficient numbers could only be recruited through conscription. Clark, after removing Miles's name, had several thousand copies of the letter mimeographed and sent to NEC members around the country, urging "a counterattack in the shape of a wave of letters to Congress." Ralph Barton Perry of the Harvard Defense Group mailed similar letters to the thirteen hundred academicians who had signed an earlier petition in support of the Burke-Wadsworth bill.[31] It was doubtful, however, that such improvised efforts to encourage letters and wires could match the longer-established techniques of the peace groups. Secretary Stimson also fretted. Opposition to the draft, he wrote in his diary, was fomented by "the well organized groups of pacifists and aided by the fact that the Germans have not been making any invasion of Great Britain," thus suggesting "a lull in the war." He also noted that "the president has taken no striking lead in regard to the Selective Service law and that is reflected in the Congress."[32]

Stimson did not err in thinking that the draft bill faced trouble. The atmosphere had definitely changed when the Senate committee met on 30 July for what was supposed to be the formal endorsement of the Burke bill. Partisan feeling, remarkably absent during earlier hearings, suddenly came to a boil as Styles Bridges demanded that the president clarify his position on the bill before the committee took action. Fellow Republicans Gurney of South Dakota and Thomas of Idaho immediately supported Bridges. Thereupon Democrats Minton and Lee accused the Republicans of playing politics with national defense. Amid such pyrotechnics, agreement became impossible, and the committee postponed consideration of the draft bill to meet the White House request, reiterated that morning, for authorization to call the National Guard into federal service.[33]

Bridges's demand evidently nettled the president. In his press conference that afternoon, FDR snapped that he had already said what he was going to say about draft legislation. As to whether senators were really delaying because of his own silence, Roosevelt doubted that he was the real cause of the slowdown.[34]

The president's comment about previous remarks referred to an earlier statement on manpower in his message of 10 July. FDR had prepared this presidential message prior to the confirmation of Stimson and Knox, and only a last-minute suggestion from Budget Director Harold Smith had prompted the president to consult with his new appointees.[35] Stimson received Roosevelt's draft message on 9 July, the afternoon the Senate confirmed Stimson. Studying the speech that night, the new secretary of war saw no comment on the draft. When he pointed out this omission the next morning, FDR asked him to compose a paragraph for inclusion in the address, which Stimson did.[36] Although the president softened Stimson's language considerably, it represented his strongest statement to date. After a long discussion of armaments and equipment, Roosevelt said: "The Congress is now considering the enactment of a system of selective training for developing the necessary manpower to operate this materiel and manpower to fill army non-combat needs. In this way we can make certain that when this modern materiel becomes available, it will be placed in the hands of troops trained, seasoned, and ready, and that replacement materiel can be guaranteed."[37]

But neither this general statement nor his somewhat facetious comment about the "draft" in accepting his third-term nomination two weeks later constituted the vigorous and specific endorsement of the Burke-Wadsworth bill that its sponsors were seeking. Undoubtedly, FDR was still feeling his way politically, not wanting to commit himself prematurely. He told his budget director on 30 July that he still hoped to combine "universal military and civilian training . . . in connection with the pending compulsory service legislation."[38] He wrote in a similar vein to Norman Thomas a day later.[39] Roosevelt also showed annoyance that Wadsworth and, especially, Burke had cosponsored the bill.[40] He had even suggested to Stimson the desirability of attaching the names of two administration supporters to the measure. Clark took the matter up with Burke and Wadsworth. "They are such fine men," he reported to Stimson, "that they care nothing about getting credit, and Burke said he was willing to take his name off the bill entirely and was sure Mr. Wadsworth would also."[41] But Clark himself stood flatly opposed. Their bill had been publicized throughout the nation as the Burke-Wadsworth bill, he argued, and a new label would cause confusion in the public mind, thus weakening, rather than strengthening, its chances for passage. The NEC refused even to consider FDR's roundabout proposal.

The president, one should remember, had other important policy decisions pressing on him in addition to the draft. Bottlenecks in the defense industry were awaiting White House judgments in regard to excess profits and other tax legislation. Japanese demands against French Indo-China and Burma posed new problems.[42] Most important, the vital issue of aid to England was still hanging fire. Earlier British requests for destroyers, torpedo boats, and military aircraft had been blocked by the Walsh amendment to the appropriations bill of 28 June, which prohibited the sale of any United States equipment unless the chiefs of staff certified that it was "not essential to U.S.

defense.''[43] Despite importunities from cabinet ''hawks'' and old friends such as Felix Frankfurter and Benjamin Cohen, Roosevelt refused to ask Congress to approve special aid to England—at least not until he had received assurances about the British fleet and believed that England had a fair chance of surviving a German attack.[44] Meanwhile, armed with classified information from the British ambassador about naval losses, William Allen White's committee and the Century Group stepped up public agitation for the transfer of fifty destroyers to the British.[45] When FDR embarked on a three-day cruise down the Potomac from 28 to 30 July, he undoubtedly talked about more than fishing and poker with fellow passengers Frank Knox and Carl Vinson, chairman of the House Naval Affairs Committee. FDR probably discussed the status of the draft bill with Senator Morris Sheppard, the other congressional guest aboard the presidential yacht.[46] On returning to the White House, Roosevelt received the strongest message yet from Prime Minister Churchill requesting naval assistance: ''Mr. President, with great respect I must tell you that in the long history of the world this is a thing to do now.''[47] Pressed by friends and foes alike, FDR would not move until he was ready. ''I am feeling a good deal like an early Christian martyr,'' he joked to an old friend.[48]

Whatever the precise reasons for Roosevelt's cautious approach, there was truth in Arthur Krock's judgment that his ''do nothing attitude'' was ''endangering the passage of a good conscription act.''[49] To counteract what seemed a flabby stand on the part of the chief executive, Stimson appeared personally before the House committee on 31 July to argue for the bill. After braving the flash bulbs of photographers, the grim-faced Secretary spoke about the nature of public office. Describing both himself and the committee members as ''trustees of the safety and protection of this country,'' he said that a trustee must follow the lessons of America's past military experiences. ''We have always had a penchant for volunteering,'' Stimson declared. ''That system has been tried again and again, and in very serious wars as well as some wars that have not been serious it has proved a costly failure.''[50]

If some form of selective draft offered the only effective method, Stimson claimed that it also guaranteed the fairest system. Selective service ''distributes the primary duty of national defense upon every citizen and . . . distributes that duty so that every man may serve where he is most effective.''[51] The draft would also make it possible, if necessary, to wage modern war without too severely disrupting the economic and industrial life of the nation. ''The real question,'' he told the committee, ''is, 'Are we in peril today; do we need to prepare?' If so, it is an imperative first step . . . to make available the manpower necessary.''[52]

Impressive in his formal statement, the secretary proved to be equally eloquent in answering questions. At one point, Congressman Charles A. Clason tried to pin him down:

"Do I understand," the Massachusetts isolationist asked, "that you believe that this conscription bill should be made a permanent policy of the United States?"

"I have not said anything about it," Stimson replied, "and I do not intend to answer that. We are talking about a problem that confronts us now and you are asking me a hypothetical question that only God Almighty can answer."

"There is a date set in this bill, 1945," Clason persisted, "at which time it shall terminate. Do you feel that that is a proper provision in this bill?"

"I think that it is a very modest provision," parried Stimson, "designed to disarm the criticisms of such gentlemen as yourself."[53]

The secretary also dealt with the inevitable question of a further trial for volunteers. Congressman Albert G. Rutherford stated at one point: "If the public is satisfied that after a definite effort by the War Department it is impossible to obtain voluntary enlistments, then they will fall in with this policy much more readily. And I believe it would be a good thing to satisfy the people that such could not be done. It would place the committee in a position to. . . ." Stimson interrupted: "I think you have only to call the members of the War Department and ask them that. It is the same kind of dilatory question which has been shown to be incompatible with modern war, the danger of modern war, in the case of all those countries that I enumerated in my statement. It was always a question of wait—wait—wait—not realizing that they were confronted by an enemy who does not wait."[54]

Waiting was becoming more and more attractive, however, as evidenced by the delays in the Senate committee. "There is strong opposition developing to this bill within the committee," Senator Tobey confided to one of Clark's friends. "Some modifications seem probable."[55] The Washington rumor mill was buzzing loudly. An officer of the General Staff told journalist Frank Hanighen that General Marshall and the other military witnesses still had doubts about conscription. "I knew their heart wasn't in it. They were carrying out orders," he said to Hanighen.[56] One of Major Hershey's assistants attended a congressional cocktail party at the Army and Navy Club and reported unanimous sentiment that "the War Department is intentionally putting the wet blanket on volunteering and is cooperating in a new Roosevelt something-or-other." He noted that "whenever the word 'emergency' is used, the men would fly into convulsive speeches. Apparently they consider the word as meaning 'a phoney Rooseveltian-created status.' "[57] Conversely, some New Deal loyalists thought the bill a plot concocted by Republicans and the army and urged the White House to deny being its parent.[58] Such confusion, reinforced by the upsurge of opposition mail, caused the Senate committee to back away from a bill that it had been ready to approve a week earlier. The first serious display of doubt came in an amendment by Austin of

Vermont to require only males in the age range of twenty-one to thirty-one to register.[59]

Such a change had been brewing for several days. Major Hershey and one or two aides had been attending the executive sessions of the committee, and on 29 July, Hershey told Stimson that the senators had complained about a wide range of registration. Hershey urged that the army accept a narrower age range. Stimson, however, told Hershey to stand firm and talk the matter over with Clark by telephone.[60] The General Staff, of course, had no objection to the 21–31 age range, since that provision had been in the original Joint Army and Navy Committee bill. Army spokesmen had argued all along that registration for ages eighteen to sixty-four would prove unpopular, unnecessary, unwieldy, and expensive. This predilection for their own program, plus Hershey's sensitivity to the political pressures on the committee, meant that army representatives did little to oppose, and probably even encouraged, Austin's amendment.

The differences between the NEC and the General Staff went deeper than a mere dispute over mechanics. The army remained interested primarily in the easiest, quickest, and most efficient method of procuring manpower. In carrying out its mission of hemispheric defense, General Marshall and his staff were not planning to build a large army for service abroad in 1940. The Plattsburg sponsors, however, had not only seen their bill as being necessary for creating a much-larger army but also for the psychological preparation of the entire nation. Interventionists at heart, Clark and his NEC associates envisioned the draft as the first step in a redefinition of national security that posited the survival of England as being more important than the defense of South America. Narrowing the age limits meant that only eleven to twelve million men would register, as compared to forty-two million.[61] To the civilian sponsors, such a change would have destroyed the secondary purpose of their bill by leaving a majority of the male population unaffected. Their insistence on wide age limits also reflected their belief in national service, nurtured since Plattsburg days, as well as their romantic notion that veterans of World War I could still perform useful military service. What they found difficult to comprehend, however, was that the eighteen to sixty-four provision made for bad politics, that people confused registration with actual induction, and, as FDR told his cabinet a few days later, "a great many old people" thought they would "find themselves in a military training camp."[62] Moreover, from the isolationist perspective, what Clark and his friends considered psychological preparation for national unity and national service was deemed psychological preparation for a war that the United States had no business to enter.

Clark gathered some of the NEC officers in Adler's downtown office. Convinced that a complete inventory of national manpower was in fact "the heart of the bill," they wired Hershey, urging that "the legislation should be dealt with . . . from the standpoint of pulling the whole nation together for the national effort which . . . we may be obliged to make. . . . Nothing can do that so effectively as the wide registration provisions of the present bill.'' As to Hershey's prediction that wider limits would hurt the chances of passing the bill, they remained ''unanimously unconvinced.'' Relying on their own soundings among like-minded elites, they contended: ''Quite to the contrary we have found that these very provisions have brought strong support to the bill . . . [and] have given confidence to the youth . . . that no effort is being made to foist the whole burden of military service on the young alone. These provisions have also appealed to those who . . . would be left out if a narrow registration . . . were enacted.''[63]

But the tide had turned against them. In the face of the president's vacillation, Democratic ranks began to waver. Senator Byrnes told reporters that he thought registration of men eighteen to sixty-four would be unnecessarily expensive; Barkley similarly admitted that he saw no reason for registering men in their sixties.[64] The youthful California Congressman Jerry Voorhis, one of the New Deal's strongest supporters, circulated a memorandum calling the Burke-Wadsworth bill ''the most fundamental departure from American Democracy as we have known it . . . in 150 years.'' Voorhis advocated a combination of vocational and military training, with strong voluntary features.[65] Such pressure had its effect. Despite Chairman Sheppard's effort to hold the line, the Senate committee on 31 July approved the proposal to register only the 21–31 age group.[66]

Austin's amendment proved to be only the first of several amendments that delayed and weakened the bill. By the end of the week, the senators had, among other things, changed the title to simply ''A Bill to Provide for the Common Defense and to Increase and Train the Personnel of the Armed Forces of the United States.''[67] While the change occurred mainly for cosmetic reasons, it seemed to be further proof that the army's conception of the bill as being strictly a businesslike means of producing manpower had replaced the sponsors' objective of achieving important, if intangible, results of a broader nature. In addition, against the advice of the War Department, the committee bowed slightly to advocates of volunteering by voting to allow voluntary enlistments to continue concurrently with the operation of the draft. After consultation with army representatives, the committee did reject a proposal by Senators Lee and Bridges to limit the number of inductees in one year to eight hundred thousand or one million.[68]

Although the NEC believed the narrow age range had come close to emasculating their bill, the New Yorkers still had ideas of restoring the original provisions when the Senate began floor debate. Their hopes picked up momentarily when Gen. Hugh Johnson denounced the Austin amendment in his syndicated column of 2 August. Johnson recalled that the draft had started with the twenty-one to thirty age group during World War I, but eventually widened to eighteen to forty-five. ''Why can't we learn from past blunders?''

he asked. He pointed out that drafting the 21–30 group in 1917/18 had meant taking "key men out of necessary war industries and ruthlessly . . . invad[ing] dependent families." Johnson also cited the imperative need for "specialists of all kinds . . . right now," arguing that "registration and classification of men between 18 and 50 is far more likely to produce better and more qualified specialists more quickly than one of men between 21 and 30." Johnson's final argument stressed fairness and equity: "As long as men are equally fit and available with equally slight disruption of other national interests, their relative obligations of citizenship are equal and not to be measured by some arbitrary classification in age groups."[69]

The New Yorkers seized upon this helpful piece of propaganda, reprinting and circulating thousands of copies of it. To each member of the Senate committee they sent wires, citing Johnson's column and asking that the issue be reconsidered.[70] "Our courage here has fully revived," Clark wired Wadsworth on 3 August.[71] To General Palmer, Clark predicted: "We may get a better bill out of the House. . . . Letters and telegrams are now the big thing to concentrate on."[72] These pleas came to naught, however, as Senator Gurney wrote Clark that he agreed with the wide age range of the original bill, but "I am just as definitely convinced that [it] would have no chance of passing."[73] Even more disheartening, Congressman Wadsworth rejected the suggestion that a representative of the NEC sit alongside army drafting experts when the House committee drew up its final bill.[74] More and more, the draft bill seemed to be caught up in political machinery beyond the Plattsburgers' control.

These amendments notwithstanding, the Senate committee's favorable vote on the Burke bill on 5 August boosted some spirits. The bill went to the Senate floor endorsed by thirteen out of eighteen members, including nine Democrats and four Republicans. One Democrat, one Republican, and one Farmer-Laborite (Ernest Lundeen) were opposed, while one member, Harry Slattery of Illinois, was absent. Downey of California, still urging a "small mechanized army," abstained from voting. In its final action, the committee also voted down a motion by Johnson of Colorado to hear further testimony from former Secretary Woodring.[75]

The Majority Report gave conspicuous emphasis to the bill's defensive purposes. Obviously afraid of the charge that conscription would lead to intervention, the senators stated:

> Congress recently has made the greatest peacetime appropriations in the history of this Nation, for the purpose of providing the weapons and machines of *defense*. . . . Weapons and machines of *defense* are not enough. Weapons without men are as futile as men without weapons. Today's *defensive* weapons are complex in nature, requiring months of training to operate. It would be criminal to place these weapons and machines in the hands of untrained men for *defensive* purposes. It would be criminal to subject these

untrained men to the hazards of a *defensive* campaign without adequate training. It would be criminal to give the Nation a false sense of security by the mere possession of *defensive* armaments and a corresponding lack of trained men. [italics added][76]

In a Minority Report, Senators Johnson, Lundeen, and John Thomas of Idaho made it clear that they could support conscription as a war measure, but not in peacetime. "Regimentation of American life as provided for in the Burke-Wadsworth bill in peacetime," they protested, "is utterly repugnant to American Democracy and American traditions." In the end, they advocated a "thorough trial" of voluntary enlistment before resorting to a "Hitlerized method" with its "far-reaching implication of militarism and imperialism."[77]

In their argument, opposing senators relied heavily upon a letter that Woodring had written to Senator Vandenberg, released to the press the week before. As one who could presumably speak with authority, Woodring did not "see the need for compulsory training at this time" and urged that there be no draft until "the chief of staff of the United States Army has first advised the Senate in writing that the voluntary system has completely broken down." Woodring added that if "paternalism" had really "broken down the moral stamina and fiber of American youth" and thereby "broken down the voluntary instinct to serve in a patriotic way, we then unquestionably will have to adopt a compulsory system for the defense of this country." Woodring believed, however, that the volunteer spirit still lived. He challenged the Senate to demand from the War Department some proof that "our present quota of enlistments . . . have failed to be reached in any instance."[78]

Without consciously intending to do so, the Minority Report forecast subsequent strategy by the opposition. Just as the report did, isolationists on Capitol Hill continued to condemn the bill on many counts, especially for its "un-American" quality. But in time, sensing that they could not defeat the bill outright, they were to fall back on a crippling substitute that sought to "give the volunteer system more time" before resorting to conscription. Senator La Follette grimly confided to his wife on 5 August: "There will be a real fight on it, unless we can get an amendment in to give the voluntary method a fair trial."[79]

In New York, Clark tried to give the NEC's Steering Committee an estimate of what was happening in Washington. Some opponents, he reported, reasoned like Senator Taft, who refused to recognize any immediate threat to the United States. Many others, especially the rabid anti-New Dealers, did not trust Congress to check the chief executive and thus feared the bill for the additional power it would give to Franklin Roosevelt. Claiming that the army itself did not really desire conscription, more and more senators demanded that volunteering be tried further. Finally, in Clark's estimate, the fact that neither the president nor Willkie had made a clear-cut statement on conscription meant that strong party men on both sides were still sitting on the fence.[80]

At this critical point, with the opposition gaining strength, the president unexpectedly stepped in. Only three days before, when he had peevishly refused to comment, he had seemed less willing than ever to commit himself. Barkley and Byrnes, his chief spokesmen in the Senate, were giving ground, and the majority leader had gone out of his way to disassociate the administration from the bill. Byrnes had reportedly urged the postponement of any vote until after the fall elections.[81] The Senate committee had trimmed the bill until, as columnist Mark Sullivan wrote, with some exaggeration, "it was little more than a skeleton proposal . . . [and] the whole idea of conscription might die, unless Mr. Roosevelt came to the rescue."[82]

On 2 August an anxious Stimson decided to take matters into his own hands. Having unofficially assumed the duty of prodding the president, he and Secretary Knox went to the White House that Friday afternoon, determined to get a decision on a number of important issues, most notably conscription and naval assistance to England. Thus ensued, in Harold Ickes's words, "the most important cabinet meeting that I have attended since the president came into power."[83] Not only did FDR agree to explore a plan to exchange fifty destroyers for British bases in North America, but he surprised Stimson by his decisiveness about the draft. When the secretary mentioned "how I was getting word from some people—old McKellar particularly—that he hadn't received any orders from the White House," the president said he had dealt with the matter at length in his press conference that morning. FDR also agreed to "call some of the leaders in and make it clear to them that they must get busy on that bill," which he regarded as "one of the two great fundamental pillars of national defense," along with aid to England.[84]

Reports of the press conference, on the front pages the next day, provided welcome relief to the backers of selective service. The president had opened his session by chattering inconsequentially about weekend plans to go to Hyde Park. A pause, as if that were all. Then Fred Essary of the *Baltimore Sun* spoke up.

> "There is a very definite feeling, Mr. President, in congressional circles," he said, "that you are not very hot about this conscription legislation and, as a result, it really is languishing."
>
> "It depends on which paper you read," FDR shot back, his cigarette holder at a jaunty angle.
>
> "Well," countered Essary, "I read my own, which I believe in."

The president threw up his hands and said he was damned if he did, damned if he didn't. If he had sent up a prefabricated bill to the Capitol tagged "must" legislation, he would be criticized for playing dictator; now he was being blasted for not telling Congress what to do. Putting aside flippancy, he began to talk straightforwardly, calmly, seriously. The European war had taught fundamental lessons, he said. The public had learned not only that America must have sufficient numbers of war machines but that it must also have trained men to use them. "For purposes of defense," he continued, "we have to have men who are already trained beforehand. In doing that we save lives—we save human lives. That is the important thing. We all know from experience that in an untrained army or an untrained navy, relatively, the casualties . . . are much higher than in . . . the trained army and navy. . . . It is a case of saving lives."[85] Finally, the essential point became axiomatic: "You cannot get a sufficiently trained force of all kinds at the front, in the navy yards and the arsenals, transportation, supply system, and munitions output, you cannot get it by just passing an Act of Congress when war breaks out, and you cannot get it by the mere volunteer system." For these reasons the president favored an immediate draft.

> "There is a very quotable sentence right there, if you will permit it," Essary remarked.
> "What is it?" asked FDR.
> "That you are distinctly in favor of a selective training bill—"
> "And consider it essential to adequate national defense," the president interjected. "Quote that."[86]

Although he still had not endorsed the specific terms of the Burke-Wadsworth bill, Roosevelt's bravura performance had finally given his unequivocal approval of the draft itself.

Even though he had vacillated and hedged since the bill had been introduced in June, the president showed real political courage in coming out for the draft at this juncture. The third-term issue still loomed large, as many Democrats continued to grumble at a step that Roosevelt had justified in terms of national unity.[87] Wendell Willkie, whom FDR regarded as "at heart a totalitarian," had refused to comment publicly on all major issues until his formal acceptance speech on 17 August.[88] Moreover, many of those who were urging conscription and aid to England actually opposed Roosevelt's reelection in November.[89] Thus, when the president decided to move on both issues, he hoped to do so in a way that would minimize partisan recriminations. Much of the decisive cabinet meeting of 2 August was taken up with discussion of a plan to use William Allen White as a go-between with Willkie to obtain bipartisan approval of a destroyer/bases deal. "The feeling," wrote Harold Ickes, "was that the one preoccupying thought on the Hill is what may happen to the British navy. If we could go up with a bill frankly saying that we were going to sell fifty reconditioned destroyers in consideration of the possible coming over here of the British navy and of the granting of basing rights in British naval bases," then Congress might go along.[90] Such a quid pro quo,

FDR told Lord Lothian the next day, would serve as "molasses" to soothe congressional opposition.[91] But a resolution approving a destroyer deal was still in the talking stage, and support from Willkie and Republican congressional leaders remained problematical. Roosevelt's decision, therefore, to give public backing to the draft as "one of the two fundamental pillars of national defense" meant taking a considerable political risk.[92]

The temptation to remain aloof must have been strong for FDR. Notwithstanding favorable public-opinion polls, the opposition seemed to be gaining, rather than losing, strength. Senators Wheeler and Johnson told Howard Beale "to keep the letters and wires coming, that they are having tremendous effect . . . [and] are running 100–1 or 70–1 against the bill."[93] Loyal Democrats were urging Roosevelt to repudiate the bill. Congressman A. J. Sabath of Illinois wired the president on 2 August, the day of his press conference: "Sentiment of country and members are against the Burke-Wadsworth bill. It was cleverly concocted to create prejudice against you. . . . It would be diplomatic to first issue a proclamation for voluntary enlistment. I strongly urge you to state that the Burke-Wadsworth bill is not your bill . . . that neither Burke nor Wadsworth have consulted [you?] or were requested to introduce bill."[94] The day before, Senator Vic Donahey of Ohio pleaded with FDR in a similar fashion. Letters from his Ohio constituents were "pouring in and they show 100 to 1 against the conscription measure." The draft was "fraught with political disaster in Ohio." Without an amendment that would continue voluntary enlistments, Donahey would be compelled "to vote against and urge the defeat of the pending bill."[95] A few days later, Senator Francis T. Maloney of Connecticut warned Edwin Watson: "I don't think his [FDR's] enemies could dig a deeper pit for his burial in November than the one prepared by the Conscription Bill."[96]

The president's long reply to Donahey, which was deeply earnest and sincere, shows him in his best light: "I would be derelict in my duty if I did not tell the American people of the real danger which confronts them at the present time." FDR's warnings had been "scoffed at on many occasions." But "too many people in Scandinavia, Poland, Czechoslovakia, Holland, Belgium, and France—and in England too—looked at the danger with political eyes, injected politics into their own domestic pictures and were, therefore, totally unprepared to meet the shock and the invasion when they came." Even with the draft in 1917, it had taken a year to get an army prepared for war. Roosevelt could not "guarantee such a period free from attack in the days to come. No American can afford to bet on a repetition of such circumstances." In conclusion he appealed to Donahey's patriotism: "I want to plead with you to banish political considerations from your mind. This is the last place where any president or senator should think of national defense in terms of party advantage. Do please reconsider this whole vital matter and give me your aid for the protection of your nation and mine."[97]

Even this eloquent plea failed to convert Donahey, who remained outside the fold to the very end.[98] But the letter proved effective in a more important way. On the day it was written, FDR also dictated a letter to Senator Alben Barkley: "I enclose copy of a letter from Vic Donahey and copy of my reply. This is for your information. I am sending another copy to Jimmy Byrnes."[99] This "corking letter" (Barkley's phrase) left no doubt in the minds of Democratic wheel horses as to the president's desire for a draft bill; in essence, it was a quiet order to get to work.[100]

Roosevelt's public and private backing, coming as it did just before the Burke bill was reported out of the Senate committee, had an immediate effect. As Senator La Follette wrote to his wife, "There is a lot of sentiment in the chamber against it [conscription], but if the president puts on the heat it will eventually pass."[101] Whether FDR would apply more "heat" depended mainly on the course of debate in the Senate and on the fate of the growing air battles over the English Channel.[102] Willkie's response to bipartisan overtures from the White House would also go a long way toward determining the final outcome.[103] The Plattsburgers, having taken their bill as far as the floor of Congress, could now do little more than watch and wait on the sidelines.

10

The Dog Days of August

Whenever the Congress remains in session after August first, you can look for trouble. The fellows begin to look like Tony Galento and act like Joe Louis. They hit from any position and the referee is in as much danger as the opposing fighters.

—Senator James F. Byrnes

The shadow of war in Europe, along with the uncommonly hot summer weather, seemed to cast a surrealistic, almost paralyzing spell over Washington during late July and August of 1940.[1] President Roosevelt, whose chronic sinus problems required him to avoid air conditioning and even electric fans, sweltered in the 100-degree temperatures and longed for weekend cruises aboard the yacht *Potomac*.[2] Secretary of State Cordell Hull, worn out by the events of the spring and his attendance at the Pan-American Conference in Havana in July, spent the better part of August recuperating at White Sulphur Springs, West Virginia. Secretary Stimson managed to fly to Long Island on weekends, but he found Washington so hot and humid that he had trouble sleeping and had to forgo his usual afternoon game of bowls at Woodley.[3] So "churned up" was Stimson over preparedness and aid to England that at times he thought he should act as secretary of state in Hull's absence.[4] Frederick Libby had worked at full throttle for more than three months, but on one hot August morning he "cut my thumb shaving, scratched my wrist on the license, and bumped my forehead and cut it on a knob in the toilet," whereupon the pacifist leader and his wife decided to go to Cape Cod for a two-weeks' vacation.[5] Grenville Clark also left Washington in early August, then caught a cold and spent much of the month at his Outlet Farm in Dublin, New Hampshire.[6]

Many proponents and opponents of the draft stayed to press their opinions on Washington during August, as the House Military Affairs Committee continued hearings, even while the Senate was debating. As if affected by the summer heat, however, the media did not dwell on the thousands of concerned citizens who came to Capitol Hill to lobby, pro or con, for the draft, but chose, instead, to focus on the bizarre. Elane Summers, a nineteen-year-old sophomore from Rockford (Illinois) College, attracted considerable publicity by donning a Revolutionary War costume, mounting a horse as Pauline Revere, and riding off to Washington to warn the nation: "Mobilize for Peace—Defeat Conscription."[7] Even more curious was a group of black-veiled matrons who called themselves the Mothers of the United States of America. Led by Rosa Farber and Mary Decker of Detroit, the Mothers arrived in Washington in mid August, vowing to hold a "death watch" against President Roosevelt's return to the "politico-feudalistic system of compulsory training in peacetime."[8] Their antics included hanging a coconut-and-papier-mâché dummy of Senator Claude Pepper on one of the trees of the Capitol. The Florida Democrat hailed his mock hanging as "a splendid demonstration of . . . freedom of speech and freedom of action in the American way of doing things."[9]

To its dismay, Congress had to stagger through the August doldrums. Although many members had opposed adjournment in June for fear that President Roosevelt would somehow involve the nation in war, the reality of steamy summer sessions appealed to very few. Because of elections coming up in November, normally polite legislators grew irritable as they awaited the draft, taxes, and other items on the docket. Given the intensity of feeling aroused and the determination of opponents to prevent "rush" legislation, however, the debate over conscription promised to be loud and protracted. In addition, Vice-President John Nance Garner had gone back to Texas in a huff after the third-term nomination, and this tended to weaken FDR's ability to count votes and manage discussion on the Senate floor. Even worse, majority whip Jimmy Byrnes, increasingly becoming the chief White House manager in the Senate, usually escaped to New Hampshire after mid August to relieve his severe allergies. Byrnes agreed to stay and help with the draft, even taking an air-conditioned room at the Hotel Mayflower, but his temper suffered along with his hay fever.[10] So trying were conditions that Speaker William B. Bankhead of Alabama aggravated his high blood pressure and died of a stroke just after the final vote on conscription was taken in the House. "I shudder for the future of a country whose destiny must be decided in the dog days," one opponent commented in early August.[11] Because German attacks against British air fields were on the increase throughout the month, however, Congress could not postpone a decision much longer.

Even before the Burke bill reached the Senate floor, opposing senators doubted their chances of defeating it. "It will pass unquestionably," Hiram Johnson confided to his son, "but some heat has already got into the discussion."[12] Roosevelt's public endorsement on 2 August seemed to sway the issue in the Senate.[13] "If [only] we can keep the issue pending until the colleges open," one student peace worker wrote, then perhaps "the students will be marching on Washington.''[14] On 6 August, however, the newspaper *PM* published a preliminary survey entitled ''Poll of the Senate Shows Majority Favoring Military Draft Bill.'' Interviews with seventy-three senators indicated that thirty-four favored the bill, twenty-four opposed it, and fifteen were unwilling to commit themselves. If this tally proved accurate, then proponents needed only fifteen more votes for a majority and would likely get them.[15] On that same day, Thomas Rankin reported to Norman Thomas: ''The Senate is weakening under administration heat; the president was very sly to pretend to exert no pressure. . . . Sen. Wheeler is discouraged.''[16]

The so-called Peace Bloc in the Senate found it difficult to coordinate strategy against the draft. Conservative Republicans such as Taft and Vandenberg did not work easily with liberals such as La Follette and Wheeler. Vandenberg, for example, had discouraged the formation of an antiwar research bureau on Capitol Hill only to find at the last minute that several opposition senators lacked good speech material against the draft.[17] Howard Beale, Thomas Rankin, and others on the Washington scene hurriedly filled in; *Uncensored* sent Richard Rovere from New York to help ghostwrite speeches; and over the next two weeks, Oswald Garrison Villard, Charles Beard, Harry Elmer Barnes, and other members of the Writers Anti-War Bureau prepared antidraft statements which Senator Wheeler eventually inserted in the *Congressional Record.*[18] Wheeler did manage to gather a small group of opponents on 8 August, the day before the debate on the draft was scheduled to begin, and they agreed tentatively to speak against conscription for two weeks. ''At the end of that period, unless they have concrete evidence from their constituents that they are speaking for a sizable group,'' they proposed to drop their fight. ''If they [should] have evidence of real support by that time,'' they would continue the battle. ''Of course,'' the senators noted, ''this situation will change if the Germans invade England.''[19]

The opposition assault had already commenced somewhat unexpectedly on 6 August, when Rush Holt, the Senate's youngest member, delivered a sensational exposé about the origins of the draft bill. A lone-wolf Democrat whose abusive rhetoric had won him few friends on either side of the aisle, he depicted in lurid colors the 22 May meeting at the ''Hahva'd Club'' in New York, where the conscription conspiracy had been concocted. He proceeded down the list of ''brave patriots,'' attacking the most prominent in turn. He cited Grenville Clark, ''of the proletarian law firm of Root, Clark, Ballantine, and Buckner,'' as having evaded payment of his ''just and rightful share of taxes.''[20] Henry L. Stimson was allegedly ''carrying out in the cabinet the wishes of those who want us to go into the war.'' Gen. John F. ORyan, ''as most of you know, has already advocated the entrance of the United States into this war.'' Kenneth Budd was serving as ''a director of the North British and Mercantile Insurance Company, with headquarters in London.'' Julius Ochs Adler also wanted ''the American boy to protect his investments.'' Such men, Holt charged, had planned to raise a quarter of a million dollars to get a draft bill enacted. If this legislation were truly needed, Holt asked, would such a propaganda fund be necessary to persuade the army and the navy to request it and the Congress to vote for it? The call for conscription, he concluded, "did not come from labor . . . from the railroad brotherhoods, the C.I.O., the American Federation of Labor, the Grange, or the poor people." On the contrary, it came "from those individuals who had interests to protect in this war, and . . . will sacrifice American boys on the battlefield to protect them as they did before. . . . The call for conscription came from this international crowd which tried to get us into the League of Nations, which tried to get us into the World Court, and have gradually tried to push us into involvement in international affairs abroad."[21]

As the galleries cheered Holt's diatribe, Sherman Minton jumped to his feet. He shouted: "Mr. President, I hold no brief for the men just excoriated by the Senator from West Virginia. So far as I know, they are high-class, patriotic gentlemen, although they might belong to the Harvard Club." Minton assured his colleagues, however, that no Holts could have attended the Harvard Club meeting because the Holt family was conspicuously lacking in patriotism. The Indiana Democrat went on to charge that during the World War, Holt's father had opposed sending food to American troops abroad and had sent another son to South America to dodge the draft. Minton would listen to no lectures on national defense from the scion of "a slacker family." Holt lashed back furiously, calling the statement "a malicious lie" and saying that when the White House wanted filth thrown, it called on the senator from Indiana. Minton snapped: "When Hitler wants it thrown you throw it." Senator Barkley finally stepped in and silenced the two combatants.[22] "What a pain in the neck that little bird [Holt] turned out to be," Minton confided to a former colleague. "I did lose my head a little and spoke when I was very angry, and . . . I probably did violate the rules of the Senate, but I was angry enough to have done even more."[23]

Reached at home by the press, Clark stated that "the integrity and character of those concerned rests on many years of private and public life in their communities" and such men could "stand on their records and the patriotic nature of their motives." Clark also predicted that "every demagogic effort, every intrigue of the agents of Hitler, may now be expected to try to defeat this bill."[24] Julius Adler pointed out that Holt's speech revealed nothing that was not already on the public record; he also denied having investments in any corporation other than the New York Times Company and in government bonds.[25] Stimson refused even to hear Holt's charges when a reporter tried to repeat them to him.[26]

Holt's onslaught would have had more credibility if he had questioned, not the motives, but the methods of the Plattsburgers, for it was legitimate to ask whether any pressure group should exert such influence on governmental

Senator Sherman Minton of Indiana and Vice-President John Nance Garner looking at a copy of the draft bill. Minton was an outspoken supporter of the draft, but Garner left Washington after FDR's third-term nomination and remained absent throughout the Senate debates over the draft. (Courtesy of Dartmouth College Library)

policy. But by impugning the character of his opponents, he had laid himself open to easy counterattack. "What young Mr. Holt failed completely to recognize," the *New York Herald Tribune* editorialized, "is that the particular men whom he singled out for abuse took part . . . in the preparedness movement before the last war, and themselves served overseas honorably and gladly."[27] Stung by Holt's charges, Congressman Wadsworth wrote to a Kansas minister: "I shall be sixty-three years of age on August 12, 1940, and consequently subject to registration under the . . . bill as originally introduced. Personally, I regret exceedingly that the Senate committee has cut down the age range."[28] Walter Lippmann added an ironic twist by observing that sons of MTCA members would be more likely to see military service under a draft system, simply because "the sons of well-to-do families do not have the kind of jobs which would exempt them from military service."[29] A further irony was that Holt's labeling of the Plattsburgers as "the same international crowd" overlooked the fact that the leaders of William Allen

White's committee, which was then working assiduously to facilitate the destroyer deal with England, had purposely avoided any position on the draft because they feared that the ensuing controversy would delay assistance to Britain, their acknowledged priority.[30]

Despite Holt's obvious excesses, opposition strength in the Senate revealed itself during the debate and vote on the National Guard on 7 and 8 August. Even though the bill authorizing the president to call out the National Guard and Organized Reserves for a year's training passed by a vote of 71 to 7, it did not come without "hard sledding."[31] An amendment proposed by Alva Adams of Colorado to prohibit the president from sending the Guard outside the continental United States met defeat by the razor thin vote of 39 to 38.[32] Secretary Hull later told reporters that this vote flashed a green light to aggressors and had caused "damage he could never repair."[33] Another amendment, which would have permitted individual guardsmen to resign within twenty days of the bill's enactment, failed by only a 47 to 36 vote.[34] Such hesitation over calling up the relatively small number of men who had volunteered for the Guard and the Reserves meant that the debate over conscription would probably get even fiercer. Senator Barkley confidently predicted passage by a majority of 3 to 1, but Tom Rankin reported: "I have been cheered by contact with the various Senate offices; we are gaining converts, in spite of administration pressure."[35]

Chairman Morris Sheppard formally opened the discussion of S-4164 on the next day. His introductory remarks stressed that the "doctrines and aggressions of certain dictator-controlled nations" made it necessary for the United States to create an army of sufficient size to defend against an attack at home "or the Western Hemisphere." Voluntary enlistments had proven inadequate. Faced with the "tragic necessity" of an immediate emergency, the aging Texan could see no solution but a selective draft in which "the burdens will be borne equally by all classes, regardless of economic means."[36]

The anticonscriptionists returned fire immediately. As soon as Sheppard had completed his formal remarks, Vandenberg tried to pin him down as to concrete evidence that volunteering had failed. Every monthly quota had been met, the Michigan Republican claimed, and "innumerable" recruiting stations had allegedly turned away excessive applicants. Why the hurry? Vandenberg asked, when William Knudsen of the National Defense Advisory Commission had testified that same morning that sufficient equipment for a 750,000-man army would not come off the production lines until 1942.[37] John A. Danaher of Connecticut, a formidable debater, asked Sheppard if the navy needed more ships than it had. "We need twice that many," Sheppard replied. "Then we couldn't even spare fifty, could we?" Danaher asked gleefully.[38] From Wheeler came the familiar claim that Japan, Germany, or Italy did not pose any immediate danger and that conscription in peacetime would mean a "step away from democracy."[39] Sheppard's halting defense of the bill did little to slow the isolationist momentum.[40]

Opponents pounded away for several more days. On 10 August, Senator Wheeler proposed a nationwide referendum on the draft, since proponents had depicted the bill as being necessary for the preservation of democracy.[41] Two days later, while members of Labor's Non-Partisan League visited congressional offices to protest against conscription, Norris of Nebraska delivered a ringing declaration of his "bitter" opposition. A peacetime draft, he asserted, would "turn the clock back a thousand years." If such a bill were passed, "we shall be doing it 50 years from now, we shall be doing it 100 years from now. . . . We cannot get away from it." The old Progressive predicted that this bill would "put this country on a road which means the ultimate destruction of democracy."[42] D. Worth Clark of Idaho, following Norris, claimed that proponents were seeking to "take advantage of the hysteria . . . now sweeping over the country to engraft this as part of the permanent life of the American people, to let every boy . . . grow up to be a soldier, to be regimented and subjected to the militarism which is repugnant to every American instinct and institution."[43]

Taft's speech, which was better reasoned and less emotional, came on 14 August.[44] He warned against exaggerating the emergency: "I am convinced that to meet the threat of a totalitarian nation, we need not make ourselves totalitarian. I shudder when I hear the words 'total defense.' I do not know what 'total defense' means unless it means the subjugation of every other principle of our life to the one subject—military defense." He was certain that "our present forces can defend us against an attack across 3,000 miles of water."[45] Even though Franklin Canfield reported that "Taft is consuming the time, if not occupying the attention, of the Senate today," Taft's speech made a favorable impression.[46] Senator Austin wrote to his mother that Taft had "made a fine argument . . . the most free from the sloppy talk about 'war mongering,' 'militarizing,' 'anti-American,' etc. which has come from Senators Vandenberg, Norris and Wheeler. . . . It was refreshing to one like myself who is persuaded that the bill ought to be agreed to."[47] Grenville Clark tried to persuade Taft to tone down his criticism. "I was surprised at the complete certainty with which you expressed your point of view," he wrote, "to the effect that those who have serious apprehension, all have hysteria." Clark urged Taft to show "more *tolerance* . . . toward those with whom you so sharply disagree. . . . Isn't it just *possible* that they may turn out to be less foolish than . . . you and Senator Wheeler . . . make them out to be?"[48] Taft later thanked Clark for "taking so much time to reform the sinner who has strayed," but he remained certain that "the conscription bill is a great mistake."[49]

Lesser lights, representing a variety of viewpoints, also twinkled in the opposition galaxy. Adams of Colorado, for example, wanted to keep costs down, saw no immediate threat to the United States, and was afraid of giving the president such broad powers.[50] James Murray of Montana opposed the bill because "what we need is a highly trained, professional army like Hitler has, made up of men . . . intensely trained and . . . equipped . . . with the most modern military machinery. A conscript army made up of youths trained for a year or two, compared to Hitler's army, is like a high school football team going up against the professional teams like they have in Chicago and New York."[51] Senator Nye, however, found "laughable" any thought that the country faced a military threat: "About the only argument the friends of conscription have been able to drum up is that Hitler is going to get us if we don't watch out, and probably by tomorrow morning, or anyway come harvest time."[52]

Senator William J. Bulow of South Dakota refused to support the bill because conscription constituted the very evil that men like his father had emigrated to America to escape.[53] Arthur Capper of Kansas, who was described by one reporter as "a dried-up little old man who is going to blow away someday in a high Washington wind," wrote to Clark, saying that he favored "a program which will make it possible to defend ourselves," but thought "we can set up a program in this country without resorting to compulsory military training or conscriptive practices."[54] Walsh of Massachusetts, a believer in the militia, recalled the heroics of the Yankee Division in World War I, when he had been governor. "I am ready to conscript if we really need to," Walsh declared, "but I want proof first that there is an actual need, and I want removed from my mind . . . that enlistment today may mean participating in a foreign war, rather than in defense of America."[55] Guy Gillette of Iowa wanted preparedness but claimed that it would suffice to build up the fleet, increase the production of materiel, and train specialists in the techniques of modern warfare. Draftees under the Burke bill would receive useless training. "This idea of letting the boys sit around for a year playing stud poker and blackjack is poppycock," he snorted.[56] Danaher of Connecticut had acted cordial and respectful when Douglas Arant, his old friend and classmate at Yale Law School, had visited him, but on the Senate floor, Danaher opposed the bill forcefully. "What is back of this military conscription effort?" he asked a constituent. "Let it be noted that the very same officers who testified before our committee as to the size of our army and what it should be before Mr. Stimson became secretary have now more than trebled their estimates."[57]

The intensity of the assault did not, however, reverse the earlier judgment that some form of draft bill would go through. Even after two days of isolationist artillery, Barkley, apparently energized by a communication from the White House, repeated his prediction that the fight was already won. The opposition had admitted privately that it could not "delay the bill long," and he now prophesied that no more than a fourth of the Senate would register nay in the final vote.[58] Burke himself felt confident from the first that his bill would pass by a two-to-one vote.[59] "Norris, Vandenberg, and Wheeler have made splendid speeches against the conscription bill," Senator La Follette noted on 13 August, "but the administration forces act as though they had the votes."[60]

On 15 August, NEC workers in Washington confirmed this favorable judgment on the basis of interviews, the *PM* survey, and estimates made by Frank Kluckhohn of the *New York Times*. They now listed forty-nine senators—forty-one Democrats and eight Republicans—as definitely for the bill. They counted thirty-one as already in the nay column; this number included eighteen Democrats, nine Republicans, two Farmer-Laborites, one Progressive (La Follette), and one Independent (Norris). This summary still left sixteen senators in the doubtful category, but enough would certainly vote for the bill to assure a solid majority.[61]

Given their minority status, opposition senators faced a strategic problem. Unable to defeat the bill outright, they saw that their best chance was to use delaying tactics, to weaken the measure by amendment, as had been done in committee, and at the showdown to throw their support to a compromise. Although members of the Keep America out of War Congress sent wires "urging no compromise with the principle of conscription," opponents understood that amendments offered their only realistic hope.[62] On Saturday 10 August, Senator Wheeler announced that he and a dozen colleagues who were committed to fighting the Burke-Wadsworth bill to the very end would meet the following Monday to plan their strategy.[63]

Amendments of all kinds were already pouring into the Senate hopper. Lodge and O'Mahoney had both suggested a ceiling on the number of men inducted in any one year, and Lodge had also sponsored an important amendment to limit the service of draftees to the Western Hemisphere. Burke accepted Josh Lee's proposal to raise the base pay of all trainees to $30 per month, which eventually passed with virtually no opposition. Walsh, Guffey, and others had offered amendments relative to the exemption of ministers and theological students. Robert Wagner of New York pushed for a prohibition of racial discrimination against volunteers. Consistent with his interest in mobile mechanized forces, Downey of California proposed a system of superhighways and airfields, to be built at federal expense. Clark of Missouri wanted a unified Department of Defense, which would include as subdivisions the army, the navy, and an autonomous air force. Alexander Wiley of Wisconsin tried to cripple the bill by forbidding the president to put the draft into effect until Congress had expressly declared an emergency. A similar amendment by Johnson of Colorado stipulated that no person could be inducted under the bill until Congress had actually declared war.[64]

The amendment that eventually became the rallying point for the opposition was authored by Francis T. Maloney of Connecticut, a loyal Democrat, who by no means opposed conscription or aid to England.[65] Maloney faced a tough campaign for reelection, however, and the flood of negative mail had persuaded the former newspaperman that some sort of compromise was needed.[66] He first outlined his proposal to reporters on 3 August, intending it as an honest effort to reconcile advocates and opponents. In essence, his amendment would have authorized the president, prior to 1 December, to call for volunteers, not to exceed four hundred thousand, the number that the army planned to induct that autumn if selective service were enacted. If by 1 January the number of volunteers had not reached this figure, the president might then institute the draft. "The paramount thing is to eliminate any controversy over the defense program," Maloney explained. With so many senators saying that conscription was "both undemocratic and unnecessary," his amendment "would demonstrate whether it is necessary. It is geared to meet the demands of the army and to satisfy the argument that compulsion is not necessary."[67]

At that time, die-hards were still hoping to substitute a plan for one-year enlistments.[68] When asked about Maloney's amendment, Senator Wheeler said that his group would favor it if they could not persuade the Senate to accept the one-year volunteer proposal.[69] Before long, however, most opponents swung over to Maloney's plan as their best hope of crippling the bill, for it soon became apparent that a majority of the senators would endorse some version of the compulsory principle.

From the standpoint of the opposition, this was unquestionably a wise move. As indicated by the Senate committee's sudden capitulation on age limits, the antidraft propaganda barrage had many senators wondering about the accuracy of public-opinion polls. "Of course there is a drive against conscription, notwithstanding the Gallup Poll," snapped Hiram Johnson on 13 August.[70] A large number of senators considered that peacetime conscription was a real departure from American tradition and approved it only reluctantly as a necessary evil in an hour of crisis. "No man in the Senate . . . underneath really favors peacetime conscription," Wheeler reported to a friend, "no matter what he may say publicly, outside of Josh Lee, Pepper and Senator Burke—a strange combination."[71] Moreover, the arguments of influential men such as Vandenberg raised real doubts as to the failure of volunteer methods; and former Secretary Woodring, a man who should know, had flatly denied that there was any shortage of voluntary enlistments.[72] Many senators looked nervously at the date of 7 November on their office calendars, and Maloney's amendment provided a convenient means of dodging the issue until after the elections. Bennett Clark of Missouri professed to believe that the White House had secretly encouraged the move for delay: "Everyone has known all the time that some excuse would be found for postponing the operation of the draft. Nothing . . . would indicate that they are . . . so inept as to have hundreds of thousands of mothers going down to the stations kissing their boys good-bye . . . within three or four weeks before an election."[73]

The possibility of compromise suddenly loomed as the major threat to the bill. In the eyes of the draft's sponsors, postponement would mean a victory for the isolationists and probably for Hitler as well. Time seemed to be more urgent than ever. Colonel Donovan's return from England in early August had reversed previous predictions that the British could not withstand a German assault. Nevertheless, "the bombing attacks upon the Island have been increasing in intensity," Secretary Stimson noted on 13 August. "There have also been signs of a concerted movement of German air force with Italian air force into the Mediterranean. . . . Consequently my mind has been full of foreboding and anxiety."[74] No one had a crystal ball that could predict that the Royal Air Force would win the Battle of Britain and that Operation Sea Lion would never be launched. Notwithstanding opponents' charges about artificial hysteria, men like Clark and Stimson sincerely believed that the country had delayed too long in building up defenses, that immediate aid to England was imperative, and that further delay could prove fatal. Stimson jotted in his diary: "It is the old case of the people saying to Noah, 'Oh, get along now / with your darned old scow. / It ain't going to rain much anyhow.' "[75] But to those who lacked the sense of urgency that actuated the interventionists, postponing the draft at least until volunteering had had a further trial did not seem unreasonable. Opponents tried to exploit these feelings on the part of "middle-of-the-road" senators to the fullest. When Senator Charles L. McNary told General Marshall that he would vote for the Burke bill but expected Maloney's amendment to pass, Stimson ruefully observed: "This would be bad news, more so psychologically than in any other way. It would be just as good as giving a great many airplanes to Hitler in the shape of morale just at this time."[76]

The matter thus turned on whether the volunteer system was adequate or not. Opponents insisted that the call to colors would bring forth more than enough men to meet any attack on the United States. Proponents argued that the volunteer system had never produced enough men. Those who were on the fence, listening to what often seemed reasonable arguments on both sides, simply did not know whether the volunteer system would do the job. Hence the attractiveness of Maloney's middle course—try volunteering first; if this should fail, institute the draft.

Opponents offered evidence that voluntary enlistments could do the job. They cited the Gallup poll of early June, which indicated that 85 percent of the twenty-one to forty-five age group would volunteer if the nation were attacked.[77] On a more authoritative level, they had testimony in black and

U.S. Senate Gallery

HITLER: "KEEP THE DRAFT DEBATE GOING, BOYS."

This cartoon reflects the impatience of those who supported immediate preparedness and believed that prolonged debate encouraged Nazi Germany to launch the expected invasion of Britain. (Reprinted by permission of the New York *Daily News*)

white from the former secretary of war that the volunteer system had not broken down. Other War Department officials had told the House Military Affairs Committee in June that the army "anticipated no difficulty" in

obtaining voluntary enlistments at least up to 315,000 or 350,000 men.[78] A
Montana Democrat assured his constituents that "men are enlisting at the
rate of about 33,000 per month," which would be more than enough for
adequate preparedness.[79]

Senator Vandenberg proved to be the most compelling orator for the
volunteer system. On 12 August he said: "The army and navy have filled
every volunteer quota they have sought this year. Until larger quotas have
been tried and failed, the . . . presumption must persist that the army and
navy can get what they want by the traditional volunteer system." He asked:
"Has the president issued a ringing call for volunteers? He has not. Has there
been a persuasive fireside chat upon the subject? There has not." Volunteers
had even been turned away in August because quotas were filled, so
Vandenberg exclaimed: "My God . . . they say the system has broken
down. . . . There is no break-down in the volunteer system, but there is a
break-down in the willingness to acknowledge its success."[80]

There was no denying the fact that recruitment had increased markedly.
June had seen a new gain to the army of 16,177, and the July figures had risen
to 23,234.[81] Compared with the trickle of new men before that time (the net
gain in May had been 1,307), this seemed almost a flood; and army officers
admitted that they had not "put on the pressure" as in 1917.[82]

Further support for volunteering came from an incident that Senator
Wheeler brought to light. Thinking he had unearthed a real piece of
skulduggery, he accused the secretary of war of having eliminated two pages
from the August issue of *Recruiting News,* the official publication of the army's
Recruiting Publicity Bureau. The pages had been excised, according to
Wheeler, because they carried a statement from General Marshall congrat-
ulating the Recruiting Service for exceeding its quotas. Flourishing the
evidence, the senator further charged that "sentries were posted so that copies
did not get out until pages 13 and 14 were removed from every copy. . . .
General Marshall has been gagged and the rest of the army . . . ordered to
keep its collective mouth shut."[83]

In fact, although the incident had occurred, neither Stimson nor
Marshall had known anything about it until Wheeler delivered his blast in the
Senate. As the secretary commented in his diary, the deletion was simply a
case of "over-zeal" on the part of a subordinate in the Adjutant General's
Office.[84] The day after Wheeler's attack, General Marshall published the two
pages, openly admitting "a blunder of judgment."[85] Stimson angrily noted
that "it was typical of Wheeler. The isolationists are descending to every
possible trick and Wheeler has always had a nasty tongue. . . . I talked pretty
rough about Wheeler."[86]

The main flaw in the provolunteer argument was that the army's
recruiting successes in June and July were relatively unimportant as a gauge
of future potential. As the General Staff had testified, the army had based

those quotas, not on what it wanted, but on what it thought it could obtain. Even more important, those figures were determined by the General Staff's now-obsolete plans to raise an army of no more than four hundred thousand men. The War Department had never denied that an army of this size could be raised through voluntary enlistments, and the recruiting figures for June and July seemed to indicate that it could be done. But by August the figure of four hundred thousand no longer applied, as manpower estimates had soared to three times that number. One of Senator Taft's assistants had a long talk with officers in the War Plans Division and then reported:

> A war with Japan and Germany with possible complications in South America might require putting into operation all four augmentation plans. It might even require more than the 4,000,000 men so raised. . . . I believe that if we had a trained reserve of perhaps two million men right now, the army would not be asking for conscription. . . . The difficulty lies in the fact that we do not have such a reserve, and those who are making the policies believe, whether mistakenly or not, that there is a very real and imminent possibility of attack.[87]

If one were to reject the hemispheric strategy in favor of the isolationist premise that a strong navy and a small mechanized army would be sufficient for home defense, the advocates of volunteering may have had a valid point. But even most isolationists desired hemispheric defense, and military experts were now saying that Germany's blitzkrieg had not invalidated the old maxim that battles are won primarily with infantry.[88]

The question still remained as to whether volunteer enlistments could provide enough men for the larger forces now deemed necessary. Advocates of the draft pointed to the fact that during the twelve months from 1 July 1939 to 10 June 1940, the army had achieved a net gain of only 72,870 men, or an average of approximately 6,000 a month.[89] True enough, the lightning war in Europe had driven larger numbers to the recruiting stations, and the June-July quotas had been exceeded. But the results were uneven. "The enlistments in the Fourth Corps Area demonstrate that the boys of the South will volunteer," Senator Byrnes informed a constituent. "On the other hand, in the populous centers of the country, the recent enlistments show that they will not volunteer."[90] Just how long the peak influx would continue remained uncertain. As one officer put it, the army would have to recruit "more than 100,000 men per month for the next fourteen months. This is a sustained effort of recruiting which must bring in each month five times the net gain of the record-breaking month of July."[91]

Even to obtain some eight hundred thousand men by the following spring, recruitment would have to increase to a net monthly gain of one hundred thousand. Everything in the army's experience pointed to the impossibility of such numbers, even under the impetus of an intense nationwide campaign. The discarded Civilian Volunteer Effort had offered no hope of obtaining anything like eight hundred thousand men, and the figures for World War I were equally instructive. Notwithstanding the atmosphere of superpatriotism that stigmatized young men who were waiting to be drafted, the army had only succeeded in attracting one hundred thousand volunteers during one month, the month immediately following the declaration of war.[92] Major Hershey also made the telling point that any sustained recruiting drive would "force the army to make its main effort on recruiting rather than training. It will require a large number of officers and soldiers who are badly needed for other duties."[93]

Even if volunteers did appear in sufficient numbers, advocates of the draft still had logic on their side. Given the uncertainties inherent in the international crisis, there was no guarantee, under the volunteer system, that the army would reach its quota in each successive month. The General Staff could never be sure whether it would have, by any given date, enough manpower to accomplish its various missions. Under the draft, however, it could plan to the very man its schedule of inductions, reducing or increasing the intake according to the need. Supporters of the Maloney amendment could argue that only four months would be lost under their plan, but such a delay while the Battle of Britain was raging posed large risks. One of Hershey's assistants likened Maloney's amendment to "substitutes of every day which are almost as good and they seem cheaper. The automobile with a wooden top, almost as good, looks just the same; no one will ever know the difference. How dangerous to discover the difference when the car rolls over. How dangerous to accept substitutes when human life is involved, how much more dangerous when national life is jeopardized."[94] One did not have to advocate intervention to see the draft as a necessary insurance in a world at war. The volunteer system was at best an uncertain, inefficient method that could function only unevenly, while the draft seemed to be a sure and systematic means to a goal that had to be reached swiftly.[95]

Because Clark knew that Senator Maloney was no die-hard opponent, he tried by letter to dissuade him from pressing his compromise. Noting that the amendment ran "contrary to the considered advice of General Pershing, the secretary of war, [and] the Chief of Staff," Clark "respectfully suggest[ed] that you would be taking a heavy responsibility in failing to give weight to their judgment." He also pointed out that "any such large number of men could be secured through volunteering only by an immense and emotional recruiting campaign that would stir up and disrupt the whole country." In his estimate, "further experiment with the volunteer system" would only "create confusion and delay the orderly development of the plans which our best informed advisers tell us are necessary." Clark urged Maloney to at least "further discuss the problem in detail with the responsible officers in the War

Department, because it is hard for me to believe that after doing so, you would wish to press the proposal."[96] Maloney gave a cordial but negative response: "Until you have a chance to examine Congressional mail, I doubt that you can realize the feelings of our people and how 'bitterly' so many of them feel about immediate conscription."[97] He still believed that his proposal was "a safer and saner one" on which both friends and foes could unite.[98]

Maloney's confidence seemed to be bolstered by the growing support for his compromise. On Wednesday 14 August, despite radio and press reports of intensified Luftwaffe raids on England, Franklin Canfield wrote from Washington that the draft bill had become "more and more enmeshed in politics where it will strangle unless something can be done to pull it out."[99] The Associated Press also carried a story that ten senators, so far noncommittal, could tip the scales either way on a compromise amendment; an informal canvass revealed that a Senate that had been so apparently favorable to an immediate draft a few days earlier was now almost evenly divided on the Maloney amendment.[100] By Thursday, Canfield had grown even more pessimistic. "I saw Kluckhohn, of the *Times*," he reported to Clark, "and he said he thought the Maloney Amendment was 'in the bag' unless the Administration moved to prevent its adoption."[101] On Friday, Stimson, "backed up by Members of the Cabinet," did urge the president to make another, even stronger, statement in favor of the draft, but FDR remained silent.[102]

So far, Roosevelt had made no public comment on the Maloney amendment, which had been proposed just after his earlier press conference. Maloney himself had telegraphed the White House, urging support for his amendment, lest the Democrats face "burial" in November.[103] Roosevelt had also received a wire from Edward Taylor of Colorado, chairman of the House Appropriations Committee, asking FDR to meet personally with Willkie and to work out "a mutually satisfactory program" with respect to the draft and thus "smooth the way for this highly important and necessary legislation."[104] FDR replied on 12 August that Willkie had "no desire to cooperate and is merely playing politics. . . . The best approach is an appeal to the patriotism of Joe Martin [House Minority Leader] and Charlie McNary [Senate Minority Leader]."[105] On the next day, Senator Byrnes explained to a friend why he found Maloney's amendment so tempting: "If we do not devise some plan of this kind in the Senate, the bill may be filibustered for the next sixty days, and if voted upon by the House just prior to the election, it might not pass at all."[106]

The president's frustration at this juncture derived not only from opposition to the draft in the Senate but also from difficulties encountered in the parallel effort to secure bipartisan support for a destroyers/bases deal. Despite a nationwide radio speech by General Pershing on 4 August, urging the transfer of destroyers, initial soundings were pessimistic. Secretary Hull put the odds against any such legislation at four to one, and a straw poll of senators showed that at least twenty-three were strongly opposed to selling naval vessels to England, apparently enough senators to mount a filibuster.[107] Those individuals who were trying to smooth the way for a destroyer transaction were hampered by the president's public silence, confusion over legalities, and several different proposals for accomplishing the objective. Even worse, William Allen White's effort to gain Willkie's blessing ran into snags. "My general views of foreign policy . . . in the present international situation are known," the GOP candidate publicly announced on 9 August. "As to specific executive or legislative proposals, I do not think it appropriate for me to enter into advance commitments and understandings." White hurriedly wired to FDR at Hyde Park: "It's not as bad as it seems. I have talked with both of you on this subject during the last ten days. I know there is not two bits difference between you on the issue pending. But I can't guarantee either of you to the other, which is funny, because I admire and respect you both."[108] White did see an advance copy of the formal acceptance speech that the nominee planned to give on 17 August, and he tried to assure the White House that Willkie would say nothing in criticism of FDR's initiative. Harold Ickes urged Roosevelt to "go ahead with a bill and leave Willkie *et al.* to take it or leave it," but the president remained cautious.[109] On 12 August, Senator Pepper, who had agreed to sponsor a destroyer bill, told Stimson that such a bill had "no chance" of passing.[110]

Roosevelt could blame himself for helping to create his own dilemma. Following his cabinet meeting of 2 August, when he gave the go signal on both the draft and the destroyer plan, the president spent the next ten days either at Hyde Park or inspecting naval bases along the coast of New England.[111] Although he monitored the overtures to Willkie by phone and kept a full schedule of appointments at Hyde Park, he did not press any legislative leaders, nor did he exert any influence over the debate in the Senate. FDR did have Senator Walsh accompany him aboard the *Potomac* from 11 to 13 August, but he unaccountably said nothing to the chairman of the Naval Affairs Committee about the pending destroyer deal.[112] While it made sense to approach Willkie, the president must have known that his Republican opponent had far less influence over senators than he himself did as the incumbent. By staying in the background and trying to lead by proxy, FDR had permitted isolationists such as Wheeler, Holt, and Vandenberg to dominate the headlines. The attacks against the draft in the Senate were endangering aid to England. A British analyst gave a somber appraisal:

> The [president] . . . messed up the whole business by not sponsoring a bill of his own but letting one slip out that was badly drawn. . . . Nothing was done to create the right atmosphere and present it as a patriotic "service" bill, so that the isolationist attack on it as a "preparation for war" bill has had more

success than was necessary. . . . In the political atmosphere which exists upon the Hill at present, it doesn't look very promising for those 50 destroyers.[113]

On his return to Washington, however, Roosevelt once again displayed what Stimson called "the happy-go-luckiness of it all coupled with flashes of real genius in statesmanship."[114] On the afternoon of 13 August the president called Stimson, Morgenthau, Knox, and Undersecretary of State Sumner Welles to a "momentous conference," in the course of which FDR "drafted very hastily, but in admirable shape, the papers to constitute a message to Great Britain."[115] He read to his advisers the latest telegram from William Allen White, implying that "Willkie wouldn't give much trouble on this matter but would in no way guarantee that he wouldn't," but the president decided that he would go ahead with a destroyers/bases trade regardless. When asked about concluding arrangements with England before going to Congress, Morgenthau said FDR "ought to tell Congress first, but the undercurrent of those present seemed to be to do it first and tell Congress afterward."[116] The ostensible reason for Roosevelt's decision to by-pass Congress on the destroyer deal was the publication, two days earlier in the *New York Times,* of an elaborate legal brief, arguing that the commander in chief had the constitutional authority to do so.[117] Written by Dean G. Acheson, and signed by George Rublee, Charles C. Burlingham, and Thomas D. Thacher, the *Times* brief repeated legal arguments that FDR had rejected three weeks earlier when Benjamin Cohen had pressed them privately.[118] This time, however, in the face of urgent British needs and the apparently precarious political situation on Capitol Hill, the president decided that he could negotiate with the British through executive agreement. Two days later, on 15 August, he learned that Senator McNary, Willkie's running mate, could not support a destroyer transfer in the Senate but would not object if "plausible grounds" were found for by-passing Congress. Then, in an extraordinary move, Justice Frankfurter passed the word to the White House, via Stimson, that he, Frankfurter, found the Acheson-Rublee arguments constitutionally sound.[119] His mind made up, Roosevelt announced at his press conference on 16 August that negotiations were under way for the acquisition of British air and naval bases in North America.[120]

The president's decision to avoid Congress on the destroyer deal was not matched by a similar decisiveness on the Maloney amendment. What Willkie might say about the draft in his acceptance speech obviously worried FDR, who told Morgenthau that he "might take the wind out of his [Willkie's] sails" by supporting Josh Lee's amendment for $30 a month for draftees. He then startled the Treasury secretary by saying he really preferred national service and "sketched a system . . . where the boys through selective draft would have to come into the CCC. He had the thing worked out carefully in his mind and it sounded awfully good."[121] At the cabinet meeting on 16 August, when Stimson urged a stronger statement for the draft, Roosevelt sidestepped by saying that he would get the national commander of the American Legion to issue a statement.[122] FDR's concern that Willkie might be setting a trap for him was evident after the cabinet meeting in a conversation that he had with Ickes, which Ickes recorded thus:

> The president made a surprising statement to me at this conference. He told me that J. Edgar Hoover was devoted to him personally and that Willkie had personally asked Hoover to go on the Republican ticket with him as vice-president. Hoover refused. I have no doubt that the president believes this, but it does seem strange to me that Willkie should make such an offer to Hoover. However, it is not impossible. Willkie would be willing to take anybody on the ticket with him who might aid him in his canvass and Hoover is a very popular and romantic figure.[123]

Democratic floor managers were exhibiting similar nervousness. House majority leader Sam Rayburn told Joseph Drake, a NEC worker, that supporting the Maloney amendment would actually speed up the operation of the draft and that he did not consider the loss of several months a "very substantial matter."[124] When the Senate recessed early on Thursday 15 August, ostensibly to permit Republican senators to attend Willkie's acceptance speech in Indiana on Saturday, Franklin Canfield described Barkley as being "relieved to put off debate until after Willkie had spoken."[125] On the next day a Republican congressional aide reported "a lot of talk on Capitol Hill . . . about dropping the conscription legislation until after we convene in January."[126]

By this time the GOP candidate's opinion on the draft had become a headline topic. "What Wendell Willkie thinks of conscription," reported the Scripps-Howard Washington correspondent, "is becoming as much of a Washington puzzle as was . . . Mr. Roosevelt's third-term intentions."[127] Hiram Johnson confided to a friend that "there is anxiety here about what he [Willkie] will say. Men like Vandenberg and Taft have wired him about our foreign policy. I have talked at length with Joe Martin. . . . If he takes a position on conscription that it will heal all wounds, we'll be in a rather sorry plight."[128] Johnson of Colorado predicted that if Willkie did back the draft vigorously, "a dozen timid Democratic Senators and fifty election-conscious Congressmen will be free to support it, since it will no longer be a campaign issue." Willkie's opposition would effectively kill the bill, but if the Republican nominee sat on the fence, Johnson concluded, "Congress will follow suit by adopting some straddling amendment like the Maloney amendment."[129] Frank Kluckhohn told Canfield that Willkie's endorsement would probably have no decisive impact on Congress, whereas a strong denunciation might tip the scales against the bill.[130] A British diplomat commented that Willkie had "manoeuvered himself into a position of political prominence which is not bad for a novice."[131]

The man whose views on the draft seemed to be so crucial had spent most of his time since the nomination vacationing at the Broadmoor Hotel in Colorado Springs. Willkie had decided to remain silent on major issues until his acceptance speech, because his strong internationalist views might offend Old Guard Republicans. By staying in Colorado, he hoped to attract Democrats and independents who were disgruntled because of Roosevelt's third-term decision, while at the same time avoiding daily contact with party regulars.[132] He did not lack advice, however, for proponents and opponents of the draft showered him from afar with letters and telegrams.[133] Grenville Clark sent a long wire, urging a forthright endorsement with "no weasel words"; to do otherwise would be "wholly inconsistent with your character."[134] Frederick Libby, Oswald Garrison Villard, and other peace leaders asked Willkie to oppose the draft, while urging their local affiliates to send thousands of similar messages to the candidate.[135] The most important advice, however, seems to have been a long letter from Congressman Wadsworth. Emphasizing that "this bill did not originate in the White House," the cosponsor described in detail the army's manpower plans, the position of Secretary Stimson and General Marshall, the history and activities of the Plattsburg movement, and the urgency of the immediate enactment of selective service.[136] The letter hit home, as Willkie thanked Wadsworth for the best analysis of defense issues that he had seen. "You will be satisfied," he wrote, "with what I say on the subject in my acceptance talk."[137]

As the day of the speech at Elwood approached, however, the pressure on Willkie to hedge became enormous. House minority leader Joseph William ("Joe") Martin, whom Willkie had picked to head the Republican National Committee, was one of the few congressional leaders to make the long journey to Colorado. Martin gave sensible counsel about conscription: "These legislative issues are Roosevelt's responsibility, not yours. . . . You're still on the outside. You don't have to comment on every bill. Don't voluntarily assume positions until you have to. . . . The draft is a very unpopular issue. Naturally, people don't want their sons in uniform. Go slow on this thing. It is not necessary for you to take the initiative on selective service right now."[138] Alf Landon had a similar conversation with Willkie at the Broadmoor on 14 August. In an effort to avoid mistakes that Landon had made in 1936, he urged Willkie to coordinate with Joe Martin and Charles McNary before taking a stand on the draft. Willkie's chief speechwriter, Russell Davenport, interrupted: "Well, Governor, would it make any difference if Mr. Willkie's position were not in accord with Republicans in Congress?" Landon said it would make "all the difference in the world," because if "they are voting one way and Mr. Willkie is talking another, people are going to say: 'What does the Party stand for?' "[139] Finally, on the eve of the Elwood speech, some twenty-five Republican congressmen got together and phoned Willkie, pleading with him not to come out for peacetime conscription. When asked what the candidate had said, one of the congressmen replied: "Well, it sounded like the letters I write to my constituents."[140]

Saturday 17 August saw Elwood, Indiana, turned upside down. The temperature had already reached 102 in the shade when Willkie arrived from Rushville. Thousands of cheering, perspiring supporters kept up a steady din as the candidate's open car moved slowly down the main street, and a solid mass of thirty thousand more was waiting in front of the high school to watch Willkie shake hands with old schoolmates. Not until well past noon did he reach Calloway Park, where some two hundred thousand admirers had jammed the grounds and overflowed into the surrounding cornfields. As the GOP nominee came to the front of the speaker's platform, the chant that had swept the Philadelphia convention two months before broke out. For five minutes he stood and waved his flat straw hat, while the crowd shouted, "We want Willkie."

Shortly after 3 p.m., Willkie began to speak. The speech did not belong in the usual class of platitudinous oratory; one reporter called it "uneven, boyishly earnest in places, everywhere practical and hardheaded."[141] The heat and perspiration made it difficult for Willkie to read his speech smoothly, and millions of Americans who were listening to the radio could not always follow the hoarse, raspy voice. But the candidate made it eminently clear where he stood on aid to England, which was then undergoing the sixth straight day of heavy Nazi bombardment. Britain's defeat and the loss of the Royal Navy would constitute a "calamity" that would leave Americans "exposed to attack." He quoted Roosevelt's Charlottesville pledge to "extend to the opponents of force the material resources of this nation," and he said, "I am in agreement with those proposals, as I understand them." Willkie did not say anything specific about destroyers for England, and he wondered out loud whether Roosevelt was "not deliberately inciting us to war," but he effectively repudiated the isolationist position. When he reached the paragraphs on national defense, Willkie urged that the armed forces be strengthened so that "no nation on earth dare attack us." On conscription, without committing himself on the details of the legislation then in Congress, he said with transparent sincerity: "I cannot ask the American people to put their faith in me without recording my conviction that some form of selective service is the only democratic way to secure the trained and competent manpower we need for national defense."[142]

Willkie's somewhat ambiguous statement on the draft encountered a mixed reception. Considering it too weak, Grenville Clark immediately urged Willkie by wire to issue a stronger statement.[143] Senator Burke, however, telegraphed his congratulations. Burton Wheeler declared that Willkie had

Wendell Willkie's endorsement of selective service in August 1940 was crucial to its final passage. (Courtesy of Franklin D. Roosevelt Library)

dealt in generalities without saying whether he favored compulsory training in peacetime. Gillette of Iowa, who supported the draft in wartime but not in peacetime, noted the curious fact that both he and Burke could agree with Willkie's statement. Key Pittman told a friend that "in view of the position taken by Willkie, I don't see how it [conscription] could be much of an issue during the campaign." Pittman now "favored the Maloney amendment."[144] Although Senator Norris called the statement "too vague," Taft declared himself "satisfied." In favoring "some form of selective service," Taft argued, Willkie had not even mentioned the word *compulsory;* "that is quite different from recommending a draft."[145]

Despite his ambiguity, Willkie had nevertheless demonstrated that he would not make a campaign issue of conscription. As Stimson noted, it was "a fair, brave, and sensible speech—not a very great speech but exactly the right kind of speech. . . . He has gone far to hamstring the efforts of the little group of isolationists to play politics."[146] Several days later, Joe Martin announced that the party would take no official stand on conscription, that his congressional colleagues could vote their consciences. "The Republican party does not want rubber-stamp congressmen," he declared.[147] By the end of the month, Willkie was giving private assurances to the British ambassador that "he would not oppose the transfer of the destroyers" but could not say so publicly "because it would certainly be used against him."[148] Hiram Johnson later wrote that Willkie's speech "really broke the back of the opposition to the conscription law. He slapped every one of us . . . who were thinking American and acting American."[149] For historian Harry Elmer Barnes, the Republican candidate had proven himself "no more than a Coolidge with a goat-gland operation and a gardenia. . . . We will have to vote for Norman [Thomas] and despair for the Republic."[150]

On the day after Willkie's address, from Independence Hall in Philadelphia, with President Roosevelt's knowledge and blessing, Ambassador William C. Bullitt broadcast a fiery interventionist speech, blasting politicians for their timidity on conscription. To those senators who opposed conscription in peacetime but would accept it after a declaration of war, Bullitt charged: "The ruined homes of France, the women and children starving on the roads, cry out. . . . The dictators . . . count . . . on honorable men" like those senators. Bullitt exhorted the American people to "demand the privilege of being called into the service of the nation. Tell them [congressmen] that we want conscription."[151] This speech, which D. Worth Clark of Idaho suggested was "little short of treason," sparked isolationist fireworks when the Senate opposition returned to the attack on Monday 19 August. Claiming that Willkie had not rejected the Maloney amendment, the advocates of compromise seemed more confident than ever.

Friends of the bill made an effort to stop the swing toward volunteering. Lister Hill of Alabama, using arguments supplied by the NEC, quoted Woodrow Wilson's definition of selective service: "It is not a conscription of the unwilling but selection from a nation that has volunteered *en masse.*"[152] Unexpected support came when Tydings of Maryland, whom the sponsors had written off as being unalterably opposed, spoke out strongly for the bill. As the galleries cheered, Tydings asserted that "we would better overdo on the side of preparedness than underdo."[153] On the next day there was a bitter clash between Wheeler and Tom Connally, when the latter, defending the draft, charged Wheeler with trying "to make it just as difficult as he can for the government to get an army."[154] Burke went on national radio that night in an attempt to explain why volunteer enlistments could not fill the army's needs. On that same day in Vichy, France, Marshal Henri Philippe Pétain, in his first interview with American journalists since the armistice, spoke about Rochambeau and Lafayette and "advised the United States to take its preparedness seriously."[155]

Despite these efforts, the compromise continued to attract support, and on 20 August, Maloney persuasively argued his case before the Senate. He candidly admitted "the probability of great danger . . . and even the possibility of attack, but I am sure the time has not yet arrived to distribute gas masks, to plow up golf courses, and to build bomb shelters." He refused to condemn the Burke-Wadsworth bill. "I only point out . . . that it is not an administration bill—or even an army bill." He characterized his own proposal, not as "an anesthetic for the conscription operation," but as "a possible cushion against a shock to our national life, or to the body politic." Although neither Willkie nor the president had said anything specific about his amendment, Maloney did not think that either candidate disagreed with it.[156] After making his speech, Maloney told one reporter that fifty-six senators had promised to support his amendment, more than enough to ensure its passage.[157] James Davis of Pennsylvania found the amendment preferable to premature conscription. "Shall we gather these thousands of men and give them sticks for guns, pipes for machine guns, and trucks marked 'tanks'?" he asked. That afternoon, Paul French heard a rumor that "several southern senators plan to have the bill recommitted to committees in the event the Maloney amendment is approved, on the ground that it would be better to end the discussion on conscription until after the election if immediate conscription is not approved."[158]

Senator Barkley gave the compromise added importance by announcing that the senators would vote on all other amendments first, leaving the decision on Maloney's amendment until just before the final vote on the bill itself. He also tried ineffectively to speed things up. While the Mothers of America were hanging Senator Pepper in effigy on the lawn of the Capitol, the majority leader was threatening to hold sessions through Saturday if the Senate had not yet come to a vote.[159] Senator Theodore Green of Rhode Island complained to a constituent: "If you get impatient with delays, how do you think I feel sitting in the Senate listening to . . . all sorts of orations . . . when I firmly believe every day counts in this tremendous job of preparedness."[160]

From Franklin Canfield's perspective, administration supporters seemed to be retreating. Isolationist senators, he reported, had bragged that they had enough votes to put the compromise through, a judgment that the *New York Times* verified by noting that the White House would "not oppose" the Maloney amendment "in more than normal fashion."[161] Thinking that he had been sitting on the fifty-yard line after several days in the Senate gallery, the young NEC lawyer observed that "the 'ball' had been taken away from the sponsors of the bill and . . . its opponents were running with it for a touchdown in the form of the Maloney amendment." Mixing the metaphor, he blamed Barkley and Burke for letting the isolationists "croon themselves hoarse without opposition." Canfield also cited a "confidential report heard on good authority . . . that senators were 'free' to vote as they chose on the Maloney amendment. Officially . . . Barkley will make a speech against the amendment, but his speech will have little effect if this word has already gone around.''[162]

Encouraged by their apparent success, opposition leaders continued their delaying tactics. Despite Barkley's warning that members would forfeit the floor if they yielded for other senators to make lengthy remarks, hostile speeches strung out in an almost endless chain. One of the worst offenders was Holt, who held the floor for the entire second half of Wednesday's session, yielding to Lundeen, to Wheeler, to Clark of Missouri, and to others who wanted to prolong the oratory. ''The debate rattles on like an old lumber wagon,'' Austin wrote to his mother in Vermont, ''not much accomplished except the circulation of hot air.''[163] La Follette became so embarrassed by his colleagues' tactics that he hesitated to give his own speech against a bill that he strongly opposed.[164] On Thursday 22 August, as a dozen black-veiled Mothers of America began a ''death watch'' in the Senate antechamber, Holt again obtained the floor. Three hours later he was still speaking, yielding occasionally to other isolationists. ''To call this a filibuster,'' Harry H. Schwartz of Wyoming cracked, ''is to put it mildly. One isolationist speaks and then all the others get up and agree with him, making speeches of their own.''[165] A frustrated Canfield complained: ''It is about time that these voices were drowned out by supporters of the bill on the floor.''[166] The near filibuster was holding up not only the draft bill but other defense measures as well, most notably the $5-billion military appropriations bill and the complementary tax legislation that was expected to follow. Without these appropriations the preparedness program would come to a halt.[167]

As the week drew to a close, Senator Wheeler almost delivered a bombshell by reading a personal letter from William Allen White, praising Wheeler's stand and opposing conscription. Before doing so, however, he asked White's permission, whereupon the venerable chairman of the Committee to Defend America by Aiding the Allies politely requested that his ''personal letter to an old friend'' be kept confidential.[168] Wheeler respected White's wishes, although he did show the correspondence to some of his fellow isolationists.[169] On Friday 23 August, Charles A. Lindbergh slipped into Washington for meetings with Wheeler, Lundeen, Henrik Shipstead, Nye, and other Senate isolationists. Although the famous aviator did not oppose conscription, his outspoken pronouncements against intervention made him the ideal candidate to head up a new ''nationalist, anti-war coalition,'' soon to be called the America First Committee.[170] Meanwhile, Senator Barkley was getting nowhere in his effort to force a vote, and it looked as though the Senate debate would drag into the next week.

As the summer heat maintained its grip on Washington, the wives of senators and other administration officials fled for their usual vacation spots.[171] Mrs. Roosevelt spent most of the summer at Val-Kill cottage in

Hyde Park, while Harold Ickes and his young wife managed to sneak away to Bar Harbor, Maine, for the last two weeks of August. Howard Beale took his mother to Thetford, Vermont, where he could read graduate dissertations and follow the conscription battle from afar. Although General Marshall stayed chained to his desk at the Munitions Building, Mrs. Marshall had a pleasant week's sojourn visiting their son, Allen Brown, who had just been married in June and was working for a radio station in Poughkeepsie, New York. The family reunion included a luncheon at the rustic White Hart Inn in Salisbury, Connecticut. Then Allen spoiled everything by remarking to his mother that he saw no real reason for conscription. Katherine Marshall "nearly blew up." She proceeded to lecture her son, saying he had no idea as to "what was really going on and how dangerous it was not only with Japan and Germany, but also South America." In reporting the contretemps, Allen commented that there were "millions who know even less than I do and who are therefore quite naturally against conscription since they know no direct reason for it and at the same time will be directly affected by conscription. Why in the name of God doesn't the government tell the country what is going on?"[172] The chief of staff, having completed preparations for the induction and training of four hundred thousand draftees for the autumn, could probably sympathize with his stepson's puzzlement. Like Stimson and the Plattsburgers, he undoubtedly hoped that the president would speak out forcefully one more time and kill the Maloney amendment.

11

The Final Enactment:
"A Turning Point in the Tide of War"

President Roosevelt and Secretary Stimson spent Saturday 17 August watching First Army maneuvers in upstate New York near Ogdensburg. Driving more than seventy miles in an open car through beautiful rolling countryside south of the St. Lawrence River, Stimson and the president became exhilarated as they reviewed the largest peacetime concentration of American forces since the Civil War, some ninety-four thousand men. The secretary of war greeted many old friends, including Plattsburgers Julius Adler and Cornelius Wickersham of the New York National Guard Division. "I wished very much that I was . . . working with the troops instead of sitting in a motor car all day," Stimson wrote in his diary that night.[1] The crisp, clear weather—a sharp contrast to sultry Washington—kept the presidential party in buoyant spirits until their return in late afternoon to the special railroad car near the Canadian border.

FDR had made a last-minute decision the day before to visit northern New York, not so much to witness troop maneuvers as to confer with Canadian Prime Minister W. L. Mackenzie King about mutual defense arrangements in connection with the destroyers/bases negotiations. When King arrived at U.S. Railway Car Number 1 at exactly 7 P.M., he found the president in a jovial mood. "A happy blend of chief of state, man of the world, and host," FDR served cocktails and joked about their "stealing half the show" by holding the Ogdensburg summit on the same day as Willkie's acceptance speech, "although this was not on purpose." He talked seriously about sharing responsibility with Canada for evacuated British children and assured King that he expected a favorable opinion soon from Attorney General Robert H. Jackson, affirming the legality of a destroyers/bases transaction. Roosevelt then lightened the conversation with humorous anecdotes about Anglo-American relations. J. Pierrepont Moffat, the newly appointed United States minister to Canada, was especially amused by FDR's tale about Gen. Edward Pakenham, who had been killed at the battle of New Orleans in 1815 and whose body had been shipped back to England,

200

preserved in a cask of rum. The president quoted Pakenham's great-grandson as having said: "Yes, it's true, my great-grandfather arrived in shocking condition as the sailors had discovered there was rum in the cask and had bored a hole, inserted a tube, and drunk it all."[2]

Stimson joined the two heads of state for the second course of the meal, and there ensued "one of the momentous talks which I [Stimson] ever participated in."[3] Just as he sat down, the text of Willkie's Elwood speech began to come in over the news wire. All conversation stopped. "The first two or three pages were pretty innocuous," King later recorded. FDR remarked that the one message Willkie seemed intent on conveying was that "he, the president, was bringing the United States into the war." Then the parts about the draft and aid to England came in, and "both said at once that it was all right." Obviously relieved, Stimson commented that Willkie's support of both issues made everything fit together "like a piece in a jigsaw puzzle."[4] The rest of the evening passed in a happy discussion of the destroyers/bases agreement, which FDR thought would be concluded soon, and plans for a Joint Canadian-American Defense Board. "Almost with tears in his eyes," the Canadian leader thanked the Americans for what would be "a most tremendous encouragement to the morale of Great Britain and Canada."[5] So exhilarated was Stimson that when the meeting broke up just before midnight, he compared their gathering to the Constitutional Convention of 1787, saying: "I felt that it was very possibly the turning point in the tide of the war, and that from now on we could hope for better things."[6]

Although the Ogdensburg meeting focused on the destroyers/bases issue and joint defense planning, two days in upstate New York also underscored the importance of the draft. When Stimson had breakfast with Minister Moffat on Sunday morning 18 August, he "talked of his troubles in getting conscription through right away. . . . It must come . . . at once. The Willkie speech was a godsend." He told Moffat how he often woke up at night "in a sweat because of our poor defense posture." The draft and aid to England were very complementary policies. "The danger was very near," the secretary warned, "and only England was holding it off. We couldn't do enough for England."[7] Roosevelt also connected the draft to hemispheric defense and the war in Europe.[8] "Anybody who knows anything about the German methods of warfare," he wrote a few days later, "would know" that the ninety-four thousand troops he had seen on maneuvers "would have been licked by thoroughly trained forces of a similar size within a day or two." Not only did the American units lack "many forms of modern equipment," but also "the men were not trained in the high sense of the term to use the arms they had," and "the men themselves were soft—fifteen miles a day was about all they could stand and many dropped out at that." In the president's mind, it was now clear that even though "voluntary enlistments are running at their peak today . . . this peak is far short of the essential numbers we require." He

Henry L. Stimson, a photograph for his friend Grenville Clark, signed "with affection and gratitude." (Courtesy of Dartmouth College Library)

wished that "everybody who opposes the draft enlistment could study and see with their own eyes what has led to the present situation."[9]

Neither FDR nor Stimson, however, made any public statement about the draft while at Ogdensburg, because they did not want to shift the spotlight from the Canadian–United States defense arrangements.[10] But the two men, accompanied by Gen. Hugh Drum and Congressman Andrew May during their inspections, undoubtedly discussed the Burke-Wadsworth bill. At one point during the tour the president managed a brief conversation with Julius Adler, who reminded FDR of the necessity for a strong statement against the Maloney amendment. FDR replied: "Have someone ask me at my next press conference."[11]

In the week following the Ogdensburg meeting, no immediate presidential pronouncement came forth concerning the draft. The destroyers/bases negotiations ran into unexpected difficulties when Prime Minister Churchill balked at publicly repeating assurances about not surrendering the British fleet.[12] While debate droned on in the Senate, Stimson became immersed in the details of the destroyer discussions, airplane contracts, and Canadian-American defense issues.[13] Not until Friday morning 23 August did the secretary call to remind FDR about the Maloney amendment. The president was amenable. He was holding his usual Friday press conference in an hour. Would Stimson prepare a memorandum on the subject for him? Stimson immediately summoned General Marshall. Together they worked out an unequivocal statement entitled "Reasons Why the Maloney Amendment Must Be Defeated."[14]

When reporters arrived, Roosevelt nonchalantly announced that the only thing he had was the signing of the Investment Company Act of 1940, about which Steve Early would give the necessary details. Other than that, nothing: "Just plain ain't no news."

Then from *Times* correspondent Charles Hurd came the expected question: "Mr. President, would you care to comment on the wisdom of this Senate proposition to postpone conscription until January first and give the volunteer system a further trial?"

No hesitation. "Personally I am absolutely opposed to postponement," the president said decisively, "because it means in these days—and we all know what the world situation is—nearly a year of delay." Point by point he followed the memorandum that had been drawn up by Marshall and Stimson only an hour before. At the current rate of volunteering it would take a year to get four hundred thousand men, and twice that many men were needed. The army had to be hardened and given team training as quickly as possible. All the talk about shortages in equipment was misleading. If Congress put off the increases in manpower, the orders for other materiel would be put off until the following spring, thus wasting the entire autumn and winter. "Well, the gist of it is," he concluded, "that if we do not get a bill . . . in the next couple of weeks—we are going to have a real delay in getting our team together." The bills had been introduced in June and "they are still talking. . . . That is why I am asking for action now."[15]

Again, though only after prodding, FDR had eschewed caution when equivocation on his part would have meant real danger to the defense program. In his column the next day, Mark Sullivan blamed Roosevelt's earlier hesitation on a split personality: "Mr. Roosevelt the President, and Mr. Roosevelt the candidate for a third term. . . . On this occasion, Mr. Roosevelt the President seems to have won. . . . He is for conscription, prompt conscription, and stakes his reputation on that."[16] A more partisan witness, Steve Early, claimed that "the president is [not] bothering one bit about the November elections. He is giving himself entirely over to . . . national defense, conscription, war reports, and the delicate diplomatic issues."[17] Whatever his precise motives, FDR took a bold step even when he privately feared that it "may very easily defeat the Democratic National ticket—Wallace and myself."[18]

Notwithstanding the bugle call from the White House, the situation did not suddenly resolve itself when the Senate met on Saturday 24 August. Barkley again failed to obtain unanimous consent to limit debate (he had been trying for five days), and the *New York Times* headline reported bluntly: "Senate Dallying on Draft Continues."[19] The logjam did show some signs of breaking. In his maiden speech, Senator Ernest W. Gibson of Vermont (who had taken his late father's seat) demanded action on the draft, and immediately a number of senators walked over to congratulate him.[20] Harry F. Byrd of Virginia echoed Gibson's plea for action, and Vandenberg, fair-minded as always, admitted that the subject had been substantially exhausted.[21] After the afternoon session, Senator Wheeler told Frederick Libby and Dorothy Detzer that opponents had agreed that voting on amendments could begin on the following Tuesday or Wednesday.[22] La Follette also saw the momentum turn. "The president's statement will probably put over the draft bill," he glumly informed his wife.[23] Supporters of the Maloney amendment were now admitting that their majority of six or seven votes had evaporated.[24]

Opponents received another jolt over the weekend when Wendell Willkie, almost on cue, announced that he favored the immediate enactment of the draft. He explained that his comments at Elwood were intended as a very definite endorsement of conscription, and interpretations to the contrary completely distorted his position.[25] At a press conference on Monday the Republican nominee reaffirmed that he had never meant anything other than "Now!" when he had advocated "some form of selective service" in his acceptance speech.[26] Willkie confided to columnist Joseph Alsop that he was being "subjected to terrific pressure, designed to modify his position on conscription and foreign policy," but Alsop said that Willkie "sincerely believes in what he is saying, and does not propose to change, even if it should mean defeat."[27]

These developments enabled Barkley to predict, when the Senate reconvened on 26 August, that the compromise would lose by a close vote.[28] As crowded galleries voiced lusty approval of Senator McKellar's plea of "For heaven's sake, let's do something," the legislators finally got down to work during the Monday session. Austin wrote to his mother that because of "a limitation of 15 minutes for each speaker while on the pending amendments, we may [now] expedite the bill."[29] Continued wrangling forced the session well into the evening, but when the weary senators adjourned at 10 P.M., they could point to actual progress for the first time in three weeks.[30]

Out of the way were a number of amendments, several of which had caused much discussion and had threatened even longer delays. The first was Lodge's proposal to limit to eight hundred thousand the number of men in training at any one time; a compromise, speeded by Senator Sheppard and approved by the General Staff, set nine hundred thousand as the maximum.[31] An even-more-important amendment by Lodge, which would have limited service to the Western Hemisphere and to United States territories and possessions, went through by a vote of 67 to 4. This amendment, which had little impact on the constitutional powers of the commander in chief during wartime, at least placed the Senate overwhelmingly on record as desiring conscription for hemispheric defense, not as the basis for another AEF.[32] Lodge's attempt to narrow the age range of draftees to twenty-one to twenty-five met defeat by a vote of 60 to 19. In addition, the Senate adopted an amendment, by Wagner of New York, prohibiting racial discrimination against Negroes who volunteered for the armed forces, and another by Gurney of South Dakota, making the courts responsible for handling cases of reemployment.[33]

The next morning brought a dying burst of isolationist oratory. "Right now," Austin wrote disgustedly, "Sen. Johnson of Colorado is on the floor with what looks like the manuscript of a two-hour speech, which will not add a new thought or clarify an old one."[34] Johnson was followed by McCarran and then Lundeen, all of whom read diatribes to a nearly empty chamber.[35] Again Barkley held the Senate into night session to get constructive action, for the only votes during the day had come on three relatively minor amendments. The first significant test occurred early in the evening. Walsh of Massachusetts offered a substitute that would have allowed registration to continue but would have forbidden the induction of any men "unless and until the Congress shall have declared that a state of war exists, or has declared that the United States is threatened with invasion." In a short debate, Henry F. Ashurst, Wheeler, and Danaher supported Walsh, while Barkley and McKellar both asked, "Why pass the Bill at all, if the amendment is agreed to?"[36] When the vote was tallied, the opposition could muster only 29 backers; 54 voted nay.

The next contest came on an amendment by Taft, who proposed to limit the Regular Army to five hundred thousand and establish a special army training corps of one and a half million volunteer reservists. Except for the Ohio senator's short speech of explanation, no one debated, and the proposal died by a vote of 55 to 22.[37] The Walsh and Taft amendments, both of which would have eliminated the draft completely, verified earlier predictions that some form of conscription would pass and that the critical battle would come on a proposal to postpone its operation. By the time the Senate had acted on Taft's substitute amendment, it was 10:30 P.M. To the disappointment of spectators who had packed the galleries to witness the all-important roll call, Barkley moved to proceed to executive business and to adjourn. Since he had finally obtained a limitation of debate, he announced that the bill could easily be disposed of the next day.[38]

Victory did not come easily. Until the very end of the nine-hour session that closed the long debate on 28 August, the fight raged bitterly, with the issue still in doubt. As before, one delay followed another. Although the fifteen-minute limit curtailed windy oratory, legislators still had to thread their way through a labyrinth of amendments before coming to the final decision that evening.

The first important amendment, sponsored by Senators Richard Russell of Georgia and John H. Overton of Louisiana, gave the president authority to seize industrial plants that refused to cooperate in the defense program. This amendment encountered surprisingly little opposition, partly because many opponents thought they saw in it a way of striking back at the sponsors of the draft. "The financial crowd in New York, who are parading and shouting for this bill in the interest of doing patriotic service," mocked Wheeler, "will raise a howl when this amendment is put into the bill."[39] Alexander Wiley of Wisconsin, a Republican who voted nay on the final bill, thought the Russell amendment was "an omen of what is coming—total conscription of men, property, labor. . . . Every citizen must be on guard to see that we do not lose our freedoms through the 'back door' . . . [and] be prepared so we won't lose them through the 'front door.' "[40] Presented during the afternoon, the Russell-Overton proposal passed by a wide margin, 69 to 16.[41]

Oddly enough, the climax came, not on the Maloney amendment, toward which Senate momentum had been building for weeks, but on an eleventh-hour substitute offered by Carl Hayden of Arizona. This happened simply because Hayden's amendment incorporated the essential principle of Maloney's, thus anticipating the much-publicized compromise. Once the senators had voted on the Hayden proposal, the fate of the Maloney amendment, purposely held until last, became a foregone conclusion.

The issue remained the same—should Congress postpone the operation of the draft until volunteering had received a further trial? The Maloney amendment provided a trial until 1 January 1941; the Hayden amendment called for only sixty days. Like his Connecticut colleague, the Arizonan sought both preparedness and Democratic unity, and he believed that Congress could have both. "Enough voluntary enlistments could be secured within the next two months to fill the immediate needs of the War Department," he assured a constituent.[42] Why not authorize two separate calls, each for four hundred thousand one-year volunteers, one immediately upon enactment, the other on 1 January? If the quotas for either call had not been filled after sixty days, the draft would automatically operate to make up the difference. In this way, Hayden argued, the army could be certain of obtaining the desired number of recruits on its specified dates; at the same time the adequacy or inadequacy of the volunteer system could be demonstrated to everyone's satisfaction.

Apparently answering the argument of urgency, since the army would require at least a few weeks to get the draft under way in any event, the seductive proposal attracted even some senators who opposed Maloney's substitute. Hayden found an able ally, for example, in Tydings, who argued that the amendment would prove once and for all that volunteering could not do the job. Resistance to the new proposal, however, grew more vociferous than had earlier discussion on Maloney's amendment. Sheppard, the first to speak against it, was quickly followed by fellow southerners Connally of Texas, Allen Ellender of Louisiana, and Carl A. Hatch of New Mexico. Bailey of North Carolina passed the word to Edwin Watson that southern Democrats would be "voting right and with the president on every question before the Senate, particularly conscription."[43] From Austin and Barkley came other persuasive arguments. The former pointed out that the bill itself provided just what Hayden was urging: the dual operation of the volunteer and compulsory system, for immediately upon enactment, men from eighteen to thirty-five could enlist for one year. The more volunteers, the lower the draft quotas. Barkley spoke bluntly: "I am one of those who believes that if there is any need for this legislation the need exists now." The amendment was simply more temporizing, with a method that would be "the wrong way to raise an army" even if it produced sufficient numbers.[44]

This was an essential point. The Senate had tended all along to look mainly in terms of numbers, forgetting the vital consideration of efficiency. The primary justification for selective service lay in its ability to furnish the desired quantity of men to the armed forces. But the secondary justification, almost as important, came from its ability to furnish the right recruits, leaving in their civilian occupations those men who would be more valuable to the total defense effort at home than in the military service.

By the time of Barkley's speech, however, the moment for changing votes by argument had passed. The decision on the Hayden amendment was close. Twelve senators did not vote. Of the remaining 84, 41 voted for the proposal, 43 against. As expected, party lines meant little. The defection of several senators who later supported the bill itself—as, for example, William H. King, Maloney, Mead, Neely, Pittman, Tobey, Tydings, Wagner, and White—indicated strong reluctance to take the irrevocable step.[45]

Ironically, the Hayden amendment would have passed if the anticonscriptionists had not split on the issue. The opposition, as always, included too many individualists. As Hiram Johnson explained to his son, many opponents voted for the Russell-Overton, Hayden, and Maloney amendments to embarrass the bill's sponsors. "I would have voted for any amendment that would have smeared the bill," he wrote.[46] But Senator Taft found himself voting with Barkley and Burke; he announced at the last moment that he opposed both the Hayden and Maloney proposals "because they are simply advanced as a means of proving that the volunteer system will not work. . . . Of course it will not work under those conditions."[47] Either because they thought as Taft did or because they firmly opposed a draft bill in any form, Clark of Idaho, Danaher of Connecticut, and Schwellenbach of Washington joined Taft in answering no to the roll call.[48] The amendment lost by only two votes. Had one of these four men changed his mind, there would have been a tie, and had two voted yes, the amendment would have carried.

The rest seemed anticlimactic. The Hayden amendment had cut the ground from under the Maloney plan. If the Senate opposed postponement for only sixty days, it would hardly approve a delay until 1 January. The Maloney amendment thus went down by a vote of 50 to 35, 22 Democrats, 10 Republicans, 1 Independent (Norris), 1 Progressive (La Follette), and 1 Farmer-Laborite (Lundeen) voting for it. Effective opposition had dissipated; but even here the anticonscription forces might nearly have won if they had held ranks, for the 50 nays included 6 consistent foes of the draft principle—Ashurst, Clark of Idaho, Clark of Missouri, Danaher, Schwellenbach, Taft, and Thomas of Idaho.[49]

Just before the final roll call, Senator Danaher asked the majority leader to refute, for the record, the charge that the Senate had "unduly prolonged" consideration of the bill. Barkley replied, somewhat charitably, that "it had been an intelligent debate. It has probably been a little longer than some of us would have preferred, but it has been a legitimate debate."[50] With this gesture and with special recognition for the performance of Senator Sheppard as chairman of the Committee on Military Affairs, Barkley called the final vote. Eight Republicans joined the 50 Democrats voting aye, while 17 Democrats, 10 Republicans, 2 Farmer-Laborites, 1 Progressive, and 1 Independent voted nay.[51] Geographically, the strongest support for the bill came from southern and border states, with New England and Middle Atlantic not far behind. Mountain-state senators divided evenly on the measure, while only one-third from the West Coast, Plains, and Great Lake states voted for the final bill.[52]

The bill's sponsors were jubilant. "The Senate's action by such a decisive majority," Grenville Clark exulted, "is now proof that the American system is still capable of meeting a crisis."[53] For Senator Barkley, it was, "politically speaking, one of the most extraordinary pieces of legislation ever enacted by Congress in time of peace."[54] Julius Adler wrote Senator Sheppard how "fortunate that in this emergency you were directing consideration of the measure."[55] Senator Bailey, for one, thought the lengthy debate had proven beneficial in the long run. He confided: "If I had made a decision three weeks ago, it would have been different from the decision I will make now. Altogether, I consider these matters as being of a great deal more importance than any matters . . . in my lifetime. Some of the people in North Carolina have written to me quite impatiently, but I have thought . . . they would have been as deliberate as I have been."[56] The antiwar newsletter *Uncensored* agreed with Bailey's judgment. Its editor, Sidney Hertzberg, wrote: "At a time when representative government is everywhere in question, the Senate debate on conscription provided striking proof of the intelligence, the sincerity and the sense of democratic responsibility with which a freely elected legislature can face a great decision. The decision itself may have been a blow to democracy; but the process of reaching it was democracy's triumph."[57] For the bitter Hiram Johnson, however, it was "the most insidious act that has been passed in my long service here."[58]

Passage of the Burke bill caused some advocates of the draft to get overconfident. During the last days of the Senate debate, the National Emergency Committee forwent lobbying for the moment and attempted to prove that much of the opposition to the draft came from subversive sources. Angered by charges of Wall Street and Jewish machinations, some NEC leaders, especially Perley Boone, overreacted. While Franklin Canfield talked to the FBI and the House Un-American Affairs Committee, Boone assembled an impressive display of reprints from the *Daily Worker,* handbills from the Young Communist League, and photostats of party circulars suggesting that Communists had inspired at least some of the letters, wires, and postcards pouring into Washington. The governing committee in New York talked about sending a well-documented letter to each congressman and senator, requesting a formal investigation. Congressman Wadsworth, however, strongly opposed this, saying that no investigation could begin before the final vote on the bill. Such a move, he thought, would look like cheap theatrics.[59] The NEC thus dropped the idea of an investigation, although Boone did send documented letters to members of the House Military Affairs Committee, calling attention to Communist influence.[60] These charges of subversive collusion, while they enraged patriotic opponents of the bill, probably made some legislators question more critically the mass of opposition mail. With this parting shot, NEC workers in Washington, again on advice from Wadsworth, closed down their headquarters at the Carlton because they did not think it prudent or necessary to lobby further in the House.[61]

President Roosevelt seemed pleased by passage of the Burke bill, even as he fretted and worried about the final details of the still unannounced destroyers/bases transaction. He told intimates that Britain had only a "fifty-fifty" chance of survival and that he must go ahead with naval assistance, even if it cost him the election.[62] Before journeying first to Hyde Park and then to Tennessee over the long Labor Day weekend, he told his wife that he might make a speech linking the draft to the destroyer deal, or he might possibly dramatize the acquisition of new bases by making a personal inspection tour. "Good for him," Eleanor wrote to their daughter, Anna, "but I tell him he must explain to the people first or they will say 'Ah ha!' "[63] Secretary Stimson and his wife also left Washington after the Senate vote on 28 August, flying to St. Hulbert's in the Adirondacks for a week of hiking, golfing, and relaxation.[64] Meanwhile, rumors circulated that Senators Minton and Pepper were informally polling their colleagues, at the request of the White House, to determine the sentiment for a declaration of a "state of war"—not against

Germany—but a declaration that might justify further steps away from strict neutrality.[65]

The House of Representatives, except for sporadic outbursts, had been waiting throughout the Senate debate for action from the other wing of the Capitol. Individual congressmen, of course, had been subject to the same barrage of mail, telegrams, and pamphlets as had their Senate colleagues.[66] The Committee on Military Affairs had continued open hearings until mid August and since that time had been meeting in executive session. This was by conscious design. Majority Leader Sam Rayburn, working closely with Wadsworth, had advised Chairman Andrew May to hold the bill in committee until the Senate had acted.[67] In this way they could make the majority report conform more or less with the amended Senate measure, thereby avoiding complications with two radically different bills. The House committee, however, did not act as a mere rubber stamp. Much to the satisfaction of Stimson and the Plattsburgers, the committee followed "good Jim Wadsworth" and retained the twenty-one to forty-five age provision, despite the Senate's retreat to twenty-one to thirty-one.[68] "Pressure is tremendous here," wrote one congressman who opposed conscription, "and no one knows what kind of draft bill will pass . . . but some kind of draft bill is going to pass."[69] Moreover, a last-minute attempt by one committee member to elicit a negative opinion from General Marshall brought forth a firm answer from him: "It is not fair to the country or to the men themselves to await an actual emergency to commence their training. I do not think we can afford to speculate with the safety of the United States."[70]

May's committee lost no time. On Friday 30 August, less than two days after the roll call on the Burke bill, May brought his report to the floor. A minority of eight members, including five who had reversed themselves since the day before, opposed the bill, not only because it constituted a "distinct and dangerous departure" from American practice but also because it marked the first step towards a "totalitarian military economy." This last concern arose from the adoption of the Russell-Overton amendment to allow the conscription of industry. The majority, however, expressed confidence that the general public would "hail the enactment and completion of this legislation as a distinct triumph for America."[71]

To minimize delay, May went before the House Rules Committee the same day and obtained, despite strenuous objections from Republican members, a special "gag rule," limiting general debate to only two days.[72] This meant that formal consideration would begin the following Tuesday, 3 September, and would last only until Wednesday night. Thursday and Friday would be devoted to a section-by-section reading of the measure and to the proposal of amendments. Rayburn predicted that the bill would pass easily by a two-to-one margin on Friday night.[73]

Outside Congress, opponents of conscription redoubled their efforts to block the hated measure. In special Labor Day radio broadcasts, both William Green and John L. Lewis assailed the bill, with the latter damning it as "one of the major planks in the platform of reaction."[74] That Friday, unsubdued by the passage of the Burke bill in the Senate, two thousand demonstrators streamed into Chicago for the three-day Emergency Peace Mobilization, sponsored by the newly formed Committee to Defend America by Keeping out of War and by the People's Peace Federation.[75] Infiltrated by Communists and enthusiastically backed by the *Daily Worker,* the Chicago rally repelled most of the better known peace organizations, and its headline speakers, Senators Nye and D. Worth Clark, thought it wise to cancel their appearances at the last minute. But Joseph Curran of the National Maritime Union, Michael Quill of the Transport Workers Union, and Ben Gold of the International Fur and Leather Workers Union provided plenty of oratorical power. Hundreds of young zealots, wearing "Stop Conscription" buttons, then traveled eastward to flood the House galleries when debate commenced on Tuesday. Actor-singer Paul Robeson led this Washington mobilization.[76]

More than a thousand young Americans also attended the National Conference of Methodist Youth, at Lake Winona in Indiana over the Labor Day weekend. Exhorted by pacifists Kirby Page and John Swomley, the Methodists passed antidraft resolutions and mailed out at least one hundred thousand stickers. According to one delegate, they made stencils and, "using poster-card paints, transferred the words 'Stop Conscription—Write Your Congressman' in big letters on at least 150 cars. . . . Caravans of a sort were organized, with the cars decorated. I got only two hours of sleep."[77] Nor did Frederick Libby sleep very much on returning to Washington from his New England vacation. Over the Labor Day weekend the peripatetic peace worker raised $1,000, gave a detailed interview against the draft to the *Washington Post,* debated against naval aid to England over the American Forum of the Air, transcribed another interview on the draft, to be sent to some seventy radio stations, and mailed out anticonscription pamphlets to approximately thirty-two thousand opinion leaders around the country.[78] Ever optimistic, Libby thought that "the addition of conscrip[tion] of industry to the bill has given us a good chance to defeat it in the House—at least 50-50."[79] Dorothy Detzer also believed there was "still a chance to defeat this bill in the House." Urging as many members as possible of the Women's International League to come to Washington, the "queen of the Hotspurs" emphasized that "the entire House must be re-elected. Therefore the members of the House are much more sensitive to public pressure at this time than the Senate. So your efforts now should be more than doubled."[80] While Thomas Rankin helped to arrange more radio time for antiwar senators, Libby and Detzer mailed out to local affiliates more than forty thousand copies of Senator Wheeler's latest speech.[81]

Other peace leaders were less sanguine. Ed Johnson of the Committee on Militarism in Education admitted: "It looks as though we're licked on conscription. I fear nothing short of a miracle will prevent approval by the House."[82] Norman Thomas's Socialists gave out a formal statement, saying that the Senate bill, as passed, "will make for war rather than peace."[83] But instead of stepping up lobbying efforts in Washington, Thomas set out on a series of campaign speeches around the country, and party workers seemed mesmerized by the possibility that their candidate, as the only presidential hopeful "unqualifiedly opposed to peacetime military conscription," might actually win a substantial percentage of the vote in November.[84] For Socialists, the fight over conscription began to take a back seat to the presidential race. As for the small group of pacifists who were working primarily for a strong conscientious-objector clause, the efforts of Paul French and Raymond Wilson had not succeeded in broadening the grounds for objector status beyond that of religious beliefs. Despite appeals to Eleanor Roosevelt and a personal interview with Secretary Stimson, the CO clause in the Senate bill failed to cover humanitarian or "absolutist" objectors. The Quakers thus asked Howard Beale to cut short his Vermont holiday to help prevent further erosion in the House bill.[85]

When the House reconvened on 3 September, it seemed to be staging a much faster rerun of the previous three weeks in the Senate. Hamilton Fish of New York led off with the first of many anticonscription attacks. May quickly defended the bill on behalf of the Military Affairs Committee. All through the afternoon the oratorical winds blew back and forth. "If you read all the speeches," one New York congressman later observed, "I'm afraid you would have been asphyxiated."[86] The chamber burst into an uproar at one point when a youth from the Emergency Peace Mobilization shouted from the crowded gallery: "American conscription is American fascism."[87] Such demonstrations did little for the pacifist cause, as Congressman Eugene Cox of Georgia called the protesters "Communist bums and bohunks," and a Pennsylvania Democrat boasted: "I don't depend on bastards like you to get elected."[88] A worried Frederick Libby did a hurried canvass and counted: "189 for us on conscript[ion]. A House majority is 218. But we shall do our best." Libby sent another telegram to Wendell Willkie, urging him "in view of FDR's obvious trend toward dictatorship to call for postponement of draft action until Jan. 15."[89]

The next morning, just as debate was to begin anew, President Roosevelt stunned Washington by announcing the acquisition of eight British bases, from Newfoundland to British Guiana, in exchange for fifty United States destroyers of World War I vintage. When asked if the Senate needed to ratify the agreement, FDR snapped: "It is all over; it is all done."[90] Although the transaction had been rumored for weeks, the president's timing and methods irritated his political opponents.[91] Nearly every congressman was buzzing over the news when James Wadsworth rose to speak on his bill early in the afternoon. Like many other Americans, he confessed, he had been too complacent about Hitler before 1939; but now the aggressive designs had become too plain for anyone to miss. The United States could not take chances. He characterized his bill as an emergency measure, aimed at meeting an authentic danger: "It is not an attempt to establish a permanent policy in the United States. It is meant to meet . . . the immediate future and to put the country in a position to meet that situation promptly. In my humble judgment, we cannot afford to indulge in a 'wait and see' policy. Others have indulged in that and they have perished."[92] Throughout, the speech was interrupted by bursts of applause, and when Wadsworth had finished, the entire House rose in spontaneous ovation.[93]

Speaking immediately after Wadsworth, Vito Marcantonio represented the opposite extreme. The fiery New Yorker hailed his older colleague from upstate New York as one of the most "honest and able" men in Congress but said that his bill would lead to a war that a majority of Americans abhorred. Marcantonio shouted: "Despite the controlled press and the controlled polls, you must admit that the AF of L, the CIO, the churches, the youth organizations, and the Farmers Union do represent a far greater number of people in their opposition . . . than do the organs of propaganda . . . hysterically clamoring for its passage." Cries of "wolf" only masked ulterior motives. Marcantonio warned: "You are not fooling the American people. The day is not far off when these weapons of destruction and this army built by conscription will be used not for defense but for participation in an imperialist war."[94] A more reasonable isolationist, Clifford Hope of Kansas, told his constituents that he could see himself voting for peacetime conscription "if England should go down," but "Germany has not been able to cross the twenty miles of the English Channel."[95]

Packed galleries, including both supporters and critics of the bill, frequently had to be admonished as the debate raged on. In a highlight of the session, Congresswomen Clara G. McMillan of South Carolina and Frances P. Bolton of Ohio, both of whom had sons of draft age, took the floor to speak on opposite sides. McMillan supported the draft as a means of ensuring that untrained men would not have to go into battle; she said that while she would vote for the bill with a heavy heart, she would do so with conviction. Representative Bolton, making her maiden speech after assuming her late husband's seat, argued that conscription would bring "more danger than defense, more dictatorship than democracy. . . . If Mr. Roosevelt can do what he wants with our destroyers without consulting Congress, and we give him our boys, God alone knows what he will do with them."[96] Both women received standing ovations.

The speechmaking continued until well into the evening. Just prior to adjournment, Martin Sweeney of Cleveland delivered a vitriolic speech in which he damned conscription as part of an administration plot to get the United States into the war on England's side. Although nominally a Democrat, Sweeney elicited cheers from the Republican side when he condemned not only FDR but also Woodrow Wilson for entering World War I. When Sweeney sat down, Democratic Congressman Beverly Vincent of Kentucky loudly remarked that he refused "to sit by a traitor." Sweeney thereupon threw a punch at Vincent, who retaliated with a staggering right to the jaw, the best punch landed in the past fifty years according to the House's doorkeeper.[97] After colleagues had rushed in to separate the two pugilists, Sweeney expressed regret at what had happened; Vincent tried to explain his behavior but stopped short of making a formal apology. The House voted the next day to expunge Vincent's "traitor" remark from the *Congressional Record*. "And so the disgraceful episode ended," noted Congressman Lawrence Lewis, who had helped to break up the fight.[98]

Beneath the fireworks of the two-day debate, it became apparent that members of the House disagreed with the senators on two significant points—age limits and the industrial draft. On age, House members remained firm in insisting that all males between the ages of twenty-one and forty-five be liable for training. "It is difficult to convince me that *I* would not make a better soldier" than younger men, Lyle Boren of Oklahoma boasted.[99] In the final decision, after voting down Clinton Anderson's amendment to accept the Senate's age limits of twenty-one to thirty-one, the House also rejected Anderson's compromise proposal to register men twenty-one to forty-five but to make only those aged twenty-one to thirty-one subject to induction.[100] In regard to the Russell-Overton amendment, House members objected principally to the president's authority to take over factories for an indefinite time. Many congressmen, for whom Cox of Georgia acted as spokesman, saw this as further evidence of the country's turning to the left. According to Cox, the provision was "undesirable, unnecessary, Un-American, and . . . unconstitutional."[101] Robert Doughton of North Carolina, the powerful chairman of the House Ways and Means Committee, told his constituents that Republican opposition to the industrial draft was "only a political move" to discredit the New Deal.[102] To placate such opposition, May announced, prior to the House debate, that he would recommend a milder substitute for the Senate's industrial draft.[103]

Meanwhile, in response to needling from Wendell Willkie, new controversy over the industrial draft broke out in the Senate. Having made conscription itself a nonpartisan issue, the GOP candidate seized upon the hastily passed Russell-Overton amendment as one point he could criticize. Willkie charged that such a provision would "sovietize" American industry, and he challenged the president to make clear his own preference.[104] FDR ducked at his press conference, by saying disingenuously that he never commented on pending legislation.[105] Democrats in the Senate, however, had a field day heckling Willkie's willingness to draft men but not wealth. Jimmy Byrnes suggested that since thirteen senators of Willkie's own party had voted for the amendment, Willkie could find among his Republican cohorts plenty of opponents to debate. Sherman Minton brought guffaws when he remarked that "Indiana chiggers" must be "eating on Willkie a little."[106]

In accordance with his promise to propose a milder substitute, May's committee presented an amendment by Congressman Joseph Smith of Connecticut, which provided for the mandatory rental, rather than the outright seizure, of noncooperating industries.[107] Although Smith's amendment went beyond the Senate version by authorizing the criminal prosecution of violators, the House eventually accepted it. This meant that differences on both the industrial draft and age limits would require settlement by a House-Senate conference committee.

Although these two issues seemed to be the only areas of contention, opponents suddenly sprang a surprise by resurrecting a new version of the Hayden amendment. The calendar called for little more than a routine reading of the bill for Thursday 5 September. No sooner had the clerk of the House begun to read than the burly six-foot-five-inch figure of Hamilton Fish interrupted, offering as his own amendment the same plan that had failed by only two votes in the Senate. The Republican congressman from President Roosevelt's own home district proposed to delay the draft for sixty days while four hundred thousand volunteers were being sought; if the numbers failed to appear, the president could then fill the quotas by draft. The amendment provided for a second similar call on 1 January 1941.[108] That Hamilton Fish should sponsor such an amendment presented a real irony, for twenty-five years earlier, Fish had worked closely with DeLancey Jay, Grenville Clark, Philip Carroll, and the other young professional men who had founded the Plattsburg Movement. Himself a Plattsburg graduate, Fish had commanded a Black National Guard regiment during World War I, had won the Croix de Guerre, had attained the rank of major, had been elected to Congress in 1919, and had supported Leonard Wood for the presidency in 1920. During eleven terms in Congress, however, Fish had broken ties with most of his old Plattsburg associates. A staunch anti-Communist, Liberty Leaguer, and champion of veterans' causes, by the mid 1930s the former All-American football player had become the ranking Republican on the Foreign Affairs Committee and a chief spokesman for what historian Manfred Jonas has called "belligerent isolationism."[109] Although Fish was usually a consistent supporter of strong national defense, he opposed the bill because he believed that FDR would use a conscript army to form a second AEF. The president had an equally low opinion of Fish. "I wish this great Pooh-bah would go back to Harvard and play tackle on the football team,'' FDR had commented only a few months earlier.[110]

Fish had done his homework well. By using peace workers as researchers and go-betweens, the aristocratic Fish formed a temporary alliance with such liberal Democrats as Jerry Voorhis and John Coffee of Washington.[111] Caught off guard, Wadsworth, May, and Rayburn did their best to rally their wavering colleagues. "Time there was for England, for Belgium, for France," warned Rayburn, "and they didn't use it. Sixty days would have meant a great deal." May charged political cowardice: "My God, men and women, have we come to the day in this country when we are afraid to vote until after the votes are counted in November?" Wadsworth said that the amendment would jam the entire machinery of army expansion, while R. E. Thomason of Texas tersely noted: "If you [Fish et al.] are opposed to this bill, this is one of the best means I know to scuttle it." But the House had taken the bit in its teeth. When both sides had argued themselves dry, the chair put the question. A solid chorus of nays seemed to match the shouts of aye. Unable to decide, the chair directed a teller vote. With Fish and May acting as tellers, the legislators slowly filed past. The final count went 185 to 155 in favor of Fish's amendment.[112]

Whether or not the House would retain Fish's amendment on final reading remained problematical. Ninety congressmen had not voted; and members, who were sometimes inclined to vote with reckless abandon in teller counts, might well reconsider when forced to put their names on record. The estimated forty-five Democrats who had voted aye might vote differently once May and Rayburn cracked the whip. Nevertheless, if Fish's amendment did pass on the roll call, this would revive the compromise that had apparently been throttled earlier in the Senate. Opponents in the upper chamber, thus emboldened by a favorable vote in the House, might succeed in winning the two or three votes necessary if and when the Senate considered a conference bill.[113]

The already tense atmosphere on Capitol Hill now grew tauter. On the evening of 5 September, the Detroit minister Owen Knox led a group of draft protesters in a prayer vigil on the Capitol steps, even though the sergeant at arms of the Senate had expressly denied them permission to do so. Standing firm, Knox and his followers began singing "We Shall Not Be Moved." Soon the police moved in, swinging their nightsticks. Knox was arrested, more police arrived, and the rest of the demonstrators scattered. One policeman tried to calm the unruly onlookers by getting the crowd to sing "My Country 'Tis of Thee," a form of riot control that the *Washington Post* considered a "very interesting and important contribution to police science."[114] That same evening, Senator Taft delivered an effective speech over a nationwide radio hookup, in which he cleverly used the destroyer deal to discredit the draft. He reasoned: "If Hitler were about to overwhelm England and attack the United States, the president obviously could not weaken our navy by depriving it of 50 destroyers now in active service. The alleged need immediately for a huge army is based on the theory that our navy is inadequate. The president has just determined that the navy is completely adequate and can even afford to surrender 50 of its fighting craft."[115]

Dorothy Detzer found the last few days of the House debate almost unbearable. Carloads of women from the eastern branches of the WILPF, including the organization's secretary, Mildred Scott Olmsted, had come to help lobby, but it became almost impossible to talk to congressmen face-to-face. "The crowds were so big and the feelings were so intense" that it reminded Detzer of the Bonus March, eight years earlier. The Capitol police, puffed up with authority, seemed especially insolent to opponents of the draft. "Only those who have known the provocative behavior of police handling a picket line," Detzer recorded, could imagine the "pushing and shoving, the sneering comments about the crowd, the inciting actions—such as fingering a revolver while taunting . . . 'this would be a swell bunch of communists on which to do some target practice.' " The doorkeepers, whose duties included carrying cards from constituents to their representatives, acted equally offensive. They often tore up the cards or refused to take them in, sometimes telling people to go home, the bill was going to pass anyway. At one point, Detzer and Olmsted went to the office of the sergeant at arms and appealed for protection from his own police. They assured him that they understood the problems created by the large crowds and tense atmosphere, but they insisted that he should instruct his men not to increase tensions themselves. "The sergeant at arms never rose from his seat," Detzer reported, "and he exchanged winks with other police officers who were lolling in their chairs. . . . I myself feared violence. . . . The ugly, sinister atmosphere of war is already here."[116]

The House did not come to the third reading of the measure until Saturday 7 September. Events abroad still shared the spotlight with domestic news. King Carol II of Rumania, forced by Germany to cede half of Transylvania to Hungary, had abdicated in favor of his son Michael. From Moscow came the announcement of a series of new government appointments, one of which made Andrei Vishinsky the assistant to Foreign Minister V. M. Molotov.[117] With the biggest air battles of the war raging over London, the Royal Air Force was more than holding its own.[118] In Washington, President Roosevelt refused to comment on the Fish amendment at his Friday press conference. He did, however, remark, with a wry smile, *"Tempus fugit,"* and again pointed out the seriousness of any delay in the defense program.[119]

This gentle prodding failed to produce the desired effect on the wayward House, despite the fact that "the Democrats were present in full force."[120] Ratifying earlier tentative decisions, the House, during its Saturday session, adopted the Smith amendment for conscription of industry and upheld the liability of men from the ages of twenty-one to forty-five.[121] Then came the roll call on the Fish amendment. As in the Senate, the vote for compromise was razor thin; but in this case the opposition won by a tally of 207 to 200.[122] Hiram Johnson wrote gleefully: "I am glad the House . . . stuck to their decision to give sixty days for voluntary enlistment. I am glad of this not . . . because it will accomplish in the long run any results, but for the reason that I would do anything . . . that might smear it, or might demonstrate its uselessness. . . . It does make the progenitors of the bill perfectly furious."[123]

Again the final decision on the bill came as an anticlimax. With one member voting present, the vote showed 263 for and 149 against the Burke-Wadsworth bill. For passage were 211 Democrats and 52 Republicans; opposed were 33 Democrats, 112 Republicans, 2 Progressives, 1 Farmer-Laborite, and 1 American Laborite. Geographically, the House vote followed the earlier pattern in the Senate, with southern and border-state delegations almost unanimously supporting the draft, followed by members from the New England and Middle Atlantic states. Mountain and Pacific congressmen, many of them Democrats, tended to vote for both the Fish amendment and the final bill, while those from the Great Lakes and Great Plains mostly voted nay on the final bill but supported the Fish amendment.[124] More than in the Senate, however, partisanship seemed to determine votes. Outside the eastern states, GOP representatives opposed the draft by a vote of 88 to 7, while at the same time supporting the Fish compromise by 91 to 3. Such a pattern probably reflected suspicion of President Roosevelt as much as it did hard opposition to the principle of the draft. Wadsworth, who did his best to line up Republican support, confided to a friend that "if any other man had been in the White House, there would not have been 25 or 30 votes against the bill on the Republican side."[125] Senator Taft also observed that "the vote is really an anti-Roosevelt vote."[126]

On Sunday 8 September the press reported predictions by congressional leaders that the draft legislation, now agreed to in preliminary form by both houses, would be completed and passed by the following Saturday. Speaker Will Bankhead had already appointed the House conferees, the Senate would name theirs the next day, and discussion by joint committee would begin on Tuesday. Of the three major issues—age limits, the industrial draft, and the Fish amendment—only the last promised real trouble.

Acceptance of the compromise seemed so likely that the army had already begun to work out procedures for the sixty-day volunteering period. On Monday, General Marshall outlined to Stimson a plan to eliminate "some of the evils of the Fish amendment and reduce delay to a small amount." Since nothing prohibited the establishing of local draft boards at once, he explained, these agencies could handle volunteer enlistments; then, if and when the volunteer system failed to meet quotas, the same draft boards could immediately select men under the draft. After going over this plan with Shedd and Hershey, Stimson called Wadsworth, who thought it acceptable.[127]

At this point, Grenville Clark, who had a knack for stepping in at such moments, got wind of what was going on at the War Department. Immediately he telephoned Stimson. As with the Civilian Volunteer Effort in June, he again interceded to prevent temporizing. "We must not compromise," he insisted to the secretary. "The psychological effect would be bad, very bad." If they were to retain the Fish amendment, Clark argued, registrants would already have their numbers, and they would know whether they were likely to be drafted. Those whose numbers stood near the top would volunteer so as to avoid being drafted later, thus repeating the experience of 1917 and unjustly casting a stigma on those who waited for induction. Most important, this forced volunteering—a most undesirable and inefficient method of compulsion—would confuse the public, for the artificial success of a volunteer drive would raise doubts about the necessity of the draft when international events were making it more imperative all the time.[128]

Although Stimson thought " 'Grenny' was wildly excited about the situation," the action of the Senate on Monday justified Clark's counsel to stand firm.[129] When Adams of Colorado, who had voted against the bill, offered a motion to eliminate a conference by accepting the House's version, he was promptly voted down. Even more striking evidence that draft supporters had gained strength came on two other motions by Bennett Clark of Missouri. The first proposed that Senate conferees be instructed to insist on limiting registration to men between the ages of twenty-one and thirty-one. Despite Senator Wheeler's assertion that wider limits amounted to "a club to hold over all American working men," the motion went down, 44 to 23. Next, Clark moved that the Senate instruct its conferees to accept the Fish amendment. A close vote seemed likely; but the opposition, unable to coordinate, had fallen apart. Barkley jibed that the amendment was aptly named, since its real design was to "fish for votes in November." Hill and Connally followed with equally sharp attacks. Only Carl Hayden took the floor to speak for Clark's motion, which was rejected by the surprising vote of 48 to 19.[130]

The Fish amendment received two more telling blows that day, when Henry Wallace and Willkie both condemned it. In a speech at Hastings, Nebraska, Wallace charged that the Republicans, the "party of appeasement," were purposely delaying the defense program.[131] Though hardly agreeing with this analysis, Willkie nevertheless expressed, at Rushville, Indiana, his hope that the conference committee would eliminate the Fish amendment. This comment evoked a violent denunciation from Fish, who charged that Willkie had "fallen for the propaganda of the interventionists and the eastern press and columnists."[132] That evening, one participant told columnist Raymond Clapper that the president had phoned every conferee, saying that "the bombing of London was much worse than the newspapers say and urged them [to] get conscription bill out of conference today and pass it tomorrow."[133]

Such pressure had a demonstrable effect on the Conference Committee, and agreement on all three issues came on Wednesday 11 September. Thinking they had a strong bargaining chip in the Fish amendment, House members had adamantly stuck to the twenty-one to forty-five age limits. But on Wednesday night, in return for giving up the volunteering proposal, they accepted the senators' compromise to extend the age range of the Senate bill to twenty-one to thirty-five. This last agreement came about in a somewhat unorthodox manner. Major Hershey, waiting outside the conference room, encountered an exasperated Walter C. ("Ham") Andrews, who threw up his hands and asked Hershey the oldest age that a man could volunteer for the army. Hershey said "35 years," whereupon the New York congressman went back inside and the conferees immediately settled on the age range of twenty-one to thirty-five. The senators then agreed to eliminate the Russell-Overton amendment, substituting for it the House plan for the mandatory forced rental of defense industries. Both sides decided to strike out the provision for criminal prosecution of plant owners.[134] Thus the bill went back to the Senate without the Fish amendment, with the age limits twenty-one to thirty-five, and with the Smith plan replacing the Russell-Overton forced-seizure plan. "I fought myself hoarse yesterday," conferee Elbert Thomas reported, "but I had my way in everything so I certainly shall not complain if it keeps up that way."[135]

With passage of an immediate draft bill now assured, James Wadsworth wrote to the man who had planted the original seed. Although annoyed at the narrow age range, Wadsworth noted that "twenty-one to thirty-five is not so bad" and "I am really somewhat astounded that our bill has not suffered more." He predicted that the bill would "be sent to the Senate today and acted upon. It will be submitted to the House tomorrow, Friday, and acted upon. I am confident the votes in both houses will be heavily in its favor. In other words, our job is over."[136]

In the Senate on Thursday, things went momentarily awry as a group of southern Democrats balked at the revised industrial draft. They did not object to forced rental, but they complained that the conferees had pulled all the teeth from the Smith plan. As House members, waiting at the other end of the Capitol for the bill, began to drift over to the Senate to see what had gone wrong, the dissenters insisted that criminal penalties for offenders be restored to the section in question. Congressman Lewis, after reassuring a worried officer of the General Staff that the House had more than enough votes, looked in on the "Cave of the Winds [Senate] where they were still talking."[137] Finally, the Senate took the usual action of sending the bill back to the Conference Committee.[138] The committee, which met as soon as the Senate recessed, resubmitted the original language of the Smith amendment and had the bill ready when the Senate reconvened on Saturday morning.[139]

In half an hour on Saturday 14 September the Senate approved the revised bill and sped it along to the House. The final count, 47 to 25, showed 40 Democrats and 7 Republicans in the affirmative and 13 Democrats, 10 Republicans, 1 Progressive, and 1 Independent in opposition. While few senators felt disposed to make speeches at this late juncture, Burton Wheeler issued one last lurid prediction: "You will have a country of Al Capones. You will have a country where robbery and murder will run riot."[140]

Passage in the House followed similar lines, the great majority of Democrats supporting the measure, the Republicans opposing it about two to one. The final tally counted 232 yes, including 186 Democrats and 46 Republicans, and 124 nays, including 32 Democrats, 88 Republicans, 1 American Laborite, 1 Farmer-Laborite, and 2 Progressives. Senator Key Pittman, president pro tem of the Senate, and Sam Rayburn, acting Speaker of the House during the sudden illness of Will Bankhead, attested to the authenticity of the engrossed copy of the bill and forwarded it to the White House. The president announced that he would formally sign the measure into law on Monday.[141]

The small band of pacifists who had worked so assiduously for a strong CO clause followed these last two weeks of the legislative process with mounting apprehension. When the House debate began right after Labor Day, Raymond Wilson and Paul French, who had assumed responsibility for the objectors when Howard Beale had gone to Vermont, had hopes that they could broaden the definition beyond the language contained in the Senate bill. Congressman Jerry Voorhis offered to sponsor an amendment on the floor, and he even introduced his own bill for voluntary national service along the lines of FDR's pronouncements earlier in the summer.[142] The pacifists faintly hoped that the president might still support such a measure.[143] Once debate had started, however, the Friends huddled with Voorhis and decided against any new amendment. As the California congressman later explained, the German blitz of London and the growing impatience of Congress as a whole made them realize that if they raised "this question at all [it] might lead to somebody making a counter proposition to render the whole section . . . less liberal than it was in the first place."[144] Major Hershey also assured the Quakers that under administrative regulations to be set up under the Selective Service Act, the authorities would bend over backwards to protect absolutist objectors and anyone who was sincerely opposed to military service on nonreligious grounds. Hershey told both Beale and French that if he, Hershey, were to be put in charge of selective service, no conscientious objectors would ever go to jail.[145] With such assurances and with the political momentum swinging unmistakably toward swift passage, the pacifists thought that they could live with the language of the Senate bill.

Then disaster apparently struck. Howard Beale was sitting in the House gallery on Friday evening 6 September, when, without warning, Pennsylvania Democrat Francis Walter rose and offered an amendment to eliminate the role of the Justice Department in dealing with the claims of conscientious objectors. The chair—Lindsay Warren of North Carolina—asked for the unanimous approval required for floor amendments. Voorhis jumped up and objected furiously. Warren struck the gavel, saying "without objection, consent is granted." "But I objected, Mr. Chairman," Voorhis pleaded. "I did not hear your objection," the chair replied.[146]

Beale sat there flabbergasted. "I suppose they learned the trick from old Joe Cannon," he later wrote.[147] The pacifists soon learned what had happened. Because Justice Department lawyers feared that as many as one-tenth of all registrants would claim conscientious-objector status, they had written the amendment to give local draft boards the primary jurisdiction. The pacifists objected to such an arrangement, for they believed that local boards would show more prejudice and that only the Justice Department could ensure equal and fair treatment. A frustrated Paul French wrote in his diary: "It is curious how a few minutes can undo the work of a month or more."[148]

The peace lobby did not give up. In a meeting held on Sunday afternoon at Frederick Libby's headquarters, its members vowed to press the Conference Committee to restore the Senate version, which they proceeded to do.[149] Beale again took the lead and immediately buttonholed Elbert Thomas, Warren Austin, and Styles Bridges. By Wednesday morning he could telegraph Roger Baldwin: "Six [out of eleven] conferees pledged to retain Senate provision."[150] Andrew May said that he would present the House version but would not argue for or against it, an assertion that Beale doubted in view of May's reputation as a "hard-boiled militarist." Beale's hopes seemed dashed, however, when the conference report came back on Thursday morning. Instead of accepting the Senate version, the conferees offered a new provision for objectors, again suggested by the Justice Department, that tried to split the difference. The new clause provided that local boards should decide the case of each conscientious objector, but in the event of an appeal, the appeals board of the Selective Service Administration should hear each appeal first; in each case, however, the Justice Department would also hold a hearing and make recommendations that the regular draft appeals board should consider but would not be bound to follow. Roger Baldwin took the first train to Washington and had a long talk with Attorney General Robert Jackson that same afternoon. Jackson again promised that his department would do all that it could to treat conscientious objectors with "great fairness" and that all regulations for determining objector status would be drawn up in cooperation with prominent religious spokesmen and lay leaders "like Roger Baldwin."[151]

The pacifists were not mollified. They saw little chance that they could get the bill sent back to the Conference Committee because of the objector clause alone. The president seemed to be their best hope, and Wilson, French, and Clarence Pickett spent most of Friday 13 September seeking an audience at the White House by way of Mrs. Roosevelt.[152] But FDR could not see them; his appointments were full.[153] That afternoon, however, Senator Wheeler told Beale that he might be able to get enough votes at the dinner hour to recommit the bill because of the clause about the conscription of industry "and that perhaps we could at that time . . . get our clause changed" as well. Beale got hold of French, and they agreed that someone should be at the Senate in the late afternoon and early evening. Unfortunately, both men had already made dinner engagements, so that when Beale arrived, "the bill had been recommitted and the Conference Committee was sitting and it was too late to do anything." Beale and French tried to reach individual conferees the next morning before the Senate reconvened. But "the people we knew best were out of town. No one was available. I tried to find Austin of Vermont but he too was gone from town. So I went up to Johnson of Colorado for advice. He felt there was nothing we could do." Beale called Baldwin, who again telephoned the attorney general. Beale then hunted down Major Hershey and had another "long and very satisfying talk." Again the pacifists were assured that the army and the Justice Department would do their utmost to protect conscientious objectors through administrative regulations. Convinced that they had done all they could, Beale and French went over to the Senate wing of the Capitol at eleven o'clock and "got ourselves slipped into a gallery reserved for parties with guides, by a friendly doorman Paul French had gotten to know. . . . We slid in to see the final session that was to make the Burke bill law."[154]

President Roosevelt formally affixed his signature to the Selective Training and Service Act at 3:08 P.M., on 16 September, in an impressive ceremony in the Cabinet Room of the White House. The chief executive spoke solemnly of peace and sacrifice. "America stands at the crossroads of its destiny," he proclaimed. "Time and distance have been shortened. A few weeks have seen great nations fall. We cannot remain indifferent to the philosophy of force now rampant in the world. . . . We must and will marshal our great potential strength to fend off war from our shores. We must and will prevent our land from becoming a victim of aggression." The Congress had enacted, without partisanship, he claimed, a fair and democratic method of building United States forces. At the time of registration, young men would come from the factories and the fields, the cities and the towns, to enroll their names. He concluded: "On that eventful day, my generation will salute your

President Roosevelt signing the Selective Service and Training Act of 16 September 1940. Behind him, left to right, are Henry L. Stimson, James W. Wadsworth, General George C. Marshall, and Senator Morris R. Sheppard. (Courtesy Dartmouth College Library)

generation. May we all renew within our hearts that conception of liberty and that way of life we have all inherited. May we all strengthen our resolve to hold high the torch of freedom in this darkening world so that our children and their children may not be robbed of their rightful inheritance."[155]

Afterwards, with movie cameras whirring away and flash bulbs popping, Roosevelt laughed and joked with fellow Democrats as he signed the bill with first one pen, then another. Grim-faced, Stimson, Marshall, and Wadsworth stood stiffly by.[156] (Marshall later told Howard Petersen that "Grenville Clark should have been here instead of me.")[157] After smiling for numerous photographers, the president gave Wadsworth one of the ceremonial pens, whereupon the New York Republican took it home and casually dropped it in the wastebasket.[158]

The victors saved their congratulations for private. The day after the signing, Stimson wrote to Clark, "I want to tell you what a fine job—in fact unique job—you have done in getting it drafted and passed. If it had not been for you no such bill would have been enacted at this time. Of this I am certain."[159] Wadsworth expressed similar sentiments:

> I have one thing on my mind just now, and that is admiration and gratitude to you and those who worked with you in starting this thing and carrying on the battle so bravely. Your emergency committee has performed a vital public service. It performed it unselfishly and with a vision not often possessed by any group in these hectic days. You paid me a high compliment in asking me to introduce the bill, and what is more important, you gave me a chance to serve in a great cause. I rejoice at the opportunity, and not the least part of my satisfaction is my better acquaintance with you and your fellows.[160]

A warm letter came back from Clark in Dublin, New Hampshire. "I think time will show," Clark replied, "that it was a *sine qua non* to any real effort to stand up to Hitler et al. Much more needs to be done to that end but without this I don't think we'd have got to first base."[161]

12

Epilogue:
The Ambiguous Legacy

Some years after the end of World War II, Lewis Hershey asked Grenville Clark for a photograph to hang in his office at selective-service headquarters in Washington. The selective-service director thought it was only appropriate that the man who had done so much to get the draft law enacted in 1940 should be so recognized. Clark, even though he had worked closely with Hershey during the war and had developed a real fondness for the man whom most Americans thought of as "Mr. Selective Service," declined the request, saying that his own role had been "only minor."[1]

Clark's modest assessment may have been a polite way of paying tribute to Hershey, who was to run the machinery of selective service for some thirty years, but possibly Clark's refusal more accurately reflected his own doubts about the long-term legacy of 1940. Notwithstanding his herculean efforts for selective service in 1940 and for national service after Pearl Harbor, the old Plattsburger took up a new cause, world federalism, and became an increasingly vocal critic of American policies during the Cold War. When the Truman administration asked Congress to renew the draft in March 1948, Clark sent a wire to his old foe Robert Taft: "Hope you will insist on much clearer evidence that war is unavoidable before approving either selective service or universal training. The assumption that Russian policy aims at world domination rather than defense against Western attack is surely not valid."[2] Initially, Clark was concerned with the impact of the draft on what he considered an overly aggressive United States foreign policy, and his writings and backstage activities during the late 1940s and 1950s were aimed primarily at such global changes as reform of the United Nations Charter and intricate plans for nuclear disarmament.[3] In reaction to United States involvement in Vietnam, however, the man who wrote the Burke-Wadsworth bill came to be critical of the draft as an institution, particularly its channeling and deferment practices that seemed to discriminate on the basis of class and educational background.[4] Clark died in 1967, but before that, he advised the son of a close friend to claim conscientious-objector status, even though the courts did not yet recognize the validity of selective objection to unjust wars such as the one in Vietnam.[5] Although Clark and Hershey never exchanged any harsh words, the Plattsburg founder and the one-time "Hoosier isolationist" followed separate paths after World War II.[6]

It does not detract from the ironic legacy of 1940 that Clark was alone among Plattsburg leaders in joining the peace movement after World War II and in working alongside such former opponents as Norman Thomas, Roger Baldwin, Jeannette Rankin, and Abraham J. Muste.[7] Clark often sought younger lawyers to assist him in his various causes, and such close associates after the war included Thomas Rankin, Kingman Brewster, and several others who had worked against the draft in 1940.[8] As for Archie Thacher, Kenneth Budd, Julius Adler, and the rest of the Plattsburg crowd, after the war they pushed vigorously for a permanent system of universal military training, a cause that was also supported from inside the government by President Truman, General Marshall, Congressman Wadsworth, and such former Plattsburgers as Robert Patterson, Howard Petersen, and John McCloy. Again, however, partly because of opposition from labor, farmers, peace groups, and higher education and mainly because of the costs involved, the country failed to adopt UMT. Instead, the military raised active forces to meet its far-flung commitments through a combination of selective service and voluntary enlistments.[9] A modified version of the system that had worked so well in the two world wars lasted from 1948 to 1972.

Ironically, the draft became the most conspicuous casualty of the Vietnam War. Notwithstanding the dispatch of more than 2.5 million troops to Vietnam over the course of a decade, the United States failed to achieve its political and military goals. As casualty lists rose after 1965, political protest against the war tended to focus on the draft. Some 70 percent of the fifty-six thousand Americans who died in Vietnam were draftees. Students on college campuses burned their draft cards in symbolic protest, and Catholic priests poured blood on selective-service files in Catonsville, Maryland. Fully thirty thousand youths of draft age fled the country, while as many as half a million avoided induction through various illegal means. General Hershey, who tried to defend the system that he had administered since 1940, became the target of much vitriol. When Richard M. Nixon became president and began to withdraw United States forces from Vietnam, he removed Hershey from office and pledged to end the draft. In a further irony, when the Nixon administration moved to an All-Volunteer Force (AVF) in 1973, it did so by arguing that a leaner professional force that would emphasize firepower over manpower could meet all defense needs. Although the AVF would number more than two million uniformed personnel, the argument was reminiscent of the pacifist/ isolationist opposition of 1940. A subtle philosophical shift also occurred, as military service was seen, not as an obligation, but as a tax. According to the presidential commission that recommended the AVF: "When not all our citizens can serve, and when only a small minority are needed, a voluntary decision to serve is the best answer, morally and practically, to the question of who should serve."[10]

Whether or not the kind of military system that had proved so successful in two world wars should necessarily apply to the nuclear age was a question the Plattsburgers left unanswered. The political scientist Eliot A. Cohen has argued that once the United States achieved the status of a world power, it had to be prepared to fight two kinds of wars—the large conventional total wars that require full mobilization, as in 1917 and 1941, and smaller, peripheral wars and police actions that are fought with limited forces, as in Korea and Vietnam. Comparing the American experience in Korea and Vietnam with nineteenth-century Britain's small wars in Africa and Asia, Cohen contends that Anglo-Saxon countries can engage in such conflicts with greatest military success and least disruption of domestic tranquility by relying on professional forces.[11] Yet Cohen also notes that the All-Volunteer Force, which is so dependent on superior American technology, would prove deficient in the event of a conventional war in Europe against Warsaw Pact forces. Eventually, he concludes, "demography, strategic necessity, and economic recovery will conspire to force a return to the draft. What kind of draft, however, remains as open a question as it was almost forty years ago."[12]

Of course, the enormous changes wrought by World War II make it difficult to apply any solutions or techniques from an earlier era. Just as nuclear weapons and other technological advances shrank the globe and expanded American power and commitments, the sheer size of government after World War II automatically diminished the influence of small elite groups such as the Plattsburgers. In terms of methods, 1940 marked the last time when a dedicated layman like Clark could effectively propose national solutions while still maintaining his amateur status. Thereafter the Plattsburg tradition of national service meant that the Ivy League/Wall Street elites had to go to Washington to man the machinery of government from within. It disappointed Robert Patterson, for example, that he could not lead troops into battle during World War II; instead, he had to stay at his desk in the new Pentagon Building and direct industrial mobilization. When Patterson succeeded Stimson as secretary of war in the autumn of 1945, the Plattsburg flag passed to a different generation. Others in the Plattsburg lineage, such as John McCloy, Howard Petersen, and Lewis Douglas, stayed on as insiders, as "national security managers," who easily shuttled between high positions in government, academia, and business.[13] Grenville Clark, in continuing his role as an elder statesman incognito for two decades, found that he could still communicate with his friends on the inside, but their views and objectives had changed. "Tell Grenny we still love him," was a message that came from National Security Adviser McGeorge Bundy in the early 1960s. "They have a funny way of showing it," Clark responded.[14]

Passage of the draft in 1940 did have a more immediate connection with United States involvement in World War II. As a direct reaction to Hitler's blitzkrieg victories in Europe, the success of the four-months' campaign for selective service marked the beginning of the end of isolationist assumptions in the United States. Despite the claims of a Nye or a Taft that Hitler posed no immediate strategic threat, enactment of the draft in peacetime showed that totalitarian aggression, whether through invasion or fifth-column uprisings, seemed real and frightening enough to prepare for such eventualities. Congress, by passing the Lodge amendment, did hope to confine the deployment of draftees to defense of the Western Hemisphere, but the concurrent destroyers/bases transaction implied that defense of the hemisphere was linked to the survival of the British Empire and of the Royal Navy. Indeed, the successful and simultaneous accomplishment of the draft and of the destroyer deal set in motion a redefinition of national security that blurred the distinction between war and peace and eventually required vast increases in United States power to defend bases and allies abroad. The draft could provide the manpower for this expansive vision.[15]

President Roosevelt's indirect style of leadership tended to obscure the relationship between defense and foreign policy in 1940. Confused at first by the implications and extent of Germany's triumphs, the president proceeded cautiously in May and June, emphasizing rearmament needs, keeping his options open and his political fences mended, hoping to minimize isolationist obstruction, and all the while gauging events abroad in terms of naval power. Because FDR delayed making any firm decision on either the draft or the destroyer deal until early August, both policies took shape and gathered momentum along different lines in ways that sometimes confused the public debate and made it difficult to coordinate policy. He allowed the debate in Congress over conscription (a desirable goal, but not the top priority for him) to endanger any forthright policy of aid to England, so much so that he nearly backed off from both policy options in the midst of a presidential campaign against an opponent whom he mistakenly viewed as a potential Fascist. Moreover, the president's unwillingness to give clear clues to the civilian groups that were pushing both the draft and the destroyer deal meant that the main arguments for the two policies tended to contradict each other. As Taft and others pointed out, it was inconsistent to urge peacetime conscription on the grounds that the hemisphere would be immediately threatened if Britain should fall, while at the same time transferring fifty naval vessels to that same country because the latest intelligence indicated a better than 50 percent chance that it could withstand a German invasion.

By the time FDR finally acted on the destroyers/bases transaction, both the fierce public debate over conscription and Willkie's unwillingness to cooperate publicly persuaded the president that the only way to avoid an interminable filibuster was to proceed through an executive agreement.

Roosevelt's decision to back both measures took political courage, for he honestly believed that it could lead to his defeat in November, or possibly even to his impeachment. So he moved obliquely, deviously, successfully, not revealing his full motives and increasing his opponents' suspicions. That he needed to act in such a circuitous manner is not at all certain.

This is not to suggest that FDR was secretly plotting intervention on the side of Britain in 1940. If anything, the president's inattention to the details of the draft bill, his greater concern for keeping Britain in the war, his unwillingness to propose wartime economic mobilization, even his pledges not to send American boys into foreign wars—all point to the sincerity of Roosevelt's belief that the best way to avoid war was for the United States to become the "arsenal of democracy."[16] To be sure, FDR understood that by giving aid to Britain, he ran the risk of war. In fact, German naval planners reacted to the destroyer deal by proposing Operation Felix, the projected occupation of Gibraltar, the Canaries, the Cape Verde Islands, and the Azores, to be carried out "before the USA steps in."[17] A more prudent statesman might have employed "worst case analysis" and ordered his military advisers to prepare for war with Germany in 1941, but Roosevelt did not.[18] Nor did he try to dispel Winston Churchill's illusions that the United States would become a belligerent after the president had been reelected.[19] Even during the lend-lease debates in February and March 1941, when FDR declared that the survival of Britain was vital to United States defense, he did not make public the strategic discussions that were then taking place in Washington between British and American staff officers on a contingency basis.[20] Animated by what Anthony Eden was later to call "cheerful fecklessness," the president continued until Pearl Harbor to attempt to satisfy the twin impulses of most Americans—namely, to help Britain beat Nazi Germany, while at the same time avoiding formal participation in the war.[21] An improviser at heart, the president preferred to move in a forward direction but without any predetermined destination.

Given FDR's hesitant leadership and the army's preoccupation with hemispheric defense during the spring of 1940, the Plattsburgers' proposal for peacetime conscription came at a fortuitous time. By introducing the Burke-Wadsworth bill on their own and by attracting wide publicity, the NEC leaders initiated a national debate on a controversial and vital issue without forcing the president to commit himself prematurely during an election year. The Plattsburgers' single-minded dedication to a strong draft bill with broad registration, and particularly their steadfast opposition to the Civilian Volunteer Effort and other proposals for voluntary enlistments, virtually ensured that some form of military conscription would emerge intact from the legislative process. While the debate over the draft did not always clarify the links between national defense and the war in Europe, it did awaken the country to international dangers, and it did prepare individuals for necessary sacrifices. If NEC leaders became diverted at times in a quixotic quest to revive Plattsburg-style officer camps, even to the point of alienating the General Staff, this did not in the end detract from their main objective of obtaining a draft law. Just as their Puritan ancestors sometimes pursued God's grace too single-mindedly, so, too, did these twentieth-century aristocrats occasionally project their own vision of military conversion in ways that were not always appropriate or universal. Nevertheless, as General Marshall instinctively guessed, proposals for peacetime conscription and other forms of military expansion stood a much better chance of public acceptance if they came from civilian, rather than from military, authorities.

The army certainly profited from the Plattsburg initiative. By letting civilians lead before he took up the cudgels, General Marshall obtained the one mechanism necessary for raising forces that would be large enough to provide for hemispheric defense or to wage war in overseas theaters. For the remaining year of peace the army used manpower from the draft to enlarge and reorganize its structure, adapt to modern weapons and tactics, and carry out large-scale maneuvers during the summer of 1941.[22] After Pearl Harbor, selective service permitted the army to expand enormously. Draft calls reached a peak of five hundred thousand a month by late 1942. By registering 45 million men and drafting 10 million, the system enabled the army to reach its top strength of eighty-nine divisions and 8.3 million men in 1945. More than 5 million draftees served overseas in Europe, Asia, Africa, and the Pacific, by far the most extensive war effort ever undertaken by the United States.

Even though the Plattsburg sponsors did not envisage such a large army when they introduced their bill in June 1940, they essentially planted a seed that grew in accordance with administration policy and bureaucratic blueprints. They urged the draft in 1940 on the unstated assumption that the United States should intervene in the European war on the side of Britain, but these foreign-policy desires did not dictate the outcome in 1940 or afterward. The Plattsburgers scored by getting their proposal before Congress at a crucial moment, but once it became a national issue, control slowly slipped from their hands. Just as they could not persuade the General Staff to reinstitute Plattsburg officer camps, NEC leaders could not guarantee that the draft would be used to "stand up to Hitler, et al." simply by advocating it.[23] The waning of their influence became evident even during the congressional debates, for it was Hershey and his aides, not Clark and Petersen, who drafted the final amendments to the bill. Once selective service had passed, the NEC disbanded most of its organization, except for a small subcommittee that pushed futilely for officer training in 1941. Grenville Clark remained influential as an unofficial adviser to Stimson and as a founder of the interventionist Fight for Freedom Committee in 1941. Yet Clark, even as he backed lend-lease, convoys, repeal of the Neutrality Act, and other steps toward war, was always careful not to advocate publicly any premature entry into the war.[24] His chief concern was that the United States be prepared for war if it came. As a War Department consultant, Clark helped to draft a resolution for a declaration of war on 8 December 1941, but it can hardly be said that he or the Plattsburg crowd had guided United States policy to that fateful result.[25]

Passage of the Burke-Wadsworth bill also proved to be a turning point for the opposition. College students, as historian Justus D. Doenecke has pointed out, returned to their campuses that fall with a "certain fatalism. . . . They were not militantly interventionist but they often found isolationism futile."[26] The peace groups in particular took their defeat as a sign that United States intervention in the war against Hitler was only a matter of time. The Committee on Militarism in Education formally dissolved itself on the fatalistic assumption that the draft had militarized all education.[27] Pacifists redoubled their efforts at counseling conscientious objectors, and Paul French, Raymond Wilson, Roger Baldwin, and others worked with the Selective Service System in setting up and administering Civilian Public Service Camps, wherein some twelve thousand COs who refused to do noncombatant service worked without pay during the war on projects involving reforestation, agricultural experimentation, and soil-erosion control.[28] The KAOWC did remain in operation, and such individuals as Libby, Detzer, Villard, and Thomas kept up their own crusades against war until Pearl Harbor. Almost as soon as the draft bill became law, however, the new and more conservative America First Committee became the chief vehicle for opposing intervention. Unlike the peace organizations and the KAOWC, America First favored a strong national defense.

The changed priorities became obvious in the summer of 1941, when the KAOWC network tried to reconstitute the antidraft lobby to oppose the Roosevelt administration's bill to extend the period of service for draftees under the Selective Training and Service Act. Norman Thomas asked Howard Beale to coordinate the opposition as he had done the year before. This time Beale said no, that he had worked himself to exhaustion the previous summer, and he absolutely had to finish his research on Theodore Roosevelt.[29] The America First Committee, while opposing any new American Expeditionary Force, took a neutral position on extension of the draft.[30] The legislation, which authorized an additional eighteen months of service for all inductees, eventually passed by a 50 to 35 vote in the Senate and by a bare 203 to 202 in the House. The close vote did not so much reflect strong opposition to the draft as it reflected erratic leadership by FDR, who failed to explain the necessity for longer service and who left Washington during the final voting to meet secretly with Winston Churchill off Newfoundland. Ironically, because of the 203 to 202 vote, the 1941 legislation extending the period of service has often been confused with the Selective Training and

Service Act of the preceding year. The draft itself, mandated by law to continue to 1945, was not being extended in 1941; rather, it was the twelve-months' training period that was being extended. Even if the vote on extending service for eighteen months had been negative, almost certainly a compromise would have been reached at twelve or six months. Not even the most inveterate isolationists were proposing to terminate the draft in 1941. It had become, as FDR had said the year before, the "pillar of national defense."[31]

The Plattsburg effort also helped to sustain faith in American institutions at a moment of peril. Germany's sudden victories in Europe produced a crisis of confidence among Americans, a sense of despair that democratic governments could not defend against the totalitarian juggernaut. The comment by Senator Minton about adopting Hitlerism to defeat Hitlerism was an extreme example. Young John F. Kennedy's slim volume *Why England Slept*, published at the height of the selective-service debate, echoed the gloomy analysis that totalitarian states that are geared to war had clear advantages over democracies, where "the cry of 'warmonger' will discourage any politician who advocates a vigorous arms policy." Nevertheless, Kennedy thought that the United States could still profit from Britain's example by getting "our armaments *and the people behind these armaments* . . . prepared . . . even to the ultimate point of war." In the next-to-last paragraph of the book, the future president concluded: "What we need is an armed guard that will wake up when the fire first starts or, better yet, one that will not permit a fire to start at all."[32] In a symbolic sense the old Plattsburg crowd provided the United States with such an armed guard in 1940, by writing and by lobbying through the legislation that eventually raised the military forces necessary to triumph over the Axis war machines. And by stressing the principle of national service and a citizen's obligation in a democracy, Clark and his colleagues articulated a rationale for military reform that harmonized with American traditions and values.

But the initiative of the Plattsburgers in 1940 has a broader implication for Americans nearly half a century later. The trauma of the Vietnam War, the end of the draft, and a nuclear arms race have diminished the links between the people, the armed forces, and the government. John Kennedy's 1940 comment that "there is no lobby for armaments" makes for quaint reading in an era when the common defense no longer seems to be the responsibility of every citizen but instead is provided by hundreds of billions of tax dollars, technical experts, and esoteric systems and strategies.[33] But if the 1940 experience means anything, it suggests that the questions of national security are too important to be left to experts and machines. Just as the Plattsburgers and their opponents thrashed out the pros and cons of a military draft in 1940, it is still the obligation of citizens to think and debate anew the dilemmas posed by global commitments in an age when nuclear weapons can obliterate, for all time, the distinction between citizens and soldiers.

Notes

Acronyms used in the notes

ACLU	American Civil Liberties Union
AFSC	American Friends Service Committee
CDGA	Document group at Swarthmore College, Swarthmore, Pa.
COHP	Columbia Oral History Program, Columbia University, N.Y.
DG	Document Group
FDRL	Franklin D. Roosevelt Library, Hyde Park, N.Y. ·
FO	Foreign Office
GRB	Georgia Robison Beale
HHPL	Herbert Hoover Presidential Library, West Branch, Iowa
KAOWC	Keep America out of War Congress
LC	Library of Congress, Washington, D.C.
MSS	Manuscripts
MTCA	Military Training Camps Association
NA	National Archives, Washington, D.C.
NCPW	National Council for the Prevention of War
NYPL	New York Public Library
OF	Official File
PPF	Personal Papers File
PSF	President's Secretary's File
RBFO	Records of the British Foreign Office, Public Record Office, Kew, England
RG	Record Group
SCPC	Swarthmore College Peace Collections, Swarthmore, Pa.
SHSW	State Historical Society of Wisconsin, Madison
YCAW	Youth Committee against War
WILPF	Women's International League for Peace and Freedom

CHAPTER 1. THE LOTTERY OF WAR

1. *The Public Papers of Franklin D. Roosevelt,* ed. Samuel I. Rosenman, 13 vols. (New York, 1939-50), 9:510-14.

2. Since the army planned to call only 800,000 draftees by June 1941, registrants with high induction numbers were not likely to be drafted in the near future. In fact, Roosevelt, in his speech, said that "only the first ten per cent will be considered as the 'first drawn' 1,640,000 out of the total 16,400,000. If your number is drawn after the first ten per cent of the numbers, you will not be called into this year's service" (Roosevelt, *Public Papers,* 9:511-12).

3. YCAW news release, c. Nov. 1940, box 35, America First Committee Records, Hoover Institute, Stanford University, Stanford, Calif. See also John L. O'Sullivan, "From Voluntarism to Conscription: Congress and Selective Service" (Ph.D. diss., Columbia University, 1971), 136-37; also *Time,* 11 Nov. 1940, 24-25; George Q. Flynn, *Lewis B. Hershey: Mr. Selective Service* (Chapel Hill, N.C., 1985), 73.

4. The most publicized cases involved eight students at the Union Theological Seminary, who refused to register. Among the eight was David Dellinger, who later rallied draft protesters against the Vietnam War during the 1960s and 1970s (see David Roberts, "The Case of the Union Students," *Christian Century,* 30 Oct. 1940, 1340-42).

5. Quoted in *Time,* 11 Nov. 1940, 24.

6. Geoffrey Perrett, *Days of Sadness, Years of Triumph: The American People, 1939-1945* (New York, 1973), 40.

7. Roosevelt, *Public Papers,* 9:517.

8. Oswald Garrison Villard to Porter Sargent, 27 Aug. 1940, Oswald Garrison Villard MSS, Houghton Library, Harvard University, Cambridge, Mass.

9. Quoted in Richard Lowitt, *George W. Norris: The Triumph of a Progressive, 1933-1945* (Urbana, Ill., 1978), 302.

10. Clifford Hope, Jr., to Earl C. Richardson, 27 July 1940, Clifford Hope MSS, Kansas State Historical Society, Topeka.

11. Grenville Clark to James W. Wadsworth, 17 Sept. 1940, Wadsworth Family MSS, LC.

12. Forrest C. Pogue, *George C. Marshall: Ordeal and Hope* (New York, 1966), 62.

13. Quoted by James N. Rosenau in *Public Opinion and Foreign Policy* (New York, 1961), 62.

14. *Complete Works of Abraham Lincoln,* ed. John G. Nicolay and John Hay (New York, 1905), 6:312; Grenville Clark, *A Plan for Peace* (New York, 1949), 3.

15. Lord Halifax to Sir John Simon, 21 Mar. 1941, reel 2, Hickleton MSS, Churchill College Archives, Cambridge University, Cambridge, England.

16. "Movements of Opinion in the United States in the First Year of War, September 1939-September 1940," compiled by the Survey Department, the British Press Service, New York, 1940—(received in FO on 16 Nov. 1940), A4694/131/45, RBFO.

17. Ibid.

CHAPTER 2. PLATTSBURG REVISITED

1. Hadley Cantril, ed., *Public Opinion, 1935-1946* (Princeton, N.J., 1951), 970-71.

2. John F. Kennedy to Joseph P. Kennedy, n.d. (c. Apr. 1940), JFK Personal Papers (correspondence, 1939-40), box 1, John F. Kennedy Presidential Library, Boston, Mass. Another college student and future United States senator, Claiborne Pell of Princeton, was also writing perceptively about American attitudes in 1940 to his father, the United States ambassador to Portugal (see Claiborne Pell to Herbert Pell, 20 May, 17 and 23 June, 21 July, 26 Aug. 1940, box 18, Herbert Pell MSS, FDRL).

3. Herbert S. Parmet, *Jack: The Struggles of John F. Kennedy* (New York, 1980), 68.

4. Diary entry, 16 Apr. 1940, in Anne Morrow Lindbergh, *War Within and Without* (New York, 1980), 79. FDR's own thinking during the Scandinavian campaign is seen in a candid talk with Canadian Prime Minister Mackenzie King: "When speaking of the British and French being hard pressed, he [FDR] said he might

find it desirable to send some destroyers and cruisers across the Atlantic to assist the Allies. . . . [As in the Quasi-War with France in 1798–1800] there had been no declaration of war, and there would be no declaration this time. . . . He spoke of the danger to South America if the Germans were to succeed. Of the ease with which Mexico might be occupied by the Germans if they got a foothold in South America. Of the short distances from there to ports of the middle states for aeroplanes. . . . He spoke of the dangers to the Atlantic Coast cities, of gas as well as bombs. . . . He knew exactly . . . about the nature of the coasts, harbours, etc. He regarded facilities for communication as most essential of all'' (diary of Mackenzie King, memorandum of conversation with President Roosevelt, 23–24 Apr. 1940, microfiche no. 147, King papers, Public Record Office, Ottawa, Canada).

5. Lothian to FO, 7 June 1940, no. 531, A333/2961/45, RBFO.

6. Mark L. Chadwin, *The Warhawks: American Interventionists before Pearl Harbor* (New York, 1970 ed.), chap. 2.

7. Carter Glass to Wallace Tiffany, 15 May 1940, box 385, Carter Glass MSS, Alderman Library, University of Virginia, Charlottesville.

8. Joseph C. O'Mahoney to Jay Smith, 30 June 1940, box 49, Joseph C. O'Mahoney MSS, Western Historical Collections, Coe Library, University of Wyoming, Laramie.

9. Theodore G. Bilbo to O. M. Patton, 19 June 1940, Theodore G. Bilbo MSS, University of Southern Mississippi Library, Hattiesburg, Miss. (from the notes of David Porter).

10. "American Preparedness," British Library of Information Report no. 221, 24240/131/45, RBFO.

11. Henry A. Wallace, diary, 24 May 1940, copy in possession of Theodore A. Wilson, Lawrence, Kans.

12. "British Fleet," British Library of Information Report, 24240/131/45, RBFO.

13. Mark S. Watson, *Chief of Staff: Prewar Plans and Preparations* (Washington, D.C., 1950), 94–97, 107–10; David A. Haglund, *Latin America and the Transformation of United States Strategic Thought* (Albuquerque, N. Mex., 1984), chap. 9.

14. Henry Morgenthau, Jr., presidential diary, 10 May 1940, Henry Morgenthau, Jr. MSS, FDRL.

15. Henry Morgenthau, Jr., diaries, 14 May 1940, vol. 262, pp. 252–57, Morgenthau MSS, FDRL.

16. Arthur H. Vandenberg to Hiram H. Walker, 22 May 1940, Arthur H. Vandenberg MSS, Bentley Library, University of Michigan, Ann Arbor.

17. "The Suggestion of Conscription in the U.S.A.," British Library of Information Report no. 278, 24240/131/45; Robert E. Wood to Bertie McCormick, 3 June 1940, box 11, Robert E. Wood MSS, HHPL.

18. Hiram Johnson to Hiram W. Johnson, Jr., 18 May 1940, pt. 6, box 8, Hiram Johnson MSS, Bancroft Library, University of California, Berkeley.

19. Charles Edison to FDR, 14 June 1940, PSF-Senate, FDRL.

20. Clarence Brown to Alice Zartram (copy), 18 June 1940, box 5, John W. Vorys MSS, Ohio Historical Society, Columbus.

21. Karl Mundt to Herbert Hoover, 8 June 1940, box 449, Post-presidential Files, Individuals, Herbert Hoover MSS, HHPL.

22. FDR to Lewis Douglas, 7 June 1940, PPF 1914, FDRL.

23. Roosevelt, *Public Papers,* 9:264.

24. William Allen White to FDR, 5 June 1940, quoted in Walter Johnson, *The Battle against Isolation* (Chicago, 1944), 82: "Had splendid conference at the White

House. Effect distinctive progress is being made and additional progress will be made next week." Senator Claude Pepper to Clark Eichelberger, 7 June 1940, wire, Clark Eichelberger MSS, NYPL.

25. FDR to Pa Watson, 14 June 1940, OF 4065, FDRL.

26. *New York Times,* 2 and 12 June 1940.

27. Cantril, *Public Opinion,* 458; George Gallup message for Julius Adler, 18 June 1940, box 171, Henry L. Stimson MSS, Sterling Library, Yale University, New Haven, Conn.

28. Pa Watson to War Department, 13 and 16 June 1940, OF 1413, FDRL.

29. Executive Committee, Second Corps Area, MTCA, "Minutes of Meeting of May 8, 1940," Grenville Clark MSS, Baker Library of Dartmouth College, Hanover, N.H.

30. Telegram to Woodrow Wilson, 10 May 1915, copy in Clark MSS.

31. Hermann Hagedorn, *Leonard Wood: A Biography,* 2 vols. (New York, 1931), 2:155.

32. Diary entry of 23 Mar. 1917, in *The Cabinet Diaries of Josephus Daniels, 1913–1921,* ed. E. David Cronon (Lincoln, Nebr., 1963), 120.

33. Russell F. Weigley has written that "because he was the kind of man he was, Leonard Wood [would] have infuriated [people] if he had done no more than urge that infantrymen go on carrying rifles" (*History of the United States Army* [New York, 1967], 327).

34. For the origins of the 1915 Plattsburg camp see John Garry Clifford, *The Citizen Soldiers: The Plattsburg Training Camp Movement, 1913–1920* (Lexington, Ky., 1972), chap. 3.

35. Leonard Wood, "Report on Military Instruction Camps," 16 Nov. 1915, Adjutant General Files, RG94, AG2310060, NA.

36. Assistant Secretary of the Navy Franklin D. Roosevelt apologized that a recent appendectomy had prevented him from attending Plattsburg (FDR to Leonard Wood, 16 Aug. 1915, Leonard Wood MSS, LC).

37. See Clifford, *Citizen Soldiers,* 63, 65.

38. "Remarks of Grenville Clark . . . First Training Regiment," 1 Sept. 1915, Clark MSS.

39. John W. Chambers, "Conscription for Collossus: The Adoption of the Draft in the United States during World War I" (Ph.D. diss., Columbia University, 1973).

40. Clifford, *Citizen Soldiers,* 229–33.

41. R. R. Palmer, B. I. Wiley, and W. R. Keast, *The Procurement and Training of Ground Combat Troops (The United States Army in World War II)* (Washington, D.C., 1948), 95.

42. Henry L. Stimson and McGeorge Bundy, *On Active Service in Peace and War* (New York, 1948), 349; see also Pogue, *George C. Marshall: Ordeal and Hope,* 461 n; Palmer et al., *Procurement,* 107; Bundy-Stimson transcript, c. 1946, box 188, Stimson MSS.

43. John P. Finnegan, *Against the Specter of a Dragon: The Campaign for American Military Preparedness, 1914–1917* (Westport, Conn., 1974), 66–67.

44. John W. Chambers, "Conscripting for Colossus: The Progressive Era and the Origin of the Modern Military Draft in the United States in World War I," in *The Military in America: Essays and Documents,* ed. Peter Karsten (New York, 1980), 277.

45. Michael Pearlman, "Leonard Wood, William Muldoon and the Medical Profession: Public Health and Universal Military Training," *New England Quarterly* 52 (Sept. 1979): 327; see also Pearlman, *To Make Democracy Safe for America: Patricians and Preparedness in the Progressive Era* (Urbana, Ill., 1984).

46. See Richard Gillam, "Plattsburg Redivivus," *Yale Review* 62 (Mar. 1973): 472–77.

47. "Bob Patterson has a one-track mind; fortunately the one track is for war. He has been fighting the world war over and over again ever since he was in it" (Lloyd K. Garrison to Charles C. Burlingham, 4 Aug. 1940, box 6, Charles C. Burlingham MSS, Harvard Law School Library, Cambridge, Mass.). Keith Eiler is completing a scholarly biography of Patterson.

48. Leonard Wood, "Heating Up the Melting Pot," *Independent* 87 (July 1917): 15.

49. *New York Times,* 9 May 1916.

50. Clark, "Remarks . . . to First Training Regiment," 1 Sept. 1915, Clark MSS.

51. Theodore Roosevelt, quoted in Chambers, "Conscripting," 279.

52. The rank and file of the Seventy-seventh Division consisted of ethnic groups speaking forty-four different languages. Their theme song was "The Jews and the Wops,/ And the Dutch and the Irish Cops;/ They're All in the Army Now." Thirteen MTCA executives served as officers in the Seventh-seventh, including Henry L. Stimson, Theodore Roosevelt, Jr., Robert Patterson, and Julius Ochs Adler (see the brilliant discussion in Pearlman, *To Make Democracy Safe,* chap. 7; see also Richard Weiss, "The Patrician as Patriot," *Reviews in American History* 13 [Sept. 1985]: 404–8).

53. Pearlman, *To Make Democracy Safe,* chap. 9.

54. G. Clark to Ralph Barton Perry, 28 Jan. 1921, Perry MSS, Pusey Library, Harvard University, Cambridge, Mass.

55. See Clifford, *Citizen Soldiers,* 296–98.

56. See R. A. Hill, "Reserve Policies and National Defense," *Infantry Journal,* Jan. 1935, 59–61.

57. As quoted in MTCA, *Eight Years of the CMTC* (Chicago, 1930), 7–8. It should be emphasized that the Organized Reserves, the ROTC, and the National Guard were the primary civilian reserve components under the National Defense Act of 1920.

58. *Annual Report of the Secretary of War, 1930* (Washington, D.C., 1930), 153.

59. "Statesman Incognito," *Fortune,* Feb. 1946, 110–15.

60. Elting E. Morison, *Turmoil and Tradition: A Study of the Life and Times of Henry L. Stimson* (Boston, 1960), 396–97. Forrest Pogue has described Clark thus: "A lifelong sponsor of worthy causes, he gave the same single-minded efforts to military preparedness that other equally sincere men gave to vegetarianism, the single tax, and planned parenthood" (*George C. Marshall: Ordeal and Hope,* 56).

61. See Norman Cousins and J. Garry Clifford, eds., *Memoirs of a Man: Grenville Clark* (New York, 1975), 111–12.

62. Cleveland Amory has told the story of how Clark, who had invited General Pershing to lunch at the Porcellian Club after World War I and had invited General Eisenhower for a similar visit after World War II, was roundly admonished by one of the crustier members for abusing his guest privileges (*Proper Bostonians* [New York, 1947], 29).

63. Martin Mayer, *Emory R. Bucker* (New York, 1968).

64. Henry L. Stimson, diary, 1–2 Dec. 1941, Stimson MSS.

65. See Irving L. Janis, *Victims of Groupthink: A Psychological Study of Foreign Policy Decisions and Fiascoes* (Boston, 1972).

66. Quoted in Robert Dallek, *Franklin D. Roosevelt and American Foreign Policy, 1932–1945* (New York, 1979), 278.

67. See Porter Sargent to Oswald Garrison Villard, 19 July 1945, Oswald Garrison Villard MSS, Houghton Library, Harvard University.

68. See Clifford, *Citizen Soldiers,* 89 n.

69. Ralph Barton Perry, *The Plattsburg Movement* (New York, 1921), vi.

70. William E. Leuchtenberg's forthcoming study of the 1937 Court fight will detail Clark's role.

71. Byron Fairchild and Jonathan Grossman, *United States Army in World War II: The War Department, the Army and Industrial Manpower* (Washington, D.C., 1959), 219.

72. Felix Frankfurter to Jean Monnet, 29 Sept. 1952, Felix Frankfurter MSS, LC. For Clark's activities as a World Federalist see John F. Bantell, "The Origins of the World Government Movement: The Dublin Conference and After," *Research Studies* 42 (Mar. 1974): 20–35, and "Grenville Clark and the Founding of the United Nations: The Failure of World Federalism," *Peace and Change* 10 (Fall/Winter 1984): 97–116.

73. The most scholarly account of the interventionist movement is that by Chadwin in *The Warhawks.*

74. Executive Committee, Second Corps Area, MTCA, "Minutes of Meeting of 8 May 1940," Clark MSS.

75. *New York Times,* 9–11 May 1940.

76. Clark to Tom R. Wyles, 16 May 1940, Clark MSS.

77. Tom R. Wyles to Clark, 21 May 1940, Clark MSS. Some of the resentment felt by Wyles and Jamison at being pushed can be seen in the records of the national MTCA headquarters at the Chicago Historical Society (see, especially, Wyles to Chester D. Heywood, 28 May 1940, MTCA files, 1940, Chicago Historical Society).

78. Clark to White (wire), 10 May 1940, White to Clark (wire), 20 May 1940, both in Clark MSS.

79. Spencer interviews with Grenville Clark (1947), in Clark MSS.

80. Palmer to Clark (wire), 16 May 1940.

81. See Robert Charles Erhart, "The Politics of Military Rearmament, 1935–1940: The President, the Congress, and the United States Army" (Ph.D. diss., University of Texas, 1975, chap. 9).

82. Clark to FDR (wire), 16 May 1940, Clark MSS.

83. FDR to Clark, 18 May 1940, in *FDR: His Personal Letters,* ed. Elliott Roosevelt, 4 vols. (New York, 1948), 2:1026.

84. Entry of 19 May 1940, Charles A. Lindbergh, *The Wartime Journals of Charles A. Lindbergh* (New York, 1970), 349–50.

85. *New York Times,* 13–23 May 1940.

86. Ibid., 23 May 1940.

87. As members of the Century Club, Lewis Douglas and William J. Donovan played principal roles in the effort of that group to facilitate the destroyers-for-bases deal during the summer (see Chadwin, *Warhawks,* chap. 3; interview with Lewis Douglas, 1 July 1947, Robert E. Sherwood MSS, Houghton Library, Harvard University).

88. Henry S. Hooker to Marguerite Le Hand, 23 May 1940, PPF 482, FDRL.

89. *New York Times,* 23 May 1940.

90. See Ernest Denham, Jr., "The *New York Times* and Peacetime Conscription: An Interpretive Study of an Editorial Crusade" (Master's thesis, University of Georgia, 1959).

91. Quoted in Charles W. Kegley and Eugene R. Wittkopf, *American Foreign Policy: Pattern and Process* (New York, 1979), 225.

92. Clark to Adler, 24 May 1940, Clark MSS.

93. Henry A. Wallace, diary, 22 May 1940.

94. Lothian to FO, 23 May 1940, A3297/2961/45, RBFO; and James R. Leutze, *Bargaining for Supremacy: Anglo-American Naval Collaboration, 1937-1941* (Chapel Hill, N.C., 1977), 78-79.

95. Nicholas Harmon, *Dunkirk: The Patriotic Myth* (New York, 1980).

96. Karl Mundt Weekly Newsletter, 23 May 1940, Karl Mundt MSS, Karl Mundt Library, Dakota State College, Madison, S. Dak. (from notes of David Porter).

CHAPTER 3. GENERAL STAFF PLANNING:
THE BACKGROUND OF SELECTIVE SERVICE

1. See the excellent discussion in John W. Chambers, ed., *Draftees or Volunteers: A Documentary History of the Debate over Military Conscription in the United States, 1787-1973* (New York, 1975), 41-45; and the excellent new work by Fred Anderson, *A People's Army: Massachusetts Soldiers and Society in the Seven Years' War* (Chapel Hill, N.C., 1984).

2. Quoted in Chambers, *Draftees,* 47.

3. Richard H. Kohn, *Eagle and Sword: The Federalists and the Creation of the Military Establishment in America, 1783-1802* (New York, 1975).

4. Joint Army and Navy Selective Service Committee, *American Selective Service* (Washington, D.C., 1939), 7.

5. See Harry Ammon, *James Monroe: The Quest for National Identity* (New York, 1971), 338-40.

6. The most eloquent speech opposing conscription in 1814 was made by Daniel Webster, a speech reprinted by opponents of the draft in 1917 and afterward. Ironically, Webster himself, in his later "nationalist" period, had second thoughts about his 1814 speech and had it deleted from the *Annals of Congress.* It can be found in *The Letters of Daniel Webster,* ed. Claude H. Van Tyne (New York, 1902), 56-68.

7. Weigley, *History of the United States Army,* 175.

8. The standard account is by Albert B. Moore, *Conscription and Conflict in the Confederacy* (New York, 1924).

9. Eugene C. Murdock, *One Million Men: The Civil War Draft in the North* (Madison, Wis., 1971).

10. Adrian Cook, *The Armies of the Streets: The New York City Draft Riots of 1863* (Lexington, Ky., 1974).

11. Chambers, *Draftees,* 182-88.

12. Quoted in Chambers, *Draftees,* 199.

13. Stephen E. Ambrose, *Upton of the Army* (Baton Rouge, La., 1965).

14. Russell F. Weigley, *Towards an American Army* (New York, 1962).

15. Graham A. Cosmas, *An Army for Empire: The United States Army in the Spanish-American War* (Columbia, Mo., 1971).

16. Martha E. Derthick, *The National Guard in Politics* (Cambridge, Mass., 1961), 29-32.

17. John McAuley Palmer, *America in Arms* (Washington, D.C., 1943), 101-24.

18. Weigley, *History of the United States Army,* 339-40.

19. George C. Herring, Jr., "James Hay and the Preparedness Controversy, 1915-1916," *Journal of Southern History* 30 (Nov. 1964): 383-404.

20. Palmer, *America in Arms,* 138-52.

21. John P. Finnegan argues that prior to 1917, most advocates of preparedness never seriously thought of sending an expeditionary force to Europe. "Its thrust was isolationist, not interventionist, despite the personal attitudes of many supporters. In a

collapsing world, America was arming against nameless dangers which would follow the end of the European war'' (*Against the Specter of a Dragon,* 4).

22. *The Public Papers of Woodrow Wilson: War and Peace,* ed. Ray S. Baker and William E. Dodd, 8 vols. (New York, 1927), 1:10.

23. One of the great ironies of the Selective Service Act of 1917 is that Woodrow Wilson chose conscription, rather than volunteering, partly to thwart his great antagonist, Theodore Roosevelt. Faced with a request from the old Rough Rider that he be permitted to raise and lead a volunteer division in France, Wilson decided to prohibit volunteer regiments and to maintain central and professional control over all forces (see Daniel R. Beaver, *Newton D. Baker and the American War Effort, 1917-1919* [Lincoln, Nebr., 1966], 28-30).

24. See Chambers, ''Conscripting,'' 280-87.

25. Joint Committee, *American Selective Service,* 12-13; and Edward Fitzpatrick, *Conscription and America* (Milwaukee, Wis., 1940), 28-29.

26. Russell Weigley has written that ''the success of the Selective Service Act of 1917 surely owed much also to the discipline implicit in industrial society, to the consequent immense power of the modern state, and to the modern mass media of communication and publicity, upon which neither George Washington nor Abraham Lincoln had been able to draw'' (*History of the United States Army,* 358).

27. Such examples included prohibition, the Civilian Conservation Corps, and the Motor Carrier Act and the Public Utilities Act of 1935. Gen. Hugh S. Johnson, a high official in the Selective Service System, used techniques similar to Draft Registration Day in arousing public support for the National Recovery Act in 1933 (see John Chambers's forthcoming book *To Arm a Nation: The Origins of the Modern Military Draft*).

28. *Arver* v. *United States,* in *U.S. Reports* 245 (1918): 366-67.

29. Edward M. Coffman, *The Hilt of the Sword: The Career of Peyton C. March* (Madison, Wis., 1966), 175-77.

30. Palmer, *America in Arms,* 168.

31. James W. Wadsworth, Jr., ''Memoir,'' Columbia Oral History Project, 308-9.

32. James W. Wadsworth, Jr., ''Introduction,'' in John McAuley Palmer, *Statesmanship or War* (Garden City, N.Y., 1927), xv.

33. Palmer, *America in Arms,* 166.

34. Ibid., 173.

35. Ibid.

36. Palmer to Grenville Clark, 26 Apr. 1920, Clark MSS. On Wadsworth see Martin L. Fausold, *James W. Wadsworth, Jr.: The Gentleman from New York* (Syracuse, N.Y., 1974), 117-22.

37. Watson, *Chief of Staff,* 87, 103-4.

38. One of the thorniest issues of selective service in war or peace was deciding who was to be drafted or deferred and under what criteria. Perhaps the main reason that selective service aroused little public protest during the 1950s and 1960s—at least until the Vietnam War grew hot—was the fact that draft calls remained relatively low and most citizens of military age did not have to serve (see the classic study by Albert Blum, *Drafted or Deferred: Practices Past and Present* [Ann Arbor, Mich., 1957]).

39. See the standard work by Robert D. Ward, ''The Movement for Universal Military Training in the United States, 1942-1952'' (Ph.D. diss., University of North Carolina, 1957).

40. Horace Stebbins to A. G. Thacher, 27 Jan. 1920, Clark MSS.

41. According to a *Literary Digest* poll in 1935, about 81 percent of American college students said they would not bear arms if the United States invaded another country, while 16.5 percent indicated that they would refuse to serve even if America was invaded (Charles Chatfield, *For Peace and Justice: Pacifism in America, 1914–1941* [Knoxville, Tenn., 1971], 259–60).

42. *Annual Report of the Secretary of War, 1934,* 34.

43. Johnson Hagood to Hermann Hagedorn, 15 Dec. 1928, Hermann Hagedorn MSS, LC.

44. Daniel H. Lew, "A History of the Selective Service and Training Act of 1940" (Ph.D. diss., Harvard University, 1941), 121–38.

45. There were also proposals in the late thirties, tied in with the so-called Ludlow Amendment, calling for a national referendum on conscription in the event of war (see Ernest C. Bolt, Jr., *Ballots before Bullets: The War Referendum Approach to Peace in America, 1914–1941* [Charlottesville, Va., 1977], 146, 149–50, 179–81).

46. Lord Lothian to Minna Butler-Thwing, 21 June 1940, GD40/17/470, Lothian MSS.

47. Weigley, *History of the United States Army,* 402–3. "In the zany era of flappers and flagpole sitters, wild-sounding jazz and soaring stock values, America merrily made herself more impotent militarily than any other major nation, with even Germany, saddled by peace-treaty restrictions, having a larger army" (D. Clayton James, *The Years of MacArthur: 1880–1941,* 3 vols. [Boston, 1970–85], 1:312).

48. "Military considerations were far from the mind of the president and Congress during the depression. Their first order of business was the economic well-being of the nation and the effects of government pay cuts, the CCC, and relief measures on the army were of secondary or even tertiary concern" (Robert K. Griffith, Jr., "Quality Not Quantity: The Voluntary Army during the Depression," *Military Affairs,* Dec., 1979, 176).

49. *Annual Report of the Secretary of War, 1935,* 42.

50. Robert E. Sherwood has written that the service departments moved "at a glacial pace—when the time demanded jet propulsion." The cardinal principle of career officers was "Never stick your neck out" (*Roosevelt and Hopkins* [New York, 1948], 159).

51. *War Department Annual Report, 1934,* 54.

52. Robert Miller, "The United States Army during the 1930s" (Ph.D. diss., Princeton University, 1973), 14.

53. "It is unwise, from the point of view of national finances, and incidentally, from the point of view of public opinion, for me to recommend additional increases over those contained in the budget" (FDR to Secretary of War, 15 Jan. 1936, PSF [War Dept., 1934–36], FDRL).

54. Erhart, "Politics of Military Rearmament," 88.

55. See Pogue, *George C. Marshall: Ordeal and Hope,* 22.

56. *Annual Report of the Secretary of War, 1938,* 5.

57. Marvin A. Kreidberg and Merton G. Henry, *History of Military Mobilization in the United States Army, 1775–1945* (Washington, D.C., 1955), 480–92; see also Keith D. McFarland, *Harry H. Woodring: A Political Biography of FDR's Controversial Secretary of War* (Lawrence, Kans., 1975).

58. Joint Committee, *American Selective Service,* 7; see also, John O'Sullivan, "From Voluntarism to Conscription: Congress and Selective Service" (Ph.D. diss., Columbia University, 1971), 17–18.

59. Transcript of oral-history interview with Gen. Lewis B. Hershey (1973), Lewis B. Hershey MSS, Institute for Military History, U.S. Army War College, Carlisle Barracks, Pa.; see also Flynn, *Lewis B. Hershey,* chap. 3.

60. Joint Committee, *American Selective Service,* 24-25.

61. Ibid.

62. Ibid., 25-26.

63. Transcript of Hugh Johnson's lecture on "Selective Service," 23 Oct. 1939, G-1 MSS, Army War College.

64. Joint Committee, *American Selective Service,* 26-27.

65. *Annual Report of the Secretary of War, 1938,* 2.

66. G-2 memorandum of 23 May 1940, quoted by Erhart in "Politics of Military Rearmament," 305.

67. E.g., army representatives objected strenuously to the eight-months' training period specified in the Burke-Wadsworth bill. Although they would have preferred eighteen months, they eventually compromised on twelve, which they considered an irreducible minimum.

68. *Annual Report of the Secretary of War, 1934,* 34.

69. *Annual Report of the Secretary of War, 1939,* 35.

70. "Arms before Men," *Time,* 22 Aug. 1938, 23.

71. Watson, *Chief of Staff,* 158.

72. Christopher Gabel, "The U.S. Army Maneuvers of 1941" (Ph.D. diss., Ohio State University, 1981), chap. 1.

73. *Annual Report of the War Department, 1939,* 4.

74. *Annual Report of the War Department, 1938,* 30.

75. Sterling Morton to Alf Landon, 24 July 1940, Landon MSS.

76. Col. J. W. Anderson, n.d. [c. Mar. 1939], quoted by Watson in *Chief of Staff,* 88.

77. Anderson is quoted by Watson in *Chief of Staff,* 94-95; Stetson Conn and Byron Fairchild, *United States Army in World War II: The Western Hemisphere: The Framework of Hemisphere Defense* (Washington, D.C., 1960), chap. 1.

78. See Charles A. Lindbergh's speech calling for hemispheric defense on 19 May 1940; and Haglund, *Latin America,* chaps. 4-8.

79. Joint Planning Board to FDR, 26 June 1940, quoted by Erhart in "Politics of Military Rearmament," 307.

80. Pogue, *George C. Marshall: Ordeal and Hope,* chap. 3.

81. Watson, *Chief of Staff,* 145-47. See also *Berlin Alert: The Memoirs and Reports of Truman Smith,* ed. Robert Hessen (Stanford, Calif., 1984), 30-38.

82. Sherwood, *Roosevelt and Hopkins,* 136.

83. The army's discouraging response to Congressman Kent Keller's proposal for an American School Army was another case in point. The Illinois Democrat wanted to attract enlistees by promising a free college education (see General L. J. McNair to Keller, 22 Mar. 1940, box 321, Kent Keller MSS, Illinois State Historical Society, Springfield).

84. George C. Marshall, *Biennial Report of the Chief of Staff, 1939-41* (Washington, D.C., 1942), 2.

85. E.g., Marshall had a junior staff officer, Omar Bradley, accompany Senators Henry Cabot Lodge and Rufus Holman to army maneuvers in Louisiana over the weekend of 19-22 May. They could see, as Bradley later wrote, the "undistinguished and unimaginative leadership shown by the [senior] generals. . . . The 'close air support' by the air corps fighters was a joke" (Omar Bradley and Clay Blair, *A General's Life* [New York, 1983], 89; see also, Marshall to Baruch, 29 Mar., 3 and 9 April, and 15 May 1940, vol. 50, Bernard M. Baruch MSS, Seeley Mudd Library, Princeton University, Princeton, N.J.).

86. Quoted in John M. Blum, *From the Morgenthau Diaries: Years of Urgency, 1938–1941* (Boston, 1965), 141.

87. As early as 20 May 1940, Marshall asked his staff: "Assuming Congress gave us a Selective Service Act, how long would it take to procure 750,000 men?" (Watson, *Chief of Staff,* 184).

88. Transcript of an interview with George C. Marshall, 22 Jan. 1957, George C. Marshall Library, Lexington, Va.

89. Notes of interview with George C. Marshall, 23 July 1947, Robert E. Sherwood MSS, Houghton Library, Harvard University, Cambridge, Mass. Months later, Marshall told an assistant secretary of state that "one difficulty had been that the P[resident] knows the navy like a book, but he knows very little about the army" (Adolf Berle, diary, 10 Sept. 1940, FDRL).

90. Henry Wallace, diary, 17 May 1940. "The president said there was about a 50-50 chance that the French would hold out" (personal memorandum, 17 May 1940, box 45, Farley MSS).

91. Entry of 15 May 1940, Adolf A. Berle, diary, Berle MSS, FDRL. "The cries for help from the Allies are taking almost pitiable form" (J. P. Moffat, diary, 15 May 1940, Houghton Library, Harvard University, Cambridge, Mass.).

92. Statement of 30 May 1940, *Complete Presidential Press Conferences of Franklin D. Roosevelt,* 24 vols. (New York, 1972), 15:412–13. "We have reached a state now where the main type of problem to be decided is to what degree we must conserve our inherent strength for our own defensive purposes. . . . We have to face the possibility that there may be a complete German victory. . . . What this would mean in relation to the British fleet is the crux of the problem for ourselves" (Moffat, diary, 21 May 1940).

93. Roosevelt, *Public Papers,* 9:238.

94. See David Haglund, "George C. Marshall and the Question of Military Aid to England, May–June 1940," *Journal of Contemporary History* 15 (Dec. 1980): 749–53.

95. Ibid.

96. Watson, *Chief of Staff,* 106.

CHAPTER 4. WOOING THE WHITE HOUSE
AND THE WAR DEPARTMENT

1. Louis Johnson to Col. A. W. Herrington, 11 May 1940, box 13, Louis Johnson MSS, Alderman Library, University of Virginia, Charlottesville. Robert Sherwood has written about the capacity of amateurs, unfettered by "standard operating procedures," to think and act imaginatively. One such amateur was industrialist Robert T. Stevens, one of the country's leading textile manufacturers, who told procurement officers that two hundred thousand parachutes would be needed in fiscal year 1940/41, not the War Department's projected nine thousand parachutes. When asked how he arrived at such a number, Stevens replied: "The president has asked for 50,000 war planes. I just multiplied them by four," since the average requirement was four parachutes per plane (*Roosevelt and Hopkins,* 161–62).

2. Haglund, "George C. Marshall," 745–60.

3. Marshall to Emily Brown, 29 May 1940 [Larry Bland files], Marshall MSS. On the Palmer-Marshall relationship see Weigley, *Towards an American Army,* chap. 13; Pogue, *George C. Marshall: Education of a General, 1880–1939* (New York, 1963), 203–21; Palmer, *America in Arms,* 181.

4. Interview with Lewis B. Hershey, Washington, D.C., 15 Dec. 1967; see also O'Sullivan, "From Voluntarism to Conscription," 23; Palmer memo for A. G. Thacher, 27 May 1940, Clark MSS.

5. Minutes of meeting of 28 May, Clark MSS; Spencer interviews with Clark, c. 1947.

6. Notes of interview with Lewis Hershey, c. 1941, box 32, Joseph Alsop MSS, LC.

7. Hershey interview, 15 Dec. 1967; O'Sullivan, "From Voluntarism to Conscription," 22n; telephone interview with Walter Weible, 16 Dec. 1967; Hershey to Col. Arthur Vollmer, 8 Sept. 1949, file 113, box 2, Lewis B. Hershey MSS.

8. "All our plans are to get such quick increases of volunteers enlisted for the duration, as we can manage in order to avoid the necessity of calling for elements of the National Guard. Of course in all of this much will depend on the further developments abroad" (Marshall to Gen. William N. Haskell, 3 June 1940, Selected Correspondence, 1938–51, Marshall MSS).

9. Marshall, *Biennial Report*, 3.

10. Transcript of interview with George C. Marshall, 22 Jan. 1957, Marshall Library. For Marshall's cultivation of key senators see Marshall to Clement Trott, 1 Apr., to Asa Singleton, 11 Apr., to Marie Singer, 16 Apr., and to Millard Tydings, 8 June 1940 [Bland chronological file], Marshall MSS.

11. This account of the interview with Marshall is based on notes that Clark made at the time and Spencer's interviews in 1947; see also Watson, *Chief of Staff*, 190–91. Interestingly, Marshall was receiving similar advice to act boldly from Baruch: "I believe he could get at least his 330,000 [men] and even up to 400,000 if he went after it now. Now is the time for him to let the authorities know what . . . is necessary. . . . The whole country is blazing with comment . . . on the necessity for adequate defense. The country does not know how far behind we are. . . . I would like to see it so that he [Marshall] will be found fighting for whatever he thinks is necessary" (Baruch to Walter Bedell Smith, 11 May 1940, vol. 48, Baruch MSS).

12. It would be stretching the point too far to call General Marshall an isolationist in the spring of 1940. Nonetheless, his concern for hemispheric defense and his desire to place American rearmament needs ahead of military assistance to the Allies were compatible with the Gibraltar America ideas of the America First Committee that was formally organized a few months later. Although no Anglophobe himself, Marshall's confidence in such General Staff planners as Stanley Embick and Albert C. Wedemeyer did at times result in strategic designs that diverged from British aims during World War II in ways that can be characterized as "isolationist" (see Haglund, "George C. Marshall"; and Mark Stoler, "From Continentalism to Globalism: General Stanley D. Embick, the Joint Strategic Survey Committee, and the Military View of National Policy during the Second World War," *Diplomatic History* 6 [Summer 1982]: 303–21). For Marshall's opposition to transferring army bombers to England at the time of Woodring's dismissal see Morgenthau, diaries, 19 and 20 June 1940, vol. 273, 22, 181.

13. Quoted in Frank Hanighen to Cushman Reynolds, n.d. (c. July 1940), *Uncensored* MSS, New York Public Library. Although he was never directly identified, the evidence suggests that Hanighen's informant on the General Staff was Col. Truman Smith.

14. Marshall interview, 22 Jan. 1957. Marshall further commented: "I might say that I went through a very difficult period here and it was very hard to keep my temper. I was being dictated to, and I mean dictated to. I was being sent for by a conference of this important New York fellow and this other important New York fellow and they

would call me in—the New York fellows and dictated to me what I should do. I tried to listen politely, but I didn't do."

15. Watson, *Chief of Staff*, 194-95.

16. Clark to Stimson, 2 Jan. 1945, box 147, Stimson MSS.

17. By late June, after he had nominated Stimson as secretary of war, Roosevelt may have *hoped* that a draft would be passed, even though he had not publicly endorsed it (Roosevelt to Stimson, 26 June 1940, PPF 20, FDRL).

18. Entry of 7 May 1940, Henry A. Wallace, diary.

19. FDR told his four sons that he expected them to "wrestle with your own conscience" over whether to volunteer for military service or wait to be drafted (Elliott Roosevelt, *As He Saw It* [New York, 1946], 7-8).

20. Roosevelt later denied having advocated universal military training in 1919/20, when in fact he had (FDR to Norman Thomas, 12 Aug. 1940, PPF 4840, FDRL).

21. FDR to Leonard Wood, 16 Aug. 1915, Wood MSS.

22. FDR memo for E. R., 5 Aug. 1940, OF 1413, FDRL.

23. FDR to Helen Rogers Reid, 6 June 1940, Reid Family MSS, LC.

24. A. J. Sabath to FDR, 2 Aug. 1940; Vic Donahey to FDR, 1 Aug. 1940, OF 1413, misc., FDRL; Jerome Frank to Robert Jackson, 27 July 1940, box 30, Jerome Frank MSS, Yale University.

25. Eleanor Roosevelt to Harriet Aldrich, 21 May 1940, Eleanor Roosevelt MSS, FDRL.

26. White House mail in mid June was running 2 to 1 against conscription, whereas the national polls indicated better than 50 percent of the public in support (Watson to War Department, 13 June 1940, OF 1413, FDRL).

27. L. Cephus to FDR, 26 July 1940; H. Rosen to FDR, n.d. [Aug. 1940], OF 1413, FDRL.

28. See Herbert S. Parmet and Marie B. Hecht, *Never Again: A President Runs for a Third Term* (New York, 1968).

29. Roosevelt, *Public Papers*, 9:202.

30. Leutze, *Bargaining for Supremacy*, 73-79. E.g., FDR told a Canadian official on 25 May that "if Germany gets the French fleet . . . as she will doubtlessly demand, she would be superior to this continent." He urged Canada and the other dominions to press Britain "not to yield to the making of any soft peace even though it might mean the destruction of England comparable to that of Poland, Holland, and Belgium . . . but to have her fleet make its base at different outlying parts away from England and send the King to Bermuda. . . . Meanwhile, the United States could not part with any of their planes. They had not enough at the present time to meet the United States needs" (Mackenzie King, diary, 26 May 1940, King papers, microfiche no. 149).

31. On 28 May, while the fighting around Dunkirk was raging fiercely, Harry Hopkins told Henry Wallace that "it was interesting to see how the president's mind seemed to go in two directions at the same time. He has become a budget balancer again on minor matters. . . . If the international situation is as grave as you think it is—and as the president thinks it is half the time—we ought to be approaching the problem in a much bigger way" (Wallace, diary, 28 May 1940).

32. Lord Lothian to Lady Astor [c. 30 May 1940], in J. R. M. Butler, *Lord Lothian* (New York, 1960), 288.

33. See Alexander Stoesen, "The Senatorial Career of Claude D. Pepper" (Ph.D. diss., University of North Carolina, 1965), 139-50. The State Department, possibly without FDR's knowledge, advised the Foreign Relations Committee to table the resolution on the grounds that the repeal of the Neutrality Act could be considered

a *casus belli* by Germany (Key Pittman to Cordell Hull, 21 May 1940, and Green H. Hackworth to Hull, 21 May 1940, reel 20, Cordell Hull MSS).

34. Haglund, "George C. Marshall," 746. The president also "wished to go much farther" in giving aid to England at this juncture than did Secretary of State Hull (see Adolf A. Berle, diary, 13 June 1940, Berle MSS, FDRL).

35. Entry of 20 May 1940, presidential diaries of Henry J. Morgenthau, Jr., Morgenthau MSS, FDRL. For a discussion of FDR's somewhat paranoid reaction to his foreign-policy critics see Richard W. Steele, "Franklin D. Roosevelt and His Foreign Policy Critics," *Political Science Quarterly* 94 (Spring 1979); see also, William Phillips, diary, 31 May 1940, Houghton Library, Harvard University.

36. Samuel I. Rosenman, *Working with Roosevelt* (New York, 1952), 225.

37. Sherwood, *Roosevelt and Hopkins,* 132–33, 157.

38. Robert A. Divine, *Roosevelt and World War II* (Baltimore, Md., 1969), 37. James M. Burns has written graphically about FDR's pattern of "moving step by step, avoiding commitments to any one man or program, letting his subordinates feel less the sting of responsibility than the goad of competition, thwarting one man from getting too much control, preventing himself from becoming a prisoner of his own machinery, and, above all, keeping choices wide in a world full of snares and surprises" (*Roosevelt: Soldier of Freedom* [New York, 1970], 53).

39. Clark to FDR (wires), 21, 24, and 26 May 1940, Clark MSS.

40. Roosevelt, *Public Papers,* 9:230–40. The British ambassador commented: "Largely the broadcast fireside chat of the 26th May was, on the whole, a missed opportunity. It was . . . less advanced than public opinion in the country" (Lothian to FO, no. 891, 1 June 1940, A3223B/39/45, RBFO.

41. Roosevelt, *Public Papers,* 9:241–42.

42. Ibid., 251. When asked by a reporter "Is there any thought of conscription?" Steve Early gave an emphatic no (transcript of press conference, 30 May 1940, box 40, Early MSS, FDRL).

43. For a convenient listing and summary of all the various manpower plans in the spring of 1940 see "Manpower" folder, box 302, Harry Hopkins MSS, FDRL. Such plans included a proposal by FDR in April to give the rudiments of military training to three hundred thousand enlistees in the Civilian Conservation Corps (see memorandum for General Gasser and Colonel Ward, 18 Apr. 1940 [Larry Bland chronological file], Marshall MSS).

44. For the bureaucratic confusion see, especially, entries of 27 May, 3 and 4 June 1940, Harold Smith, diary, Smith MSS, FDRL.

45. Watson to Clark (wire), 29 May 1940, OF 4065, FDRL.

46. *Kiplinger Letter,* 25 May 1940.

47. Blum, *From the Morgenthau Diaries: Years of Urgency,* 165–69; and Harold L. Ickes, *The Secret Diary of Harold L. Ickes: The Lowering Clouds, 1939–1941* (New York, 1954), 136, 146, 180, 183, 189, 193, 196, 198, 207, 210, 266.

48. *New York Times,* 9 June 1940; see also transcript of oral-history interview, 3 Dec. 1958, copy in Thomas Dewey MSS, University of Rochester Library, Rochester, N.Y.

49. McFarland, *Harry H. Woodring,* 25; "Arms before Men," *Time,* 22 Aug. 1938, 23–25.

50. McFarland, *Harry H. Woodring,* 79–80.

51. Ibid., 103–10.

52. Jack Alexander, "Stormy New Boss of the Pentagon," *Saturday Evening Post,* 30 July 1949, 27.

53. McFarland, *Harry H. Woodring,* 144–45; Farley denied having made any such promise.

54. James M. Burns, *Roosevelt: The Lion and the Fox* (New York, 1956), 372.

55. "Master of the Pentagon," *Time,* 6 June 1949, 22.

56. Pogue, *George C. Marshall: Ordeal and Hope,* 20–22.

57. McFarland, *Harry H. Woodring,* 185–91.

58. Alexander, "Stormy New Boss," 70.

59. Morgenthau, presidential diary, 13 May 1940, Morgenthau MSS, FDRL.

60. Harold Smith, diary, 13 May 1940.

61. Robert Sherwood has written about FDR's reaction to his, Sherwood's, having fired an unsatisfactory subordinate: "I can't believe it. I thought you were a complete softy—like me" (*Roosevelt and Hopkins,* 72).

62. Entries of 18 and 29 Apr., 13 May, 3 and 17 June 1940, Morgenthau, presidential diaries, Morgenthau MSS, FDRL; entries of 19, 25, and 26 May, 2 June 1940, Harold Ickes, diary, Ickes MSS, LC. Supreme Court Justice Frank Murphy, a strong advocate of conscription, was one possible nominee seriously considered by FDR (see the excellent biography by Sidney Fine, *Frank Murphy: The Washington Years* [Ann Arbor, Mich., 1984], 206–9).

63. Ickes, diary, 12 June 1940, Ickes MSS, LC.

64. See Helen Woodring to Harry Woodring, 22 Mar. 1940, box 5, Harry H. Woodring MSS, Spencer Research Library, University of Kansas, Lawrence. James Farley told the following story to Henry Wallace: "The president called in Woodring and said that a list of several names had been submitted to the pope—including Woodring's, [Myron] Taylor's, and some others—and that the pope had indicated that Woodring was first on the list. Jim said, 'Of course, you and I know that the pope never heard of Woodring, or the name of anyone else in the cabinet, except possibly Hull. . . .' Harry of course knew this and said: 'Mr. President, if you want me to resign I will be delighted to do so, but I am not in the slightest interested in going to Rome. Neither is Mrs. Woodring. Rather than go there I would, of course, resign.' The president replied: 'Why of course I don't want you to resign. Just forget the whole matter' " (Wallace, diary, 18 Jan. 1940). Morgenthau later commented that Woodring "had a fourth rate mind and was stubborn" (J. P. Moffat, diary, 3 July 1940).

65. John McAuley Palmer to Lewis Hershey, 5 Aug. 1940, box 24, Selective Service Headquarters records, RG 144, Federal Archives, Suitland, Md.

66. Much of the foregoing description of relationships is based on Spencer's interviews with Clark and Frankfurter in 1947, the notes of which are in the Clark MSS. For a recent published account of the Stimson appointment that used notes of Spencer's 1947 interviews see Bruce Allen Murphy, *The Brandeis/Frankfurter Connection: The Secret Political Activities of Two Supreme Court Justices* (Oxford, 1982), 195–200.

67. *Harvard Alumni Bulletin,* 18 Apr. 1945, quoted by Arthur M. Schlesinger, Jr., in *The Crisis of the Old Order, 1919–1933* (Boston, 1957), 330.

68. Lewis Douglas, "Grenny in the 1930s and 1940s," in *Memoirs of a Man,* ed. Cousins and Clifford, 196–97.

69. Frankfurter to Clark, 16 May 1957, Frankfurter MSS.

70. Frankfurter later remembered Clark at Harvard as having "one of those deep but slow minds" (Harlan B. Phillips, ed., *Felix Frankfurter Reminisces* [New York, 1960], 13).

71. "Felix was really quite sour when I told him that I was going to settle down and said one of the things that made life possible for him was the beer and cheese we are accustomed to have together from 12 to 1 on the way home" (Clark to Fanny Dwight, 1 Sept. 1909, Clark MSS).

72. Frankfurter to Emory Buckner, June 1915, box 30, Frankfurter MSS.

73. Lowell and Frankfurter had clashed earlier over the Sacco-Vanzetti case (see Joseph P. Lash, ed., *From the Diaries of Felix Frankfurter* [New York, 1975], 124–40).

74. Ibid., 5–9.

75. Eleanor Roosevelt to Sara Delano Roosevelt, 12 May 1918, quoted in Lash, *From the Diaries of Felix Frankfurter,* 24.

76. Stimson and Bundy, *On Active Service,* 288–94.

77. See also Nelson Dawson, "Louis D. Brandeis, Felix Frankfurter, and Franklin D. Roosevelt: The Origins of a New Deal Relationship," *American Jewish History* 68 (Sept. 1978): 32–42; and Murphy, *Brandeis/Frankfurter Connection.*

78. Entry of 2 June 1940, Ickes, diary, Ickes MSS, LC.

79. Frankfurter to Lord Lothian, 3 June 1940, GD40/17/400, Lothian MSS/ papers of Philip Kerr (Lord Lothian), Scottish National Record Office, General Register House, Edinburgh.

80. Frankfurter to Harold Laski, 9 Apr. 1940, box 74, Frankfurter MSS.

81. Eliot Janeway, *The Struggle for Survival* (New Haven, Conn., 1951), 140–41.

82. Ickes, diary, 26 May 1940, Ickes MSS.

83. Quoted in Morison, *Turmoil and Tradition,* 398–99.

84. Quoted, ibid., 399.

85. Memorandum of conversation with Stimson, 17 July 1940, Morgenthau, diaries, vol. 283, 164–65.

86. Notes of interview with Felix Frankfurter, 28 Aug. 1947, Clark MSS; Stimson, diary, 25 June 1940, Stimson MSS.

87. Max Freedman, ed., *Roosevelt and Frankfurter: Their Correspondence* (Boston, 1967), 524–28; Root, memorandum, 1 June 1940, Clark MSS.

88. Although some revisionist historians after World War II tried to make a causal connection between the Hyde Park meeting of 1933 and Japanese-American relations prior to Pearl Harbor, the most important long-term consequence of the meeting was the mutual respect between Stimson and FDR (see Charles A. Beard, *American Foreign Policy in the Making, 1932–1940: A Study in Responsibilities* [New Haven, Conn., 1946], 143–44; Charles C. Tansill, *Back Door to War* [Chicago, 1952], vii). For a refutation see Robert H. Ferrell, *American Diplomacy in the Great Depression: Hoover-Stimson Foreign Policy, 1929–1933* (New Haven, Conn., 1957), chap. 14; and Frank Freidel, *Franklin D. Roosevelt: Launching the New Deal* (Boston, 1973), chap. 3.

89. Their views were similar on military matters as well. Though neither man probably remembered it, by a striking coincidence, Roosevelt and Stimson had both published articles in the April 1917 issue of *Scribner's Magazine,* advocating universal military training (O'Sullivan, "From Voluntarism to Conscription," 26n).

90. Roosevelt to Stimson, 6 Feb. 1935, PPF 20, FDRL.

91. Stimson, diary, 3 May 1940, Stimson MSS.

92. Landon to FDR, 20 Dec. 1937, PPF 3855, FDRL.

93. Ickes, *Secret Diary,* 3:23–24.

94. Landon told columnist Raymond Clapper that he had tried to get Roosevelt to promise not to run for a third term in the event of a "coalition" cabinet. He had urged Knox to insist on the same point (Raymond Clapper, diary, 22 and 23 May 1940, Clapper MSS, LC).

95. *New York World-Telegram,* 23 May 1940; Early press conferences, 21, 22, and 25 May 1940, box 40, Early MSS; Donald McCoy, *Landon of Kansas* (Lincoln, Nebr., 1966), 438.

96. The story of FDR's 1937 offer to Knox is based on Knox's account to Clark at the time (Spencer interviews with Clark, 1947).

97. Ickes, *Secret Diary,* 3:15–17, 87–89, 180–81.

98. Frank Knox to FDR, 15 Dec. 1939, PSF, FDRL.

99. FDR to Knox, 29 Dec. 1939, PSF, FDRL; see also, Farley, memorandum, 13 Dec. 1939, box 44, James A. Farley MSS.

100. Knox to FDR, 17 Jan. 1940, Frank Knox MSS, LC.

101. Knox to William Allen White, 28 May 1940, box 344, White MSS, LC. See also Knox to Landon, 8 and 11 June 1940, Landon MSS; Knox to Lord Lothian, 20 June 1940, box 402, Lothian MSS; Knox to Thomas W. Lamont, 6, 8, and 12 June 1940, box 124, Thomas W. Lamont MSS, Baker Library, Harvard Business School, Boston, Mass.

102. "At long last," Knox wrote to his wife, "we are going to take off our mental blinders and speak frankly of what most of us have recognized for a long time—that this was as much our war as it was the war of the other great democracies. I liked the way Roosevelt put it—the important thing being that there was no longer any more talk of help for the Allies *short of war,* just help to the utmost and all out for defense. From now on we are in the war until Germany and her jackal partner are licked" (Knox to Annie Knox, 11 June 1940, box 3, Knox MSS).

103. Press Conference, 24 May 1940, PFF 1-P, FDRL.

104. Ickes, *Secret Diary,* 3:215; *New York Times,* 21 June 1940.

105. Richard Barnet has depicted the Stimson-Knox appointment as a watershed event in the rise of what he calls the "national security managers." Their appointment made possible the later addition to the administration of Robert Lovett, John McCloy, Nelson Rockefeller, William Donovan, Lewis Douglas, Robert Patterson, Harvey Bundy, and countless others (see Barnet, *Roots of War: The Men and Institutions behind U.S. Foreign Policy* [Baltimore, Md., 1973], 52–55).

106. Stimson to FDR, June 1940, PPF 20, FDRL.

107. FDR to Stimson, 4 June 1940, PPF 20, FDRL.

108. Conference with representatives of the American Youth Congress, 5 June 1940, PPF 1-P, FDRL.

109. "He was the most complicated human being I ever knew" (Frances Perkins, *The Roosevelt I Knew* [New York, 1946], 3).

CHAPTER 5. NEW YORK:
THE NATIONAL EMERGENCY COMMITTEE

1. The British foreign secretary, Lord Halifax, noted in his diary that day: "[Ambassador] Joe Kennedy . . . was encouraging about the president's possible action with regard to the destroyers, and thought if and when Italy comes in this might give him the occasion, with general assent of U.S. opinion, for doing a great deal more" (3 June 1940, Halifax Family MSS, Borthwick Historical Institute, York, England).

2. *New York Times,* 4 June 1940.

3. Minutes of National Emergency Committee of the MTCA, 3 June 1940, Clark MSS; Ralph A. Lowell, diary, 3 June 1940, Lowell MSS, Massachusetts Historical Society, Boston.

4. See Mark Chadwin, *The Hawks of World War II* (Chapel Hill, N.C., 1968), chap. 4.

5. Minutes of Administrative Committee of NEC, 7 June 1940, Clark MSS; Boone's obituary in *New York Times,* 7 Sept. 1948.

6. Frederick J. Libby, "The Present Draft Law Has a Past," *Compass,* Spring 1943, DG 23, box 8, SCPC; see also O'Sullivan, "From Voluntarism to Conscription," 38 n.

7. Clark to John W. Davis (wire), 5 June 1940, and Davis to Clark (wire), 6 June 1940, box 120, John W. Davis MSS, Sterling Library, Yale University; Langdon Marvin to William Y. Elliott, 6 June 1940, box 137, William Y. Elliott MSS, Hoover Institute.

8. W. T. Stewart, memorandum of finances of NEC, Clark MSS.

9. As a writer, Clark was both meticulous and aesthetic in his methods. He often would have successive drafts printed and sent to his friends for comment. Much to the consternation of his secretaries, he liked nothing better than to mark up, in *ink,* apparently finished products just back from the printer. The many drafts of the 1940 draft act can be found in the Clark MSS. A description of Clark's writing habits is in Louis B. Sohn, "Grenville Clark: As Seen from a Co-author's Perspective," in Cousins and Clifford, *Memoirs of a Man,* 45–52.

10. *New York Times,* 21 June 1940, p. 3; Ralph A. Lowell, diary, 6–8 June 1940, Lowell MSS.

11. A direct descendant of Daniel Tompkins, the sixth vice-president of the United States, the seventy-year-old McIlvaine was probably the most ostentatiously aristocratic member of the NEC. Douglas Arant of Alabama could recall McIlvaine's lavish wine cellar more than thirty years later (interview with Arant, Birmingham, Dec. 1973). Convinced of his own expertise, McIlvaine presented his own universal-military-training bill to the War Department (see bill and accompanying "Memo as to the Experience of Tompkins McIlvaine Regarding Military Matters," 8 July 1940, RG 46, box 117, NA).

12. *Hearings before the Committee on Military Affairs, United States Senate, Seventy-sixth Congress, Third Session, on S-4164* (Washington, D.C., 1940), 38 (hereafter cited as Senate, *Hearings*).

13. Clark's preamble was dropped from the bill after it was introduced in Congress, but it posits the main reasons for selective service as conceived by the original sponsors. Incidentally, the military statutes of Henry VIII were designed to restore English archery to the proficiency of the days of Agincourt.

14. Senate, *Hearings,* 1.

15. Joint Committee, *American Selective Service,* 21–22; Selective Service System, *The Selective Service Act* (Washington, D.C., 1954), Special Monograph no. 2, vol. 3, 307.

16. Senate, *Hearings,* 1.

17. Frederick J. Libby, diary, 3 July 1940, Libby MSS, LC.

18. Morgenthau, diary, 2 Aug. 1940, vol. 288, 156–57.

19. The extension of the period of service became a critical issue in 1941, when Congress extended the period of service for eighteen more months (see O'Sullivan, "From Voluntarism to Conscription," 343–47).

20. Senate, *Hearings,* 3.

21. See James B. Conant, *My Several Lives: Memoirs of a Social Inventor* (New York, 1970), 328–39; Interview with Conant, Hanover, N.H., Aug. 1972.

22. Senate, *Hearings,* 3.

23. See George Q. Flynn, *Roosevelt and Romanism: Catholics and American Diplomacy, 1937–1945* (Westport, Conn., 1976), 73–78.

24. Senate, *Hearings,* 4.

25. Ibid., 3. Before final passage, this provision was changed to make those who failed to report for induction subject to civil, rather than military, courts.

26. Ibid., 2, 3.

27. See Theodore R. Wachs, "Conscription, Conscientious Objection, and the Context of American Pacifism, 1940–1945" (Ph.D. diss., University of Illinois, 1976), chap. 1; Chatfield, *For Peace and Justice,* 305–6.

28. "You would be amazed at the large amount of mail that every member of Congress is receiving, demanding that Congress remain in session because they do not want to trust the president and they have no confidence in him because they feel that if the United States did become involved in a war it would mean a dictatorship and they fear that after the war he would not want to give up the dictatorship" (Congressman Karl Stefan to Gene Huse, 17 June 1940, box 26, Stefan MSS, Nebraska Historical Society, Lincoln; from the notes of David Porter).

29. Senate, *Hearings,* 2, 3.

30. Ibid., 2, 5.

31. John Dickenson, *The Building of an Army* (New York, 1922), 92.

32. Marshall, *Biennial Report, 1939–1941,* 22, 28, 30–31, 39–41; Pogue, *George C. Marshall: Ordeal and Hope,* 91–103.

33. Anne Lindbergh wrote about the emotional commitment of many easterners at the time: "They are so worked up themselves that to be dispassionate is to represent the Anti-Christ. I know the 'class' well. It is 'my' class. All the people I was brought up with. The East, the secure, the rich, the cultured, the sensitive, the academic, the good—those worthy intelligent people brought up in a hedged world so far from realities" (entry of 31 May 1940, in *War Within and Without,* 96).

34. Minutes of NEC, 3 June 1940, Clark MSS; notes of Spencer interview with John Kenderdine, 23 Oct. 1947, Clark MSS; *New York Times,* 4 June 1940.

35. The 1915 Plattsburg camp had begun without official approval and was nearly canceled because of the Treasury Department's unwillingness to authorize expenditures (see Clifford, *Citizen Soldiers,* chap. 3).

36. *New York Times,* 14 June 1940. Grenville Clark, Jr., was in attendance.

37. There was a striking parallel between General Drum's participation in this project and the role played by Leonard Wood in the Plattsburg Movement of 1915/16. General Wood, then commanding the Eastern Department with headquarters at Governors Island, did everything he could to help the civilians who were organizing the Plattsburg camps, notwithstanding the apathy of his superiors and the hostility of President Wilson. General Drum similarly gave encouragement to the New Yorkers in the face of War Department disapproval. Moreover, in conducting First Army maneuvers that summer in upstate New York, Drum dramatically illustrated equipment shortages by labeling iron pipes as "cannon" and trucks as "tanks." Some members of the General Staff considered this tactic of Drum's a deliberate attempt to embarrass General Marshall, whose appointment as chief of staff in 1939 Drum had coveted for himself. Although Drum, like Wood in 1917/18, was pushed into relative obscurity after the United States entered the war, the parallel should not be strained too far. Drum was offered the China-Burma-India command in January 1942, but he foolishly turned it down (see Pogue, *George C. Marshall: Ordeal and Hope,* 90, 357–60; see also John C. O'Loughlin to Drum, 18 June 1940, box 36, O'Loughlin MSS, LC).

38. See Louis Johnson, "Hemisphere Defense," *Atlantic Monthly,* July 1940, 4.

39. Adler to Clark, 7 June 1940, Clark MSS.

40. Adler to George C. Marshall, 7 June 1940, Clark MSS.

41. Kenderdine interview, 23 Oct. 1947; Kenderdine to Adler, 12 June 1940, Clark MSS.

42. Kenderdine memorandum for Karl Behr, 15 June 1940, Clark MSS.

43. Kenderdine interview, 23 Oct. 1947, Clark MSS.

44. Marshall to Gen. Roy D. Keehn, 18 June 1940 (Larry Bland chronological file), Marshall MSS.

45. Watson, *Chief of Staff*, 192–94.

46. Marshall interview, 22 Jan. 1957, Marshall Library. Cf. "As a matter of fact, my struggle for the moment has been to get appropriations and certain legislation through Congress . . . and, *hardest of all, to meet the flood of suggestions, urgings, and enthusiasms, etc., that are aimed at the War Department these weeks, and each of them from very powerful channels. My problem has been to keep our heads above the flood of these weeks, more particularly to prevent the emasculation of most of the plans we have in favor of—to be brutally frank—a series of superficialities.* I have felt it of vital importance to do everything in my power to keep public confidence in the War Department, but it really has been hard to do this when we were involved in turning down 1,000 schemes a day" (italics added; Marshall to Bernard Baruch, 29 June 1940, vol. 48, Baruch MSS).

47. Letter AG 354.1, 14 June 1940, Subject: Special Course, CMTC, To: All Corps Area Commanding Officers, War Department files, Spencer notes, Clark MSS.

48. Some commanders would have been better off not holding such camps. Nevertheless, probably motivated by the old army maxim that a general's wish is no less a command, every commanding general made the effort.

49. Minutes of MTCA Executive Committee, 17 June 1940, Clark MSS. The MTCA civilian aide for New England, Chester Heywood, warned the Bostonians that Wyles was dead set against raising money for anything that could be considered interventionist (Lowell, diary, 11 June 1940).

CHAPTER 6. WASHINGTON:
THE BURKE-WADSWORTH BILL DEBUTS

1. Charles McNary to Mrs. Walter T. Stolz, 10 June 1940, box 2, McNary MSS, LC; J. C. O'Loughlin to John J. Pershing, 14 June 1940, box 58, O'Loughlin MSS; Oswald G. Villard to Roger Clark, 18 June 1940, Villard MSS; Cong. George H. Tinkham to Edwin M. Borchard, 5 June 1940, Borchard MSS, Sterling Library, Yale University; Sen. James F. Byrnes to Bernard Baruch, 14 June 1940, vol. 48, Baruch MSS; "Congress Stay in Session Folder," box 4, John Vorys MSS; Cong. Clare Hoffman to fellow members of Congress, 8 June 1940, box 6, T. V. Smith MSS, Regenstein Library, University of Chicago, Chicago, Ill.; Charles Tobey to W. J. Abbott, Jr., 13 June 1940, Charles Tobey MSS, Baker Library, Dartmouth College; Burton K. Wheeler to Robert E. Wood, 19 June 1940, box 21, Robert E. Wood MSS, HHPL; Cong. Frank W. Carlson to Alfred M. Landon, 12 June 1940, and Arthur Capper to Landon, 8 June 1940, Landon MSS; Clifford Hope to Robert O. Thomas, 6 June 1940, Clifford Hope MSS.

2. Minutes of NEC Administrative Committee Meeting, 17 June 1940, Clark MSS.

3. James F. Byrnes to Bernard Baruch, 14 June 1940, vol. 48, Baruch MSS.

4. Congressional Campaign file, Clark MSS; Morison, *Turmoil and Tradition,* 398. Ironically, Byrnes later wrote in his memoirs: "In Congress nothing just happens— somebody must make it happen" (*All in One Lifetime* [New York, 1958], 114; see also Byrnes to Shepard Saltzman, 25 May 1940, Nat'l. Defense file, James F. Byrnes MSS, Clemson University Library, Clemson, S.C.).

5. James T. Patterson, *Mr. Republican: A Biography of Robert A. Taft* (Boston, 1972), chaps. 14, 15.

6. Clark memorandum, 17 June 1940, Clark MSS.

7. Interview with William Chadbourne, 9 June 1947. Lewis Hershey later recalled that Palmer, who greatly admired Wadsworth, would joke that they understood one another as "gentleman farmers." "Palmer had a scrubby little farm in New Hampshire, while Wadsworth probably owned half of Genesee County in upstate New York" (Hershey interview, Dec. 1967).

8. "I do not think we shall get into this war, but if Germany wins we would better look out. Sooner or later they will try to get into Latin America, break up some of those countries with interior revolutions, get themselves established, and creep up toward the Panama Canal. The thing for us to do is stop them before they ever get in" (Wadsworth to William Beverly, 17 May 1940, box 33, Wadsworth Family MSS).

9. Wadsworth, "Memoir," COHP, 436.

10. The details of the bill's introduction in the Senate are based on Spencer's interviews with Clark, Adler, Senator Burke, Petersen, and Boone in 1947.

11. Clark memorandum for Jack Raymond, 1963, Clark MSS; Jack Raymond, *Power at the Pentagon* (New York, 1964), 44-45.

12. Clark seemed to have labored under the misapprehension that Congress would *adjourn* that day and therefore that the bill had to be introduced immediately. In fact, the Congress would only *recess,* first because of Gibson's death and then because of the Republican Convention.

13. Interview with Perley Boone, 31 July 1947, Clark MSS.

14. Frederick J. Libby, diary, 20 June 1940, Libby MSS.

15. *New York Times,* 20 June 1940.

16. Clark to Frankfurter (wire), 14 June 1940, Clark MSS.

17. Frankfurter to FDR, 13 June 1940, in Freedman, *Roosevelt and Frankfurter,* 529.

18. *New York Times,* 9 June 1940.

19. *Washington Merry-Go-Round,* 19 June 1940, quoted in McFarland, *Harry F. Woodring,* 228; Woodring to F. J. Hall of *U.S. News,* 10 June 1940, box 27, Woodring MSS.

20. *New York Times,* 19 June 1940. At the same Yale commencement, British Ambassador Lord Lothian warned Americans that the only way to ensure the British fleet's transfer to American waters in the event of a successful German invasion was for the United States to become a belligerent (Leutze, *Bargaining for Supremacy,* 88).

21. Stimson and Bundy, *On Active Service,* 318.

22. Frankfurter to FDR (wire), 19 June 1940, in Freedman, *Roosevelt and Frankfurter,* 530.

23. Stimson and Bundy, *On Active Service,* 323-24; Morison, *Turmoil and Tradition,* 398-99.

24. Knox described his appointment thus to Harold Ickes two weeks later (entry of 4 July 1940, Ickes, diary, Ickes MSS).

25. Sherwood, *Roosevelt and Hopkins,* 163.

26. Entry of 19 June 1940, Morgenthau, presidential diaries, FDRL.

27. McFarland, *Harry H. Woodring,* 228-29.

28. FDR to Woodring, 19 June 1940, box 38, PSF (Harry Woodring, 1937-40), FDRL.

29. Libby, diary, 10 June 1940.

30. *New York Times,* 21 June 1940.

31. *New York Times,* 21 June 1940.

32. J. Sterling Morton to Landon (wire), 21 June 1940, Landon MSS.

33. Amos Pinchot to Lincoln Colcord, 24 June 1940, box 67, Amos Pinchot MSS, LC.

34. *New York Times,* 22 June 1940; Ickes, *Secret Diary,* 3:215.

35. William Allen White to Landon, 5 July 1940, Landon MSS.

36. "Memorandum Re Henry L. Stimson," 21 June 1940, Warren F. Austin MSS, Guy Bailey Library, University of Vermont, Burlington.

37. *New York Times,* 21 June 1940.

38. J. C. O'Loughlin to Herbert Hoover, 22 June 1940, box 45, O'Loughlin MSS, LC.

39. *New York Times,* 23 June 1940.

40. Woodring to FDR, 19 June 1940, quoted in McFarland, *Harry H. Woodring,* 230.

41. FDR to Woodring, 20 June 1940, PSF 106, FDRL.

42. McFarland, *Harry H. Woodring,* 231. Woodring later told Arthur Vandenberg that his silence after he had resigned actually helped the isolationists. "The way I have handled the matter . . . has been very successful in modifying some of the policies of this administration to which I did not agree, and has also sobered some of the belligerent and antagonistic 'mouthing off' by some of the officials. Frankly, I believe by withholding the publication . . . [of] my letter, that it serves as a threat and as a club of restraint over some of the impetuous interventionists" (Woodring to Vandenberg, 24 July 1940, Woodring MSS; see also notes of talk with Woodring, 21 June 1940, box 48, James Farley MSS).

43. McFarland, *Harry H. Woodring,* 234. FDR may have had an additional reason for dismissing Woodring because of reports, later proven false, that the secretary of war had taken money from a German-American suspected of being a Nazi agent (see J. Edgar Hoover memorandum, 8 July 1940, no. 126-A, OF 10B, FDRL).

44. Quoted in Bernard M. Baruch, *Baruch: The Public Years,* 2 vols. (New York, 1960), 2:277.

45. Entry of 24 June 1940, in Beatrice Bishop Berle and Travis Beal Jacobs, eds., *Navigation of the Rapids, 1918–1971: From the Papers of Adolf A. Berle* (New York, 1973), 325.

46. J. C. O'Loughlin to John J. Pershing, 27 July 1940, box 58, O'Loughlin MSS. FDR told Henry Wallace that "Louis Johnson is a fine fellow and I don't like to hurt him. But obviously Stimson wants his own Asst. Secretary of War." FDR thought about making Johnson "Inspector of National Defense." FDR also confided that Johnson "didn't have a chance in a million to be vice-president" (Wallace, diary, 10 July 1940).

47. The main obstacle may have been Johnson's friendship with Farley, whose aspirations for the Democratic nomination FDR was about to thwart (James A. Farley, *Jim Farley's Story* [New York, 1948], 240–43, 294, 301, 329; see also Robert Reynolds to Johnson, 27 July 1940, and Sherman Minton to Johnson, 9 Sept. 1940, box 78, Louis Johnson MSS; and Steve Early to Johnson, 29 July 1940, box 8, Early MSS).

48. Drew Pearson to Johnson, 28 June 1940, box 24, Louis Johnson MSS.

49. Lothian to FO, no. 1204, 21 June 1940, A3223/34/45, RBFO. A Foreign Office official minuted: "Stimson recently wrote a very cordial personal and private letter to Mr. Churchill. . . . Mr. Stimson could hardly be more interventionist and Col. Knox could hardly be more bellicose" (J. V. Perowne minute, 21 June 1940, A3460/39/45, RBFO).

50. Stimson to Knox, 20 May 1940, Stimson MSS.

51. Knox's accession to the Navy Department decisively affected the other great policy initiative of the summer, namely, the destroyer deal. In his newspaper, the *Chicago Daily News,* Knox had been pushing the proposal of having the British liquidate their defaulted World War I debts to the United States by granting additional bases to

the United States Navy in the West Indies. Knox broached this idea to the British ambassador on 9 July 1940, the day of his confirmation, and his suggestion revitalized naval negotiations and linked the British request for fifty destroyers with American bases. Knox's subsequent appointment of his good friend William J. Donovan to visit England in late July, ostensibly to observe British methods for combatting fifth-column activities, eventually provided President Roosevelt with sufficient assurances that England would hold out against a German attack. Roosevelt's decision to go ahead with the destroyer deal was not made until he received Donovan's favorable report (Lothian to FO, no. 1307, 10 July 1940, A3297/2961/45, RBFO; Leutze, *Bargaining for Supremacy,* chap. 7).

52. NEC minutes, 25 June 1940, Clark MSS.

53. *New York Times,* 25 June 1940.

54. Ibid., 27 June 1940. "Taft grows in strength. Willkie grows in noise and propaganda" (Warren Austin to Mrs. Chauncey Austin, 27 June 1940, box 2, Austin MSS). "Foreign policy plank is very close to what we came to get" (Frederick J. Libby, diary, 26 June 1940, Libby MSS).

55. See Hugh Ross, "Was the Nomination of Wendell Willkie a Political Miracle?" *Indiana Magazine of History* 63 (June 1962): 79–100; Steve Neal, *Dark Horse: A Biography of Wendell Willkie* (Garden City, N.Y., 1984), chaps. 7–11.

56. Democratic Congressman Lawrence Lewis of Colorado also noted that Willkie was the only "Republican aspirant who has color and 'punch' " (diary, 27 June 1940, Lewis MSS, Colorado Historical Society, Denver).

57. Oren Root, *Persons and Persuasions* (New York, 1974), chap. 1. Among Willkie's backers were Henry Luce, Russell Davenport (editor of *Fortune*), Charlton MacVeagh, Frank Altschul, Helen Reid of the *New York Herald Tribune,* Cong. Bruce Barton, Thomas W. Lamont, and others whom the New Yorkers on the NEC knew well. Nevertheless, the manuscript evidence suggests that the Willkie campaign and the campaign for selective service proceeded on distinct and separate tracks.

58. Raymond Buell memorandum for Willkie, 27 June 1940, Wendell Willkie MSS, Lilly Library, Indiana University, Bloomington.

59. This account is based on Clark's recollections in 1947.

60. FDR's note to Stimson read: "The enclosed has just come. Please let me have your thoughts on this. As far as I know it is all right as a stopgap pending selective service legislation" (FDR to Stimson, 26 June 1940, PPF 20, FDRL).

61. On 17 May, General Marshall, who believed firmly in "gradual, planned expansion," had written that "mobilization of the National Guard . . . should be avoided until the necessity is inevitable" (Watson, *Chief of Staff,* 168, 198 n). By mid July, when Marshall was urging the activation of the entire National Guard, he wrote: "Time is the dominant factor in all this business. We cannot advertise every thought and item of knowledge we have; we are charged with the National Defense, meaning national safety. Once the dilemma has arisen, it is too late; we have to take our preliminary measures in time to reach some degree of preparation. . . . The past three months have been catastrophic in the history of the world, and the next six months may be more paralyzing" (Marshall to Gen. Roy D. Keehn, 15 July 1940 [Larry Bland file], Marshall MSS).

62. Gen. William E. Shedd, memorandum for chief of staff, 21 June 1940, and memorandum for Maj. Evert, G-2, 21 June 1940, AG 341 (7-10-39), sec. 2a, Civilian Volunteer Effort, War Dept. records, NA. The General Board of the Navy had recommended universal military training on 7 June (see memo enclosed in Edison to FDR, 8 June 1940, PSF Navy, FDRL).

63. Gen. William E. Shedd, memorandum for chief of staff, 22 June 1940, G-1/8645-289, copy in Marshall MSS; Watson, *Chief of Staff,* 11-12. For additional evidence of Marshall's determination to prevent excessive transfer of military equipment to the British see Russell A. Gugeler, "George Marshall and Orlando Ward, 1939-1941," *Parameters* 13 (Mar. 1983): 34-39.

64. It should be noted that at this meeting, FDR agreed "in general" to halt the further release of military equipment to the British on the grounds that such weapons "will seriously weaken our present state of defense and will not materially assist British forces." The president did propose a caveat, however, "that if, for example, the British displayed an ability to withstand the German assault, and it appeared that a little help might carry them through to the first of the year, then it might be desirable from the point of view of our defense, to turn over other material that would exercise an important effect on the action" (Marshall memorandum for Gen. George V. Strong, 24 June 1940, WPD 4250-3, War Plans Division, War Department Records, RG 165, NA; see also memorandum for chief of staff, 18 June 1940, White House Press Conference folder, box 84, Louis Johnson MSS; Watson, *Chief of Staff,* 112). On 3 June, General Shedd had drafted a letter for General Marshall that included these words: "Eventually the War Department must seek such [selective service] legislation; perhaps in the near future." Marshall excised this sentence (Marshall to Edwin Watson, 3 June 1940, War Department files 080, MTCA, Spencer notes, Clark MSS).

65. To their credit, even in the face of FDR's negative reaction, Marshall and Stark again recommended draft legislation in their revised "Basis for Immediate Decisions Concerning National Defense" on 27 June 1940 (Watson, *Chief of Staff,* 113).

66. Clark interviews, 1947.

67. Watson, *Chief of Staff,* 191.

68. Marshall to McCoy, 26 June 1940, box 49, Frank R. McCoy MSS, LC.

69. Marshall to Katherine Marshall, 28 June 1940 (Larry Bland file), Marshall MSS; see also, Morison, *Turmoil and Tradition,* 406 n.

70. *New York Times,* 3 July 1940.

71. "It is getting so these days that I am having difficulty in seeing anything of Katherine [Mrs. Marshall], and when I am with her I have to spend so much time relaxing that I am not very much of a husband" (Marshall to John McAuley Palmer, 24 June 1940, box 9, Palmer MSS).

72. Lothian to FO, no. 950, 8 June 1940, A3273/39/45, RBFO.

73. Mayor La Guardia, one of FDR's proposed choices for secretary of war, wrote of the NEC draft bill: "I don't think this plan is so hot. It seems to me the government is taking every precautionary means for training and providing ample funds" (La Guardia to Edwin Watson, 7 June 1940, OF 4065, FDRL).

74. The favorable *Times* editorial, incidentally, did not originate with Adler, who was scrupulous in not making the paper his own mouthpiece on military matters. Publisher Arthur Hays Sulzberger, whose views between the wars inclined toward pacifism, made the decision to support conscription in consultation with editor Charles Merz (see Meyer Berger, *History of the New York Times* [New York, 1951], 439-40).

75. Press conference, 7 June 1940, PPF 1-P, FDRL.

76. Minutes of meetings of Youth Committee against War, 7 and 14 June 1940, CDGA, box 3; minutes of meeting of Executive Committee, War Resisters League, 21 June 1940, DG 40, box 2; "Outline of a Proposed Campaign against Current Agitation for Conscription in Peacetime," enclosed in Edwin C. Johnson to Daniel L. Marsh, 17 June 1940, DG 9, box 28—all in SCPC.

77. Clark to FDR, 10 June 1940, Clark MSS; Roosevelt, *Public Papers,* 9:264.

78. FDR memorandum for Watson, 14 June 1940, OF 4065, FDRL.

79. Press conference, 18 June 1940, PPF 1-P, FDRL; see also Wallace, diary, 18 June 1940.

80. Eleanor Roosevelt had advocated a nonmilitary compulsory service program for youth as early as 3 June but had said at the time that she saw little chance of its implementation (*New York Times,* 4 June 1940). Earlier that year she had supported suggestions for voluntary military training in the CCC. "I am not in the least afraid of offering our youngsters an opportunity to learn something which will be undoubtedly valuable to them in peacetime" (Eleanor Roosevelt to Edwin C. Johnson [Committee on Militarism in Education], 20 Jan. 1940, Eleanor Roosevelt MSS, FDRL).

81. Frances Perkins to FDR, 13 June 1940, OF 504; F. C. Harrington to FDR, 15 June 1940, OF 444C; Early press conference, 19 June 1940, box 40, Early MSS; for a convenient summary of all the various manpower plans in 1940 see manpower folder, box 302, Harry Hopkins MSS—all in FDRL.

82. James Oliver to Charles Parsons, 22 June 1940, Charles Parsons MSS, Sterling Library, Yale University, New Haven, Conn.

83. Wadsworth to E. Willoughby, 21 June 1940, Wadsworth Family MSS.

84. See the numerous letters in file OF 813A, FDRL.

85. *New York Times,* 25 and 20 June 1940.

86. Ibid., 21 June 1940.

87. Representatives of the National Intercollegiate Christian Council, the National Student Federation, the American Student Union, the International Student Service, Work Camps for Democracy, the New York section of Young Judea, and the Youth Section of the League of Nations Association issued a joint press release endorsing the plan and expressing approval of Hillman as director.

88. *New York Times,* 24 June 1940.

89. Entries of 28 June and 2 July 1940, Frederick Libby, diary; minutes of National Action Committee meeting, Youth Committee against War, 8 July 1940, CDGA, box 3, SCPC; Clarence Pickett, diary, 27 June, 1, 10, and 19 July 1940, AFSC Archives, Philadelphia. FDR made similar comments about preferring voluntary national service over military conscription to such White House visitors as Fiorello La Guardia, Huston Thompson, and William Allen White (La Guardia to C. C. Burlingham, 24 June 1940, Burlingham MSS; Huston Thompson to his mother, 1 July 1940, box 1, Huston Thompson MSS, LC; William Allen White to Burton K. Wheeler, 15 and 20 Aug. 1940, box 348, White MSS).

90. *New York Times,* 10 July 1940; entry of 14 Aug. 1940, Morgenthau, presidential diaries, FDRL. Cf. FDR "was thinking in terms of a program of universal military and civilian training rather than increases in the present NYA and CCC programs. He seemed to feel there were possibilities for such training in connection with the pending compulsory service legislation. He indicated, however, that he would not object to certain specialized forms of training related to the national defense during the interim period during which the broader training programs were being worked out" (entry of 30 July 1940, Harold Smith, diary, Smith MSS, FDRL).

91. Grenville Clark became a prime mover in the post–Pearl Harbor effort for national service (see, especially, George Q. Flynn, *The Mess in Washington: Manpower Mobilization in World War II* (Westport, Conn., 1979).

92. For FDR's excessive concern with public opinion see Richard K. Steele, "Preparing the Public for War: Efforts to Establish a National Propaganda Agency, 1940–41," *American Historical Review* 92 (1970): 1640–53; and Dallek, *Franklin D. Roosevelt,* passim. For a superb discussion of FDR's cautious approach to the destroyers-for-bases deal see Leutze, *Bargaining for Supremacy,* chaps. 6–8.

93. Raymond Buell, memorandum, 27 June 1940, Buell folder, Willkie MSS; see also memorandum enclosed in Buell to S. K. Hornbeck, 25 June 1940, box 40, Stanley K. Hornbeck MSS, Hoover Institute; same memorandum, 27 June 1940, General "W" file, box 165, Roy W. Howard MSS, LC.

94. FDR to Watson, 26 June 1940, OF 4040, FDRL; Ickes, diary, 5 July 1940, Ickes MSS.

95. Wallace, diary, 28 June 1940; for an elaboration of why FDR "would hate to see Willkie as President" see James A. Farley, memorandum, 1 Aug. 1940, box 45, Farley MSS; even after the election, Mrs. Roosevelt could write to a British friend: "We now realize that Mr. Willkie was backed by forces which were a greater menace than many of us were willing to believe. There was a fascist tendency for an appeasement toward Germany which terrifies many of us" (to Florence Willert, 16 Nov. 1940, box 6, Arthur Willert MSS, Sterling Library, Yale University).

96. Sherwood, *Roosevelt and Hopkins,* 157.

97. Clark to Harry Hopkins, 28 June 1940, box 302, Hopkins MSS.

98. Sherwood, *Roosevelt and Hopkins,* 157.

CHAPTER 7. WASHINGTON: HEARINGS AND HARMONY

1. See Frank Vandiver, *Black Jack* (New York, 1977). When Pershing visited the White House, FDR asked whether he should "let the British have certain of our superior aircraft, or . . . hold them for ourselves." Pershing said he did not know (Henry Wallace, diary, 17 May 1940).

2. Pershing had served as an honorary director of the National Economy League at Clark's request in 1932/33.

3. Clark to Pershing, 13 June 1940, John J. Pershing MSS, LC.

4. Pershing to Clark, 14 June 1940, Pershing MSS.

5. Interviews with Clark and Palmer, 1947, Clark MSS.

6. Clark interviews, 1947, Clark MSS; Clark to Morris Sheppard, 22 June 1940, RG 46, box 116, NA.

7. Senate, *Hearings,* 5; Pershing to Sheppard, 3 July 1940, RG 46, box 116, NA.

8. Senate, *Hearings,* 6.

9. Ibid., 6–9.

10. Ibid., 12.

11. The argument was made by isolationists at the time and was resurrected by Bruce Russett in his provocative essay *No Clear and Present Danger* (New York, 1972) that Hitler never acquired the naval power sufficient to attack the United States and that, consequently, the physical threat to America was greatly exaggerated. Such an argument overlooks the fluidity inherent in the events of the spring and summer of 1940. At the time the NEC drew up the selective-service bill, the fall of France was imminent, and most observers believed that Germany would demand part of the French fleet in any peace settlement. Similarly, the distinct possibility that England would be invaded quickly made President Roosevelt extremely cautious about making any destroyers available to the British without an ironclad promise from Churchill that the British navy would never be surrendered. The fact that these dire scenarios did not occur does not necessarily mean that the Roosevelt administration and groups like the NEC were foolishly indulging in "worst case analysis." Whether Hitler had the capacity, or even the intention, of attacking the United States, it became increasingly prudent after the spring of 1940 to prepare for such an eventuality. For compelling

evidence that Hitler did indeed intend to attack the United States see Gerhard Weinberg, *World in the Balance* (Hanover, N.H., 1981), chaps. 3 and 4.

12. Senate, *Hearings,* 10.

13. Ibid., 27ff.

14. Ibid., 29.

15. Ibid., 48.

16. Ibid., 33.

17. Ibid., 46.

18. One scholar of selective service has written: "The effort to make Washington the father of our contemporary military ideas is somewhat too strenuous. Why don't we just leave him 'the Father of our Country'" (Edward A. Fitzpatrick, *Universal Military Training* [New York, 1945], 122-23). The most recent scholarship on Washington's "Sentiments on a Peace Establishment" indicates that the report, which emphasized federal reform of the militia, was actually drafted by Alexander Hamilton (see Kohn, *Eagle and Sword,* 45-47; and Lawrence Delbert Cress, "Republican Liberty and National Security, 1783-1798: American Military Policy as an Ideological Problem," *William and Mary Quarterly* 38 (Jan. 1981): 73-96.

19. Senate, *Hearings,* 44-48.

20. Ibid., 20.

21. Ibid., 32ff., 96ff.; Frederick Palmer to Alf Landon, 15 June and 12 July 1940, Landon MSS.

22. Senate, *Hearings,* 92-96.

23. Conant, *My Several Lives,* chap. 18; see also William M. Tuttle, "American Higher Education and the Nazis: The Case of James B. Conant and Harvard University's 'Diplomatic Relations' with Germany," *American Studies* 20 (Spring 1979): 49-70.

24. Senate, *Hearings,* 23.

25. Ibid., 13.

26. Ibid., 47.

27. Ibid., 76.

28. Entry of 1 July 1940, daily record, box 4, Harold Smith MSS, FDRL.

29. Senate, *Hearings,* 57.

30. See Jim Dan Hill, *The Minute Men in Peace and War: A History of the National Guard* (Harrisburg, Pa., 1964), 371.

31. Senate, *Hearings,* 63-64.

32. Ibid., 66.

33. Quoted in Alden Hatch, *The Wadsworths of the Genessee* (New York, 1959), 253.

34. Quoted in Watson, *Chief of Staff,* 172.

35. The official historian of the Office of the Chief of Staff later wrote of the June 1940 estimate: "It did not look toward expansion beyond the 1,000,000 man army; it did not provide except in a minor way, for new facilities; it did not provide substantially for essential items. Moreover, it did not spell out in detail the time requirements, and the hour was late" (Watson, *Chief of Staff,* 173).

36. Ibid., 172-77; Burns memo, 13 June 1940, PSF (War Department), FDRL.

37. Lothian to FO, nos. 1135 and 1269, 26 June and 7 July 1940, A3223/39/45, RBFO; Lothian also wrote: "The United States, even under Roosevelt, has made all the mistakes that all the other democracies have made. They never believed that the war could come close to themselves; they have positively allowed the democracies to be knocked out one after another. And they have postponed their own preparations until it is much too late. Hitler is not going to give us or them time to prepare if he can help

it. But the change in American thinking since May 10th has been overwhelming'' (to John Aikman, 1 July 1940, GD40/17/398, Lothian MSS).

38. Burton K. Wheeler to Robert E. Wood, 19 June 1940, Wood MSS.

39. Quoted in Watson, *Chief of Staff,* 166.

40. *New Yorker,* 10 July 1940, 35.

41. Marshall to Bernard Baruch, 29 June 1940, vol. 48, Baruch MSS.

42. Watson, *Chief of Staff,* 110–13; Pogue, *George C. Marshall: Ordeal and Hope,* 58. Years later, Marshall recalled: "The first thing he [Stimson] did when I went up to call on him, just before he accepted and came down to Washington, was to talk to them [Clark and the NEC] on the phone and press me to move ahead on this [selective service] very much more rapidly than I was willing to do'' (interview, 22 Jan. 1957). It should be noted that Marshall was still frustrated by the lack of any precise instructions about national priorities. After secret conversations with Canadian staff officers, he told the U.S. minister to Canada, J. P. Moffat, that "the administration . . . had to make up its own mind as to what it would do in very definite contingencies, such as a retreat of the British Fleet in whole or in part to North America.'' Marshall also commented: "There was no doubt that we had sold so generously to the Allied powers that our own stocks were below the safety point . . . [and] if Britain were defeated the army and the administration could never justify to the American people the risk they had taken'' (J. Pierrepont Moffat, diary, 21 July 1940, Moffat MSS, Houghton Library, Harvard University, Cambridge, Mass.).

43. *New York Times,* 7 July 1940, 17.

44. The following is based on Spencer's interviews with Clark and Petersen in 1947.

45. Report on S-4164 for the Committee on Military Affairs (not sent), file G-1/161711, War Department files; copies in Marshall MSS and Hershey MSS.

46. Woodley, purchased by Stimson for $800,000 when he was secretary of state, had been built by an uncle of Francis Scott Key's and had previously served as the summer home of four presidents (see Morison, *Turmoil and Tradition,* 254).

47. Marshall interview, 22 Jan. 1957.

48. Hershey interview, Dec. 1969.

49. Stimson, diary, 9 July 1940; Spencer's interviews with Clark, Petersen, and Hershey, 1947.

50. Hershey interview, Dec. 1969.

51. Senate, *Hearings,* 327.

52. *New York Times,* 13 July 1940.

53. Senate, *Hearings,* 327–72.

54. House, *Hearings,* 97–98.

55. Senate, *Hearings,* 347.

56. Ibid., 330.

57. Ibid., 333.

58. Lodge still remained attached to his plan and urged, through fellow Massachusetts Republican Sinclair Weeks, that Wendell Willkie come out for such a proposal (Weeks to Willkie, 13 July 1940, box 12, Weeks MSS, Baker Library, Dartmouth College, Hanover, N.H.).

59. Senate, *Hearings,* 335.

60. Ibid., 353.

61. Ibid., 350; see also Gen. E. Adams to Warren Austin, 19 July 1940, box 26, Austin MSS.

62. Marshall interview, 22 Jan. 1957.

63. Clark memorandum for Stimson, 11 July 1940, Clark MSS.

64. Committee on Military Affairs, United States Senate, S-4164: *Committee Print No. 1* (Washington, D.C., 1940), 3.

65. Senate, *Committee Print No. 1*, 4. The twelve-month period upset the device suggested by the National Guard for "commuting" at least half of a trainee's service. Originally, the bill had specified that at the end of his training, a selectee should go into the Organized Reserves for ten years, or until the age of forty-five, whichever should be earlier. Members of the inactive National Guard were eliminated from the list of those exempted from registration.

66. Senate, *Committee Print No. 1*, 5.

67. There was a minor technical change in that the limits were specified as eighteen to sixty-four inclusive, rather than eighteen to sixty-five.

68. Senate, *Committee Print No. 1*, 6.

69. Ibid., 11.

70. Ibid., 2.

71. Wadsworth to Palmer, 23 July 1940, Wadsworth MSS.

72. Reckord to May, 3 Sept. 1940; and Reckord to Wadsworth, 3 Sept. 1940, Wadsworth MSS.

73. Palmer to Wadsworth, 20 and 27 July 1940; Wadsworth to Palmer, 23 July 1940, Wadsworth MSS.

74. On this point see Hill, *Minute Men,* 372-73; and John K. Mahon, *History of the Militia and the National Guard* (New York, 1983), 179-80.

75. Stimson to Sheppard, 22 July 1940, RG 46, box 117.

76. General Andrews of the Plans and Training Division wrote in September 1940 that there were enough officers "to meet the requirements up until . . . our army exceeds a strength of two million men" (Gen. F. M. Andrews, memo for chief of staff, 19 Sept. 1940, AG 352 [9-19-40] [1], sec. 1, pt. 1, OCS, War Dept. files). As late as February 1941, the General Staff insisted that "the present pool of available and eligible officers is adequate for any situation which may arise within the next fiscal year," i.e., July 1941-July 1942 (see report of conference between staff representatives and NEC, 27/28 Feb., prepared for chief of staff by Gen. W. H. Haislip, G-1, copies in Clark MSS and Marshall MSS).

77. House, *Hearings,* 95.

78. Ibid., 102.

79. General Marshall later recalled that Martin "was being trained as a private by a corporal who had been in the army about ten years and had never been promoted from a private to a corporal—until this big change came and they had to put him in as an instructor. Well, he was no good at all at that and yet he was training Martin who was a brilliant man and who is now head of the Federal Reserve. We had nobody else to use. I wanted to go ahead as fast as we were able to manage the thing; that was all ignored. They just wanted what I call numbers—the numbers racket—which I wouldn't accept at all" (interview, 22 Jan. 1957, Marshall Library).

80. The rotund La Guardia did not emulate his tall, lean predecessor in 1915, John Purroy Mitchel, in actually taking the training course.

81. *New York Times,* 1 Aug. 1940.

82. Ralph Lowell, diary, 5 July 1940, Ralph Lowell MSS. The figures are from a report on the camps in War Dept. file 080 MTCA; Spencer notes are in Clark MSS.

83. J. D. Kenderdine to J. O. Adler, 31 July 1940, Adler MSS; Chester Heywood to Ralph Lowell, 11 July 1940, Lowell MSS.

84. Chester Davis to George C. Marshall, 18 July 1940 (Bland file), Marshall MSS.

85. *New York Times,* 2 July 1940; MTCA to Louis Johnson, 2 July 1940, Robert P. Patterson MSS, LC.

86. *New York Times,* 5 July 1940.

87. Clark to Stimson, 11 July 1940.

88. Stimson, diary, 16 July 1940, Stimson MSS; A. G. Thacher, memorandum of telephone calls and conferences, 16 July 1940, Clark MSS.

89. *New York Times,* 18 July 1940; Stimson, diary, 17/18 July 1940, Stimson MSS; Kenderdine to Adler, 31 July 1940, Clark MSS; Chester Heywood to Ralph Lowell, 22 July 1940, MTCA box, Lowell MSS.

90. Sanders to Clark, 18 July 1940, Clark MSS.

91. John P. Freeman to Clark, 29 Aug. 1940, Clark MSS.

92. Copy of telegram, undated, Clark MSS.

93. Stimson, diary, 18 July 1940; see also Wyles to William Tuttle, 9 July 1940, and Wyles to Robert Jamison, 9 July 1940, MTCA records, Chicago Historical Society.

94. *New York Times,* 25 July 1940.

95. Stimson, diary, 6 Aug. 1940.

96. Malcolm Langford memorandum for Clark, 6 Aug. 1940; and Franklin Canfield memorandum for Clark, 6 Aug. 1940, Clark MSS.

97. Stimson, diary, 8 Aug. 1940, Stimson MSS.

98. Clark to Adler, 14 Aug. 1940, Clark MSS.

99. Stimson to Clark (wire), 14 Aug. 1940, Clark MSS.

100. Stimson to Clark, 16 Aug. 1940, Clark MSS.

101. Stimson to FDR, 4 Mar. 1941, Stimson MSS.

102. Marshall interview, 22 Jan. 1957, Marshall MSS.

103. See Pogue, *George C. Marshall: Ordeal and Hope,* 102-3, 461n; Greenfield, Palmer, and Wiley, *The Organization of Ground Combat Troops,* 42, 48-51. Marshall's chief aide noted that "apparently the New York group had a 'general staff' that thought one thing, but the War Department General Staff thought another, and that he could not stay on as chief of staff if the secretary of war took the advice of the New York military group. It evidently was embarrassing to the secretary of war, but the chief of staff came out on top and it should be a red-letter day for the army. It should seat us a little firmer in the saddle. God knows, we're nearly out of it enough of the time" (Orlando Ward, diary, 27 Mar. 1941, quoted in Gugeler, "George Marshall and Orlando Ward," 33).

104. John M. Palmer to Clark, 26 July 1940, Clark MSS.

105. Clark to Palmer, 3 Aug. 1940, Clark MSS.

106. *New York Times,* 12 July 1940.

107. Ibid., 18 July 1940.

108. A good account of the 1940 convention is in Bernard F. Donohoe, *Private Plans and Public Dangers: The Story of FDR's Third Nomination* (South Bend, Ind., 1965), chap. 6.

109. Quoted in Donohoe, *Private Plans and Public Dangers,* 175.

110. For Wheeler's attitude see Burton K. Wheeler to editor, *Montana Standard* (wire), 9 July 1940, box 5, Wheeler MSS, Montana Historical Society, Helena (from the notes of David Porter).

111. *New York Herald Tribune,* 18 July 1940.

112. Ibid.

113. Roosevelt, *Public Papers,* 9:293-303.

114. *New York Times,* 19 and 31 July 1940. "The man has yet to be born of woman to whom I would vote more than eight years in the presidency" (John W. Davis to Arthur Glasgow, 15 July 1940, box 121, John W. Davis MSS).

115. *New York Times,* 26 July 1940; Johnson, daily journal, 24/25 July 1940, box 90, Louis Johnson MSS.

116. *New York Times,* 26 July 1940.

117. Henry L. Stimson to Charles C. Burlingham, 28 July 1940, box 17, Burlingham MSS.

118. Memorandum of 17 July 1940, vol. 283, 164–65, Morgenthau, diaries, FDRL.

119. Stimson, diary, 19 July 1940, Stimson MSS.

120. *New York Times,* 23 July 1940; Manfred Jonas, "Robert Porter Patterson," in *Union Worthies* (Union College, Schenectady, N.Y., 1966), 5; Keith E. Eiler, "Robert P. Patterson and U. S. Mobilization in World War II," lecture delivered at the U.S. Army Command and General Staff College, Fort Leavenworth, Kans., 30 Apr. 1984.

121. Stimson, diary, 23 July 1940; entry of 24 July 1940, Morgenthau, presidential diaries, Morgenthau MSS, FDRL.

122. Entry of 24 July 1940, Morgenthau, presidential diaries, FDRL.

123. "Exit Johnson," *Time,* 5 Aug. 1940, 11–12. According to Johnson's chief patron, James Farley, President Roosevelt said: "Louis talked too much" (*Jim Farley's Story,* 326). In regard to Johnson's interventionist attitude, it should be noted that the two chief "hawks" in the cabinet in 1940, Ickes and Morgenthau, both distrusted Johnson as an inveterate schemer.

124. *New York Times,* 24 July 1940.

125. Memorandum of phone conversation with Stimson, 15 Aug. 1940, vol. 294, 71–77, Morgenthau, diaries, FDRL.

126. *New York Times,* 16 Aug. 1940.

127. Gary R. Hess, *American Encounters India, 1941–1947* (Baltimore, Md., 1971), chap. 2.

128. Perley Boone interview, 1947; *Time,* 5 Aug. 1940, 11.

129. *New York Times,* 26 July 1940.

130. Sherman Minton to Louis Johnson, 9 Sept. 1940, box 78, Louis Johnson MSS.

131. Ickes, *Secret Diary,* 3:303.

132. Memorandum of Morgenthau phone conversation with Stimson, 15 Aug. 1940, vol. 294, 71–77, Morgenthau, diaries, FDRL.

133. FDR to J. Mayhew Wainwright, 2 Aug. 1940, PPF 1678, FDRL.

134. Copy of Patterson's address over CBS Radio, 4 Aug. 1940, RG 46, box 117, NA.

CHAPTER 8. THE ORGANIZED OPPOSITION:
"A GOOD SHIP WITH NOT ENOUGH CREW TO MAKE IT SAIL"

1. Roger Baldwin, memo of conversation with Paul C. French, 27 Aug. 1940, Baldwin folder, Howard Beale MSS, in possession of Georgia Robison Beale (hereafter cited as GRB).

2. Beale to Baldwin, 26 July 1940, vol. 2189, ACLU records, Seeley Mudd Library, Princeton University.

3. Baldwin to Charles Ellwood, 20 June 1940, ACLU records.

4. John Nevin Sayre to Edwin C. Johnson, 25 June 1940, DG 9, box 28, SCPC.

5. Beale to Baldwin, 26 July 1940, ACLU records.

6. Beale to Baldwin, 9 and 16 Aug. 1940, ACLU records; Beale to Baldwin, 11 and 21 Sept. 1940, Beale MSS/GRB; Beale, mimeographed letters, 15 and 27 July 1940, and Beale to Peter Wallenborn, 10 Sept. 1940, Beale MSS, SHSW.

7. Beale to Baldwin, 9 Aug. 1940, vol. 2189, ACLU records.

8. Beale to Baldwin, 23 July 1940, ACLU records.

9. "We discovered to our horror that a man named Evans was down professing to speak for the Congregationalists in favor of the conscientious objector and *for* the bill, and his conception of a good clause on the conscientious objector was one that would permit the CO not to pull the trigger but would force him to hold the gun while somebody else did. Ray Wilson worked most of one evening on him to try and make him see the light and I wired New York to get Allen Chalmers, the New York Congregationalist minister down to refute his testimony. Chalmers came and worked and counseled with us a whole day, but in the end though Evans still testified in favor of the bill, he was persuaded and much good Quaker persuasion had been practiced on him to accept our whole British bill including the non-religious and absolutist and to testify for that. Then the Seventh Day Adventist had to have his 7th Day Sabbath protected, and he professed to speak for all CO's. In the questioning the Committee got him gladly making munitions, driving ambulances, carrying munitions to the front, putting the gun in the soldier's hand, and doing everything but fire it. And we had to persuade the committee that this man did not represent all conscientious objectors" (Beale to Baldwin, 9 Aug. 1940, ACLU records).

10. Beale to Baldwin, 26 July 1940, ACLU records.

11. Baldwin to Beale, 30 July 1940, Beale MSS/GRB.

12. Chatfield, *For Peace and Justice,* 310.

13. Wachs, "Conscription," 56–65; see also E. Raymond Wilson, "Evolution of the C.O. Provisions in the 1940 Conscription Bill," *Quaker History* 64 (Spring 1975): 3–15; and John M. Glen, "Secular Conscientious Objection in the United States: The Selective Service Act of 1940," *Peace and Change* 9 (Spring 1983): 55–71.

14. Wachs, "Conscription," 66–67.

15. Beale to Baldwin, 23 and 26 July, 9 Aug. 1940, vol. 2189, ACLU records.

16. Wachs, "Conscription," 67. The amendment at one point was worded to protect COs on the basis of "religious training *or* belief" and thus might have extended status to nonreligious objectors. The final wording, at Colonel O'Kelliher's insistence, reverted to "religious training *and* belief." Beale had the distinct impression that Hershey, whose ancestors included Mennonites, was more sympathetic than his superior, O'Kelliher. Interestingly, Ray Wilson attributed Senator Minton's more tolerant attitude to hundreds of letters from Indiana's Friends and Mennonites (see Wilson to William C. Dennis, 23 Aug. 1940, Ray Wilson/Peace Sections, 1939–43, AFSC archives).

17. May initially reacted to their request to testify by shouting: "What do you mean witnesses against the bill? Who would oppose defending America?" (Beale to Baldwin, 26 July 1940, ACLU records). French later suspected that May deliberately delayed the printing and distribution of opposition testimony in the House hearings until after the final passage of the draft law in mid September (Wachs, "Conscription," 74; Paul French, diary, 16 Aug. 1940, SCPC).

18. Beale to Baldwin, 26 July 1940, ACLU records; Beale to Byron, 29 July 1940, Beale MSS/SHSW; Ray Wilson to Jerome Britchey, 28 July 1940, Ray Wilson/Peace Section, AFSC archives.

19. Beale to Baldwin, 9 Aug. 1940, Beale MSS/SHSW.

20. Paul French, diary, 6 Aug. 1940.

21. John E. Wiltz, *In Search of Peace: The Senate Munitions Inquiry, 1934-1936* (Baton Rouge, La., 1963); Ernest C. Bolt, Jr., *Ballots before Bullets: The War Referendum Approach to Peace in America, 1914-1941* (Charlottesville, Va., 1977); Robert A. Divine, *The Illusion of Neutrality* (Chicago, 1962).

22. Warren I. Cohen, *The American Revisionists: The Lessons of Intervention in World War I* (Chicago, 1967); Eileen Egan, *Class, Culture, and the Classroom: The Student Peace Movement of the 1930s* (Philadelphia, 1981).

23. See Robert D. Accinelli, "Militant Internationalists: The League of Nations Association, the Peace Movement, and U.S. Foreign Policy, 1934-1938," *Diplomatic History* 4 (Winter 1980): 19-38.

24. Chadwin, *Hawks of World War II*.

25. Chatfield, *For Peace and Justice*, 312.

26. Ibid., 300. "[Pacifists] had no immediate solutions to cope with the aggressive world of angry power relationships [they] confronted" (Lawrence S. Wittner, *Rebels against War: The American Peace Movement, 1941-1960* [New York, 1969], 33).

27. Mildred Scott Olmsted to Dorothy Hummel, 5 July 1940, DG 23, box 2, WILPF MSS, SCPC.

28. Wachs, "Conscription," 39-42; Chatfield, *For Peace and Justice*, 298-304; Betty Lynn Barton, "The Fellowship of Reconciliation: Pacifism, Labor and Social Welfare, 1915-1960" (Ph.D. diss., Florida State University, 1974); Glen Zeitzer, "The Fellowship of Reconciliation on the Eve of the Second World War: A Peace Organization Prepares," *Peace and Change* 3 (Summer/Fall 1975): 46-51.

29. House, *Hearings*, 453-56, 653; John Haynes Holmes to Morris Sheppard, 10 July 1940, box 24, Holmes MSS, LC.

30. Report of War Resisters' League delegation to Washington, 25 July to 2 Aug. 1940, DG 40, box 2, SCPC.

31. Stimson, diary, 22 Aug. 1940, Stimson MSS.

32. Justus D. Doenecke, "Non-intervention of the Left: 'The Keep America out of War Congress,' 1938-1941," *Journal of Contemporary History* 12 (Apr. 1977): 221-36.

33. Warren Cohen, "The Role of Private Groups in the United States," in *Pearl Harbor as History: Japanese-American Relations, 1931-1941*, ed. Dorothy Borg and Shumpei Okomoto (New York, 1973), 456.

34. Frank Hanighen to Sidney Hertzberg, 4 July 1940, *Uncensored* MSS, NYPL.

35. Edwin C. Johnson to Beard (wire), 19 June 1940; Beard to Johnson, 20 June 1940, DG 9, box 28, SCPC.

36. Senate, *Hearings*, 201-8.

37. Ibid., 235ff.

38. *New York Times*, 14 July 1940.

39. See Johnson's correspondence during the conscription fight, in DG 9, box 29, SCPC.

40. Johnson to Norman Thomas, 21 Aug. 1940, reel 40, American Socialist Party MSS, Perkins Library, Duke University, Durham, N.C.; Daniel W. Barthell, "The Committee on Militarism in Education, 1925-1940 (Ph.D. diss., University of Illinois, 1972), 314.

41. Frederick J. Libby, *To End War* (Nyack, N.Y., 1969); and George Mirabell, "Frederick Libby and the American Peace Movement, 1921-1941" (Ph.D. diss., Michigan State University, 1975); interview with Ruth Searles Benedict, Washington, D.C., Aug. 1985.

42. A. Lindbergh, *War Within and Without*, 150.

43. Chatfield, *For Peace and Justice*, 297-98.

44. Libby, diary, 10 June 1940, Libby MSS.

45. Villard to Joseph Martin, 12 July 1940, DG 23, box 300; Libby to Willkie (wires), 23 July, 29 Aug., 3 Sept., 9 Oct. 1940, DG 23, box 302, SCPC. Dorothy Detzer also had her "fingers crossed about him [Willkie], but he certainly is an attractive personality. . . . He might be ready to commit himself on a war referendum" (to Villard, 1 July 1940, Villard MSS; see also Libby, diary, 23 and 24 July, 3 Sept. 1940, Libby MSS).

46. Libby, diary, 30 June to 9 July 1940, Libby MSS.

47. Senate, *Hearings,* 182-83.

48. Libby, diary, 16 July 1940, Libby MSS.

49. Ibid., 17 July 1940, Libby MSS.

50. "I did not realize that conscription was going to become the burning issue immediately. We had defeated the proconscription plank at Chicago and we thought it was shelved until the next session of Congress. The president's action in his speech of acceptance in throwing the antiwar plank adopted by his party into the waste basket and coming out for immediate passage of conscription legislation has so altered the situation that we must focus all our attention at present on the conscription bill" (Libby to R. Douglas Stuart, 23 July 1940, box 68, America First Committee, Hoover Institute, Stanford University, Stanford, Calif.).

51. Libby, diary, 26 July 1940, Libby MSS.

52. Ibid., 22 and 27 July, 2 Aug. 1940, Libby MSS.

53. Ibid., 23-31 July 1940, Libby MSS; Beale to Baldwin, 23 and 26 July 1940, ACLU records.

54. Thomas to FDR, 24 July 1940, PPF 4840, FDRL.

55. FDR to Thomas, 31 July 1940, PPF 4840, FDRL.

56. Libby, diary, 27-31 July 1940, Libby MSS; minutes of Strategy Conference against Conscription, 1 Aug. 1940, CDGA, box 3, SCPC; branch letter no. 92, 31 July 1940, WILPF MSS, SCPC.

57. Branch letter no. 91, 3 July 1940, WILPF MSS, SCPC.

58. House, *Hearings,* 375; see also, Dorothy Detzer, *Appointment on the Hill* (New York, 1948).

59. Branch letter no. 92, 31 July 1940, WILPF MSS, SCPC.

60. *Washington Post,* 2 Aug. 1940; Libby, diary, 1 Aug. 1940, Libby MSS.

61. Minutes of Special Strategy Conference, 1 Aug. 1940, CDGA, box 3, SCPC.

62. Minutes of YCAW meetings, 7 and 14 June, 8 July 1940, CDGA, box 3, SCPC.

63. Minutes of KAOWC meetings, 9 July, 9 Aug., 9 Sept. 1940, CDGA, box 1, SCPC.

64. Fay Bennett to S. Hertzberg, 26 Aug. 1940, *Uncensored* MSS, NYPL.

65. F. Bennett to R. Rovere, 18 and 29 July, 3 Aug. 1940, Richard Rovere MSS, SHSW.

66. Rovere, who had written for the *New Masses* during the late 1930s, quit in disillusionment following the Nazi-Soviet Pact in August 1939. During the summer of 1940 he was moving toward mainstream liberalism, albeit of the antiwar persuasion (see Rovere's correspondence for this period with Granville Hicks in the Hicks MSS, Arents Library, Syracuse University, Syracuse, N.Y.).

67. Hertzberg to Villard, 22 Aug. 1940, *Uncensored* MSS, NYPL.

68. Hanighen's raw reports are in *Uncensored* MSS, NYPL.

69. Interview with Thomas V. Rankin, Feb. 1982. The Veterans of Future Wars sought to satirize regular veterans' organizations by calling for bonuses *now*—before they died in battle. A related group, the Future Gold Star Mothers, demanded

expense-paid trips to Europe to see the unexcavated graves of their yet unborn sons (Egan, *Class,* 186-87).

70. Rankin to Hertzberg, 31 July, 2, 8, and 9 Aug. 1940; Hanighen to Hertzberg, n.d. [late July 1940]—all in *Uncensored* MSS, NYPL.

71. Rankin to Hertzberg, 5 Sept. 1940, *Uncensored* MSS, NYPL.

72. Press release, 19 July 1940, reel 39, American Socialist Party MSS.

73. Norman Thomas to Emily Eaton, 11 July 1940, box 17, Thomas MSS, NYPL.

74. Thomas's statement, 11 July 1940, reel 39, American Socialist Party MSS.

75. Thomas to Wheeler, 31 July 1940, and Thomas to Siegfried Ameringer, Philip Murray, R. J. Thomas, and Morris Ernst, 24 July 1940, box 17, Thomas MSS.

76. Quoted by Bernard Johnpoll in *Pacifist's Progress: Norman Thomas and the Decline of American Socialism* (Chicago, 1970), 218.

77. Hanighen to Hertzberg, n.d. (c. 25 July 1940), *Uncensored* MSS, NYPL; Senate, *Hearings,* 267-68.

78. Senate, *Hearings,* 240-41. For background on Villard see Michael Wreszin, *Oswald Garrison Villard: Pacifist at War* (Bloomington, Ind., 1965); and Ronald Radosh, *Prophets on the Right* (New York, 1975), 67-118.

79. *New York World Telegram,* 4 Sept. 1940. For background on Flynn see Michele Flynn Stenehjem, *An American First: John T. Flynn and the America First Committee* (New Rochelle, N.Y., 1976).

80. Milo Shattuck to FDR, 2 Aug. 1940, OF 1413, FDRL. See the records of the Massachusetts Committee to Defend America at the Massachusetts Historical Society, Boston, Mass.; also Roger Greene to Kate Greene, 29 Aug. 1940, box 38, Roger Greene MSS, Houghton Library, Harvard University, Cambridge, Mass.

81. *World Affairs,* Sept. 1940, 128-29.

82. *National Peace Conference Bulletin* 2 (12 Sept. 1940), copy in Alfred Bingham MSS, Yale University, New Haven, Conn.

83. Raymond Moley, Jr., *The American Legion Story* (New York, 1963), 242-43; Elton Atwater, *Organized Efforts in the United States toward Peace* (Washington, D.C., 1936); House, *Hearings,* 486-91, 620-21; Senate, *Hearings,* 119; *New York Times,* 11 Aug. 1940.

84. *World Affairs,* Sept. 1940, 129.

85. Irwin Ross, "College Students and the War," *New Republic,* 15 July 1940, 79-80.

86. Foster Stearns to Ernest Hopkins, 4 June 1940, Ernest Hopkins MSS, Baker Library, Dartmouth College, Hanover, N.H.

87. *New York Times,* 26 May 1940.

88. FDR to Merriman, 20 May 1940, PPF 962, FDRL.

89. *New York Times,* 20 June, 14 July 1940; *New York Herald Tribune,* 5 and 8 July 1940.

90. Joseph P. Lash, *Eleanor and Franklin* (New York, 1971), 604-5.

91. House, *Hearings,* 443.

92. Ibid., 449.

93. Senate, *Hearings,* 176-77.

94. Ibid., 166.

95. Ibid., 251.

96. House, *Hearings,* 426.

97. Wayne S. Cole, *America First: The Battle against Intervention* (Madison, Wis., 1953).

98. Correspondence between Stuart, Wood, and La Follette in box 136, Philip La Follette MSS, SHSW; see also Justus D. Doenecke, "General Robert E. Wood: The Evolution of a Conservative," *Journal of the Illinois State Historical Society* 71 (Aug. 1978): 162–75.

99. Ford, who had good political instincts as a young man, asked that his name be kept off America First literature lest his football job be jeopardized. "This however will not in the least impede my work for the organization. As a matter of fact I shall probably spend more time just as a bit of spite. . . . Let me reiterate that I shall continue my efforts" (Jerry Ford to "Bobbie," n.d. [c. July 1940], box 66, America First Committee MSS).

100. Stuart to Libby, 29 July 1940, box 68, America First Committee MSS.

101. Thomas V. Rankin to Stuart, 9 Sept. 1940, box 65, America First Committee MSS; interview with Rankin, Feb. 1982.

102. Frankfurter to H. Laski, 20 June 1940, box 74, Frankfurter MSS.

103. *New York Times,* 24 May 1940. "I can't quite understand those resolutions coming out of . . . Dartmouth and Yale—apparently opposed to our arming even for defense. And yet, I guess I do understand it a little. Do you realize that all young people in this country . . . have grown up in an antiwar psychology hearing their elders say they were tricked into the last war, etc., etc., And I believe most of the kids . . . have read 'The Road to War' " (Lorena Hickock to Eleanor Roosevelt, 27 May 1940, box 7, Lorena Hickock MSS, FDRL).

104. Eleanor Roosevelt announced her belief in "the selective draft" on 7 August, even though her friend May Craig reported that the whole Washington press corps thought she would be "bucking the old man on conscription" (May Craig to Eleanor Roosevelt, 6 Aug. 1940, ER MSS; see also Joseph P. Lash, *Eleanor Roosevelt: A Friend's Memoir* [Garden City, N.Y., 1964], chaps. 8–12).

105. Neal A. Scott, the commencement orator at Davidson College in June 1940 and a close friend of coauthor Spencer, killed when a kamikaze plane struck his destroyer in the Battle of Santa Cruz Island in October 1942, was among the first of his class to lose his life in military service.

106. *Washington Post,* 20 June 1940.

107. *New York Times,* 6 June 1940. The records of the Harvard Student Defense League for 1940/41 in the Harvard University archives have extensive correspondence with interventionist groups at other universities during 1940/41.

108. *New York Times,* 15 July 1940.

109. W. R. Bowie, "Some Choose Jail Rather Than Register," *Living Age,* Dec. 1940, 330–33; Marie Dellinger to E. Roosevelt, 6 Nov. 1940, and E. Roosevelt to Dellinger, 11 Nov. 1940, ER MSS. Approximately twelve thousand conscientious objectors were assigned to Civilian Public Service Units during the war, while an estimated twenty-five thousand to one hundred thousand were granted noncombatant status within the armed forces. About six thousand, including more than four thousand Jehovah's Witnesses, went to prison as "absolutist" objectors (see Wachs, "Conscription," passim).

110. Cantril, *Public Opinion,* 459–63.

111. *Washington Post,* 12 Aug. 1940.

112. Alfred Kazin, *Starting out in the Thirties* (New York, 1980 ed.), 153, 166.

113. Interview with T. Rankin, Feb. 1982.

114. *Commonweal,* 21 June 1940, 177–78.

115. Ibid., 23 Aug. 1940, 357.

116. Ibid., 5 July 1940, 226–29.

117. Senate, *Hearings,* 119.

118. Flynn, *Roosevelt and Romanism,* 73-74.

119. Senate, *Hearings,* 250.

120. Ibid., 285; Ready to FDR, 8 July 1940, OF 1413, box 6, FDRL; several letters from Ready to Farley, July-Aug. 1940, box 10, Farley MSS.

121. Flynn, *Roosevelt and Romanism,* 75-77.

122. Beale to Peter Wallenborn, 20 Sept. 1940, Beale MSS, SHSW. For a broader focus see Edward W. Orser, "World War II and the Pacifist Controversy in the Major Protestant Churches," *American Studies* 14 (Fall 1973): 5-24.

123. House, *Hearings,* 359-60.

124. *New York Herald Tribune,* 17 June 1940.

125. Holmes to Villard, 14 June 1940, Villard MSS. Holmes's long friendship with Rabbi Stephen S. Wise suffered during this period because of Holmes's continued pacifism and Wise's turn toward intervention (see the correspondence in the Wise MSS, American Jewish Historical Society, Brandeis University, Waltham, Mass.).

126. House, *Hearings,* 604-10.

127. Oxnam, diary, 24 Sept. 1940, G. Bromley Oxnam MSS, LC.

128. "Manning Endorses the Draft," *Christian Century,* 4 Sept. 1940, 1069.

129. *New York Times,* 26 Aug. 1940.

130. Coffin to Thomas, 3 Aug. 1940, box 18, Thomas MSS.

131. Henry P. Van Dusen, "Irresponsible Idealism," *Christian Century,* 24 July 1940, 924-25. Van Dusen and Coffin actively participated as members of the Century Club group in the back-stage negotiations leading to the destroyer deal later in the summer. Episcopal Bishop Henry W. Hobson of Ohio also associated with this group and later became chairman of the Fight for Freedom Committee in 1941, the most outspoken interventionist group prior to Pearl Harbor. Much of the correspondence among the interventionist clergy can be found in the records of the Fight for Freedom Committee, Seeley Mudd Library, Princeton University, Princeton, N.J.

132. A. W. Palmer, "A Road away from Way," *Christian Century,* 19 June 1940, 793-95.

133. "An Ominous Nomination," *Christian Century,* 25 Sept. 1940, 1168-70.

134. William Hubben, "If Conscription Comes," *Christian Century,* 14 Aug. 1940, 994-95.

135. "Conscription and the Churches," *Christian Century,* 25 Sept. 1940, 1168-70.

136. Because they feared being charged as conspirators in bringing the United States into the war against Germany in order to rescue their coreligionists, most American Jewish leaders carefully refrained from taking any public position on selective service. Justice Frankfurter, for example, avoided any public pronouncements in favor of the draft or aid to England, notwithstanding his vital behind-the-scenes support of both actions. Sidney Hertzberg was probably representative of the dwindling numbers of Jewish pacifists in the KAOWC who tried futilely "to do something about Frankfurter, who seems to be the prime mover behind the Administration's moves" (minutes of KAOWC Governing Committee, 9 Aug. 1940, CDGA, box 1, SCPC). The correspondence in the *Uncensored* MSS files and in the American Socialist Party MSS reveals the agony of many American Jews who opposed war before 1940 but tended to turn interventionist after Hitler's blitzkrieg (see also Michael Young, "Facing a Test of Faith: Jewish Pacifists and the Second World War," *Peace and Change* 3 [Summer-Fall 1975]: 34-40).

137. Senate, *Hearings,* 132.

138. Ibid., 124; Zook to Charles Seymour, 28 June 1940, box 182, Charles Seymour MSS, Yale University, New Haven, Conn. For a broader focus see Joseph L.

Jaffe, "Isolationism and Neutrality in Academe, 1938-1941" (Ph.D. diss., Case Western Reserve, 1979).

139. Senate, *Hearings,* 136.

140. Ibid., 132; Snavely to Ernest Hopkins, 28 June 1940, National Defense, 1940, folder, E. Hopkins MSS.

141. House, *Hearings,* 251-56; "Recommendations of Two Commissions for Defense Program," *School and Society,* 10 Aug. 1940, 86-87.

142. Charles A. Beard, *A Foreign Policy for America* (New York, 1940).

143. Inscription in *A Foreign Policy for America,* in PPF 3847, FDRL.

144. C. Hartley Grattan, *The Deadly Parallel* (New York, 1940); Cohen, *American Revisionists,* chap. 8; Justus D. Doenecke, "Harry Elmer Barnes," *Wisconsin Magazine of History,* Summer 1973, 311-23.

145. Walter Millis, "1939 Is Not 1914," *Life,* 6 Nov. 1939, 69ff.; *New York Times,* 27 June 1940. One prominent historian who did not join the White Committee was the Sterling Professor at Yale, Samuel Flagg Bemis (Bemis to William Allen White, 20 May 1940, Bemis MSS, Yale University, New Haven, Conn.).

146. President Hopkins of Dartmouth discouraged similar speeches by alumni at Hanover, not because he opposed the draft and aid to England, but because he wished to avoid stirring up more undergraduate protest (Hopkins to Sumner Emerson, 6 and 8 June 1940, war issues folder, E. Hopkins MSS).

147. Formation of the Harvard group had the confidential approval of FDR (see James Rowe to James Landis, 15 July 1940, Landis correspondence, Harvard Defense Group MSS, Pusey Library, Harvard University, Cambridge, Mass.).

148. *New York Times,* 14 July 1940.

149. Ibid., 9 July 1940.

150. "Notes of Conference," 8 July 1940, war issues folder, E. Hopkins MSS; "Compulsory Conscription Arouses Discussion," *School and Society,* 27 July 1940, 53-54.

151. Beale to Ralph Barton Perry, 23 Aug., 30 Oct. 1940, Perry correspondence, Harvard Defense Group MSS.

152. Wechsler, in *PM,* 6 Aug. 1940. For a broader study of labor see Timothy R. Dzierba, "Organized Labor and the Coming of World War II, 1937-1947" (Ph.D. diss., SUNY, Buffalo, N.Y., 1983).

153. Interview with Archibald Thacher, July 1947.

154. House, *Hearings,* 553; see also Hugh Ross, "John L. Lewis and the Election of 1940," *Labor History* 17 (1976): 160-89.

155. James A. Wechsler, in *PM,* 6 Aug. 1940; *New York Times,* 21 Aug. 1940; *New York Herald Tribune,* 21 Aug. 1940.

156. *New York Times,* 4 Aug. 1940.

157. J. A. Phillips, A. Johnston, D. B. Robertson, and A. F. Whitney to Morris Sheppard and Andrew May, Senate 76A-E1, box 116, RG 46, NA.

158. *New York Times,* 26 Aug. 1940; memo, n.d. (Aug. 1940), box 35A, La Follette Family MSS.

159. *New York Times,* 19 Sept. 1940.

160. *New York Times,* 4 Aug. 1940; Leonard Woodcock to Ben Fischer, 6 Aug. 1940, reel 40, American Socialist Party MSS.

161. *New York Herald Tribune,* 18 July 1940.

162. See efforts to boycott the Chicago mobilization by socialist-pacifists (Sidney Hertzberg to Harry Elmer Barnes, 12 and 22 Aug. 1940, Barnes MSS, Coe Library, University of Wyoming, Laramie; Minutes of KAOWC, 9 Sept. 1940, CDGA, box 1,

SCPC; Travers Clement to H. L. Schlug, 15 Aug. 1940, reel 40, American Socialist Party MSS).

163. *New York Times,* 27 Aug. 1940.

164. Quoted in Matthew Josephson, *Sidney Hillman: American Statesman of Labor* (Garden City, N.Y., 1952), 485.

165. Senate, *Hearings,* 293; Executive Board, National Farmers' Union, to all members of Congress, 24 Aug. 1940, copy in box 99, George Norris MSS.

166. *New York Herald Tribune,* 9 Aug. 1940.

167. House, *Hearings,* 459-60.

168. Ibid., 373, 451.

169. Senate, *Hearings,* 278-84; *New York Times,* 22 Aug. 1940.

170. *PM,* 27 Aug. 1940.

171. O. Rogge, *The Official German Report* (New York, 1961), 266-73; Neil M. Johnson, *George Sylvester Viereck: German-American Propagandist* (Urbana, Ill., 1972), 217-21.

172. New York Committee to Keep America out of War to Members of Congress, 12 Sept. 1940, copy in box 8, Robert Crosser MSS, Ohio Historical Society, Columbus, Ohio.

173. *New York Herald Tribune,* 23 Aug. 1940; copy of brief in box 7, OF 1413, FDRL.

174. Copy of booklet in folder for 11 July 1940, Charles W. Halleck MSS, Lilly Library, Indiana University, Bloomington.

175. House, *Hearings,* 431.

176. Ibid., 478-80.

177. Ibid., 440-42.

178. Arthur M. Schlesinger, Jr., *The Politics of Upheaval* (Cambridge, Mass., 1960), 82.

179. Sam Porter to Clark, undated, Clark MSS.

180. This certificate carried the signatures Milt Hicks and Baron Roorback (Clark MSS). Ernest Hopkins received an identical certificate (war issues folder, E. Hopkins MSS).

181. Robert Parker to Clark, 7 Sept. 1940, Clark MSS.

182. "A Mother" to FDR, undated, box 6, OF 1413, FDRL.

183. "Americans You Are Called Upon to Defend the Constitution," undated flier in Clark MSS.

184. The best study of these groups is Geoffrey S. Smith, *To Save a Nation: American Countersubversives, the New Deal, and the Coming of World War II* (New York, 1973).

185. For an excellent monograph see David H. Culbert, *News for Everyone: Radio and Foreign Affairs in Thirties America* (Westport, Conn., 1976).

186. Quoted in Charles J. Tull, *Father Coughlin and the New Deal* (Syracuse, N.Y., 1965), 225.

187. *Social Justice,* 9 Sept. 1940.

188. The scholarship on this issue is large: see Alton Frye, *Nazi Germany and the Western Hemisphere, 1933-1941* (New Haven, Conn., 1967); Leland V. Bell, *In Hitler's Shadow: The Anatomy of American Nazism* (Port Washington, N.Y., 1973); Ronald W. Johnson, "The German-American Bund and Nazi Germany, 1936-1941," *Studies in History and Society* 6 (1975): 31-45; Sander A. Diamond, *The Nazi Movement in the United States, 1924-1941* (Ithaca, N.Y., 1974). For a recent study that argues that American Fascists were not Fascists "in any meaningful sense of the term" see Allen Brinkley's

excellent *Voices of Protest: Huey Long, Father Coughlin, and the Great Depression* (New York, 1982), especially app. 1.

189. See the diary of Adolf A. Berle for 1940 (at FDRL) for concern about fifth-column activity after the fall of France.

190. Orville H. Bullitt, ed., *For the President: Personal and Secret* (Boston, 1972), 498-502; cf. Frederick Libby, diary, 18-20 Aug. 1940, Libby MSS.

191. Smith, *To Save a Nation*, chap. 11.

192. Martin Dies, *The Trojan Horse in America* (New York, 1940), 306.

193. Bell, *In Hitler's Shadow*, 99.

194. Ibid., 100.

195. Ibid.

196. Franklin Canfield to Clark, 24 Aug., and Canfield memo to Clark, 26 Aug. 1940, Clark MSS; Perley Boone to Steve Early, 4 Sept. 1940, box 7, OF 1413, FDRL; see also J. Edgar Hoover to attorney general, 16 Aug. 1940, Grenville Clark file, Robert Jackson MSS, LC.

197. See Frank A. Warren, *Liberals and Communism: The "Red Decade" Revisited* (Bloomington, Ind., 1966); Ralph B. Levering, *American Opinion and the Russian Alliance, 1939-1945* (Chapel Hill, N.C., 1976); and Maurice Isserman, *Which Side Were You On? The American Communist Party during the Second World War* (Middletown, Conn., 1982).

198. *New York Times,* 2 June 1940.

199. Ibid.

200. *New York Herald Tribune,* 9 Aug. 1940.

201. "Conscription, Straitjacket for 42,000,000," *New Masses,* 6 Aug. 1940, 3-5.

202. *Daily Worker,* 25 July 1940.

203. "Stop Conscription," handbill in Clark MSS.

204. "People of Red Hook Want Overalls, Not Uniforms," handbill in Clark MSS.

205. Jerry Wadsworth to James W. Wadsworth, 26 Aug. 1940, box 21, Wadsworth Family MSS.

206. Trotsky to Comrade "Al," 9 July 1940, in *Fourth International,* Oct. 1940, 125, copy in box 150, Dwight Macdonald MSS, Sterling Library, Yale University, New Haven, Conn.; see also Constance A. Myers, *The Prophet's Army: Trotskyists in America, 1928-1941* (Westport, Conn., 1978).

207. Internal bulletin, 29 Aug. 1940, copy in Macdonald MSS.

208. Macdonald, "The Willkievelt Campaign," *Fourth International,* Oct. 1940, 182-85, 192; copy in Macdonald MSS.

209. Geoffrey Smith has written: "Isolationism had been a comparatively respectable term during the 1920s and early 1930s, but as America drew closer to war it actually became an epithet. The failure of noninterventionists to free themselves from pejoratively imputed totalitarian sympathies provided incontrovertible evidence of this progression" (*To Save a Nation,* 9); see also G. F. Smith, "Isolationism, the Devil, and the Advent of the Second World War: Variations on a Theme," *International History Review* 4 (Feb. 1982): 55-89; and Leo P. Ribuffo, *The Old Christian Right: The Protestant Right from the Great Depression to the Cold War* (Philadelphia, 1983).

210. Villard to Thomas, 16 July 1940, Villard MSS.

211. House, *Hearings,* 473-77; see also George Leighton to Sidney Hertzberg, 1 July 1940, *Uncensored* MSS, NYPL.

212. Manfred Jonas, *Isolationism in America, 1935-1941* (Ithaca, N.Y., 1966), 125.

213. Senate, *Hearings,* 70.

214. Ibid., 142.

215. Ibid.

216. Quoted by Libby in Senate, *Hearings,* 186.

217. Ibid., 247-48; Libby, diary, 11 July 1940, Libby MSS.

218. *Uncensored* called Baldwin "apparently the one factor that keeps the Times Annex from taking off down 43d Street and bombing Berlin with Sunday supplements" ("Conscripting Conscription," *Uncensored,* 27 July 1940).

219. House, *Hearings,* 554.

220. Ibid., 148. Opponents tried to get Baldwin to testify himself before the House committee, but the military analyst declined (H. Baldwin to Thomas Rankin, 13 Sept. 1940, *Uncensored* MSS, NYPL).

221. Senate, *Hearings,* 256.

222. Ibid., 185.

223. Ibid., 238; Villard to J. Howard Whitehouse, 14 Aug. 1940, Villard MSS.

224. House, *Hearings,* 553.

225. Ibid., 424-25.

226. *New York Herald Tribune,* 13 Aug. 1940.

227. FDR to L. B. Sheley, 26 Aug. 1940, PSF; War Department, draft folder, box 39, FDRL.

228. Entries of 18 and 19 July 1940, in William Henry Chamberlin, diary, Chamberlin MSS, Providence College Library, Providence, R.I.

229. Villard to William Allen White, 19 June 1940, Villard MSS.

230. House, *Hearings,* 459.

231. Senate, *Hearings,* 145.

232. Ibid., 184, 187.

233. Ibid., 255-56.

234. Ibid., 194.

235. Libby, diary, 10 July 1940; NCPW Newsletter, 19 July 1940.

236. Senate, *Hearings,* 244.

237. Ibid., 165.

238. Ibid., 158-59.

239. Ibid., 172, 176. For books that exemplified the isolationist perspective on conscription and national defense see Fleming MacLeish and Cushman Reynolds, *Strategy for the Americas* (New York, 1941); Hanson Baldwin, *United We Stand! Defense of the Western Hemisphere* (New York, 1941); Oswald Garrison Villard, *Our Military Chaos: The Truth about Our Defense* (New York, 1939); Johnson Hagood, *We Can Defend America* (Garden City, N.Y., 1937); Hoffman Nickerson, *The Armed Horde, 1793-1939* (New York, 1940).

CHAPTER 9. PRELUDE TO THE CONGRESSIONAL DEBATES

1. J. W. Forrestal to Baruch, 30 July 1940, vol. 47, Baruch MSS.

2. Baruch to Forrestal, 1 Aug. 1940, Baruch MSS.

3. FDR to J. Mayhew Wainwright, 2 Aug. 1940, PPF 1678, FDRL.

4. *New York Times,* 28 July 1940. See the criticism of the *Times*'s overly optimistic reportage in *Uncensored,* 3 Aug. 1940.

5. *New York Times,* 27 July 1940.

6. Ibid., 28 July 1940.

7. Clark to Lewis Sanders, 23 July 1940, Clark MSS. On that same day, Clark erroneously reported to Stimson that the bill had "successfully passed" the Senate committee (Stimson, diary, 23 July 1940).

8. See "Washington Correspondents Name Ablest Members of Congress in *Life* Poll," *Life,* 20 Mar. 1939, 13-17.

9. Interview with Hershey, Dec. 1967. Canfield left the NEC in 1941 to become U.S. consul in North Africa; he later joined the OSS. Other helpers were Joseph Drake, of Sherman and Sterling, who filled in for Langford in mid August, and Isadore Bleiberg, who as general secretary took responsibility for getting out the reams of letters, reports, and memoranda that left headquarters in the Hotel Carlton.

10. Clark to Douglas Arant, 24 July 1940, Clark MSS.

11. There are several copies of this mimeographed document in the Clark MSS; see also Clark to Stimson, 25 July 1940, box 378, Stimson MSS.

12. Sanders to Clark, 1 Aug. 1940, Clark MSS.

13. Allen Drury, *A Senate Journal: 1943-1945* (New York, 1963), 25.

14. "I have had many confidential conversations with the president. I know, too, that he knows where I stand on this war question. I know that he knows I would not follow him into war. I know that he has this in writing. But in all my conversations with him, I have never detected the slightest indication that he is not sincere, and so far as I am able, he has no intention of leading us into this war" (Norris to Grace Shellenberger, 26 June 1940, box 410, Norris MSS).

15. Minton later remarked: "Van Nuys voted against conscription and all Indiana members of House are against it. . . . Nobody in Indiana is for conscription except me and Willkie!" (n.d. [Aug. 1940], Clapper notebooks, box 25, Clapper MSS).

16. Stimson, diary, 14 Aug. 1940, Stimson MSS.

17. Robert P. Bass to Grenville Clark, 5 Aug. 1940, Bass MSS, Baker Library, Dartmouth College, Hanover, N.H. As for Truman, he was writing that "this conscription bill is liable to be a pain in the neck, but the Gallup poll shows Mo overwhelming for it this morning in the [Washington] *Post.* I don't like it but I guess I'll have to be for it. We are going to offer some amendments that may help it" (to Bess Truman, 11 Aug. 1940, family correspondence, Truman MSS, Harry S. Truman Library, Independence, Mo., David Porter's notes).

18. The above information is drawn from the files of memoranda in the Clark MSS.

19. *PM,* 30 July 1940.

20. Escal Franklin Duke, "The Political Career of Morris Sheppard" (Ph.D. diss., University of Texas, 1958), 510.

21. Much of this material is based on Spencer's interviews with Clark and Arant in 1947.

22. Joseph Alsop to Hulbert Taft, 9 Aug. 1940, box 78, Joseph and Stewart Alsop MSS, LC.

23. Taft to Clark, 13 Sept. 1940, Clark MSS.

24. Thomas to FDR, 24 July 1940, PPF 4840, FDRL.

25. Libby, diary, 27-28 July 1940; WILPF branch letter no. 92, WILPF MSS, DG 43, SCPC.

26. Beale to Roger Baldwin, 26 July, 9 Aug. 1940, ACLU MSS; Beale mimeographed letter, 27 July 1940, Beale MSS, SHSW.

27. Villard to W. Sprague Holden, 30 July 1940, Villard MSS.

28. *Peace Action,* Aug. 1940, clipping in box 8, Crosser MSS.

29. Libby, diary, 29 July 1940, Libby MSS.

30. Ibid., 1 Aug. 1940. There is a copy of Wheeler's speech at the Hotel Raleigh, 1 Aug. 1940, in box 17, Wheeler MSS (David Porter's notes).

31. Clark to Kenneth Budd (wire), 1 Aug. 1940; Sherman Miles to Clark, 29 July 1940, Clark MSS; Clark to Ralph Barton Perry, 3 Aug. 1940; Franklin Canfield to Perry, 5 Aug. 1940; Warren Seavey mimeographed letter, 7 Aug. 1940, in Ralph Barton Perry correspondence, Harvard Defense Group MSS.

32. Stimson, diary, 1 Aug. 1940.

33. *New York Times,* 31 July 1940.

34. Press conference, 30 July 1940, PPF 1-P, FDRL.

35. Entry of 8 July 1940, daily record, box 4, H. Smith MSS.

36. Stimson, diary, 9 July 1940, Stimson MSS.

37. Roosevelt, *Public Papers,* 9:290.

38. Harold Smith, diary, 30 July 1940, box 3, H. Smith MSS.

39. "I do believe that because of the lessons of this war it is necessary for every man to fit into the defense place for which he is best suited. Some will make food crops; some will work in normal peace-time industries; some will work in war-time industries; some will work in transportation; some will work in the service of supply; some will work as mechanics to keep war machines going; and others will be part of the combat forces" (Roosevelt to Thomas, 31 July 1940, PPF 4840, FDRL).

40. Burke did not help matters by publicly announcing his support for Willkie after FDR's third-term nomination. Asked to comment on Burke's bolting the Democratic party, FDR quipped that the party seemed rather to have bolted Burke—a reference to Burke's defeat in the Democratic primary in Nebraska that spring.

41. Clark to Stimson, 22 July 1940, Clark MSS.

42. See Stimson, diary, 23 July to 2 Aug. 1940; even for Stimson the draft bill was only one issue among many, and aid to England assumed increasing urgency.

43. William L. Langer and S. Everett Gleason, *The Challenge to Isolation, 1937-40* (New York, 1953), 521-22. The Walsh amendment came about largely as a reaction to FDR's attempt a week earlier to sell brand-new motor torpedo boats to England on the grounds that they were surplus. Attorney General Jackson declared the sale illegal. "He [Jackson] wished the president would stop doing things like this. Jackson is for the president at all times, 1000%, and his statement was meant merely to indicate how anxious he was to have the president take a course that would enable him, the attorney general, to keep the president out of trouble" (Henry Wallace, diary, 20 June 1940).

44. Cohen to FDR, 19 July 1940, PSF 81; FDR to Knox, 22 July 1940, PSE 82, FDRL.

45. Chadwin, *War Hawks,* chap. 4; Johnson, *Battle against Isolation,* chap. 5.

46. White House appointment logs, 28-30 July 1940, PPF 1, FDRL.

47. Churchill to FDR, 31 July 1940, quoted in David Reynolds, *The Creation of the Anglo-American Alliance, 1937-1941* (Chapel Hill, N.C., 1982), 124.

48. FDR to Mrs. Charles Hamlin, 2 Aug. 1940, PPF 2704, FDRL.

49. Arthur Krock, in *New York Times,* 1 Aug. 1940.

50. House, *Hearings,* 382.

51. Ibid., 384.

52. Ibid.

53. Ibid., 396.

54. Ibid., 400; Stimson, diary, 31 July 1940, Stimson MSS.

55. Tobey to Robert Bass, 30 July 1940, box 39, Bass MSS.

56. Frank Hanighen to Cushman Reynolds, n.d. (late July 1940), *Uncensored* MSS, NYPL. "So far as this conscription business is concerned, the great mystery to me is why the army has changed its tune. As late as last May or June, I was told by more than one ranking officer that conscription was neither wanted nor needed. But I suppose army discipline requires ditto marks when the commander in chief says

'forward march!' '' (Arthur Vandenberg to Harry Woodring, 7 Aug. 1940, box 27, Woodring MSS).

57. Francis V. Keesling, memorandum, 2 Aug. 1940, 113 file, Lewis Hershey MSS. "Among army people, the bets are 60–40 that England may not be able to hold out against the German blitzkrieg, in which case this country would be in a serious condition, especially should the English navy be captured or destroyed. The army boys are not talking neutrality any more . . . but in private conversations they told me we had better quit kidding the American people and tell them that neutrality is out of the window and we are in this war up to our necks. . . . There is a jittery feeling in Washington on the part of all officials, and the opinions on the neutrality question which were so bright a year ago are entirely changed now'' (Stefan to W. B. Sadilek, 30 July 1940, box 24, Stefan MSS, David Porter's notes).

58. Jerry Voorhis, memorandum on Burke-Wadsworth bill, n.d. (c. 26 July 1940), and Jerry Frank to Robert Jackson, 27 July 1940, Jerome Frank MSS, Sterling Library, Yale University, New Haven, Conn.; James O'Connor to John R. Yates, 17 Sept. 1940, box 1, James O'Connor MSS, Montana State University Library, Bozeman, notes by David Porter; Kent Keller to W. H. Henderson, 31 July 1940, box 322, Keller MSS.

59. Austin, notes on Burke-Wadsworth bill, box 26, Austin MSS.

60. Stimson, diary, 29 July 1940, Stimson MSS.

61. The army's selective-service machinery had already obtained from the Bureau of Census the figure of 11,300,000 for the 21 to 31 age group (memorandum for Maj. Joseph Battley, 18 July 1940, Selective Service System central files, 1940, no. 001.2-002, box 25, RG 147, Federal Archives Building, Suitland, Md.). Secretary Morgenthau also received a report from the FBI to the effect that men between the ages of 21 and 31 were being denied credit by banks because of "anticipation of the enactment of the Conscription Act" (J. Edgar Hoover to Morgenthau, 31 July 1940, vol. 288, 139, Morgenthau, diaries, FDRL).

62. Entry of 2 Aug. 1940, vol. 288, 156–57, Morgenthau, diaries, FDRL.

63. Clark to Hershey (wire), 29 July 1940, Clark MSS.

64. Clark to Kenneth Budd, 1 Aug. 1940, Clark MSS; *New York Times,* 31 July 1940.

65. Jerry Voorhis, memorandum on Burke-Wadsworth bill, n.d. (c. 25 July 1940), Frank MSS. Frank passed the memo on to Attorney General Robert Jackson, noting "Jerry is of the opinion (a) that this is a very bad bill and (b) that almost all the members of Congress think it is an administration measure. I really think Jerry has something of very great importance here and I agree with him that prompt action seems to be necessary'' (to Jackson, 27 July 1940, Frank MSS).

66. *New York Times,* 1 Aug. 1940.

67. The original title had been "A Bill to Protect the Integrity and Institutions of the United States through a System of Compulsory Military Training and Service."

68. *New York Times,* 1–4 Aug. 1940; Elbert Thomas to Will Cates, 15 Aug. 1940, box 129, Elbert Thomas MSS, FDRL.

69. Hugh Johnson, in *New York World Telegram,* 2 Aug. 1940.

70. Clark to Morris Sheppard et al., 2 Aug. 1940, Senate 76-E, box 116, Senate records, NA.

71. Clark to Wadsworth (wire), 3 Aug. 1940, Clark MSS.

72. Clark to Palmer, 3 Aug. 1940, Clark MSS.

73. Gurney to Clark, 6 Aug. 1940, Clark MSS.

74. Malcolm Langford to Clark, 5 Aug. 1940, Clark MSS; for the role played by Hershey and his staff in drafting amendments see Captain Howard, memo for Colonel Fitzpatrick, 1 Sept. 1944, historical papers file, Hershey MSS.

75. *New York Times,* 6 Aug. 1940.

76. Ibid.

77. Ibid.

78. Ibid., 3 and 6 Aug. 1940; Woodring to Edwin C. Johnson and Arthur Vandenberg, 1 Aug. 1940, copy in box 71, J. Cal O'Loughlin MSS; Woodring to O'Loughlin, 2 Aug. 1940, box 71, J. Cal O'Loughlin MSS; see also Woodring to Vandenberg, 5 Aug. 1940, box 27, Woodring MSS.

79. Robert M. La Follette, Jr., to Dear Ones, 5 Aug. 1940, box 47, ser. A, La Follette Family MSS.

80. Minutes of Steering Committee to NEC, 1 Aug. 1940; and Arant to Clark, 8 Aug. 1940, Clark MSS.

81. Press Secretary Steven Early did not deny the rumors about Byrnes's position (stenographic notes of press conference, 31 July 1940, box 40, Early MSS). Byrnes had a lengthy discussion with FDR at the White House that afternoon (White House appointment log, 31 July 1940; Rexford Tugwell, diary, 31 July 1940, Tugwell MSS, FDRL). Byrnes remained noncommittal in his private correspondence (Byrnes to Bishop E. M. Walsh, 2 Aug. 1940, Byrnes MSS).

82. Mark Sullivan, in *New York Herald Tribune,* 3 Aug. 1940.

83. Ickes, *Secret Diary,* 3:288. "We had one of the most serious and important debates that I ever had in cabinet meeting" (Stimson, diary, 2 Aug. 1940, Stimson MSS).

84. Stimson, diary, 2 Aug. 1940, Stimson MSS.

85. Lauchlin Currie, memorandum for FDR, 31 July 1940, OF 1413; FDR, memorandum for Frank T. Hines, 2 Aug. 1940, OF-8, FDRL.

86. Roosevelt, *Public Papers,* 9:317-25.

87. "This business of calling for 'unity' when almost every step the administration takes is all bound up with its political effect actually becomes hypocrisy of the rankest sort. Even the Democrats, as distinguished from those in control of the administration, will privately voice their disgust, and while many will not 'take a walk,' I predict several severe cases of laryngitis between now and November" (see John Danaher to Edwin M. Borchard, 5 Aug. 1940, box 3, Borchard MSS).

88. Henry Wallace, diary, 18 June 1940.

89. Grenville Clark and William Allen White were both Willkie supporters, as were Burke, Wadsworth, and former Budget Director Lewis Douglas. Moreover, the fact that Knox, Stimson, and William J. Donovan were working for FDR did not necessarily mean they would vote for him in November.

90. Ickes, *Secret Diary,* 3:292-94.

91. Lothian to FO, no. 1606, 4-5 Aug. 1940, FO 371/24241/A3670.

92. Stimson, diary, 2 Aug. 1940.

93. Howard Beale to Roger Baldwin, 9 Aug. 1940, vol. 2189, ACLU files.

94. A. J. Sabath to FDR (wire), 2 Aug. 1940, box 8, OF 1413, FDRL.

95. Vic Donahey to FDR, 1 Aug. 1940, box 8, OF 1413, FDRL.

96. Francis T. Maloney to Edwin Watson, 5 Aug. 1940, box 7, OF 1413, FDRL.

97. FDR to Vic Donahey, 3 Aug. 1940, box 8, OF 1413, FDRL.

98. Ironically, Donahey was defeated for reelection by Republican Harold Burton, who spoke in favor of the draft during the campaign (see radio speech, 11 Sept. 1940, box 1, Harold Burton MSS, LC).

99. FDR to Alben Barkley, 3 Aug. 1940, box 7, OF 1413, FDRL.

100. Barkley to FDR, 8 Aug. 1940, box 7, OF 1413, FDRL.

101. Robert M. La Follette, Jr., to Dear Ones, 5 Aug. 1940, ser. A, box 47, La Follette Family MSS.

102. See Key Pittman to John E. Robbins, 3 Aug. 1940, box 1, Pittman MSS, LC.

103. A poll taken by Market Analysts, Inc., in early August listed thirty-nine senators as awaiting word from either Roosevelt or Willkie before taking a position on a destroyer agreement (copy enclosed in Benjamin Cohen to Harold Ickes, 8 Aug. 1940, box 371, Ickes MSS).

CHAPTER 10. THE DOG DAYS OF AUGUST

1. The epigraph is from Byrnes to Bernard Baruch, 22 July 1939, vol. 44, Baruch MSS.

2. Rosenman, *Working with Roosevelt,* 204. One observer believed that "fall of France knocked R from moorings, gave [him] a feeling of tiredness and hopelessness. This feeling persisted, in varying degrees, right through summer" (Joseph Alsop, notes of interview with William C. Bullitt, 10 Dec. 1940, Alsop MSS).

3. Stimson, diary, 20 July to 15 Aug. 1940, Stimson MSS.

4. Memorandum of phone conversation 13 Aug. 1940, vol. 292, 157-58, Morgenthau, diaries, Morgenthau MSS.

5. Libby, diary, 8 Aug. 1940, Libby MSS.

6. See Clark, diary, for Aug. 1940; Lothian to Minna Butler-Thwing, 7 Aug. 1940, box 470, Lothian MSS.

7. *Time,* 12 Aug. 1940, 11-12; *Washington Post,* 8 Aug. 1940.

8. Rosa Farber and Mary Decker to FDR (wire), 26 Aug. 1940, OF 1413, box 7, FDRL.

9. Stoesen, "Claude Pepper," 154.

10. Byrnes to John Nance Garner, 9 Aug. 1940, Byrnes MSS.

11. Thomas V. Rankin to Sidney Hertzberg, 8 Aug. 1940, *Uncensored* MSS, NYPL.

12. H. Johnson to Hiram Johnson, Jr., 31 July 1940, pt. 6, box 8, H. Johnson MSS.

13. J. Cal O'Loughlin to Herbert Hoover, 10 Aug. 1940, box 45, O'Loughlin MSS.

14. T. Rankin to S. Hertzberg, 2 Aug. 1940, *Uncensored* MSS, NYPL.

15. *PM,* 6 Aug. 1940.

16. Rankin to Norman Thomas, 6 Aug. 1940, Thomas MSS.

17. Frank Hanighen to Sidney Hertzberg, 6 Aug. 1940, and Thomas Rankin to Hertzberg, 8 and 9 Aug. 1940, *Uncensored* MSS, NYPL.

18. Hertzberg to Rankin, 10 Aug. 1940, Beard to Hertzberg, 12 Aug. 1940, and Barnes to Hertzberg, 15 Aug. 1940 *Uncensored* MSS, NYPL; Beale to Roger Baldwin, 9 and 16 Aug. 1940, ACLU MSS; Barnes to Villard, 16 Aug. 1940, Villard MSS.

19. French, diary, 8 Aug. 1940; minutes of Friends War Policy Committee, 9 Aug. 1940, DG 47, box B, SCPC; minutes of Governing Committee of the Keep America out of War Congress, 9 Aug. 1940, CDGA, box 1, SCPC; Libby, diary, 8-9 Aug. 1940, Libby MSS.

20. This referred to a charge, falsely made against him during the court fight, that Mr. and Mrs. Clark had established a series of sixteen family trusts to avoid paying some $90,000 in taxes.

21. *Congressional Record,* 6 Aug. 1940, 9921-23. On Holt see William Coffey, "Rush Dew Holt: The Boy Senator, 1905-1942" (Ph.D. diss., West Virginia University, 1970). John A. Danaher, a Republican senator from Connecticut in 1940

who opposed the draft, later recalled that Holt had virtually no friends in the Senate, largely because of his abuse of Senate etiquette in impugning the motives of his colleagues (interview with John A. Danaher, 12 May 1980).

22. *Congressional Record,* 6 Aug. 1940, 9923–25. "Read Rush Holt's disclosure of what's back of it [conscription] in August 6 or 7 of the Congressional Record, and also his debate with Minton. I happened to be in the Senate and heard all of it. It was 'hot!'" (Cong. Merlin Hull to Jess and Lois, n.d. [c. 12 Aug. 1940], M. Hull MSS, SHSW.

23. Sherman Minton to William G. McAdoo, 22 Aug. 1940, box 473, McAdoo MSS, LC. McAdoo had written to Minton: "I am glad you tore that fellow to pieces in the Senate not long ago, and, personally I don't give a damn whether you violated the rules of the Senate or not because you had complete justification" (17 Aug. 1940, box 472, McAdoo MSS).

24. *New York Times,* 7 Aug. 1940.

25. Ibid.

26. Ibid.

27. *New York Herald Tribune,* 8 Aug. 1940.

28. Wadsworth to the Rev. Charles P. Knight, 9 Aug. 1940, Wadsworth Family MSS.

29. Lippmann, column in *New York Herald Tribune,* 10 Aug. 1940.

30. William Allen White to Clark Eichelberger, 31 July 1940, box 97, Eichelberger MSS; Eichelberger to White, 12 Aug. 1940, and White to Eichelberger, 15 Aug. 1940, box C341, White MSS.

31. *Congressional Record,* 8 Aug. 1940, 10068; Warren Austin to Mrs. Chauncey Austin, 7 Aug. 1940, box 2, Austin MSS.

32. *Congressional Record,* 8 Aug. 1940, 10066–67.

33. Notes of interview with Cordell Hull, 4 Sept. 1940, Raymond Clapper notebooks, box 25, Clapper MSS.

34. *Congressional Record,* 7 Aug. 1940, 9990.

35. Rankin to S. Hertzberg, 8 Aug. 1940, *Uncensored* MSS, NYPL.

36. *Congressional Record,* 9 Aug. 1940, 10092–96.

37. Ibid., 9 Aug. 1940, 10096; see also Stimson, diary, 9 Aug. 1940, Stimson MSS.

38. *Washington Post,* 10 Aug. 1940.

39. *Congressional Record,* 9 Aug. 1940, 10097ff.

40. Sheppard, who died within the next year, had few skills as a debater, but his popularity was such that his bumbling guidance of the draft bill did not really hurt its chances for passage. According to Lewis Hershey, every time "a boy got up and got the old man confused, he lost two or three votes" from senators who "disliked seeing Sheppard made to look foolish" (quoted in O'Sullivan, "From Voluntarism to Conscription," 68n).

41. *New York Times,* 11 Aug. 1940.

42. *Congressional Record,* 12 Aug. 1940, 10013–20; see also Norris to Julian M. Snyder, 27 July 1940, Norris MSS.

43. *Congressional Record,* 12 Aug. 1940, 10117–18.

44. For Taft's preparation for his speech on the draft see Selective Service folder, box 791, Robert A. Taft MSS, LC.

45. *Congressional Record,* 14 Aug. 1940, 10296–311.

46. F. Canfield to Clark, 14 Aug. 1940, Clark MSS.

47. Warren Austin to Mrs. Chauncey Austin, 14 Aug. 1940, quoted in David L. Porter, *The Seventy-sixth Congress and World War II, 1939–1940* (Columbia, Mo., 1979),

146; see also Walter Lippmann to Mrs. William B. Meloney, 20 Aug. 1940, box 89, Lippmann MSS.

48. Clark to Taft, 16 Aug. 1940, Clark MSS.

49. Taft to Clark, 13 Sept. 1940, Clark MSS.

50. Malcolm Langford, memorandum, 31 July 1940, Clark MSS. Adams's Democratic colleague in the House, Lawrence Lewis of Denver, saw in conscription an opportunity to obtain more money for defense installations in Colorado, including a training center at Winter Park (Lewis, diary, 17 and 19 Aug., 15 Sept. 1940, Lewis MSS).

51. James Murray to Hugh Daly, 31 Aug. 1940, box 208, Murray MSS, University of Montana Library, Missoula, notes by David Porter.

52. *New York Times,* 27 Aug. 1940.

53. Malcolm Langford, memorandum, 31 July 1940, Clark MSS.

54. Drury, *Senate Journal,* 16; Capper to Clark, 19 Aug. 1940, Clark MSS; see also John W. Partin, "The Dilemma of a 'Very Good Man': Capper and Non-interventionism, 1936–1941," *Kansas History* 2 (Summer 1979): 86–96.

55. Quoted in Dorothy Wayman, *David I. Walsh: Citizen-Patriot* (Milwaukee, Wis., 1952), 284; see also Walsh to Robert Norton, 29 Aug. 1940, David Walsh MSS, Dinard Library, Holy Cross College, Worcester, Mass.

56. *New York Times,* 4 Aug. 1940.

57. Danaher to John T. Wood, 16 Aug. 1940, Danaher MSS; Danaher, interview, 12 May 1980.

58. *New York Post,* 11 Aug. 1940.

59. Burke, interview, July 1947.

60. Robert M. La Follette, Jr., to Dearest Ones, 13 Aug. 1940, box 47, ser. A, La Follette Family MSS.

61. Memorandum, "Stand of Senators on the Burke-Wadsworth Bill," 15 Aug. 1940, Clark MSS. The number of negative votes predicted—31—proved to be the exact total in the final vote, although the summary was wrong on three individuals: Andrews of Florida, Chavez of New Mexico, and Tydings of Maryland. The opposition count was reinforced by three from the "doubtful" column.

62. Frederick Libby, who attended the KAOWC meeting on 9 August that pledged a "no-compromise" fight, told Warren Mullen to put such a statement in the NCPW newsletter; see also Libby, diary, 9 Aug. 1940, Libby MSS. Paul C. French estimated that no more than twenty senators would vote no in the end (diary, 14 Aug. 1940, French MSS).

63. *New York Times,* 11 Aug. 1940.

64. For a compilation with short summaries of all the important amendments see *Selective Service in Peacetime,* first report of the director of selective service, 1940–41 (Washington, D.C., 1942).

65. Drury, *Senate Journal,* 341. Maloney's position on international and defense issues in 1940 is conveniently traced in letters to Walter Batterson, the head of the Hartford Chapter of the Committee to Defend America by Aiding the Allies (Maloney to Batterson [with enclosures], 23 July, 3 Oct. 1940, Committee to Defend America, Hartford Chapter, records, Sterling Library, Yale University, New Haven, Conn.).

66. See Maloney to Watson, 5 Aug. 1940, box 7, OF 1413, FDRL.

67. *New York Times,* 4 Aug. 1940.

68. Pacifists were still urging a voluntary national service bill in which youths could opt for nonmilitary service (see Paul C. French and E. Raymond Wilson to Jerry Voorhis, 2 Aug. 1941, in Wilson, "Occasional Papers," vol. 2 [1931–41], DG 70, SCPC).

69. *New York Times,* 4 Aug. 1940.

70. Johnson to Frank Doherty, 13 Aug. 1940, ser. 3, box 19, Johnson MSS.

71. Wheeler to Tom Stout, 24 Aug. 1940, box 7, Wheeler MSS, notes by David Porter.

72. Anticonscriptionists were also urging the House committee to call Maj. Gen. James K. Parsons as a witness. In a speech urging UMT for twenty-one year olds, Parsons had opposed the "conscription of ungainly numbers" (*Christian Century,* 14 Aug. 1940, 990; Villard to Andrew May, 15 Aug. 1940, Villard MSS).

73. *New York Times,* 14 Aug. 1940.

74. Stimson, diary, 13 Aug. 1940, Stimson MSS.

75. Ibid., 22 Aug. 1940, Stimson MSS.

76. Ibid., 15 Aug. 1940, Stimson MSS.

77. *New York Times,* 9 June 1940.

78. Ibid., 11 June 1940.

79. Cong. James O'Connor to John R. Yates, 17 Sept. 1940, box 1, folder 52, O'Connor MSS, Montana State University Library, Bozeman, notes by David Porter.

80. *Congressional Record,* 21 Aug. 1940, 10123–28; see also Vandenberg to Kerr, 24 July 1940, Vandenberg MSS, Bentley Historical Library, University of Michigan, Ann Arbor.

81. NEC, *Why the Volunteer System Is Inadequate* (New York, 1940).

82. *New York Times,* 30 July 1940, 7.

83. *Congressional Record,* 21 Aug. 1940, 10663–65.

84. Stimson, diary, 22 Aug. 1940, Stimson MSS.

85. *New York Journal American,* 23 Aug. 1940; Pogue, *George C. Marshall: Ordeal and Hope,* 61.

86. Stimson, diary, 22 Aug. 1940, Stimson MSS.

87. J. R., memorandum for Taft, 20 Aug. 1940, box 791, Taft MSS.

88. Sherman Miles's letter to Clark, mimeographed and sent out by the Harvard Defense Group, made this essential point forcefully (Burke-Wadsworth folder, Ralph Barton Perry correspondence, Harvard Defense Group MSS).

89. NEC, *Why the Volunteer System Is Inadequate.*

90. Byrnes to the Rev. Henry F. Wolfe, 13 Aug. 1940, Byrnes MSS; see also Charles O. Andrews to W. J. Steed, 2 Sept. 1940, box 43, Charles O. Andrews MSS, University of Florida Library, Gainesville, Fla., notes of David Porter.

91. Hershey, memorandum for Morris Sheppard, 17 Aug. 1940, box 24, Selective Service Headquarters records, RG 144; see also Gen. E. S. Adams to Warren Austin, 19 July 1940, box 26, Austin MSS.

92. The figures for the first six months of World War I showed a steady decline: May—119,400; June—95,815; July—73,887; August—59,556; September—24,367.

93. Hershey, memorandum for Sheppard, 17 Aug. 1940, box 24, RG 144.

94. Francis V. Keesling, memo on Maloney amendment, Trip file, Hershey MSS.

95. Clark and his friends, under no illusions as to the strength of the Maloney proposal, worked hard to counteract it. One result was the publication of the pamphlet *Why the Volunteer System Is Inadequate.* In addition to arguments against volunteering, the pamphlet included quotations from Roosevelt, Willkie, Stimson, Patterson, Knox, Pershing, Marshall, and others. Some 133,000 copies were mailed by Perley Boone to a list that included members of Congress, Washington correspondents, 2,000 daily newspapers, 1,000 columnists, 700 radio stations, college presidents, American Legion posts, service clubs, Chambers of Commerce, and clergymen. This coverage was typical of the scale on which the NEC operated.

96. Clark to Francis T. Maloney, 12 Aug. 1940, Clark MSS.

97. Maloney to Clark, 16 Aug. 1940, Clark MSS.

98. Maloney to Clark, 29 Aug. 1940, Clark MSS.

99. Canfield to Clark, 14 Aug. 1940, Clark MSS.

100. *New York Times,* 14 Aug. 1940; WILPF branch letter no. 93, 13 Aug. 1940, SCPC.

101. Canfield to Clark, 15 Aug. 1940, Clark MSS; see also George Norris to Maurice Clark, 15 Aug. 1940, box 410, Norris MSS.

102. Stimson, diary, 16 Aug. 1940.

103. Maloney to Edwin Watson (wire), 5 Aug. 1940, box 7, OF 1413, FDRL.

104. Edward Taylor to FDR (wire), 5 Aug. 1940, PPF 5665, FDRL.

105. FDR to Taylor, 12 Aug. 1940, PPF 5665, FDRL.

106. Byrnes to Wilton Earle, 13 Aug. 1940, national defense, legislative file, Byrnes MSS.

107. Reynolds, *Creation of the Anglo-American Alliance,* 124–25. E.g., Roger Greene, who headed the Washington office of the Committee to Defend America, was in constant contact with officials in the Justice Department, the State Department, Interior, Navy, and Congress with respect to the destroyers. His correspondence shows the confusion over what was being proposed and, hence, whether the straw polls of the Senate could accurately gauge votes on a bill or resolution that had not yet been formalized (see Greene, letters to his wife, Kate, 5, 6, 7, 8, 9, 11, 12, 13, 14, and 15 Aug. 1940, Roger Greene MSS).

108. Quoted by Philip Goodhart in *Fifty Ships That Saved the World* (London, 1965), 156; see also White to Thomas W. Lamont, 13 Aug. 1940, box 124, Lamont MSS.

109. Ickes, diary, 10 Aug. 1940, Ickes MSS.

110. Stimson, diary, 12 Aug. 1940, Stimson MSS.

111. White House appointments log, 1940.

112. Davis Walsh to FDR, 19 Aug. 1940, PSF Senate, FDRL. "He [Walsh] says there is not a man in the Senate who would deny that Roosevelt is determined to get this country into war for the sake of his own election. He has been with him on one or two of his inspection trips and says it made him sick, that these trips are not for the sake of preparedness, except insofar as the pictures taken everywhere may be used for such a purpose, that they are silly political trips which can be taken on the tax payer without comment because they are inspection trips. He was just three days with the president last week, said that he was gay and amusing, never mentioned the war, that at the camps he did nothing of value except to talk to the mechanics and people who had votes, occasionally to say to one of the officers, 'I hope that warehouse is big enough,' or something equally unimportant. I have seldom seen a man as bitter as Walsh is and he was first for Roosevelt. He thinks the most inexcusable thing of all is that the money voted for preparedness has been wasted, that Roosevelt has done a good deal of talking and practically no acting. He thinks that if he should be reelected by some unhappy chance the Germans would eat us at their leisure" (William R. Castle, Jr., diary, 24 Aug. 1940, Houghton Library, Harvard University, Cambridge, Mass.).

113. "Washington Letter," 14 Aug. 1940, British Library of Information no. 362, FO 371/2421/131, RBFO. "Congressmen are frightened by their mail which is overwhelmingly against the bill and they don't trust the straw polls which indicate the country approves. They feel that even if not faked they don't take into consideration the fact that a man sufficiently interested in a public question to write about it, is a man prepared to turn out and vote, while a man who has to be hunted up and asked his opinion by a canvasser is likely to stay at home. The issue is the kind congressmen hate

more than any other because they are bound to offend some powerful groups whatever side they take.''

114. Stimson to Charles C. Burlingham, 25 Aug. 1940, Burlingham MSS.

115. Stimson, diary, 13 Aug. 1940, Stimson MSS.

116. Morgenthau, presidential diary, 14 Aug. 1940, Morgenthau MSS.

117. *New York Times*, 11 Aug. 1940. Cohen had helped Acheson draft the letter. ''I had seen two earlier drafts . . . here in Washington. I am afraid that the argument will not be very convincing to most of its readers, but it may help to smooth the way for legislation'' (Roger Greene to Kate Greene, 11 Aug. 1940, Greene MSS; Oscar Cox, daily calendar, 12 Aug. 1940, Cox MSS, FDRL; Charles C. Burlingham to Dean Acheson, 9 and 30 Aug. 1940, box 4, Acheson MSS, Sterling Library, Yale University, New Haven, Conn.).

118. Benjamin Cohen to FDR, 19 July 1940, PSF 81, FDRL; see also Cohen to Robert Jackson, 11 Aug. 1940, enclosing mimeographed copy of Acheson-Burlingham letter, box 88, Jackson MSS.

119. Reynolds, *Creation of the Anglo-American Alliance*, 125; Stimson, diary, 15 Aug. 1940. It should be noted that Frankfurter spent the night of 6 August as FDR's guest at Hyde Park, and six days later, accompanied by C. C. Burlingham, one of the signers of the Acheson letter, the Supreme Court justice again saw the president during his tour of the New London, Connecticut, naval installation (Burlingham, desk diary, 12 Aug. 1940; see also Murphy, *Brandeis/Frankfurter Connection*, 210–12).

120. By stressing the acquisition of bases and not mentioning the destroyers, FDR began his public campaign of selling the destroyer deal as the greatest accomplishment for national defense since the Louisiana Purchase. ''I've been very busy trying to get the destroyers over and I think it is now settled. The P thought so this morning'' (Lothian to Cecil Kerr, 16 Aug. 1940, box 470, Lothian MSS; see also Morgenthau, presidential diary, 16 Aug. 1940; Early to FDR, 16 Aug. 1940, box 24, Early MSS).

121. Morgenthau, presidential diary, 14 Aug. 1940, Morgenthau MSS.

122. Stimson, diary, 16 Aug. 1940, Stimson MSS.

123. Ickes, *Secret Diary*, 3:303; Morgenthau, presidential diary, 16 Aug. 1940.

124. Drake, memorandum on Rayburn, 13 Aug. 1940, Clark MSS.

125. F. Canfield to Clark, 15 Aug. 1940, Clark MSS.

126. George R. Reid to Clifford Hope, 16 Aug. 1940, box 82, Hope MSS; see also J. C. O'Loughlin memo for Herbert Hoover, 15 Aug. 1940, box 45, O'Loughlin MSS; and memorandum for secretary of war, 16 Aug. 1940, box 24, Selective Service records, RG 144.

127. *New York World-Telegram*, 8 Aug. 1940.

128. Hiram Johnson to Frank Doherty, 13 Aug. 1940, pt. 3, box 19, H. Johnson MSS.

129. *New York Herald Tribune*, 14 Aug. 1940.

130. Canfield to Clark, 15 Aug. 1940, Clark MSS.

131. ''Washington Letter,'' 14 Aug. 1940, British Library of Information no. 362, FO 371/2421/131, RBFO.

132. Notes of interview with Gardner Cowles, 23 Jan. 1952, Ellsworth Barnard MSS, Lilly Library, Indiana University, Bloomington.

133. Sinclair Weeks to Willkie (with enclosure from Henry Cabot Lodge), 13 July 1940, box 12, Weeks MSS; Taft to Willkie, 13 Aug. 1940, box 142, Taft MSS; Charles Halleck to Willkie, 7 Aug. 1940, Halleck MSS; Walter Lippmann to Willkie, 30 Aug. 1940, Lippmann MSS; box 3, national defense folder, Willkie presidential MSS, Yale University, New Haven, Conn.; Franklin Canfield to Oren Root, 31 July 1940, Clark MSS.

134. Clark to Willkie (wire), 2 Aug. 1940, Clark MSS.

135. Libby to Willkie, 23 July, 23 Aug., 3 Sept. 1940, DG 23, box 302, SCPC; see also John Nevin Sayre to Villard, 9 Aug. 1940, DG 13, box 13, SCPC.

136. Wadsworth to Willkie, 24 July 1940, Wadsworth Family MSS.

137. Willkie to Wadsworth, 5 Aug. 1940, Wadsworth Family MSS.

138. Joseph W. Martin (as told to Robert J. Donovan), *My First Fifty Years in Politics* (New York, 1960), 110.

139. Landon to John T. Flynn, 29 Oct. 1941, Landon MSS.

140. Quoted in "Washington Notes," *Uncensored,* 31 Aug. 1940; Paul C. French, diary, 16 Aug. 1940, French MSS.

141. Quoted in Joseph Barnes, *Willkie* (New York, 1952), 195.

142. *New York Herald Tribune,* 18 Aug. 1940; Ellsworth Barnard, *Wendell Willkie: Fighter for Freedom* (Marquette, Mich., 1966), 200–208; Neal, *Dark Horse,* 133–36.

143. Clark to Willkie, 18 Aug. 1940, Clark MSS.

144. Key Pittman to Joe McDonald, 20 Aug. 1940, box 16, Pittman MSS.

145. *New York Herald Tribune,* 18 Aug. 1940; *New York Times,* 19 Aug. 1940.

146. Stimson, diary, 20 Aug. 1940, Stimson MSS.

147. *New York Herald Tribune,* 24 Aug. 1940. "As national chairman," Martin later recalled, "I simply could not hand the Democrats any such plum as a vote by me against this issue" (*My First Fifty Years,* 111).

148. "He was personally in favor of doing everything possible to see that Great Britain did not get beaten in the war because he realized the continued existence of Great Britain and its navy was essential to the security and safety of the United States" (Lothian to Lord Halifax, 29 Aug. 1940, vol. 324, Halifax MSS, FO/800, RBFO.

149. Hiram Johnson to Hiram Johnson, Jr., 30 Aug. 1940, box 8, pt. 6, H. Johnson MSS.

150. Harry Elmer Barnes to Villard, 16 Aug. 1940, Villard MSS.

151. Bullitt, *For the President,* 498–502; *New York Times,* 19 Aug. 1940; *Time,* 26 Aug. 1940, 14; see also Bullitt to Herbert Feis, 26 Aug. 1940, box 12, Feis MSS, LC, and Bullitt to Henry Morgenthau, 23 Aug. 1940, vol. 295, Morgenthau, diaries.

152. *Congressional Record,* 19 Aug. 1940, 10473.

153. Ibid., 10491.

154. Ibid., 20 Aug. 1940, 10563.

155. Transcript of news broadcast, 20 Aug. 1940, box 11, Raymond Gram Swing MSS, LC.

156. *Congressional Record,* 20 Aug. 1940, 10553–62.

157. "Washington Notes," *Uncensored,* 29 Aug. 1940, 1.

158. Paul French, diary, 20 Aug. 1940; Davis to Gifford Pinchot, 20 Aug. 1940, box 751, Gifford Pinchot MSS, LC.

159. *New York Times,* 21 Aug. 1940; see also Robert M. La Follette, Jr., to Dear Ones, 23 Aug. 1940, ser. A, box 47, La Follette Family MSS.

160. Theodore Green to Alan R. Wheeler, 21 Aug. 1940, box 143, T. Green MSS, LC.

161. Canfield to Elihu Root, Jr., 20 Aug. 1940, Clark MSS; *New York Times,* 21 Aug. 1940.

162. Canfield to Root and William J. Donovan, 21 Aug. 1940, Clark MSS.

163. Austin to Mrs. Chauncey Austin, 20 Aug. 1940, box 2, Austin MSS.

164. La Follette to Dear Ones, 27 Aug. 1940, box 47, La Follette Family MSS.

165. *New York Times,* 24 Aug. 1940.

166. Canfield to Root, 22 Aug. 1940, Clark MSS.

167. David L. Porter, *Congress and the Waning of the New Deal* (Port Washington, N.Y., 1980), chap. 7. "At the moment it looks as though there were a filibuster on against the military service bill" (Joseph C. O'Mahoney to Carl Arnold, 22 Aug. 1940, box 50, O'Mahoney MSS). Although the opposition was certainly prolonging the debate, there was in fact no concerted attempt at a filibuster. In particular, Senator Wheeler was anxious to bring a transportation bill, cosponsored by himself and Harry Truman, to the floor for a vote, and so he worked hard behind the scenes to have fellow opponents of the draft keep their speeches to reasonable lengths (see Harry S. Truman to Bess Truman, 20 and 29 Aug. 1940, Truman MSS, David Porter's notes).

168. White to Wheeler, 15, 20, and 24 Aug. 1940, box 348, White MSS.

169. Wheeler to White, 19, 24, and 28 Aug. 1940, box 348, White MSS. White commented: "The only difference between you and me probably is that you think we can keep out of war by letting Hitler smash himself to pieces against England and I want to keep out of the war by helping England smash him and save us the trouble" (to Wheeler, 28 Aug. 1940, box 348, White MSS).

170. Lindbergh, *Wartime Journals,* 380–81.

171. Fortunately for historians, the absence of their families led the usually uncommunicative Taft and La Follette to write numerous letters to their wives during the summer of 1940.

172. Allen Brown to George C. Marshall, 19 Aug. 1940, Marshall MSS, Larry Bland file.

CHAPTER 11. THE FINAL ENACTMENT:
"A TURNING POINT IN THE TIDE OF WAR"

1. Stimson, diary, 17 Aug. 1940, Stimson MSS.

2. Entry for 17 Aug. 1940 in Nancy Harvison Hooker, ed., *The Moffat Papers: Selections from the Diplomatic Journals of Jay Pierrepont Moffat, 1919–1943* (Cambridge, Mass., 1956), 325–26.

3. Stimson, diary, 17 Aug. 1940, Stimson MSS.

4. Mackenzie King, diary, 17 Aug. 1940, microfiche no. 151; see also J. W. Pickersgill, *The Mackenzie King Record* (Toronto, 1960), 131.

5. Stimson, diary, 17 Aug. 1940, Stimson MSS.

6. Ibid.

7. Entry for 18 Aug. 1940 in Hooker, *Moffat Papers,* 327.

8. The two most recent studies of the Ogdensburg meeting and the destroyers/ bases negotiations stress FDR's cautious, defensive motives in the summer of 1940 (see Reynolds, *Creation of the Anglo-American Alliance,* chap. 5; and Fred E. Pollock, "Roosevelt, the Ogdensburg Agreement, and the British Fleet: All Done with Mirrors," *Diplomatic History* 5 (Summer 1981): 203–19.

9. FDR to L. B. Sheley, 26 Aug. 1940, PSF, War Department, box 39, FDRL.

10. See Arthur Vandenberg to F. W. Newton, 24 Aug. 1940, Vandenberg MSS.

11. Interview with Perley Boone, 31 July 1947, Clark MSS.

12. Churchill was also reluctant to make his offer of British bases a direct exchange for American destroyers. In order to gain the consent of the chief of naval operations, Admiral Stark, that the transfer of American destroyers would not impair national defense, however, a direct relationship between the bases and destroyers became necessary. State Department legal adviser Green Hackworth eventually broke the logjam by suggesting that some British bases be regarded as gifts and some be

direct exchanges (Leutze, *Bargaining for Supremacy,* 123; Reynolds, *Creation of the Anglo-American Alliance,* 130-31).

13. Stimson, diary, 19-22 Aug. 1940, Stimson MSS.

14. Ibid., 23 Aug. 1940, Stimson MSS; Stimson to FDR, 23 Aug. 1940, PSF, War Department, box 39, FDRL.

15. Roosevelt, *Public Papers,* 9:337-40.

16. *New York Herald Tribune,* 24 Aug. 1940; see also notes on selective-service bill, box 36, Mark Sullivan MSS, Hoover Institute, Stanford University, Stanford, Calif.

17. Early to Mary Holmes, 23 Aug. 1940, box 7, Early MSS.

18. "You may be right from the point of view of votes this fall but if you were in my place you would realize that in the light of world conditions it is, for the sake of national safety, necessary for us to prepare against the attack just as fast and as sensibly as we can. . . . There are some occasions in the national history where leaders have to move for the preservation of American liberties and not just drift with what may or may not be a political doubt of the moment. . . . I do hope you will think this thing through in terms of national safety and not just in terms of votes" (FDR to L. B. Sheley, 26 Aug. 1940, PSF, War Department, box 39, FDRL). This private letter to a small-town Democratic editor in Illinois—the clearest, most cogent, most eloquent statement by FDR on the draft—probably reveals the president's honest belief in conscription, while also setting forth the reasons for his earlier political caution.

19. *New York Times,* 25 Aug. 1940. "The conscription debate goes on, thank God, . . . despite the ukase from on high yesterday. Walsh is getting pretty sore about it all" (Frank Hanighen to S. Hertzberg, 24 Aug. 1940, *Uncensored* MSS, NYPL).

20. Ernest W. Gibson to Lawrence Turgeon, 28 Aug. 1940, Congress 1940-41 box, Ernest W. Gibson, Jr., MSS, Guy Bailey Library, University of Vermont, Burlington.

21. *Congressional Record,* 24 Aug. 1940, 10856-57.

22. Libby, diary, 24 Aug. 1940, Libby MSS.

23. La Follette to Dear Ones, 24 Aug. 1940, ser. A, box 47, La Follette Family MSS.

24. *New York World-Telegram,* 26 Aug. 1940; Paul French, diary, 26 Aug. 1940, French MSS.

25. *New York Sun,* 26 Aug. 1940.

26. *New York Herald Tribune,* 27 Aug. 1940.

27. Alsop to Wesley Stout, 29 Aug. 1940, box 34, Alsop MSS.

28. *New York Times,* 26 Aug. 1940.

29. Austin to Mrs. Chauncey Austin, 26 Aug. 1940, box 2, Austin MSS.

30. "We are doing all we can to get the conscription bill passed. We worked three solid weeks in committee on the bill and we have a good bill now and I believe it will pass. . . . Last night we started night sessions in our endeavor to get the bill through this week. So, you see, we are trying!" (Elbert Thomas to Mrs. Joseph E. Jones, 27 Aug. 1940, box 129, E. Thomas MSS, FDRL).

31. Shedd, memorandum for chief of staff, 26 Aug. 1940, box 24, Selective Service System central files, RG 147, Federal Records Center, Suitland, Md.

32. Assistant Secretary of State Breckinridge Long recorded a conversation with Secretary Hull the following day. "It is not that he [Hull] wants to send an army abroad—and I quite agree with him, but it is the effect on Germany and Japan at the present moment of notifying them officially and positively that they may do as they please anywhere in Europe and Asia with American rights and that they will have no interference whatsoever from the Government of the United States" (entry of 27 Aug.

1940, in *The War Diary of Breckinridge Long,* ed. Fred Israel [Lincoln, Nebr., 1966], 124; also quoted in O'Sullivan, "Voluntarism to Conscription," 83 n).

33. Richard M. Dalfiume, "Military Segregation and the 1940 Presidential Election," *Phylon* 30 (Spring 1969): 42-55.

34. Austin to Mrs. Chauncey Austin, 27 Aug. 1940, box 2, Austin MSS.

35. In a bit of bad prophecy, Lundeen observed: "If Japan ever fights America, it will not be in the Hawaiian region; it will not be off San Francisco and San Diego and Portland. . . . The Japanese are too clever to come over and tackle us here" (*Congressional Record,* 27 Aug. 1940, 11014-15).

36. Ibid., 11033.

37. Ibid., 11035-36.

38. *New York Times,* 28 Aug. 1940; La Follette to Rachel La Follette, 27 Aug. 1940, ser. A, box 47, La Follette Family MSS.

39. *Congressional Record,* 28 Aug. 1940, 11103.

40. Wiley to M. B. Stegner, 29 Aug. 1940, Alexander Wiley MSS, SHSW.

41. *Congressional Record,* 28 Aug. 1940, 11112. "I could never accept the philosophy that any industry should refuse to cooperate in the defense program while we are drafting men to serve for a dollar a day" (Richard Russell to Redden Smith, 5 Sept. 1940, ser. 6, Russell MSS, Richard Russell Library, University of Georgia, Athens, David Porter's notes).

42. Hayden to Mrs. Edwin Pendleton, 23 Aug. 1940, quoted in Porter, *Seventy-sixth Congress,* 152.

43. Watson, memorandum of phone conversation with Josiah Bailey, 27 Aug. 1940, OF 1413, FDRL. Only a few days earlier, Bailey had thought he would support the Maloney amendment (Bailey to Clayton Miller, 23 Aug. 1940, box 425, Bailey MSS, Southern Historical Collections, William Perkins Library, Duke University, Durham, N.C.).

44. *Congressional Record,* 28 Aug. 1940, 11117. "Both Pres. Roosevelt and Mr. Willkie sent word to me—the one thro' Sen. Gibson, the other thro' Sen. Bridges—commending my service for National Defense" (Austin to Mrs. Chauncey Austin, 27 Aug. 1940, box 2, Austin MSS).

45. *Congressional Record,* 28 Aug. 1940, 11124.

46. Johnson to Hiram W. Johnson, Jr., 1 Sept. 1940, pt. 6, box 8, H. Johnson MSS.

47. *Congressional Record,* 28 Aug. 1940, 11116.

48. Danaher, who saw the draft bill as a step toward intervention, opposed even an amended version. Years later, Danaher remembered that the Senate opposition in 1940 had too many "prima donnas." "We had no concerted action. The rate of discussion was almost nil among senators. . . . On the Democratic side I had more real friends than on the Republican side" (interview, 20 May 1980). Schwellenbach had such strong feelings against the draft that he delayed accepting an appointment to the federal bench until he had recorded his negative vote (*Congressional Record,* 30 Aug. 1940, copy in box 14, Lewis Schwellenbach MSS, LC).

49. *Congressional Record,* 28 Aug. 1940, 11137-38.

50. Ibid., 11141.

51. Ibid., 11142.

52. See table in Porter, *Seventy-sixth Congress,* 197.

53. Clark to members of the House of Representatives, 3 Sept. 1940, Clark MSS.

54. Quoted in Peggy Ann Davis, *Alben W. Barkley: Senate Majority Leader and Vice President* (New York, 1979), 99.

55. Quoted in Porter, *Seventy-sixth Congress,* 157.

56. Bailey to Frank Hopgood, 26 Aug. 1940, box 436, Bailey MSS.

57. *Uncensored,* 31 Aug. 1940, 3.

58. Johnson to Hiram Johnson, Jr., 1 Sept. 1940, pt. 6, box 8, H. Johnson MSS.

59. Canfield to Clark, 26 Aug. 1940, Clark MSS. Elihu Root, Jr., memorandum, 27 Aug. 1940, Clark MSS. Curiously, Clark had phoned Attorney General Robert Jackson earlier in the month about subversive opposition to the draft. Jackson passed the complaint on to FBI Director J. Edgar Hoover, who produced a voluminous report of more than one hundred pages on the activities of the various groups, including the Bund and the Emergency Peace Mobilization, that opposed the draft. Jackson apparently did not make these reports available to Clark (see J. Edgar Hoover to attorney general [with enclosures], 16 Aug. 1940, Attorney General's files, Grenville Clark folder, Jackson MSS).

60. Minutes of the NEC Steering Committee, 28 Aug. 1940, Clark MSS; Boone to Steve Early, 4 Sept. 1940, OF 1413, misc., FDRL.

61. Canfield to Clark, 27 Aug. 1940, Clark MSS.

62. Gifford Pinchot, diary, 27 Aug. 1940, Gifford Pinchot MSS; Grace Tully, *FDR: My Boss* (New York, 1949), 244.

63. Eleanor Roosevelt to Anna Boettiger, 30 Aug. 1940, box 52, Anna Roosevelt Halstead MSS, FDRL.

64. Stimson, diary, 29 Aug. to 4 Sept. 1940, Stimson MSS.

65. *Uncensored,* 31 Aug. 1940, 1; Ed Cooper to S. Hertzberg, 3 Sept. 1940, *Uncensored* MSS, NYPL.

66. In addition to thousands of genuine letters of protest, the authors came across numerous examples of "manufactured" opposition. E.g., in the State Historical Society of Wisconsin are the papers of Congressmen Merlin Hull and Stephen Bolles, both of whom opposed the draft. Seven identical postcards protesting conscription were postmarked 27 July 1940, from Abbotsville, Wis., in box 115, Hull MSS. Similarly, four identical cards in the same handwriting from Racine went to Bolles, postmarked 12 Aug. 1940, box 3, Bolles MSS.

67. Drake, memorandum of talk with Rayburn, 13 Aug. 1940, Clark MSS.

68. Stimson, diary, 22 Aug. 1940, Stimson MSS.

69. Karl Stefan to Art Thomas, 27 Aug. 1940, box 27, Stefan MSS, David Porter's notes.

70. Marshall to Robert W. Kean, 29 Aug. 1940, reel 21, item 799, Marshall MSS.

71. *New York Times,* 31 Aug. 1940.

72. Lawrence Lewis, diary, 30 Aug. 1940, Lewis MSS; J. Hardin Peterson to Peter Perry, 31 Aug. 1940, Peterson MSS, David Porter's notes; Walter Pierce to A. J. Moore, 2 Sept. 1940, Walter Pierce MSS, University of Oregon Library, Eugene.

73. *New York Times,* 31 Aug. 1940.

74. Ibid.

75. *Daily Worker,* 30 Aug. 1940; Samuel Walker, "Communists and Isolationism: The American Peace Mobilization, 1940–1941," *Maryland Historian* 4 (1973): 1–5; Egan, *Class, Culture, and the Classroom,* 188–92; Isserman, *Which Side Were You On?* chap. 4.

76. Folder on emergency peace mobilization, 1940, box 42, Gerald P. Nye MSS, HHPL; Fay Bennett to Robert Kramer, 28 Aug. 1940, DG 43, ser. C-4, box 3, WILPF MSS, SCPC; S. Hertzberg to Dorothy Detzer, 20 Aug. 1940, ser. C-1, box 32, DG 43, ser. C-4, box 3, WILPF MSS, SCPC; Hertzberg to Harry Elmer Barnes, 12 and 22 Aug. 1940, Barnes MSS; "You Can Still Stop the Conscription Bill," flier in box 161, *National Journal* MSS, Hoover Institute, Stanford, Calif.

77. Bob Marshall to Bob Parker, 3 Sept. 1940, reel 40, American Socialist Party MSS.

78. Libby, diary, 27 Aug. to 2 Sept. 1940.

79. Ibid., 31 Aug. 1940.

80. Branch letter no. 94, 29 Aug. 1940, WILPF MSS, SCPC; Warren Cohen, "The Role of Private Groups in the United States," in *Pearl Harbor as History*, ed. Borg and Okamoto, 423.

81. Libby, diary, 31 Aug. 1940, Libby MSS; Rankin to Hertzberg, 28 Aug. 1940, *Uncensored* MSS, NYPL.

82. Edwin C. Johnson to Kenneth Walker, 3 Sept. 1940, reel 70.20, SCPC. Johnson did send every congressman a reprint of a British editorial titled "Call Big Army Theory Obsolete" (Johnson letter, 31 Aug. 1940, copy in box 8, Robert Crosser MSS, and in box 115, M. Hull MSS).

83. Press release, 28 Aug. 1940, reel 40, American Socialist Party MSS. In fact, Thomas later won less than 100,000 votes out of nearly 50 million cast, the smallest the Socialist party had ever polled (Johnpoll, *Pacifist's Progress*, 217).

84. See Socialist party correspondence from national headquarters in late August and early September (reels 40-41, American Socialist Party MSS).

85. Baldwin to Beale, 27 Aug. 1940, Baldwin to Clark, 30 July 1940, Baldwin to William J. Donovan, 2 Aug. 1940, vol. 2189, ACLU records; A. J. Muste to E. Roosevelt, 8 Aug. 1940, DG 50, box 16, SCPC; Beale to Baldwin (wire), 11 Sept. 1940, Beale MSS, GRB, and Beale to Peter A. Wallenborn, Jr., 20 Sept. 1940, Beale MSS, SHSW.

86. Ralph A. Gamble to Archibald Thacher, 2 Oct. 1940, Clark MSS.

87. *New York Herald Tribune,* 4 Sept. 1940.

88. Quoted in Walker, "Communists and Isolationism," 4; "A lot of 'bums' and the hoodlum element, pacifists, and Communists are doing more for the bill by fighting it than they are doing against it. I don't think the opposition will get over 100 votes now" (J. Wilburn Cartwright to Carrie et al., 4 Sept. 1940, Cartwright MSS, University of Oklahoma Library, Norman, David Porter's notes).

89. Libby, diary, 3 Sept. 1940, Libby MSS; Libby to Willkie (wire), 3 Sept. 1940, Willkie MSS.

90. Roosevelt, *Public Papers,* 9:379. FDR evidently had last-minute trepidations. During his trip to Tennessee over the Labor Day weekend, Bernard Baruch found the president preoccupied, unable to talk about politics. "He said twice on the journey that he might get impeached for what he was about to do" (quoted by David E. Lilienthal in *The Journals of David Lilienthal,* vol. 1: *The TVA Years, 1939-1945* (New York, 1964), 209.

91. See Hiram Johnson to John Bassett Moore, 4 Sept. 1940, box 79, Moore MSS, LC. "I suspect that one of the reasons there has been a noticeable absence in Congress of comment on the destroyer deal is because most members felt it would serve no good purpose, particularly at this time" (Ed Cooper [aide to Burton Wheeler] to S. Hertzberg, 16 Sept. 1940, *Uncensored* MSS, NYPL).

92. *Congressional Record,* 4 Sept. 1940, 11439-41.

93. *New York Times,* 5 Sept. 1940.

94. *Congressional Record,* 4 Sept. 1940, 11441-43; Alan Schaffer, *Vito Marcantonio: Radical in Congress* (Syracuse, N.Y., 1966), 70-71.

95. C. Hope to the Rev. J. S. Phoughe, 3 Sept. 1940, and to Frank W. Russell, 20 Sept. 1940, Hope MSS.

96. *Congressional Record,* 4 Sept. 1940, 11448-51; constituent newsletter, 5 Sept. 1940, box 1, Frances Bolton MSS, Western Reserve Historical Society, Cleveland,

Ohio; see also Edith Nourse Rogers to Ralph Barton Perry, 10 Sept. 1940, Perry correspondence, Harvard Defense Group MSS.

97. O'Sullivan, "From Voluntarism to Conscription," 102.

98. Lawrence Lewis, diary, 4-5 Sept. 1940, Lewis MSS. "Saw fight in House late last night—example of chauvinist war nerves" (Rankin to Hertzberg, 5 Sept. 1940, *Uncensored* MSS, NYPL).

99. Lyle Boren to Hec Bussey, 12 Aug. 1940, quoted in Porter, *Seventy-sixth Congress,* 163.

100. *New York Times,* 7 Sept. 1940.

101. *Congressional Record,* 7 Sept. 1940, 11732.

102. Doughton to C. A. Millsaps, 9 Sept. 1940, Robert Doughton MSS, Southern Historical Collection, University of North Carolina Library, Chapel Hill.

103. *New York Times,* 31 Aug. 1940.

104. Ibid., 30 Aug. 1940; James M. Drought to Carl Ackerman, 2 Sept. 1940, box 155, Ackerman MSS, LC.

105. *New York Herald Tribune,* 31 Aug. 1940; Burton Wheeler to Amos Pinchot, 11 Oct. 1940, box 68, Amos Pinchot MSS.

106. *New York Times,* 31 Aug. 1940.

107. *Congressional Record,* 4 Sept. 1940, 11446-47.

108. *New York Times,* 6 Sept. 1940.

109. Jonas, *Isolationism in America,* 52-54; see also Richard Hanks, "Hamilton Fish and American Isolationism, 1920-1944" (Ph.D. diss., University of California at Riverside, 1971).

110. FDR to Bernard Baruch, 1 Nov. 1940, vol. 45, Baruch MSS.

111. Rankin to Hertzberg, 5 Sept. 1940, *Uncensored* MSS, NYPL.

112. *Congressional Record,* 5 Sept. 1940, 11603-4.

113. "I think . . . a big mistake was made yesterday, and the Republicans and Ham Fish scored very heavily against us" (Walter Pierce to Gen. Charles Martin, 6 Sept. 1940, Pierce MSS; Porter, *Seventy-sixth Congress,* 162-63).

114. *Washington Post,* 7 Sept. 1940; O'Sullivan, "From Voluntarism to Conscription," 105.

115. Reprint of Taft's radio address of 5 Sept. 1940, copy in Clark MSS. "I listened to your radio speech last week against the current Conscription Bill and regard it as a masterpiece of logical reasoning. Disagreeing with your conclusion, at the outset, I found myself more and more impressed with the arguments—and you certainly posed a delightful dilemma for Mr. Roosevelt in your analysis of the existence of the American emergency as contrasted with the gift of the destroyers" (Thomas E. Dewey to Taft, 10 Sept. 1940, Dewey MSS).

116. WILPF branch letter no. 95, 28 Sept. 1940, SCPC; Detzer to Mrs. J. Beardsley, 5 Sept. 1940, DG 43, C-1, box 32, SCPC; Mildred S. Olmsted to Dorothy Hummel, 9 Sept. 1940, DG 23, box 2, SCPC; Detzer to S. Hertzberg, 9 Sept. 1940, *Uncensored* MSS, NYPL.

117. *New York Times,* 7-9 Sept. 1940.

118. Entry of 7 Sept. 1940, in *The Diaries of Sir Alexander Cadogan, 1938-1945,* ed. David Dilks (New York, 1972), 325ff; see also Stimson, diary, 7 Sept. 1940, Stimson MSS.

119. *New York Times,* 7 Sept. 1940.

120. Lewis, diary, 7 Sept. 1940, Lewis MSS.

121. *Congressional Record,* 7 Sept. 1940, 11749-50.

122. Ibid., 11748-49.

123. Johnson to H. Johnson, Jr., 9 Sept. 1940, H. Johnson MSS. "Considering the temper of the congressmen, it is wonderful that we were able to hold even the Fish amendment" (Mildred Olmsted to Dorothy Hummel, 9 Sept. 1940, DG 23, box 2, SCPC).

124. *Congressional Record*, 7 Sept. 1940, 11754-55; see table in Porter, *Seventy-sixth Congress*, 199.

125. Wadsworth to J. Mayhew Wainwright, 17 Sept. 1940, Wadsworth Family MSS.

126. Taft to Paul Walter, 11 Sept. 1940, box 31, Paul Walter MSS, Western Reserve Historical Society, Cleveland, Ohio.

127. Stimson, diary, 9 Sept. 1940, Stimson MSS; Hershey memorandum on Fish amendment, 113 file, Hershey MSS.

128. Stimson, diary, 9 Sept. 1940, Stimson MSS; H. Petersen (for Clark) to Stimson, 9 Sept. 1940, Clark MSS.

129. Stimson, diary, 9 Sept. 1940, Stimson MSS.

130. *New York Times,* 10 Sept. 1940.

131. Ibid.

132. Ibid.

133. R. Clapper, notebook, 9 Sept. 1940, box 25, Clapper MSS.

134. *New York Times,* 12 Sept. 1940; Hershey, interview, Dec. 1969; O'Sullivan, "Voluntarism to Conscription," 114; "Memorandum on Conference Report," n.d. (c. 12 Sept. 1940), Hershey MSS.

135. Elbert Thomas to Will Cates, 12 Sept. 1940, box 29, Thomas MSS, FDRL.

136. Wadsworth to Clark, 12 Sept. 1940, Clark MSS.

137. L. Lewis, diary, 12-13 Sept. 1940, Lewis MSS.

138. *New York Times,* 13 Sept. 1940.

139. Ibid., 14 Sept. 1940.

140. Ibid., 15 Sept. 1940.

141. Ibid.

142. French, diary, 28-29 Aug. 1940; Voorhis to FDR, 29 Aug. 1940; FDR to Voorhis, 3 Oct. 1940, PPF 5595, FDRL.

143. T. Rankin to S. Hertzberg, 5 Sept. 1940, *Uncensored* MSS, NYPL.

144. Voorhis to Baldwin, 19 Sept. 1940, vol. 2189, ACLU MSS. French saw the destroyer deal as the "last move before actual involvement in the European War," and on 5 Sept. he had lunch with a State Department official who told him that FDR had acquired the bases to provide a line of retreat for the British Navy, to protect America's east flank, and to allow the United States Navy to operate in the Pacific, where a showdown with Japan was imminent. The same State Department official (unidentified) predicted that the United States would soon acquire new bases in Brazil, Greenland, and the Azores (Paul French, diary, 4-5 Sept. 1940, French MSS).

145. Beale to Baldwin, 21 Sept. 1940, Beale MSS, GRB; Beale to P. A. Wallenborn, Jr., 20 Sept. 1940, Beale MSS, SHSW; French, diary, 10-11 Sept. 1940, French MSS; Clarence Pickett, diary, 17 Sept. 1940, Pickett MSS.

146. *Congressional Record,* 6 Sept. 1940, 11689.

147. Beale to Wallenborn, 20 Sept. 1940, Beale MSS, SHSW.

148. French, diary, 7 Sept. 1940, quoted in Wachs, "Conscription," 69.

149. Libby, diary, 8 Sept. 1940, Libby MSS; French, diary, 8 Sept. 1940, French MSS.

150. Beale to Baldwin (wire), 11 Sept. 1940, Beale MSS, GRB. John Haynes Holmes and Roger Baldwin wires to conferees, 10 Sept. 1940; Elbert Thomas to Holmes (wire), 11 Sept. 1940; Burton Wheeler to Baldwin, 10 Sept. 1940—all in vol.

2189, ACLU MSS; Ray Wilson to A. J. Muste, 10 Sept. 1940, Ray Wilson Peace Sections, AFSC archives.

151. Beale to Wallenborn, 20 Sept. 1940, Beale MSS, SHSW.

152. "Sometimes I wonder if the conscientious objector is not a trifle snobbish in his belief that he is so far above the ordinary mortals that they can fight for a world in which he will continue to placidly live up to his ideals" (E. Roosevelt to Ensley Tiffin, 16 Sept. 1940, box 1581, ER MSS, FDRL).

153. Robert Jackson to FDR, 13 Sept. 1940, OF 10, FDRL; White House appointment log, 13 Sept. 1940; Clarence Pickett, diary, 13–14 Sept. 1940; J. J., memorandum, 14 Sept. 1940, box 3, Edwin Watson MSS, University of Virginia.

154. Beale to Wallenborn, 20 Sept. 1940, Beale MSS, SHSW.

155. Roosevelt, *Public Papers,* 9:428–31; Stimson, diary, 16 Sept. 1940, Stimson MSS.

156. A Democrats-for-Willkie Committee circulated a photograph of the president hamming things up during the signing ceremony (Pogue, *George C. Marshall: Ordeal and Hope,* 62).

157. Petersen to Clark, 23 Sept. 1940, Clark MSS.

158. Hatch, *Wadsworths,* 255.

159. Stimson to Clark, 17 Sept. 1940, Clark MSS. Stimson's letter continued: "I can realize that from the difficulties I myself met in pushing behind your efforts. The officers in the department around me from General Marshall down agree that . . . none of them expected that the passage of such a bill would be possible, and if it hadn't been for the efforts of you and your associates, they would have been right. As it is, an unprecedented feat has been accomplished in obtaining a service bill before war has actually broken out." Clark's close friend DeLancey Jay wrote: "It is an extraordinary achievement for a private citizen to have pulled off in a few months. . . . Your passion for anonymity was getting to be a bit overdone!" (to Clark, 17 Oct. 1940, Clark MSS).

160. Wadsworth to Clark, 12 Sept. 1940, Wadsworth Family MSS.

161. Clark to Wadsworth, 17 Sept. 1940, Wadsworth Family MSS.

CHAPTER 12. EPILOGUE: THE AMBIGUOUS LEGACY

1. Interview with Lewis Hershey, 15 Dec. 1967. It should be noted that Clark never regretted his role in the 1940 draft, and his association with Samuel Spencer in 1947/48 was originally intended to produce a memoir on the 1940 campaign for conscription.

2. Clark to Taft, 17 Mar. 1948, Clark MSS.

3. See, especially, Clark, *A Plan for Peace* (New York, 1949); Clark and Louis B. Sohn, *World Peace through World Law* (Cambridge, Mass., 1958).

4. See Lawrence M. Baskir and William A. Strauss, *Chance and Circumstance* (New York, 1978).

5. Confidential interview, 1973.

6. Flynn, *Lewis B. Hershey,* 65–66.

7. See essay by Baldwin in Cousins and Clifford, eds., *Memoirs of a Man.*

8. See Brewster essay in Cousins and Clifford, *Memoirs of a Man;* Rankin interview, Feb. 1982. Rankin became the principal attorney assisting Clark during the 1950s and early 1960s in the effort to bring suit against Harvard over the Arnold Arboretum.

9. Flynn, *Lewis B. Hershey,* chap. 7.

10. As quoted in Eliot A. Cohen, *Citizens and Soldiers: The Dilemmas of Military Service* (Ithaca, N.Y., 1985), 168-69.

11. Ibid., chap. 4.

12. Ibid., 182.

13. Barnet, *Roots of War*, chaps. 3 and 4.

14. Interview with John S. Dickey, Hanover, N.H., Jan. 1973.

15. See Melvyn P. Leffler, "The American Conception of National Security and the Beginnings of the Cold War, 1945-48," *American Historical Review* 89 (Apr. 1984): 346-81.

16. On FDR's indifference to details see Flynn, *Lewis B. Hershey*, 70-71.

17. Holger Herwig, *Politics of Frustration: The United States in German Naval Planning, 1889-1941* (Boston, 1976), 212.

18. "President Roosevelt's policy, for all the linearity later imposed on it, was actually a series of fits and starts whose interconnection the president himself denied at the time" (Mark M. Lowenthal, "Roosevelt and the Coming of the Second World War: The Search for United States Policy, 1937-42," *Journal of Contemporary History* 16 (1981): 413.

19. See David Reynolds, "Churchill and the British 'Decision' to Fight in 1940: Right Policy, Wrong Reasons," in *Diplomacy and Intelligence during the Second World War*, ed. Richard Langhorne (Cambridge, Eng., 1985), 160-65.

20. Leutze, *Bargaining for Supremacy*, chap. 15; Reynolds, *Creation of the Anglo-American Alliance*, chaps. 6-8.

21. Anthony Eden, earl of Avon, *The Eden Memoirs: The Reckoning* (Boston, 1965), 374.

22. See Gabel, "U.S. Army Maneuvers of 1941," passim.

23. Clark to Wadsworth, 17 Sept. 1940, Wadsworth Family MSS.

24. "I'm not certain that I'm an advocate of going to war immediately. Even if I were maybe I'd be slow to speak up with a 21 year old boy (no logic in this but it tends to make one pause on *taking the lead* in advocating war). But I certainly am for *discussing* openly or frankly the pros and cons of *going to war* instead of skirting all around the real issue by casting the talk in terms of 'aid,' 'support' etc." (Clark to Ralph Barton Perry, 2 Oct. 1940, Harvard Defense Group MSS).

25. Stimson, diary, 7-9 Dec. 1941, Stimson MSS.

26. Doenecke to Clifford, Feb. 1985.

27. Barthell, "Committee on Militarism," conclusion.

28. The great majority of the 40,000 conscientious objectors served as noncombatants in the medical corps of the various services during the war. Despite the efforts of the pacifist leaders, more than 5,000 nonreligious objectors and absolutists went to federal prison during the war, the largest number being Jehovah's Witnesses, who claimed exemption as ministers. Not until the Vietnam War did nonreligious objectors gain recognition as legitimate COs (see Mulford Q. Sibley and Philip E. Jacob, *Conscription of Conscience: The American State and the Conscientious Objector, 1940-1947* (Ithaca, N.Y., 1952).

29. Beale to Thomas, 19 June 1941, and Thomas to Beale, 22 June 1941, Thomas MSS.

30. Wayne Cole, *Roosevelt and the Isolationists, 1932-1945* (Lincoln, Nebr., 1983), 436-41; O'Sullivan, "From Voluntarism to Conscription," 343-47.

31. Stimson, diary, 2 Aug. 1940, Stimson MSS.

32. John F. Kennedy, *Why England Slept* (Garden City, N.Y., 1961 ed.), 180, 184-85, italics in original.

33. Ibid., 180.

A Note on Manuscript Sources

The principal source for this study was the Grenville Clark MSS in the Baker Library of Dartmouth College, Hanover, New Hampshire. A huge collection, the Clark papers were first used by Samuel Spencer in 1947, while they were still at Clark's home in Dublin, New Hampshire. Spencer's notes and transcripts of interviews, NEC records, Clark's Plattsburg papers, and even carbons of correspondence belonging to A. G. Thacher and Julius Adler are all easily located through an extensive index and finding aid. Charles Tobey's papers, a most revealing isolationist collection, are also at the picturesque Baker Library.

Several other sets of papers provide insight into the inner workings of the conscription campaign. The Harvard Defense Group MSS in the Pusey Library show the connection between the NEC and its principal academic auxiliary. The Ralph Barton Perry files are quite rich. Henry L. Stimson's diaries and papers at Yale are indispensable to understanding the Plattsburgers' efforts to influence the Roosevelt administration. Transcripts of McGeorge Bundy's postwar interviews with Stimson for their collaborative book *On Active Service in Peace and War* have some useful information on the abortive officer camps. Ralph Lowell's diaries and correspondence at the Massachusetts Historical Society trace the activities and views of an original Plattsburger from Boston. The organizational records of the Military Training Camps Association, at the Chicago Historical Society, while thin, bring out the differing perspectives of the NEC and of the Chicago headquarters in 1940.

Several manuscript collections at the Roosevelt Library in Hyde Park, New York, help to reconstruct the decision-making process within the administration. FDR's complex motives are sometimes apparent in his White House files (PSF, OF, and PPF), but presidential conversations recorded in the diaries of such close associates as Henry Morgenthau, Adolf Berle, and Harold Smith often reveal more. The papers of Harry Hopkins, Stephen Early, Eleanor Roosevelt, Elbert Thomas, and Samuel Rosenman—all at Hyde Park—were also useful for this study. The president's private assessments are also available in the manuscript diaries of Henry Wallace (copy in the possession of Theodore Wilson), diplomat J. Pierrepont Moffat (Houghton Library, Harvard), and Interior Secretary Harold Ickes, whose manuscripts at the Library of Congress are even more indiscreet than the famous *Secret Diary* published in the 1950s. The interplay between foreign-policy concerns and the draft in FDR's thinking can also be traced in the diaries of Canadian Prime Minister Mackenzie King (available on microfiche from the Canadian Public Records Office in Ottawa) and in the reporting of the British Embassy in Washington (available at the Public Record Office in Kew, England). The private correspondence of British Ambassador Lord Lothian, in the Scottish Record Office in Edinburgh, contains some candid appraisals of United States policy in 1940. There are memoranda of cabinet meetings and other political assessments in the papers of James A. Farley at the Library of Congress.

Revealing material also surfaced in the papers of journalists and other members of the fourth estate. Notes of interviews with administration officials can be found in the papers of columnists Joseph Alsop, Raymond Clapper (both at the Library of Congress), and Arthur Krock (in the Seeley Mudd Library at Princeton). The J. Callan O'Loughlin papers at the Library of Congress contain lengthy, gossipy letters written each week by the editor of the *Army and Navy Journal* to former President Hoover, General Pershing, and General David Sarnoff. William Allen White's papers at the Library of Congress fully reflect his dual role as editor of the *Emporia* (Kans.) *Gazette* and as head of the Committee to Defend America by Aiding the Allies. White's correspondence with Senator Burton Wheeler during the selective-service debate is especially illuminating. Inside information on the mounting opposition to the draft in Washington dominates the editorial correspondence of the antiwar newsletter *Uncensored* (at the New York Public Library), particularly the many background reports of Frank Hanighen. Oswald Garrison Villard's papers at Harvard document the dissension at the *Nation* over the war and the draft, and Villard's extensive correspondence provides an excellent cross section of the liberal/pacifist opposition in 1940. The papers of publishers Roy Howard, Joseph Pulitzer II, and Eugene Meyer, all at the Library of Congress, contain some pertinent items, as does the diary of William Henry Chamberlin at Providence College.

Of the many papers of congressmen and senators who were serving in 1940, several proved especially valuable. The Wadsworth Family MSS at the Library of Congress detail the activities of the cosponsor of the Burke-Wadsworth bill. Also at LC, the Robert A. Taft, Robert La Follette, Jr., and George Norris papers have extensive materials on the Senate opposition to the draft. The details of Taft's search for an alternative to conscription are quite poignant. Hiram Johnson's vituperative "diary" letters to his son are highlights of the Johnson collection at the Bancroft Library of the University of California, Berkeley. Arthur H. Vandenberg's papers at the University of Michigan and John A. Danaher's at Yale also contain excellent correspondence from the anticonscription perspective. Danaher, the last surviving Senate opponent of United States intervention in World War II, was kind enough to supplement the record in several conversations about the pre–Pearl Harbor era. Among supporters of the draft in Congress, the Warren Austin MSS at the University of Vermont were particularly helpful because of the Republican senator's habit of writing letters to his mother during floor debates. Although thin for his Senate years, the James F. Byrnes papers at Clemson include evidence of the Senate whip's (and presumably the president's) political doubts about the draft in mid August 1940. The Josiah Bailey MSS at Duke University fully document the evolving views of a one-time southern isolationist. Also revealing for what he did not know about White House plans is the diary of assistant Democratic whip Lawrence Lewis at the Colorado Historical Society in Denver. Clifford Hope's papers at the Kansas State Historical Society are quite good from the perspective of a moderate isolationist congressman.

The army's position on the draft can be traced in the official military records in the National Archives. Record Group 165, the files of the War Plans Division of the General Staff, is the best source for the army's strategic planning in reaction to Hitler's conquests. The complex tasks of reevaluating and putting mobilization plans into operation, meeting White House requests for emergency aid to England, and maintaining good relations with Congress and pressure groups appear in full detail in General Marshall's papers at the Marshall Library in Lexington, Virginia. The chief of staff's sometimes bitter memories of dealing with Secretary Stimson's Plattsburg friends are also documented in the transcript of an interview conducted by biographer Forrest Pogue in 1957. There is one important Marshall letter in the Frank R. McCoy papers at the Library of Congress. The collections of Harry H. Woodring (University of Kansas), Louis Johnson (University of Virginia), and Robert P. Patterson (Library of Congress) were only marginally useful. The Selective Service System Records (RG 147) at the federal records center in Suitland, Maryland, contain a few pertinent items for 1940; these can be supplemented by the Lewis Hershey papers at the U.S. Military Institute in Carlisle, Pennsylvania.

Manuscript sources for the antidraft opposition are numerous. The hospitable Swarthmore College Peace Collections house the organizational records of the Committee on Militarism in Education, the Fellowship of Reconciliation, the War Resisters League, the National Council for the Prevention of War, and the Women's International League for Peace and Freedom. Dorothy Detzer's feisty personality emerges in her letters to WIL branches and national officers. Swarthmore also holds the diary of Paul French, which offers illuminating detail on the Friends' legislative efforts during the summer of 1940. Although several pages have been scissored out, Frederick J. Libby's handwritten diary at the Library of Congress is a gold mine of information. Clarence Pickett's diary at the American Friends Service Committee archives in Philadelphia reflects a prominent Quaker's impression that the Roosevelt administration preferred voluntary national service to military conscription. The fullest reports of anticonscription activities in 1940, however, are found in Howard Beale's voluminous letters to Roger Baldwin, copies of which are in the American Civil Liberties Union files at Princeton, a small collection of Beale papers at the Wisconsin Historical Society, and in Beale family papers in the possession of his widow. Beale, who felt guilty about not having made progress on his biography of Theodore Roosevelt, kept a meticulous historical record of what was diverting him from his scholarly tasks. The America First Committee papers in the Hoover Institute at Stanford have some gems for 1940. There is also good material on the attitudes and activities of American Socialists/pacifists in the Norman Thomas MSS (New York Public Library) and in the papers of the American Socialist party and in the records of the Keep America out of War Congress at Duke University.

Several other manuscript collections yielded important insights. The Wendell Willkie papers at Indiana University's Lilly Library, although incomplete for the 1940 campaign, contain fascinating memoranda about a bipartisan approach to FDR to reach an agreement on foreign-policy and defense issues prior to the president's renomination. The papers of Willkie's biographer Ellsworth Barnard, also at the Lilly Library, include interview notes and important correspondence with close associates of the GOP candidate in 1940. Princeton's Seeley Mudd Library holds the organizational files of the principal interventionist groups, the Committee to Defend America by Aiding the Allies and the Fight for Freedom Committee, both of which contain important documents pertaining to the destroyer deal. Even more revealing regarding the behind-the-scenes efforts to push for aid to England are the diarylike letters written to his wife by Roger Greene, the Washington representative of the Committee to Defend America; Greene's papers are in Harvard's Houghton Library. Alfred M. Landon's correspondence at the Kansas State Historical Society contains numerous incoming letters from GOP friends in 1940, giving him the latest political gossip; Landon's efforts at influencing Willkie to play safe on conscription are also detailed. Herbert Hoover's postpresidential papers at the Hoover Library in West Branch, Iowa, similarly contain much information from Washington insiders who regularly kept their "Chief" up to date. The diary of Hoover's former undersecretary of state, William R. Castle, now available at the Houghton Library, is full of fascinating details, including a revealing conversation with Senator D. Walsh about his relations with the president at the time of the destroyers/bases negotiations.

A complete listing of manuscript collections, arranged geographically, follows.

American Friends Service Committee Archives, Philadelphia, Pa.
    Clarence Pickett, diaries
    Raymond Wilson MSS

American Jewish Historical Society, Waltham, Mass.
    Stephen S. Wise MSS

Borthwick Historical Institute, York, England
    Edward Wood, Lord Halifax, diaries

Cambridge University
    Churchill College Archives
        Sir Alexander Cadogan MSS and diaries
        Hickelton MSS (microfilm)
        Robert Vansittart MSS

Canada
    Public Record Office, Ottawa
        Mackenzie King, diaries (microfiche)

Chicago Historical Society, Chicago, Ill.
    Military Training Camps Association, records
    J. Sterling Morton MSS

Clemson University, Clemson, S.C.
    James F. Byrnes MSS

Colorado State Historical Society, Denver
    Lawrence Lewis, diary

Columbia University, New York, N.Y.
    Butler Library
        Nicholas Murray Butler MSS
        Allan Nevins MSS
        James W. Wadsworth, oral history memoir

Cornell University, Ithaca, N.Y.
    Collection of Regional History and Archives
        Sterling Cole MSS
        Frank Gannett MSS
        Daniel Reed MSS
        John Taber MSS
        Louis Taber MSS

Dartmouth College, Hanover, N.H.
    Baker Library
        Robert P. Bass MSS
        Grenville Clark MSS
        Ernest Hopkins MSS
        Charles Tobey MSS
        Sinclair Weeks MSS

Duke University, Durham, N.C.
    William Perkins Library
        Josiah W. Bailey MSS

Dwight D. Eisenhower Presidential Library, Abilene, Kans.
    C. D. Jackson MSS

Franklin D. Roosevelt Presidential Library, Hyde Park, N.Y.
    Adolf A. Berle MSS and diary
    Francis Biddle MSS and diary
    Democratic National Committee Records
    Stephen Early MSS
    Anna Roosevelt Halstead MSS
    Harry Hopkins MSS
    Lowell Mellett MSS
    Henry Morgenthau, Jr., diaries
    Eleanor Roosevelt MSS
    Franklin D. Roosevelt MSS
    Harold D. Smith MSS and diaries
    Elbert H. Thomas MSS
    Rexford G. Tugwell MSS and diaries
    Claude G. Wickard MSS and diaries

Great Britain
  Public Record Office, Kew, England
    Foreign Office Records, FO 371—United States
    FO/800 Lord Avon MSS (microfilm)
    FO/800 Lord Halifax MSS

Harry S. Truman Presidential Library, Independence, Mo.
    Harry S. Truman MSS

Harvard University, Cambridge and Boston, Mass.
  Baker Library, Harvard Business School (Boston)
    Thomas W. Lamont MSS
  Houghton Library
    William R. Castle, diary
    Roger Greene MSS
    J. Pierrepont Moffat MSS
    William Phillips, diary
    Robert E. Sherwood MSS
    Oswald Garrison Villard MSS
  Law School Library
    Charles C. Burlingham MSS
    James A. McLachlan MSS
  Pusey Library
    Harvard Defense Group MSS
    Harvard Student Defense League MSS
    Ralph Barton Perry MSS

Herbert C. Hoover Presidential Library, West Branch, Iowa
    William R. Castle MSS
    Herbert Hoover postpresidential MSS
    Hanford MacNider MSS
    Verne Marshall MSS
    Gerald P. Nye MSS
    Westbrook Pegler MSS
    Robert E. Wood MSS

Holy Cross College, Worcester, Mass.
  Dinan Library
    D. I. Walsh MSS

Hoover Institution on War, Revolution, and Peace, Stanford, Calif.
    America First Committee, records
    William Y. Elliot MSS
    Hugh Gibson MSS
    Stanley K. Hornbeck MSS
    Ernest Lundeen MSS
    Raymond Moley MSS
    National Committee to Feed the Small Democracies, records
    National Journal MSS
    Mark Sullivan MSS

Illinois State Historical Society, Springfield
    Kent Keller MSS
    Scott Lucas MSS

Indiana University, Bloomington
  Lilly Library
    Ellsworth Barnard MSS
    Claude Bowers MSS
    Charles Halleck MSS
    Louis Ludlow MSS
    Paul McNutt MSS
    Wendell Willkie MSS

John F. Kennedy Presidential Library, Boston, Mass.
    John F. Kennedy MSS
    James P. Warburg MSS

Kansas State Historical Society, Topeka
    Arthur Capper MSS
    Clifford Hope, Jr., MSS
    Alfred M. Landon MSS

Massachusetts Historical Society, Boston
    Committee to Defend America by Aiding the Allies, Massachusetts chapter
    Henry Cabot Lodge, Jr., MSS
    Ralph A. Lowell MSS

Memphis Public Library, Memphis, Tenn.
    Kenneth T. McKellar MSS

New York Public Library, New York, N.Y.
    Clark Eichelberger MSS
    Norman M. Thomas MSS
    Uncensored MSS

Ohio State Historical Society, Columbus
    John W. Bricker MSS
    Clarence Brown MSS
    John W. Vorys MSS

Princeton University, Princeton, N.J.
  Seeley Mudd Library
    American Civil Liberties Union MSS
    Roger Baldwin MSS
    Bernard M. Baruch MSS
    Committee to Defend America by Aiding the Allies MSS
    Fight for Freedom Committee MSS
    Arthur Krock MSS

Providence College, Providence, R.I.
Library
William Henry Chamberlin, diary

Scottish Record Office, Edinburgh, Scotland
Philip Kerr (Lord Lothian) MSS

Stanford University, Stanford, Calif.
Library
Bernard De Voto MSS
Francis V. Keesling, Jr., MSS

State University of New York at Buffalo
Anson Conger Goodyear MSS

Swarthmore College, Swarthmore, Pa.
Swarthmore College Peace Collections
American Friends War Problems Committee, records
Committee on Militarism in Education, records
Fellowship of Reconciliation, records
Paul C. French, diaries
A. J. Muste MSS
National Council for the Prevention of War, records
Jeannette Rankin MSS
Women's International League for Peace and Freedom, records
War Resisters League, records

Syracuse University, Syracuse, N.Y.
George Arents Library
Granville Hicks MSS
Dorothy Thompson MSS

United States
Federal Records Center, Suitland, Md.
Record Group 144—Headquarters of the Selective Service System
Library of Congress, Manuscripts Division, Washington, D.C.
Carl Ackerman MSS
Joseph Alsop MSS
John Balderston MSS
Henry C. Breckinridge MSS
Harold Burton MSS and diaries
Raymond Clapper MSS
Thomas Connally MSS
Elmer Davis MSS
James J. Davis MSS
Norman Davis MSS
James A. Farley MSS
Herbert Feis MSS
Henry P. Fletcher MSS
Felix Frankfurter MSS
Theodore Francis Green MSS
John Haynes Holmes MSS
Roy S. Howard MSS
Cordell Hull MSS
Robert Jackson MSS
Philip Jessup MSS
Frank Knox MSS
La Follette Family MSS
Emory Land MSS
James Landis MSS

Frederick J. Libby MSS
Breckinridge Long MSS
William G. McAdoo MSS
Frank R. McCoy MSS
Archibald MacLeish MSS
Charles S. McNary MSS
Benjamin C. Marsh MSS
Eugene Meyer MSS
John Bassett Moore MSS
George Norris MSS
John Callan O'Loughlin MSS
Robert P. Patterson MSS
John J. Pershing MSS
Amos Pinchot MSS
Gifford Pinchot MSS   .
Key Pittman MSS
Ralph Pulitzer II MSS
Francis B. Sayre MSS
Lewis Schwellenbach MSS
Raymond Gram Swing MSS
Robert Alonzo Taft MSS
Huston Thompson MSS
Wadsworth Family MSS
Wallace A. White MSS
William Allen White MSS
Leonard Wood MSS
National Archives, Modern Military Branch, Washington, D.C.
Record Group 165—War Plans Division
Record Group 107—General Correspondence of the Secretary of War and Assistant
Secretary of War

United States Military Institute, Carlisle, Pa.
Lewis B. Hershey MSS
U.S. Army War College lectures and records

University of California, Berkeley
Bancroft Library
Sheridan Downey MSS
William Randolph Hearst MSS
Hiram Johnson MSS

University of Chicago, Chicago, Ill.
Regenstein Library
William Benton MSS
Robert Hutchins MSS
Thomas V. Smith MSS
Quincy Wright MSS

University of Connecticut, Storrs
Wilbur Cross Library
Francis T. Maloney MSS

University of Kansas, Lawrence
Spencer Research Library
Doris Fleeson MSS
Harry H. Woodring MSS

University of Michigan, Ann Arbor
  Bentley Library
    Prentiss Brown MSS
    Fred Crawford MSS
    Frank Murphy MSS
    Thomas W. Spaulding MSS
    Arthur H. Vandenberg MSS and diaries

University of Missouri, Columbia
  Library: Western Historical Manuscripts Collection
    C. Jasper Bell MSS
    Marion T. Bennett MSS
    Clarence Cannon, Jr., MSS
    George Peek MSS

University of North Carolina, Chapel Hill
  Library: Southern Historical Collections
    Robert Doughton MSS
    Carl Durham MSS
    John H. Kerr MSS
    Lindsay C. Warren MSS

University of Oregon, Eugene
  Library
    John T. Flynn MSS
    Samuel Pettengill MSS
    Samuel Pierce MSS

University of Puget Sound, Tacoma, Wash.
    Homer T. Bone MSS

University of Rochester, Rochester, N.Y.
  Library
    Thomas E. Dewey MSS

University of Vermont, Burlington
  Guy Bailey Library
    Warren R. Austin MSS
    Ernest W. Gibson MSS

University of Virginia, Charlottesville
  Alderman Library
    Carter Glass MSS
    Louis Johnson MSS
    Francis P. Miller MSS
    Edwin Watson MSS

University of Wyoming, Laramie
  Coe Library
    Harry Elmer Barnes MSS
    Joseph C. O'Mahoney MSS

Virginia Military Institute, Lexington
  George C. Marshall Research Library
    George C. Marshall MSS

Western Reserve Historical Society, Cleveland, Ohio
    Frances P. Bolton MSS
    Paul Walter MSS

Wisconsin State Historical Society, Madison
    Bruce Barton MSS

Howard K. Beale MSS
Stephen Bolles MSS
Merle Curti MSS
Ludwell Denny MSS
Merlin Hull MSS
Philip La Follette MSS
Raymond Robins MSS
Alexander Wiley MSS

Yale University, New Haven, Conn.
  Sterling Library
    Dean G. Acheson MSS
    Hanson W. Baldwin MSS
    Walter Batterson MSS
    Samuel Flagg Bemis MSS
    Alfred M. Bingham MSS
    Edwin M. Borchard MSS
    John A. Danaher MSS
    John W. Davis MSS
    Jerome Frank MSS
    Walter Lippmann MSS
    Dwight Macdonald MSS
    Charles Parsons MSS
    Charles Seymour MSS
    Henry L. Stimson MSS and diary

When we have used notes from other manuscripts that have been researched by David Porter, we have cited the original documents and manuscript repositories, along with a reference to Porter's notes. We are most grateful for Porter's generous assistance.

Index